On The March With Kenny's Army

*How Liverpool FC overcame tragedy and despair to win
the League and FA Cup Double - 1985/86*

by Gary Shaw and Mike Nevin

First published in November 2011 by Gary Shaw

Copyright © 2011 Gary Shaw and Mike Nevin

ISBN 978-0-9557283-2-7

Printed and bound by the MPG Books Group Bodmin and King's Lynn

Published privately by
Gary Shaw

Contents

On The March With Kenny's Army

Acknowledgements

When the idea for this book was first conceived - in the Railway Hotel in Tithebarn Street, Liverpool over a pint or two before the Reds' meeting with Benfica in the 2009 Europa League quarter-final - little did we know that by the time we were ready for publication, Kenny Dalglish would have returned to the Liverpool managers' chair. The first notes of thanks therefore go to the King himself - and to John W Henry - for assisting with a fortunate and welcome piece of historical symmetry.

While it has been a pleasure researching, writing and bringing to life one of Liverpool FC's most fascinating seasons – and, hopefully, an illuminating and interesting piece of Merseyside social history - we are indebted to a whole host of people who have helped us to create such an in-depth, and, hopefully, vivid portrayal of not only a memorable football story, but also more than just a whiff of mid-1980s Liverpool air; a period not everyone in the city will remember with complete fondness, despite the footballing dominance of both Liverpool and Everton.

For their contributions, quotes, anecdotes and above all, their enthusiasm, we would like to thank (in no particular order) Kevin Sampson, Sean Doyle, David Swift, John Bradley, Steven Kelly, Nicky Allt, Stephen Conchie, John Joynt, David Brennan, David McKearney, Chris Maguire, Chris Hannaway, Wilko from Skem, Martin Jones, Maca from Huyton, Whitey from Wavertree, "Upsetter", Peter Furmedge, Dave Hardman, and Phil Allan and Bernard Nevin - who was also responsible for ferrying one of the co-authors to at least half these games – thanks Dad. Also, thanks to Stephen Hughes, who had put up with his (no doubt irritating) younger cousin at almost every home game – and a few aways – this season too. It was worth it though.

Particular acknowledgement and heartfelt thanks also goes to Tony Barrett for his eloquent foreword and kind review, Mark Platt - c/o Steve Newton - for the two 'shining' examples (they'll know what we mean), Peter Hooton and all at 'The End', Ron Noon, Jenny van Deursen and Dan Millington, The Voice of Anfield - George Sephton, Sam Nevin for his help with Twitter, and last but not least Paul Sullivan and Craig Pennington at the Static Gallery for their hospitality.

In our research we leaned on the excellent work of journalists covering matches for the Liverpool Echo, in particular Ian Hargraves, Ken Rogers and Ann Cummings. We should also mention contributors to the Football Echo letters' page, and thank those whose names appear in the book via this medium - even Len Griffiths, whose longevity and capacity for letter-writing never ceases to amaze.

We are also indebted to the 1985/86 Liverpool players, not just for doing the Double but – for those who published them - their autobiographies, which were a useful port of reference; Craig Johnston's in particular is worthy of a read even some 25 years after it was penned. In a similar vein, it would be remiss not to mention John Keith's compilation, 'Liverpool Supreme' which provided another useful reference tool as well as quotes from a variety of contemporary national journalists. For statistics, we thank Arnie Baldursson for his superb website lfchistory.net, and in a similar vein, all at liverweb.com.

Special mentions must also be given to our respective wives, Karen and Ursula, who have listened patiently, and impatiently, to our discussions and discoveries over the past two years - even occasionally feigning interest in our recollections of semi-flared cords, adidas polo necks, upturned bucket hats and tachini tops, ordinary trains, Ace Lager and Higsons Bitter. Not to mention the wild, but real, fantasy of touching Jan Molby after his League Cup goal against United, and whether or not Ron Atkinson actually did wear a hairpiece.

Whilst every effort has been made to ensure all information is correct, some factual errors may occur. Liverpool might even lose the odd game. If so, we hope that this does not detract from your enjoyment of the book. Likewise, every care has been taken to ensure all photographs have been used correctly; if any institution feels that they may have an issue over use of a particular photograph, please do not hesitate to contact us.

Gary Shaw & Mike Nevin - November 2011

Foreword

If a poll was ever conducted to determine Liverpool's greatest ever season there would be eighteen obvious and immediate contenders. Title winning campaigns are almost impossible to top, although all those who were fortunate enough to be in Istanbul on May 25 2005 would be well placed to state a case for the 2004/05 season being the most magical in the club's history given the incredible events that occurred on that unforgettable night in Turkey and in the weeks and months leading up to it.

When it comes to discussions about Liverpool's finest team those that won the English league title in 1978/79 and 1987/88 are always amongst the first mentioned and rightly so given their absolute dominance and the style of football they played. Few clubs in this country have ever had one team of such a high standard that they not only stand comparison with any in European football past or present, they arguably stand above most of them in the hierarchy of greatness, so for Liverpool to have had two, at the very least, illustrates their standing both domestically and abroad.

If there is a problem with having enjoyed so much success and witnessing a succession of great teams is that it can sometimes be easy to overlook times that supporters of other clubs would regard as comfortably the best in their history. The 1985/86 season falls into that category where Liverpool are concerned, a campaign that yielded the club's first ever League and FA Cup double no less and featured an unforgettable Wembley win over Everton as the icing on the most wonderful of cakes.

For Tottenham Hotspur and Arsenal, the double years of 1961 and 1971 stand out like none others, but for Liverpool there is a tendency for 1986 to blend into their lexicon of greatness, particularly as it came slap, bang in the middle of a decade in which major trophies were gathered with such a glorious monotony that success was the norm rather than the exception.

But just the merest details should be sufficient to convince that both the 1985/86 season and team stands comparison with even the very best in Liverpool's history. In many respects, it captured exactly what the club is all about with glory being earned, regardless of adversity and results achieved, through sheer force of will as much as collective talent. There were numerous occasions during that season when Liverpool's hopes were written off, not just by their rivals and the media, but also by at least some of their supporters.

It wasn't a lack of faith that caused such doubts to emerge, it was a basic appreciation of sport and a realisation that even the most dogged and determined of teams can sometimes give themselves too much to do. Ten points behind Manchester United by early autumn, eight behind reigning champions Everton with just eleven games left to play following a derby day reversal at Anfield, a goal behind and staring FA Cup Final defeat in the face against their Merseyside rivals – each and every one an obstacle that would have derailed the trophy hopes of most other teams but Liverpool managed to overcome all of them; a tribute to their talent, their mental strength, their team spirit and also to their player-manager Kenny Dalglish in his very first season at the helm.

With Dalglish now back in charge at Anfield, there is no better time to relive the 1985/86 season and also for its status as one of the greatest in the club's history to be underlined.

There may well have been campaigns when Liverpool have played better football and there may also have been ones where they won more than two trophies, but for sheer drama and magical occasions this one takes some beating.

Any season that concludes with Liverpool relegating Everton to the runners up spot in the league has to be special so for that to also happen in the FA Cup makes it truly remarkable and that makes this book a more than welcome and long overdue addition to the Liverpool library.

Tony Barrett
Liverpool fan and journalist

Introduction

"A slum game played in slum stadiums watched by slum people."

Sunday Times, 19 May 1985

Viewed from a distance of over a quarter of a century, the sight of an inconsolable Joe Fagan, hands held to a face dripping with tears, being helped down aircraft steps and across the tarmac of Speke Airport the day after Heysel, one could be forgiven for thinking that the disaster was the reason he retired as Liverpool manager. The truth however, is not as dramatic, nor as depressing.

The much loved Fagan, then aged 65, had joined the Anfield coaching staff on the recommendation of his great friend Harry Catterick in 1958. Former teammates at Manchester City during and just after the Second World War, Catterick had asked Fagan to become his trainer when the future Everton boss was appointed manager of Rochdale in 1953 and, together, the duo had spent five Third Division North years together at Spotland before the latter moved to Anfield.

18 months after Fagan's arrival Bill Shankly - who had tried to sign Joe from Manchester City when he was in charge at Grimsby - was appointed Liverpool manager and, before embarking on a journey that would propel both him and the club to legendary status, immediately assured the club's entire back-room staff that their jobs were safe.

An avuncular figure - affectionately known as 'Uncle Joe', - Fagan began his rise through the famed Anfield 'Boot Room' hierarchy at this time. After a spell as reserve team manager he was appointed first team trainer in 1971.

Following Shankly's shock resignation three years later he became Chief Coach and five years after this was named assistant manager to Bob Paisley. When Paisley retired in 1983, Fagan, who had seen and helped engineer Liverpool's rise from Second Division mediocrity to one of the most famous sides in world football, was widely viewed as the obvious candidate to succeed him.

By anyone's standards Fagan's first season in charge of Liverpool was astonishing; a Football League championship and victories in the League and European Cups providing the club with a unique treble. Fagan was quiet rightly named Manager of the Year soon after. It was a welcome and much deserved accolade for a man many had come to see as embodying the spirit of the club – loyal, modest, honest, hardworking, quiet and studious but stern when the times warranted it. Behind the scenes however, there were doubts. Like Paisley before him, Fagan had accepted the manager's job reluctantly, later remarking that he took it only, "because I was in a rut when they offered it to me. Ronnie Moran and Roy Evans were doing the training and I was just helping Bob, putting in my two pennyworth."

Perhaps overawed at the increasingly aggressive media attention the game was receiving, or maybe just thinking he was, at 64 and with a large family - five sons and a daughter - and still living in a modest semi-detached house in the city, simply not cut out to be the manager of Europe's best side with all the concomitant pressures that brought, Joe had decided to retire.

Fagan was in essence a family man and it was for this reason more than any other that, in a meeting with Chief Executive Peter Robinson and Chairman John Smith just before Christmas 1984, he informed them he wished to retire at the end of the season. As was the respected administrators' way - and as they had done previously with Shankly and then Paisley - both men pleaded with him to stay at the helm for one more season, but he was adamant. After 27 years of putting the club first Fagan had had enough. It was time to go.

Who would Liverpool turn to now? The reigning European champions should perhaps have been inundated with queries from across the globe but football was a different beast then – and managers of course could only apply for the role if they knew it existed. Showing the astuteness and acuity that had been hallmarks of their reigns, the Liverpool hierarchy somehow kept the news silent and instead discussed the matter behind closed doors. "After due consideration," Peter Robinson later said – and which took several months to finalise, "we decided to continue with our policy of promoting from within."

Ian Rush described Phil Neal as, "a vastly experienced player who had the respect of everyone in the dressing-room," and the four-time European Cup winner had seen himself as being groomed for a role in Liverpool's back-room staff, potentially even becoming manager himself. If appointed, the decision would not have been a surprise.

Ronnie Moran, with over half a lifetime at the club, was also seen as a more than capable replacement. There was even talk amongst some journalists that Graeme Souness, sold by Fagan the season before, might return as player-manager from Sampdoria, or that a young, ambitious, self-confident manager from North of the border - who had broken the stranglehold the Old Firm had on Scottish football at the time, even winning the European Cup Winners Cup in 1983 - would be asked to replace Fagan.

Any notion that Souness or Aberdeen's Alex Ferguson would become Liverpool's next manager were never really taken seriously however, and, in the build up to the ill-fated 1985 European Cup Final, it was left to Smith to phone Kenny Dalglish and ask if he and Robinson could call in at the striker's Southport home to discuss some 'urgent club business'. "I said aye that was alright," Dalglish later recalled. "Then they told me what it was about and I said they could still come."

Dalglish was offered the position and accepted it immediately. "This may have surprised some people at the time," said Robinson, "but we had every confidence that he had the ability to become a sucessfull manager. Everyone involved agreed that an official announcement of the managerial change should be delayed until after the European Cup Final had been played. Unfortunately, the terrible events at Heysel overshadowed everything else."

Kenneth Mathieson Dalglish, acknowledged even during his playing career as one of the best players to have ever represented the club, was Liverpool's 12th manager in just over 90 years – and its first ever player-manager. His appointment was met with both surprise and delight - and in Neal's case bewilderment ("For a time, Neal refused to refer to Dalglish as 'Boss'" - Roy Evans) - but the club he inherited, although still one of the top sides in the country, were in a state of perplexing though necessary transition.

The sale of Souness the season before had left a huge hole, one that had yet to be filled. Some had seen a young Danish protégé signed by Joe Fagan in 1984 as a replacement for the fiery Scot, but Jan Molby was not that type of player. Phil Neal and Alan Kennedy, with a combined 18 years and almost 700 appearances at Anfield between them, had come in for criticism by fans and so-called experts alike the previous season, whilst a number of players had even contemplated retirement after the horrors of Heysel.

In short, the squad looked old when compared to its rivals, especially Everton. More significantly it appeared to be dangerously lacking in both direction and depth, with youngsters such as Steve Nicol, Jim Beglin, Kevin MacDonald, Craig Johnston and Paul Walsh either unknown, untried or, arguably, untrusted.

If on the field problems were seen by some to be adversely affecting the club, there was no doubt that almost every observer saw problems off the field. The city was haemorrhaging not only jobs and people, but also respect. Just a few years earlier, The Daily Mirror, perhaps the only national media outlet that supported the Labour Party at the time, had gone as fas as to say, "they should build a fence around [Liverpool] and charge admission. For sadly, it has become a 'showcase' of everything that has gone wrong in Britain's major cities." Few social commentators would have disagreed; riots, unemployment, crime, violent hooligans, striking workers, benefit cheats, unrealistic and unreliable local politicians - this was the perceived view of the city and its inhabitants.

As the new season dawned however, it would be football once more through which the city would regain at least some respect in the eyes of the rest of the world. Liverpool and Everton were, by far, the two best sides in the country, and even though the irony of the sports' popularity being at its lowest ebb wasn't lost on them, the two clubs, the two sets of fans, and the city as a whole, would ensure - through one of the greatest title battles ever seen - that football and the city could hold its head up high once again.

Gary Shaw - November 2011

Who's Who

Liverpool FC First Team Squad, August 1985

Bruce Grobbelaar
Born: Durban, South Africa 6 October 1957

Signed from Vancouver Whitecaps by Bob Paisley as understudy to Ray Clemence in March 1981 for £250,000, Grobbelaar became the club's number one just a few months later when Clemence moved to Spurs.

Although the extrovert, ex-Rhodesian soldier had his critics, Grobbelaar won successive League titles, a trio of League cups and the European Cup in his first three seasons at the club.

His occasional handling errors belied a unique willingness to advance from goal at set pieces to relieve pressure on his defence. In addition, his sharp reflexes and superlative shot stopping made him the undisputed first-choice between the posts.

Due to his eccentric behaviour and a penchant for talking to the crowd during quieter moments, he was also popular with most supporters.

Was badly shaken by the Heysel tragedy and initially threatened to retire from football before relenting and returning to training in time for the new season.

Phil Neal
Born: Irchester, England 20 February 1951

Signed from Northampton Town for £66,000 in 1974 by Bob Paisley – the legendary manager's first signing after taking over from Bill Shankly - Neal uniquely featured in all four of Liverpool's European Cup triumphs between 1977 and 1984. Played an astonishing 417 games in a row for the Reds between October 1976 and September 1983 – a Liverpool record.

His Anfield testimonial - a fiercely contested pre-1985/86 season affair won 3-2 by neighbours Everton - was a reward for 11 seasons of consistency and excellence.

Behind the scenes however, club captain Neal – christened 'Zico' by the fans - was disappointed to have been passed over for the player-manager position for Dalglish, a situation that was likely to prejudice his position as the season began.

Steve Nicol
Born: Irvine, Scotland 11 December 1961

Signed from Ayr United in October 1981 by Bob Paisley – where he was only a part-time player and out of work labourer - the versatile Nicol could play in midfield or defence and, at the start of the 1985/86 season, had already played over 50 League games in a variety of positions under both Paisley and Joe Fagan.

Played in 32 out of Liverpool's 67 games the previous season, coming second to Paul Walsh in the PFA's vote for the Young Player of the Year.

An energetic substitute in the 1984 European Cup Final against Roma, Nicol volunteered to take the opening kick in the vital penalty shoot-out – and missed.

Possessed with great stamina – arguably due to his voracious appetite for potato crisps - and equally impressive with both of his size 13 feet, many felt it wouldn't be long before the 24 year-old Nicol's youthful endeavour and pace on the right became indispensable to Dalglish.

Alan Kennedy
Born: Sunderland, England 31 August 1954

'Barney Rubble' as he was affectionately known by fans, the likeable Geordie had been the unlikely goalscoring hero of two European Cup Finals - in Paris and Rome. After signing from Newcastle for £300,000 in August 1978, his Anfield career had been a huge success and, alongside his two European Cup winner's medals he could also boast five League Championships

At 31-years of age however, and having being the target for some criticism the previous season, it was clear the full-back would have to fight to reclaim his place from emerging Irishman Jim Beglin, who had been chosen ahead of him for the ill-fated 1985 European Cup final in Brussels.

Jim Beglin
Born: Waterford, Eire 29 July 1963

Bob Paisley's last Liverpool signing - from Shamrock Rovers in May 1983 – Beglin had already established himself in the first team by the end of the 1984/85 season, scoring in the European Cup semi-final against Panathanaikos.

It was predicted that Beglin's scything tackles, buccaneering runs, and powerful shooting would eventually see him command a permanent place ahead of the popular Alan Kennedy.

Alan Hansen
Born: Sauchie, Scotland 13 June 1955

Bought by Bob Paisley from Partick Thistle in May 1977 for a bargain £100,000, Alan Hansen was arguably the most graceful defender to play for the club. By the time Joe Fagan stepped down as manager 'Jocky' was 30-years of age but - at a time of unparalleled success at Anfield - had already won five League titles, three European Cups and four League Cups.

His influence in the dressing room as a senior player hadn't gone unnoticed, but it was yet to be seen how he would handle the elevation to manager - and the inevitable detachment this brought - of his close friend and colleague, Dalglish.

Mark Lawrenson
Born: Penwortham, England 2 June 1957

Liverpool's record signing when he arrived from Brighton in the summer 1981 for £900,000, but this was money well spent for a truly versatile, and incredibly gifted footballer. Lawrenson possessed superb vision and pace, was decent in the air and was renowned for his crunching, perfectly timed tackles.

Although under Joe Fagan he had become Alan Hansen's regular partner in central defence he had in fact spent much of his first Anfield season at left-back – and his second as a visionary central midfielder.

A European Cup winner in Rome in 1984, he had also won league titles in his first three seasons and had been the scorer of the often forgotten fifth goal in the 5-0 win over Everton in November 1982 – Ian Rush bagging the other four.

On the tragic night in Brussels, 'Lawro' hurt a shoulder he had dislocated three weeks previously, but was now fully recovered to take his place as one of the first names on Dalglish's team-sheet.

Gary Gillespie
Born: Stirling, Scotland 5 July 1960

Falkirk's captain at the age of 17 - the youngest in Scottish football history - before heading South to Coventry and moving to Liverpool in July 1983 at a cost of £325,000, Gillespie was a tall, elegant defender similar in style to Alan Hansen.

'Dizzy' had struggled to win a regular place under Joe Fagan and, with Hansen and Lawrenson an established pairing in his favoured position at centre-half, the role of accomplished understudy beckoned once again under the new manager.

Mark Seagraves
Born: Liverpool 22 October 1966

A product of the club's youth system, locally born Seagraves began the new season as a 19-year old reserve defender, firmly behind Hansen, Lawrenson and Gillespie in the pecking order for a place in the heart of Liverpool's rear-guard.

Many expected a bright future for the tall, elegant defender however, and should the opportunity of a place in the first-team beckon; there was no doubt it would be eagerly taken.

John Wark
Born: Glasgow, Scotland 4 August 1957

Already a proven First Division performer when Joe Fagan paid £450,000 to sign him from Ipswich Town in March 1984, Wark came with a reputation for goals from midfield and made an immediate impact when scoring on his Liverpool debut – against Watford in March 1984.

With Ian Rush absent through injury, Wark was the Reds' leading scorer in 1984/85 with 27 goals in all competitions. He missed only two matches that season and was keen for more of the same ahead of the new campaign. An injury in the 1985 pre-season in Dalglish's earliest days as manager however, threatened to rule out the prolific Scot for the opening two months.

Jan Molby
Born: Kolding, Denmark 4 July 1963

Signed from Ajax for £200,000 in August 1984, Molby initially struggled to fill the huge role left in midfield by Graeme Souness's departure to Sampdoria. There had been glimpses of his remarkable vision, passing and shooting ability during the Danish international's 24 appearances in his debut season however, and many hoped he would be given a chance to shine in the forthcoming campaign.

Dalglish and the rest of the 'Boot Room' had recognised his immense creative talent but, although he had been a regular starter in the pre-season friendlies, it wasn't obvious who would partner him in central midfield.

Kevin MacDonald
Born: Inverness, Scotland 22 December 1960

Transferred from Leicester City in November 1984, Joe Fagan's £400,000 purchase made his debut against Luton at Anfield in the last match of 1984 and made 24 consecutive appearances in the second half of the season before being injured.

Had been signed to partially fill the void left by Graeme Souness but, although he was strong in the tackle, he had yet to score his first goal and was finding it difficult to win over the Anfield crowd.

His challenge as he recovered from the injury that curtailed his first season in Liverpool was to prove he had the necessary class to merit a more permanent place in Dalglish's plans.

Ronnie Whelan
Born: Dublin, Eire 25 September 1961

Plucked from the obscurity of Home Farm in the Irish League for a bargain £35,000 in September 1979, Ronnie Whelan initially beat off the competition of future Everton star Kevin Sheedy to cement a regular Anfield first team place in 1981.

By the time Dalglish took over, 24-year old Whelan was already a veteran of three successful title campaigns - and a European Cup winner.

Although right-footed, he regularly weighed in with goals from the left of midfield including match winners in the 1982 and 1983 League Cup Finals at Wembley. As the Eire international began his sixth full season at Liverpool, his growing ability to also feature in the middle of midfield made him a prized Anfield asset.

Sammy Lee
Born: Liverpool 7 February 1959

Although still only 26, Sammy Lee was one of the most experienced players on Liverpool's staff. Having made his debut as far back as April 1978 he had become a regular during 1980/81 and had played in the European Cup triumph in Paris. Championship honours, and a second European Cup winner's medal, followed in the ensuing three seasons.

Despite his credentials however, Liverpool-born Lee's place had come under threat in Joe Fagan's second and final season, restricting him to 25 appearances and, as the new season beckoned, he was preparing to fight it out with Craig Johnston for a place on the right of the Reds' midfield.

Craig Johnston
Born: Johannesburg, South Africa 25 June 1960

A £650,000 signing from Middlesbrough in April 1981, Craig Johnston occasionally frustrated manager Bob Paisley - his individualistic, all-action style sometimes disrupting the trusted team pattern that was Liverpool's trademark.

Recognising the Australian's unpredictable talents however, Johnston struck 10 goals in Paisley's final season in 1982/83. He continued to shine in Joe Fagan's treble year - making 52 appearances - but his unpredictability and inconsistency saw him fall out of favour during Fagan's second season when he featured only 17 times.

At the start of the 1985/86 season Johnston, viewed predominately as a right winger, faced an uphill battle – or a change in managerial views - to re-establish himself as a first team regular in Dalglish's new set-up.

Kenny Dalglish
Born: Glasgow, Scotland 4 March 1951

Dalglish's appointment as player-manager was recognition not just of his remarkable football knowledge and ability to inspire those around him, but also a note of acceptance that he was nearing the end of his glorious playing career.

Since his arrival from Celtic in a £440,000 deal which many thought the most astute piece of business in Liverpool's history, Dalglish carried all before him – a three-time European Cup Winner and five-times league champion (as well as an MBE in the New Years Honours List in 1985) – before promotion to the manager's chair in the days following the Heysel tragedy.

At the age of 34 however, the regularity of his goals was on the wane - as shown by his tally of just six goals in 53 games in 1984/85 - but Dalglish remained the team's most creative attacking force and it was fully expected that he would combine his new managerial duties with the renewal of his partnership with Ian Rush up front.

There were understandable concerns the dual role would be too taxing, even for a man of Dalglish's calibre, so former boss Bob Paisley was installed as team consultant to smooth his transition into management.

Ian Rush
Born: St. Asaph, Wales 20 October 1961

Emerging into the first-team picture at the same time as Ronnie Whelan, becoming a regular in autumn 1981, Ian Rush quickly established himself as the best striker in Britain - culminating in a remarkable season in 1983/84 when his 47 goals fired Liverpool to the treble.

Having signed from Chester for £300,000 in May 1980, Rush heeded the advice of Bob Paisley to be more selfish and was unstoppable in front of goal for three seasons until a knee ligament injury forced him to miss the opening 14 matches of the 1984/85 season. Remarkably however, he recovered to score 26 goals in the remainder of that campaign.

Rush's exploits at home and abroad had not gone unnoticed and in the summer of 1984 Liverpool refused to accept a bid for his services – thought to be around £4 million - from Napoli - much to Rush's frustration. He put the disappointment of missing out on financial security offered by such a move out of his mind however, and by the time Dalglish took control his attentions were firmly re-focused on matters at Anfield – at least for the time being.

Paul Walsh
Born: Plumstead, London 1 October 1962

Another Joe Fagan signing - for £700,000 from Luton Town in May 1984 - Walsh made a dramatic start to his Liverpool career, scoring after just 15 seconds of his Anfield debut against West Ham just three months later.

The PFA Young Player of the Year – who had also helped England win the same year's European U-21 Championships with Sammy Lee - went straight into the side deputising for the absent Ian Rush. Although the Welshman's return coincided with an injury of his own for Walsh, the diminutive striker later regained his place up front - with Dalglish assuming a deeper role behind the front two.

In a promising first season, the skilful Walsh netted 13 times in 39 appearances, culminating in selection for the European Cup Final.

Already capped by England, Walsh felt he had done enough to warrant a first team place and, as the new season dawned, Dalglish faced an intriguing selection and formation dilemma revolving around the abilities of himself, Rush and the confident 22-year old Londoner.

On The March With Kenny's Army

Prologue

"In a city cast as an outsider in its own land, battered by the deliberately economic downturns and clearouts of the early 1980s, Liverpool Football Club was an enduring source of pride, a magnet for the energies and emotions of a public hungry for success."

David Goldblatt, The Ball is Round: A Global History of Football, Penguin 2007

"I remember the day perfectly. It was raining. And freezing cold. I decided to leave after New Year and although I didn't think it would be my last Christmas living with my family, it was one of the worst. I knew I was leaving from about August '85 when my YTS at Yew Tree finished. It was a typical Maggie Job share - give two men one job and make them share it. There were fellas 30+ on it and I was only 19. I didn't look down on them or pity them, I just wanted a proper job, with proper money. I wanted a car or a bike and I wanted to be able to go out and buy clothes.

"As with everyone else at the time, life was hard. I remember a typical family meeting where it was decided we had to get rid of the telly or the stereo, so we voted. All hands bar mine went up to get rid of the telly, I was f**king devastated, I used to lie to me mates about what I watched and would just join in conversations about TV shows and films. All I wanted was a fair crack of the whip, a chance to do something. I had no hatred - bar footy related - to London and I had been a few times with Liverpool. We never just went on the day, we would always make a weekend of it.

"I told no-one I was thinking of leaving. I was the baby of the house, the youngest of seven and I knew that they would try and talk me out of it. So Christmas came and went and on 2 January 1986 and after a brief conversation with my family I left home on a National Express coach bound for London. I have no shame in saying I was upset. I knew what I was doing. I knew what I was leaving behind - but I was one of the lucky ones. I met my wife a year later while selling ice creams in Hyde Park.

I remember siting and looking out of the window of the coach going around Hyde Park Corner with my Head bag, a few clothes and Level 42 playing on my second-hand walkman that my Mum had got me for Christmas. And I cried like a f**king baby.

"Its 25 years later now and I'm married with three lads. Its been hard, but I've been lucky. I met lads in London who'd been here for years and they took me under their wings and showed me how to survive in the beginning. I met the wife a year later and her big Irish family also looked out for me.

"I left Liverpool at 19 with £12. Norris Green was being savaged by drugs and it seemed everyone was on the dole. My eyes were only truly opened to the North-South Divide when I walked into a Job Centre by Victoria Station and there where hundreds of jobs on the boards. Within two days I had a bedsit and was working on the British Library, Kings Cross as an unskilled labourer - getting £120 a week. The irony is that I got the job, the car, the bike and the clothes, but I paid for it by losing my identity, my city. Even now I'm very bitter about that.

"I'm 44 and still go the games - aways only. I love our end and listening to the everyday conversations that go on from lads who live at home, but at the end of the game they all go home and I travel back to Wembley, no tears this time, but still the same feeling of sadness."

Sean Doyle, exiled Liverpool fan. Summer 2011

On The March With Kenny's Army

*How Liverpool FC overcame tragedy and despair to win
the League and FA Cup Double - 1985/86*

by Gary Shaw and Mike Nevin

Chapter One
No Need to Run and Hide

Liverpool v Arsenal
Saturday 17 August 1985

"In Liverpool itself, sentiments after Heysel were mixed, ranging from deep shock and real shame that some people from the city were directly involved in such an appalling football tragedy, to open anger at the predictably spiteful and vicious press coverage that football, and especially the city, attracted as a result of the disaster."

John Williams, "Passing Rhythms, Liverpool FC and the Transformation of Football. John Williams, Stephen Hopkins and Cathy Long (eds.), Berg, 2001.

The first post-Heysel season was always going to be emotionally confusing, perplexing and contrasting for not only the club's fans in particular but also for the city of Liverpool in general.

In later years, Liverpool supporters would have to contend with unsavoury taunts and chants regarding their role in the disaster by fans of most clubs - including their city rivals – but in the immediate aftermath of the tragedy, the Red half of the city received sympathy and understanding from their Evertonian friends, neighbours and colleagues. When news filtered through of the amateurish organisation, farcical policing and crumbling Brussels venue, educated followers of other English clubs accepted that it could just have easily been them - and their club's reputation - at the wrong end of the moral outrage now sweeping the country.

That the target was enlarged to include the city itself only lent an extra fortitude to Merseyside's shared resistance. The defiance – to outsiders in general, but towards right-wing politicians, journalists and social commentators in particular - that typified the city in the 1980s was evident most glaringly in the continued support for a far-left council that, in the eyes of many, was almost single-handedly fighting the worst ravages of Thatcherism.

The, "spiteful and vicious press," coverage referred to by Williams, would continue to be directed toward Liverpool well into the new season, especially when the left-wing council versus right-wing central government saga was played out again, but nothing highlighted it more than the vitriol that followed Liverpool's first home game of the season, when an embarrassing, innocuous and seemingly banal technical problem at Anfield suddenly evolved, with the help of the right-wing press, into a torrent of media-led criticism. In the eyes of the London-based media and political class, the moral panic caused by the supposed rise of yobbish behaviour and terrace culture at the country's most successful club, added yet more fuel to discussions surrounding Liverpool's seemingly proud rise to the forefront of contemporary urban decline.

"The city's strong self-identity," Williams also wrote, "its semi-Celtic local culture, it's long-term industrial decline and depopulation, and its social, cultural and geographical relative isolation from the mainstream of Englishness, all allied to a formal and deep popular isolation to the politics of national government in Britain in the 1980s," meant however, that what followed a fine opening game win at Anfield, was not unexpected.

In the eyes of many Scousers, they had been forgotten by central government, by the establishment, by England in general. In return, many viewed any focus on the city with rapidly growing scepticism. After a fine opening day win over Arsenal was overshadowed by a non-story that criticised their behaviour before the game, many Kopites felt rightly aggrieved.

The story in question focused on the nature and - in light of recent events - alleged lack of respect shown by the Kop, a terrace that up until May 1985 had been regularly lauded by the press for its passionate support, sense of fair play, and self-effacing wit.

Their offence? Singing the club anthem, You'll Never Walk Alone, when they should have sang - as directed by the opening games' programme notes - the much more establishment-friendly Abide With Me, a hymn that in Liverpool at least, was viewed as a bucolic, pious, little-Englander tract that was rarely, if ever, sung on the frequent trips to the national stadium made by Everton and Liverpool fans alike.

Indeed, just a year before, at the 1984 Milk Cup Final, and even at the curtain raiser to the 1985 season, the Charity Shield, both sets of fans had ignored the hymn and sang instead a defiant, "Merseyside, Merseyside, Merseyside," – a reminder to the rest of the nation it seemed, that the provincial city in the North-West of England still existed for other reasons beyond biting over-critical degradation. That the accusations of ill-timing, callous disrespect, loutishness and a subsequent fierce defence of their alleged misbehaviour, were played out in the media, was reflective of the broad feeling of neglect and disenchantment with those who administered and wrote about the sport.

"With the eyes of Europe on Anfield, it is vital for football everywhere that this game provides a memorable afternoon's entertainment," was Liverpool Echo reporter Ian Hargraves' take on the Red's opening fixture of the season. In his 'My View' column he also took the opportunity to call for wholesale reform of UEFA on the grounds that their conduct over Brussels, "has been nothing less than disgraceful, and must leave everyone questioning their ability to act as the ruling body of the European game."

Whilst he noted that, together with their indefinite European ban for Liverpool, "our government [also] seem determined to make them the scapegoats as well," Hargraves nevertheless insisted that, "had Liverpool's advice been taken [on the game] there would have been no Heysel disaster, just as there had been no serious trouble at any European game either Liverpool or Everton had ever staged."

Asking that a club, "be allowed some say in how the events they compete in are promoted," does not seem that much of a radical idea today, but in the aftermath of Heysel to advocate such a stance was almost incendiary. The chances of just such a shift in UEFA's policy was not that remote the respected reporter added, especially as, "even Juventus stand behind Liverpool on this issue." Eventually clubs would have a say in policing, ticketing and other issues surrounding the final, but it would take many years for such reforms to benefit English sides.

Kenny Dalglish's programme notes echoed Hargraves initial pre-match assessment. The new player-manager acknowledged that, although, "this is a season with a difference, in many ways," – his appointment itself being the most notable change – he also hoped that the club could, "get the legacy of Brussels out of our system," as quickly as possible.

Liverpool Chairman John Smith, arguably one of a handful of Conservative supporters whose views were listened to for more than a second on Merseyside, and one of the most respected men in English football administration was however, unequivocal in his condemnation of, "the minority who have brought violence, hooliganism, intimidation and disgrace to far too many matches."

"Last season was a disaster for English football," he wrote in the match programme. The domestic game, "simply cannot go through another season like it, if it is to survive as a sport." Smith and prominent Club Secretary Peter Robinson had publicly asked UEFA to move the European Cup final from the Heysel Stadium as soon as Liverpool emphatically won their semi-final first leg against Greek side Panathanaikos. In the view of the Liverpool officials there were grave concerns over the inadequacies of the stadium, policing and ticket arrangements.

Smith had informed Merseyside Police that they had the full backing of the club, "in taking firm action against anyone who steps out of line," this season. Anyone who entered the field of play would be immediately ejected from the ground, stadium CCTV had been extensively increased, whilst the club would fully enforce the new Sporting Events (Control of Alcohol) Act – a law still in place today – that forbade anyone from entering a football ground drunk or even to view an area of the pitch whilst being served with alcohol.

The rule still differentiates from other sports however, and one can still drink freely at rugby or cricket games – even if held in a football stadium – whilst corporate hospitality companies simply ensure a piece of glass is between the drinker and the action in order to adhere to the wording, if not the nature, of the law.

If the words of their chairman and manager were not enough to capture the mood, those who chose to pay 50p for the Anfield Review were left in no doubt as to their standing in the public's and the media's eye when they opened it to find a flyer from Merseyside Police fall from its pages – mug-shots of fans in differing states of violent action from Brussels with an appeal for their identity. "Do you know these men?" it asked. Looking at the single A5 sheet even now, some 25 years later, instils a chilling sense of reflected guilt.

Before a ball had even been kicked then, it was as ignominious a start to the new campaign as you could have wished for. However, more was to follow. Almost laughable for its hyperbole when reviewed today, the 'tannoy incident' nevertheless serves as a reminder of the depth of disgust in which football fans in general where held at the time, and Liverpool fans – from the city – in particular.

Also listed in the programme for the Arsenal game was an Order of Service for a short ceremony, "of prayer and dedication," to be held, "with the memory of Brussels still very much in our minds." Liverpool's three religious leaders; the Most Rev. Derek Warlock, Roman Catholic Archbishop of Liverpool; the Right Rev. David Sheppard, Anglican Bishop of Liverpool; and the Rev. John Williamson, Moderator of the Free Churches, were each to say short prayers in front of the Anfield Road end of the ground before a rendition of Abide With Me was to be sung by the crowd. Amongst the first religious leaders to acknowledge the role social deprivation, unemployment and inequality played in creating and prolonging many problems the inner cities faced during the social and political upheaval of the 1980s, Warlock and Sheppard were well respected in Liverpool.

Rarely seen in public without each other, the two men were extremely close and had fully endorsed a recent report into the Churches role in the inner cities, commissioned by the Archbishop of Canterbury Robert Runcie. Faith in the City would be published, amid great controversy, just a few months later, with many on the left seeing it as a vindication of their attacks on what they saw as unjustified and unsustainable Conservative attacks on the ordinary people of Merseyside. Few men then, were better qualified to give such an address in the memory of what happened at Heysel, but even they could not have foreseen the furore that would follow their role in a well-intentioned service arranged by the club.

Never the most audible tannoy, the public address system at Anfield completely failed this day. Those entering the ground later on in the afternoon, particularly in the Kop, at the other end of the pitch and adorned by numerous Juventus flags that day – the terrace's own tribute to the dead - had little idea a service was being conducted as only muffled noise made its way onto the home terracing.

Indeed, in the absence of any decipherable sound even those who had bought match programmes found the order of service difficult to follow, so, when a few hundred supporters in the remaining stands began to sing – badly - Abide with Me, the Kop did what it knew best – and simply sang its own anthem, loud and clear, as a mark of respect to those who had died. Few singing You'll Never Walk Alone with such intensity and passion that day could have envisaged the debate that would follow their actions after the game – nor the obvious class connotations it almost inevitably raised.

As for the game itself, few observers expected Arsenal to offer any real threat to a Liverpool side that had been installed as second-favourites for the title behind champions Everton, and this turned out to be the case.

Managed by their loyal, former player and coach Don Howe – in his second extended spell with the club - Arsenal were a solid though unspectacular side, far removed from the mercurial, flamboyant foreign legion we are accustomed to today.

Indeed, recent success had been conspicuous by its absence for the Gunners and it had been seven years since silverware of any description had found its way to the Highbury trophy room, whilst their last league championship was in their famous 1970-71 'double' winning season. In that time their near neighbours Tottenham Hotspur, with successive FA Cups in 1981 and 1982 and UEFA Cup success in 1984, had overtaken them as the dominant footballing side in North London. Whereas Arsenal could only finish seventh in 1984/85, Spurs finished in third - with the same number of points as second-placed Liverpool.

Player-manager Dalglish named himself at no. 7 in a familiar looking Liverpool line-up that read: Grobbelaar, Neal, Kennedy, Lawrenson, Whelan, Hansen, Dalglish, Nicol, Rush, Molby, Beglin. Youngsters Nicol and Beglin would occupy the wide positions in midfield with Whelan and Molby in the middle. For defender Mark Lawrenson, who had played in bigger games both domestically and internationally with the Republic of Ireland, this match, "was the most nerve-wracking of my career…I cannot recall a more tense occasion than our first game after Heysel. It seemed that the world's press was at Anfield that day, and no team has been subjected to such an intense glare of publicity." Lawrenson also wondered how the new Reds' manager was coping with all this pressure. "We were all churning inside," he said, "but if he felt the same way, he did not let on to any of us."

In bright, early autumn sunshine however, Dalglish's first competitive game in charge of the Reds ran as smoothly as the new player-manager could have wished. If he was nervous at taking charge of his beloved Reds for the first time – and with such intense media interest in the game – then he didn't show it. With the emphasis very much on smooth, flowing, attacking football, Liverpool were simply too good, too fast, and too tactically astute for Don Howe's seemingly straight jacketed Arsenal side.

In Charlie Nicholas and Tony Woodcock the Gunners had arguably two of the best centre-forwards in the country but, against as good a defence the English game has ever seen in Lawrenson, Hansen, Neal and Kennedy, they were always fighting a losing battle. In the summer of 1983 Nicholas had famously tuned down a move from Glasgow Celtic to Bob Paisley's perennial title challengers in favour of a move to London's bright city lights. Mindful of the high standards required at Anfield he instead chose to join Arsenal - who had failed to register a trophy since their victory in the 1980 FA Cup Final. His decision to turn Liverpool down – and the four League titles, a League Cup, an FA Cup and a European Cup the Reds subsequently won in the time he spent at Highbury - given his supposed position as an 'expert' football pundit, still forces wry smiles and raised eyebrows on Merseyside. In his time at Arsenal Nicholas won just the one trophy – the 1987 League Cup.

Coupled with a midfield that paled in comparison with the talent Liverpool could call on; the sublime passing and ball control of Danish international Jan Molby, "who on this form will be an influential figure,"; the never-say-die attitude of Whelan and Nicol; and a strike partnership as imperious and clinical as Dalglish and Rush, Arsenal were lucky to be only a goal down at half-time.

The Gunners actually started the game well, forcing two corners in the first 10 minutes but these failed to threaten Grobbelaar and it was as close as the Londoners would get in the first half. On 12 minutes Alan Hansen brought the ball out of defence in his usual graceful manner, as far as the edge of the Arsenal penalty area and, after exchanging a one-two with Rush, just failed, "by inches to reach the return pass before goalkeeper Lukic."

Eight minutes later, "the ball was moved briskly between Molby, Whelan, Dalglish and Beglin," before Whelan curled a 25-yard shot just wide. Seconds later Kennedy set Whelan free on the left and the Irishman did well to find Molby inside the area but the Dane's low shot was smothered by Gunners' keeper John Lukic – who had been born in Chesterfield to Yugoslav parents. This move, "seemed to inspire Liverpool," and within minutes both Rush and Kennedy were extremely unlucky not to score. Nicholas and Allinson then briefly threatened the Liverpool goal but Hansen, "refused to panic under pressure," and he, "played the ball quietly out of defence." On the half-hour mark Molby shot a free-kick - following a foul on Dalglish outside the area - just over the bar.

Liverpool were finding it difficult to turn chances into goals, but five minutes later the home side's pressure told. From the right wing Nicol found Rush unmarked in the area, but the prolific Welshman missed the ball completely. Fortunately, most of the Arsenal defence were expecting the Welshman to get a shot on goal at least and they could only watch as the ball ran through the box to Beglin who sent a perfect cross into the danger area for Whelan who, appearing from nowhere, left Lukic, "helpless with a perfect header." There was time for Molby to fire a rare header wide from a Nicol free kick but the half ended with the home side a goal to the good.

Nicol showed he wasn't just a dogged, hard working influence when, early in the second-half, he went on a run down the right that had the crowd cheering as he beat England left-back Kenny Sansom not once but twice. The Scotsman's cross was eventually cleared by O'Leary. Arsenal then created a chance completely against the run of play but Robson sent his shot into the roof of the stand when under pressure from the Liverpool defence. "Nicol's torment of Sansom," seemed to never end and he again beat the Arsenal captain easily before finding Dalglish in the area only for Arsenal, "to scramble the ball away."

Minutes later the diminutive full-back showed he had had enough of being exposed by Nicol and he upended the Scot in the box after being drawn into an unwise tackle. "There were strong appeals for a penalty but ref Hutchinson settled for a corner." Soon after another penalty appeal – this time for a foul against Rush – was also waved away. On 55 minutes the referee had no option but to book Williams for a foul on Lawrenson but, with the versatile centre-half seemingly well-placed to score after coming out of defence to augment the attack, the ultimately missed free-kick by Molby was of little consolation.

Arsenal's best player was the languid Rix in central midfield, but even he could not prevent Liverpool from engineering a host of decent chances. Dalglish and Rush both went close in quick succession whilst, "Beglin forced a brilliant save from Lukic after Molby had cleverly switched the direction of the attack."

The quality of Liverpool's football temporarily banished the horrors of Heysel from the minds of fans and journalists alike and it was all Liverpool now; Anfield on a sunny opening day of a new season decorated by the forceful attacking play of the home side. Rush headed against the top of the bar from a powerful Kennedy cross but then Arsenal twice came close to an equaliser. Grobbelaar tipped a Robson shot around the post for a corner, and from the resultant kick the ball fell loose in the area but no Arsenal player could take advantage.

Seconds later the Gunners were made to pay for such profligacy as Dalglish, "dribbling brilliantly down the middle," took the ball around Lukic and, with defenders on the line, crossed to the far post, "where the incoming Nicol steered it firmly home with his head."

Liverpool were in total control. They threatened a third goal when Molby, Rush, Nicol and Dalglish – all on top of their game - combined to find Whelan on the edge of the box but, as he was about to shoot, he was fouled by a desperate lunge from Rix. The offence appeared to take place inside the box but again the referee waved away the appeals of Liverpool's players - and most of the 38,261 crowd - and gave a free-kick instead. Nicol stepped up to take it and almost scored a third only to see Lukic make a great save. There was still time for Grobbelaar to upstage Lukic as Liverpool's Durban-born goalkeeper pulled off the save of the day from a Sansom header with just five minutes to go.

Other results saw Everton draw at Leicester in a swift return to Filbert Street for Gary Lineker, and Manchester United beat Aston Villa at Old Trafford. It was an inauspicious start to the season for Ron Atkinson's side, and few commentators went overboard on what was after all the opening day of a long season, but for Bob Driscoll in the Daily Star, the manner of Liverpool's win warranted special mention. "Quite simply," he said, "Liverpool looked as good as ever they did under last season's orthodox managership."

Although there were plaudits for the team in some newspapers, few fans leaving Anfield at the final whistle could have envisioned the glut of negative comments concerning their alleged poor behaviour prior to the game that would also appear in them over the coming days. The tannoy breakdown and the pre-match confusion that ensued brought judgemental comment in the following day's papers – simplistically and wrongly reported in almost all the 'Sundays' as Liverpool fans 'interrupting' the memorial service.

If Dalglish's embryonic management had begun to restore some of Liverpool's standing on the football front, a long struggle lay ahead for Liverpool's supporters to shed their tarnished reputation. Together with the news that Kirkby-based food manufacturer Kraft was cutting a further 60 jobs – in addition to the 260 lost in the previous two years – it was yet another negative aspect of living in mid-1980s Merseyside. The Kraft plant would not survive the year.

Aston Villa v Liverpool
Wednesday 21 August 1985

"The recent youth exchange between Liverpool 28 Improvement Committee and a party of Turin youngsters was a great success. We would like to publicly thank the many organisations who helped to make the trip go smoothly, both before the Italians arrived and when they arrived in Liverpool.

Special thanks to both the city and county councils, JH Rogerson builders, The Princes Trust and The John Moores Foundation for helping to finance the trip. Also greatly appreciated were the efforts of the Holiday Inn, Bucco di Bacco, Everton FC, The State, Club Continental and the Montini and Mab Lane Youth Centres in accommodating and catering for the party. We are hoping to take the next step towards reconciliation by accepting an invitation to visit Turin before Christmas."

Letter to Liverpool Echo, Mark Fitzimmons, Cantril Farm, 17 August 1985

On the day Liverpool were despatching Arsenal with relative ease a letter from Reds' fan Mr R. Brigden of Maghull appeared in the Football Echo. As with many fans' views on team selection and potential transfer targets, Mr Brigden's views were very much hit and miss. Most Liverpool fans would have agreed with his assessment that the Anfield side had lost far too many games at home the previous season and that Dalglish had to be more, "ruthless in his team selection," in future if success was to return.

Replacing Grobbelaar with Chris Woods of Norwich would also perhaps have found more than a few advocates, but his remarks that Liverpool, having missed out on Gary Lineker, should pursue Arsenal's Charlie Nicholas however, would have been laughed at by most of the Anfield faithful.

Despite this one anomaly, it is the remaining contents of Mr. Brigden's letter that make for more interesting reading. His views that Steve Nicol's best position was right-back – at the expense of Phil Neal - and that Alan Kennedy be replaced at left-back by Jim Beglin appear, in light of subsequent events, to be strangely prophetic.

In addition, whilst lamenting that Liverpool missed Graham Souness's role as a hard-tackling midfielder a potential solution to this situation was offered. "Steve McMahon of Villa would fit the bill," Mr Brigden wrote - another example of his fortune telling skills. Next up for Liverpool? A trip to Villa Park where, even though reports intensified about a possible Anfield move for the former Everton player before the game, McMahon would play a crucial role. Whereas in today's game imminent transfer targets for clubs are routinely precluded from playing as they are often deemed 'mentally unable to play', no such worries existed in the mid-1980s.

Despite enquiries for the player having already been conducted by Liverpool's senior staff, and the view of most observers that his sale was practically imminent - possibly just days away - Steve McMahon not only played, but he was instrumental in helping Villa secure a share of the spoils in a 2-2 draw against his future employers. Prior to the game Kenny Dalglish reiterated his desire to sign the battling midfielder, but categorically stated that Villa's desire to include Paul Walsh in any deal simply would not happen. "There is no way Paul is going to leave Anfield," he told the Liverpool Echo. The Reds' management team sees, "the Rush-Walsh partnership up front as crucial to their championship challenge."

Although Walsh had played only 20 minutes of football in pre-season however, Dalglish named him in the starting 11 instead of himself. It was a decision that many felt, "imposed something of a handicap on his side," as the Londoner was, "clearly not match fit and had to be replaced by Craig Johnston on the hour, by which time he had also damaged a knee." When the substitution was made, the game, played in heavy rain that made good football difficult, was in the balance at 1-1.

After only nine minutes Grobbelaar - reinforcing Mr Brigden's view of him as untrustworthy - failed to hold an awkward, skidding cross by Mark Walters. The spill fell to former Young Player of the Year Gary Shaw [no relation to the co-author] who was making his return to the Villa starting line-up after a nightmare 18 months out following four operations on a knee injury. The one-time Liverpool target made no mistake and Villa, with McMahon, Walters and former Everton forward Andy Gray, creating problems for the Liverpool defence – both Lawrenson and Hansen would ultimately be booked - were one up.

Villa had the best of the remainder of the first-half but they failed to capitalise on their possession and, as the half wore on, Liverpool began to cope much better with both the Midlanders' forwards and the treacherous conditions.

Revelling in his new central midfield role, Ronnie Whelan was a key factor in this improvement and, on 38 minutes, it was his pass that found Walsh in space on the right wing. In attempting to close him down Villa left-back Brendan Ormsby could only foul the nimble front man however, and Molby's sublime cross from the subsequent free-kick fell, "perfectly for Rush to score with an equally good header." It was the Welshman's 11th goal in the last nine meetings between the sides.

Liverpool improved to such an extent in the second-half that, "the only surprise was that they did not score two or three times." Nigel Spink saved well from Rush whilst a Whelan shot flew just wide, but it was a Villa substitution that almost changed the game.

Gary Williams was injured when tackling Beglin and manager Graham Turner brought on teenage sensation Tony Daley, one of the fastest players in the league at the time. Daley's first touch was a warning for Liverpool – taking him on, "a spectacular run that took him through most of the Liverpool side." Seconds later it was the speedster's pass that found Mark Walters sprinting clear of Liverpool's defence to smash the ball past Grobbelaar.

With just 14 minutes to salvage a point from the game Liverpool attacked in numbers and, with just four minutes remaining, deservedly grabbed an equaliser after Molby scored following a clever one-two with Rush. Two minutes later the Welsh striker wasted a glorious chance to win the game for the Reds when his penalty, after he was pushed in the back when heading against the bar, was wonderfully saved by Spink.

Phil Neal had taken penalties throughout his Liverpool career - including two in European Cup Finals - but in this instance he deferred responsibility to prolific teammate Ian Rush. It was a spur-of-the-moment decision [to take the penalty]," Rush later said. "Phil Neal asked me if I wanted to have a go and I agreed. If I was asked to do so again I would have a go – but I doubt the lads will allow me to after this." Manager Dalglish was more upbeat about the miss however, stating he "did not regard it as a penalty missed – rather a great save."

Even this wasn't the end of the drama however. With less than 30 seconds remaining Johnston rounded the Villa keeper only to see his goal-bound shot cleared of the line by none other than Steve McMahon. The midfielder had prevented his (very) soon to be employers from winning what was an absorbing and entertaining match - albeit a frustrating one for Liverpool.

With the football press of 1985 perhaps having a more realistic view of the longevity of a football league campaign than today's media, Liverpool's result was not greeted with the kind of negative, overblown response that has now become almost commonplace. Indeed, the league table was still two games away from actually being published in most newspapers. It would not be long however, before any serious evaluation of the forthcoming campaign was forsaken for the sort of hyperbole to which football fans have now seemingly grown accustomed. The reason for this change of emphasis? Ron Atkinson's Manchester United who, in beating Ipswich Town at Portman Road the night before - on the same night Everton beat WBA 2-0 - had won their opening two games. Just three games later they would already be being talked about as champions in waiting.

Of perhaps more significance for the football fan however – although few saw it that way at the time - was the news that, in the wake of the tragedies that had befallen the game recently, Liverpool fan Rogan Taylor had set up the Football Supporters Association (now Football Supporters Federation) the forerunner to the organised supporter groups we now take for granted. Together with the fledgling fanzine movement, inspired by such music magazines such as the NME and irreverent Merseyside publication The End - with its cryptic take on Liverpool culture - it appeared that, with very few in football's hierarchy taking fans' views seriously, grass roots supporters were finally taking it upon themselves to forge an alternative, cultured and resonant force for good in the game.

Newcastle United v Liverpool
Saturday 24 August 1985

"There were 5,770 other people at the game, probably around 1,000 from Leeds. There was a noticeable absence of whole families and a curious absence of blacks. Someone had spray-gunned 'We're back, LUFC 85 National Front' on an exterior wall at the Leeds end but, if this constituted a threat, nothing came of it. The first sanction visibly to work was the banning of alcohol. In the hour before the kick-off I saw not a single drunk, nor did I see a bottle or can in the vicinity of the ground. Indeed, the only element of provocation was the presence of two TV crews and a posse of press photographers looking for violence to film.

Ian Wooldridge, The Daily Mail, writing on Fulham v Leeds, Division Two. Monday 19 August
Just six days before the season had started Jack Charlton had rocked the football world when, after a row with supporters over the sale of exciting winger Chris Waddle to Spurs, he resigned as manager of Newcastle United. Former goalkeeper Willie McFaul replaced Charlton – in a caretaker capacity - so, with two draws from their first two games, the only managerless club in the First Division hosted the only one with a player-manager.

Realising that Paul Walsh was still far from match-fit, Dalglish named himself in an unchanged starting line-up. Walsh was given a run-out for the A team whilst Craig Johnston was named substitute for the third game in a row.

Ian Hargraves noted that although Liverpool's early season form had, "settled down in most respects," it would perhaps, "be a little time before they generate as much fire-power as they would like." A consistent and recognised striker, either to partner or act as back-up to Ian Rush – who before the game had ended speculation about his future by signing a new three-year deal - was seen as a necessity. Following this game many saw Peter Beardsley as just such a player. However, it would be another two years before he would be recruited by Dalglish, albeit after the eventual sale of Rush.

Also in the Newcastle side were the stylish Glen Roeder, ex-Sunderland defender Jeff Clarke, former Everton man Gary Megson, and precocious 18-year old midfield talent Paul Gascoigne. The future darling of the national media Gascoigne enjoyed a decent enough game in midfield, but it was his fellow Geordie, Beardsley who excelled, having a hand in almost all of Newcastle's best moves.

"A thriller of a match in a cup-tie atmosphere," saw Liverpool produce few notable chances. Indeed, the Reds had only three shots in the first 45 minutes; Nicol forcing a fine save from keeper Martin Thomas early on, a long-range effort by Beglin that went wide, and Ian Rush, perhaps surprised, "when Anderson gave the ball away in a dangerous situation to the left of the penalty area," uncharacteristically scuffing a shot that he would otherwise normally have buried with ease.

The main talking point for Liverpool however, came with just 10 minutes of the half remaining, when Dalglish was injured in a tackle with McDonald, "and immediately put up his arm to signal for the Liverpool trainer." Ultimately, the player-manager would require four stitches in a knee-wound, and he was replaced by Johnston, who, "soon became Liverpool's busiest player."

Despite the Australian's energy, the Newcastle forwards were by far the more dynamic attacking force with, "Beardsley absolutely outstanding, as every Liverpool player will certainly be quick to testify." The diminutive but deceptively quick and agile forward, had caused numerous problems for the Liverpool defence in the first half - especially down the away side's left - and within five minutes of the restart Beardsley again, "showed a fine turn of speed that kept the partisan fans on their toes and raced down the right wing towards goal. Former Newcastle favourite Alan Kennedy, "managed to catch up with him to divert the ball and Beglin completed the clearance."

Soon after, Beardsley beat Hansen on the edge of the box, "with ease and got in a swerving shot," that, "Grobbelaar did well to back pedal and save." The future Liverpool star was rampant. Minutes later, "one of Lawrenson's typical saving tackles," stopped him again and it was no surprise when, in the 70th minute, "his amazing cross from one side of the field to the other," was found by MacDonald on the right. The inch-perfect cross was met at the far post by rakish, blonde-haired centre-forward George Reilly to power home a header with Grobbelaar stranded.

With 20 minutes remaining Liverpool tried desperately to score an equaliser but, despite Kennedy and Beglin beginning to get the best of a tiring Beardsley, Molby - who was again dictating Liverpool's play from the centre of the pitch - and Johnston going close after a clever Beglin through ball, Newcastle remained resolute and held on to remain undefeated.

Clearly downhearted when interviewed by the Press after the match – "it required a major physical effort [for him] to speak when asked about the game," - Dalglish lamented his side's failure to start at a high enough tempo. "We are not to happy about our performance as you might expect," he said through almost grated teeth, before adding that although, "we were second best on the day...I didn't think we deserved to lose."

Repeating the same mantra that every Liverpool manager had evoked since Bill Shankly brought a pragmatic, winning ethos to the club, Dalglish turned his attention to the next game, against Ipswich Town, just two days later. "We have to take each game as it comes and we must start all over again on Monday."

Liverpool v Ipswich Town
Monday 26 August 1985

The message came through via our trainers Roy Evans and Ronnie Moran – You will have to start calling him Boss or Gaffa, now he's the Manager. And eventually we did – unless it was on the field. He was only our equal then. Dalglish may be the greatest player I have ever played with but he's no bighead.

Ian Rush reflects on Dalglish's new status. August 1985.

Having been, "unfairly criticised after last week's game with Arsenal," Liverpool fans, "responded with a display of wit and good manners that could hardly have been bettered," in their next home game – a five-goal drubbing of a poor Ipswich side on August Bank Holiday Monday. With Dalglish injured, he named Craig Johnston for his first start of the season. Sammy Lee returned from a year beset with injury at the expense of Jim Beglin whilst Paul Walsh was named as substitute.

The visitors were in transition following their halcyon days of the late-1970s and early-80's. FA Cup winners in 1978, Bobby Robson had developed a team around the talented Dutch midfield duo Frans Thyssen and Arnold Muhren, and they narrowly missed adding to their sole League Championship - won with Alf Ramsey at the helm in 1962 - when they were runners-up to Aston Villa in 1981, and Liverpool a season later.

Their supporters could claim that they played the purest football in Division One and they also enjoyed success in Europe, winning the UEFA Cup in 1981 defeating AZ67 Alkmaar in a thrilling two-legged final. Robson's managerial abilities were recognised by the FA and, despite the offer a 10-year contract from Ipswich chairman Patrick Cobbold, he accepted the post of England manager soon after. A number of key players followed Robson's path away from Portman Road and their decline was so sharp that they finished 17th in 1984/85.

Although he had been at Anfield for four seasons, Craig Johnston had never managed to lay claim to a regular place in the starting 11. Both Bob Paisley and Joe Fagan appeared to mistrust his unpredictable talent and mazy dribbles, which didn't always fit in with Liverpool's tried and trusted pattern of play which placed a heavy emphasis on passing and moving. Johnston had come close to leaving the club in the summer, but the change of management saw him opt for one last throw of the Anfield dice. The likeable all-rounder had been rewarded with a number of appearances in pre-season - and a place on the bench - in Liverpool's three opening fixtures. This was his first start of the season.

A Liverpool player since his 1978 debut - at the age of nineteen - Sammy Lee had been sidelined by injury for most of the previous season but his skill and all-action style had never been in question. Indeed, he had enjoyed a fine summer, regaining his fitness by captaining England as an over-age player in the European U-21 Championships. The ever-popular local lad assumed a position in central midfield, with Whelan moving back to his old position on the left in place of Beglin. The change in personnel and positioning worked spectacularly however, as Liverpool, despite a slow start against the East Anglians, "clicked so well that they were three up within 27 minutes."

"Poor Ipswich just didn't know how to cope," although trying to play the same open style as Liverpool contributed greatly to their downfall. "Such a policy is easier to lay down than to execute." Perhaps a more cautious early approach from the visitors would have been advisable but, "after briefly mounting a half-hearted challenge for the opening 15 minutes of the game… [Ipswich then] spent most of their time trying to prevent Liverpool reaching double figures."

After a quarter of an hour, a superb 30-yard cross field pass by Molby found an unmarked Nicol who, after a clever one-two with Johnston, casually stroked the ball into the net from just inside the area. Eight minutes later, "Rush came in from nowhere to score," from Whelan's flick-on of Nicol's corner and just three minutes after this the game was effectively over - Molby despatching a Nicol pass from the right, "after Whelan had done much of the spade work." That the scoreline was 'just' 3-0 at half-time owed much to the agility of Ipswich custodian Paul Cooper, though the second 45 minutes brought the stocky keeper no respite.

Defending the Kop end, the home crowd (at 29, 383 it was an incredible 9,000 down on the opening home game v Arsenal) were already singing, "Going Down, Going Down," to the visiting fans – from whom came the humorous retort, "So are we, So are we" – when, following a fine scrambling save from Rush, they began to regale the visiting keeper with a rendition of the Spiderman theme, with the masked super-hero's name replaced in favour of, "Cooperman." Upon hearing his name sung in such appreciative fashion the Ipswich

No. 1 smiled and waved at the home crowd, but not even any superhuman efforts he may have had could prevent Liverpool, on 70 minutes, going 4-0 up.

"After a precise right-wing move [involving Nicol and Johnston] reminiscent of Liverpool's famous clincher in the 1974 FA Cup victory over Newcastle," Rush calmly side-footed the Australian's precise pass for his second goal of the game and his third of the season so far. Although the game was effectively over, Liverpool's ruthlessness and pursuit of more goals was evident when Neal was replaced by striker Paul Walsh five minutes later.

With Johnston moving to the right wing and Nicol dropping to right-back, Ian Hargraves noted that the new, "combination showed a zest and imagination that had the crowd roaring, and many will feel they were watching what is potentially Liverpool's strongest formation." The pace of, "Johnston and Nicol tore Ipswich's left flank to pieces," and it was no surprise when the home side scored a fifth. That it did not arrive until the final minute was a surprise however, with Cooper again making two fantastic saves from Molby and Rush respectively, before the Dane sent a fierce free-kick crashing against the bar.

Alan Hansen then, "strode majestically upfield and crossed with his left foot for Johnston to get a long-awaited reward with a powerful header." It was the Australian's 22nd goal for the club - but his first since March 1984 when he scored in a 4-1 triumph at Benfica's Stadium of Light.

After the game, manager but absent player Kenny Dalglish was full of praise for his side. Although he jokingly stated that, "I don't mind sitting it out when they play like that," he was, "especially happy for the two lads [Sammy Lee and Paul Walsh] who've been out with injury." The manager would have also been encouraged by the words of McMahon, who told reporters, "I will only move to Anfield."

The normally taciturn Scot also had words for both sets of supporters. "I think some of the criticism last week was most unfair, because we did have a problem with the microphones," he said. "Today the fans of really deserved a pat on the back and I don't just mean our fans – even the Ipswich supporters were tremendous." Despite such a resounding home victory Liverpool trailed the early league leaders Manchester United, who won 2-0 at home to West Ham and maintained their 100% record, by five points in the first published league table of the season.

West Ham United v Liverpool
Saturday 31 August 1985

"It seems that the media were simply searching for some facet of the crowd's behaviour to criticise. They were so eager to jump on any possible misdemeanour that they missed the whole reason for what was described (quite unjustly) in one paper as 'an intesive demonstration...emphasised that a hard core of Liverpool supporters are still unrepentant for the major contribution to the Heysel tragedy'...the singing of 'You'll Never Walk Alone' rather than the second or third verses of 'Abide With Me' was more in token of respect to Juventus fans rather than disrespectful."

J C Hurst, Letter to liverpool Echo, 24 August 1985

At the end of a week in which Liverpool launched an official Anfield Travel Club - that required supporters to carry a photo membership card in order to purchase tickets for or travel to, away games - Liverpool travelled to East London, and a first meeting of the season with an emerging West Ham United at Upton Park. Members of the new travel club were requested to obey club stewards at all times and refrain from drinking alcohol on coach journeys. There was a suggestion from the club that travel to away fixtures would be otherwise unavailable, but British Rail continued to run 'football specials', 'ordinary' trains to all Division One destinations continued, and there was no shortage of local firms who ran independent coaches from various pick-up points throughout Merseyside. Predictably, membership of the Anfield Travel Club never amounted to more than a few hundred - with the vast majority of away fans choosing alternative transport, and the relative freedom that went with it.

The day before Liverpool travelled to East London, the Heysel Stadium launched its first major sporting event since the European Cup Final when Zola Budd and Sebastian Coe were the star attractions at an IAAF Athletics Meeting. The same afternoon UEFA showed it had not rid itself of the anger and shame it still felt at events in May when the governing body refused point blank a proposal (from both Liverpool and Juventus officials) to a combined Reds/Juve team taking on a European-select XI in order to raise funds for the families of those killed.

Despite enduring an indifferent start to their league campaign, the Hammers boasted as promising and as potent an attack as any team in the top flight. Fed by the midfield thrusts of newly signed Mark Ward from Oldham Athletic and the longer-established though cultured wing play of Alan Devonshire, diminutive forward and lifelong fan Tony Cottee together with his new partner Frank McAvennie had already hinted at an exciting partnership.

The Hammers had lost three of their first four games, and were indebted to the Scot's opening brace in a 3-1 home win over QPR for their sole three points so far. In McAvennie however, a £340,000 summer recruit from St. Mirren in the summer, West Ham had unearthed one of the signings of the season – even if the continuing dispute with TV companies and the resulting black-out of games meant that few English fans had actually seen him play.

While the TV license-paying public may have been sorry they were unable to assess this new star of English football for themselves, Bruce Grobbelaar was certainly relieved to see the back of the troublesome, blonde-haired Scotsman until later in the season. McAvennie's efforts gave Grobbelaar - a source of ongoing debate amongst Liverpool fans for his idiosyncratic approach to the art of goalkeeping - a difficult afternoon. In the Sunday Times, respected football writer Brian Glanville wrote that the Liverpool keeper had endured, "one of his most wildly erratic days."

"On turf made slippery by early rain," Liverpool did not play well in the first-half, giving the ball away sloppily and failing to both threaten Phil Parkes in the Hammers' goal, nor contain the attacking trio of Cottee, Ward and McAvennie. Tactically, Sammy Lee and Jan Molby were playing deep, often picking the ball off the toes of their defenders just yards outside their own area. Although, "Molby never broke out of a gentle trot, let alone broke sweat [and] his use of the crossfield ball was sometimes excellent," the Liverpool midfield never seemed to combine as effectively as Devonshire and Dickens.

Even accounting for their lacklustre start it was a goal of their own making that Liverpool conceded after 21 minutes when future Everton forward Tony Cottee played a long, speculative ball down the middle of the pitch. Under no real pressure, Hansen came to collect it but, seeing Grobbelaar advancing a full 10-yards outside his area, the normally composed Scottish centre-half hesitated and, in the resultant mild panic, McAvennie nipped in between defender and goalkeeper to score into an empty goal. The goal was a blow to Hansen, whose early season form had seen increasing calls for Jock Stein to recall him to Scotland squad for the upcoming World Cup Qualifier against Wales.

17 minutes from the end of the game another Grobbelaar faux-pas - when he failed to deal with a Ward cross - allowed McAvennie to again show his opportunism when in front of goal, and he beat the Liverpool keeper to the ball once more to score West Ham's second of the game from a tight angle.

At this point Liverpool had already cancelled out West Ham's opener courtesy of a well-worked move down the right by Neal and – on the right wing - Nicol. Nicol's cross to the far post was headed into the net by Johnston whose, "tricky running plus his intelligent use of the ball... [quickly became] one of Liverpool's most potent weapons." Indeed, until McAvennie's second, Liverpool had looked by far the better side, "producing some excellent combined moves," and, "a West Ham team which had played skilfully in midfield, swiftly and incisively, lost much of its confidence."

Liverpool then rallied from the set-back of finding themselves a goal down for the second time in the match. With just six minutes remaining Rush, though bundled to the ground inside the box after good work again by Nicol on the right, recovered quickly to prod the ball towards Johnston. The Australian's cross to the same far post where he netted his side's opening goal was now met by Whelan, who nodded in another deserved equaliser.

The opening month of the season had seen Liverpool fail to win in their three games away from Anfield. They had scored 11 goals in five league games and conceded just five, but five of their goals had come in the one match against a bedraggled Ipswich. Despite the return of a number of midfielders to the first team squad, notably the bustling Sammy Lee and the attack-minded Craig Johnston - whose, "twisting and turning has given them a valuable new weapon," - it was clear the Reds needed more steel in this area if they were to mount a serious title challenge.

Indeed, although, "the new midfield formation is settling down quite well – and scoring goals," too often they were careless in possession when attempting to build an attack. It was arguable that uncharacteristic sloppiness had contributed to all the dropped points so far but, with Manchester United setting a flawless pace, the gap between Liverpool and Ron Atkinson's charges had already grown to a worrying seven points - before August was out.

Just as worrying for the new manager, Liverpool seemed unable to win the ball back as often as they gave it away, especially away from home. As easy on the eye as Jan Molby, "another man in form," was, he was not a renowned tackler. By his own admission the Dane would later state that he was bemused by early comparisons to the legendary Graeme Souness as had never been blessed with the steel of Liverpool's former captain. Fans were starting to call for a more combative midfielder to play alongside Molby. Afforded time and space on the ball in the presence of an enforcer for company, they felt that only then would the Dane be able to harness the full range of his undoubted passing skills.

It was still early days in the title race however, but if Liverpool were to settle into any sort of rhythm they needed to address the absence of a true ball-winner in midfield. The void left by Souness's departure hadn't been properly addressed in Joe Fagan's second and final season - and ultimately put paid to Liverpool's chances of silverware. Now, Dalglish was coming under increasing pressure to make his first significant foray into the transfer market and finally secure a hard-edged foil to Molby's creative talents.

Liverpool v Nottingham Forest
Tuesday 3 September 1985

"Everyone knows that the main guilty parties have not been punished. UEFA and its president are still there, in their positions, when in fact they, and only they, are the guilty parties in this affair. They were the ones who didn't have enough sense before Brussels to take the sort of preventative measures which were obviously necessary. It was easy for them to turn on the clubs afterwards."

Juventus captain Michel Platini interview to L'Equipe as reported in Liverpool Echo 9 September.

If Liverpool's at times wayward goalkeeper had arguably cost them points in at Upton Park at the weekend, it was perhaps some consolation for Bruce Grobbelaar – a spectator for much of this Tuesday evening fixture – that he wasn't the only no. 1 sometimes guilty of bizarre footballing decisions at inopportune times. One-time rival of Ray Clemence for the role of England's first choice keeper - and the bane of Liverpool strikers in the past - Peter Shilton had left Nottingham Forest for Southampton in 1982, and the former European champions – a shadow of their former selves but still under the guidance of the outspoken, mercurial Brian Clough - had yet to sign a replacement of equivalent stature.

Unchanged from their last game but with Beglin on the bench in place of MacDonald, Liverpool dominated the first half. Forest keeper Hans Segers - who, nine years later would occupy the same courtroom, charged with match-fixing along his opposite number here, Grobbelaar - was in fine form in the opening 45 minutes, thwarting a succession of Liverpool attacks.

Steve Nicol, rapidly evolving into the best attacking right-back in the country, saw a powerful shot deflected wide of the Dutchman's goal after 10 minutes. Together with Molby – a one handed tip over the bar from the Dane's free-kick – Liverpool were then thwarted by a series of excellent saves that the contemplative, midweek home crowd - a startlingly low 27,000 - could only applaud.

Ten minutes into the second half however, after smartly and rather routinely saving a Mark Lawrenson header, Segers made a critical error of judgement to show that it wasn't only Zimbabwean keepers who could cost their side three points. Attempting to find one of his own men with a quick throw, the future Wimbledon number one instead found Ronnie Whelan some 30-yards out.

With little more than a glance at the stranded keeper on the edge of the area, the Irishman - who along with Phil Neal and Alan Kennedy had undeservingly and quite inexplicably become a target for the boo-boys in the crowd - coolly and calmly lifted the ball over the back-pedalling Dutchman's head and curled an exquisite shot just under the bar and into the net. With Forest barely threatening, this solitary goal could have decided the game. Such was Whelan's versatility that Dalglish would often shift him around the field; left back, left midfield, and a more central role alongside Molby and/or McMahon. For a young player who was still adjusting to his changed surroundings, this was no mean feat – a point lost on the more impatient element in the crowd who would often seize on an early misplaced pass, or a wayward shot to lambast the Irishman.

For some fans the fickle nature of the Kop was fast becoming an embarrassment. Stating that the crowd had, "no wit anymore," B. Banks of Aughton took the time to write to the Football Echo to lambast his fellow supporters and even called for the Kop to become all-seater as all they could provide was, "just sheep-like chanting and obscenities." In contrast, some fans were – like Mr Pryer - at least able to see the future of the club in players whom many had written off almost before their Anfield careers had begun. Gill Corrin of Broad Lane wrote in to praise Ronnie Whelan, "a target last season," as well as this, and wished him a long and successful future at the club.

With further fine Segers saves from Rush – a tip over the bar from a powerful header, Nicol – touching a fierce drive onto the post and out for a corner - and even Alan Hansen, Liverpool should have added to their lead before they grabbed a second on 60 minutes – scored in spectacular fashion once again by Whelan. Bringing the ball out of defence with ease, Mark Lawrenson ran 30-yards with the ball at his feet to find Whelan on the edge of the Forest area with a straight pass through the middle. In, "a replica of the unforgettable goal he scored against Manchester United in the Milk Cup three seasons ago", Whelan curled a right-foot shot past the despairing dive of Segers - and the points were Liverpool's.

Liverpool's third game of the season at Anfield, their third win, and their third clean sheet, contrasted sharply with their away form. It was clear that more bite was needed in midfield, especially away from Anfield where Liverpool had developed a habit of losing sloppy goals.

Dalglish had recognised a lack of steel in central midfield, a problem which - following the departure of Graeme Souness to Italy - had blighted the challenge for honours in Joe Fagan's second season. Just two days later, and as expected, expected, Steve McMahon - the former Everton ball-boy who had graduated to the Goodison first team before moving to Aston Villa - finally joined the Reds in a deal reported to be worth around £350,000. Although the signing had, "been on the cards since the start of the season," thrashing out a deal with the Midlanders had been more problematic than had been first anticipated.

Dalglish favoured a straight cash deal for a player who, two years previously, had turned Liverpool down to join Villa after failing to agree terms with Everton over a new contract; "a move he has regretted bitterly." Villa manager Graham Turner however, was keen for a cash plus player deal, and had requested reserve defender Gary Gillespie or striker Paul Walsh in addition to the fee agreed.

That Dalglish did not wish to part with either, was testimony to the importance he placed in such players, providing more than adequate cover in case of injury or loss of form. The player-manager recognised the importance of fielding players who could replace those in his perceived best eleven, without impacting on the effectiveness of his line-up. As the season progressed and the inevitable injuries and loss of form took their toll, his judgement of the value of these so-called 'squad players' would be was instrumental in his team's ability to produce results in the key games during the run-in.

McMahon was, "the kind of hard tackling, competitive player able to sharpen up their

[Liverpool's] midfield," – the perfect replacement for Graeme Souness that many fans had been demanding since the mercurial Scot's quest for financial security saw him secure a move to the Genovese club, Sampdoria. McMahon's move to Anfield - which ruffled a few feathers on the other side of Stanley Park - was facilitated by Villa's move for Steve Hodge of Nottingham Forest. The Kop would have to wait to see McMahon's debut however, as he was signed too late to figure in Liverpool's second home engagement of the week – the weekend's upcoming visit of Graham Taylor's Watford.

Liverpool v Watford
Saturday 7 September 1985

"When I arrived at Anfield, racist slogans were daubed on the
stadium walls: 'NF', 'White Power', 'No Wogs Allowed', 'There's No Black In The Union Jack' and 'Liverpool
Are White'. I expected it. Evil exists in football as in life generally."

John Barnes, The Autobiography, 1999. Headline Book Publishing.

After being introduced to the Anfield crowd before kick-off – when the Kop jokingly sang 'Everton reject!' and then the much more appropriate 'Supermac' in his honour - Steve McMahon, Kenny Dalglish's first major signing, could only look on in awe as the player supposedly most under threat from his arrival masterminded a victory that, "at one time looked impossible." If Dalglish's intention with the capture of ex-Villa and Everton man McMahon was to tap into the sometimes latent ability of Jan Molby, then it had an instant and immediate effect.

For the fourth game in a row Liverpool's starting 11 was unchanged. With Kevin McDonald suffering from flu earlier in the week, Dalglish had countenanced naming young reserve Ian Fairbrother as substitute in place of Jim Beglin, but McDonald recovered sufficiently enough to enable him to wear the no.12 shirt – which had been rotated so far between himself, Walsh and Craig Johnston.

Managed by future England manager Graham Taylor, Watford had been promoted to the top flight only three years previously but, to everyone's amazement, they managed to finish second, behind Liverpool in their first season. Forerunners of Wimbledon, Sheffield Wednesday and Bolton Wanderers, their uncompromising, physical approach harnessed their strengths, with one time England striker Luther Blisset the target man for their direct, long ball style of play. Whilst such an approach did at times bypass their midfield, the 'Hornets' were still capable of playing effective football, albeit not for the purists. A 4-3 defeat in the corresponding fixture at Anfield the season before however, was testimony to their ability to feature in competitive, exciting games.

In that fixture - Liverpool's last home game before Brussels - Watford fielded a young Jamaican-born winger blessed with exceptional skill, strength, touch and balance. John Barnes was already being talked of as one of the future stars of the British game. Barnes featured again here but in a more advanced position, with Blisset surprisingly named as substitute by Taylor for, "trying too hard," to recapture his best goalscoring form.

As classy as Barnes was however, he was upstaged completely by the Liverpool player supposedly most under pressure by the arrival of McMahon. In imperious form, Jan Molby was at the centre of everything good about Liverpool during this game but, before the Dane could weave his midfield magic, Liverpool had to recover from the shock of conceding their first goal of the season in the opening minutes of the match.

The Reds had started the game strongly, winning no less than four corners in the opening 120 seconds, yet in almost their first attack of the game a perfect Barnes free-kick was headed across the Grobbelaar's goal by Smilie at the far post, and Colin West slotted the ball past the Zimbabwean from inside the six-yard area.

As a Northern British city with a higher than average number of people employed in the older manufacturing industries, Liverpool was more than susceptible to the vagaries of 1980s free-market economics practiced by the Conservative Government of the day. As such, unemployment rose, factories shut and social problems became more acute. In such scenarios the far-right normally prospers but, in Liverpool at least, formal institutions such as the National Front enjoyed little political success.

Paradoxically, this situation existed despite the Toxteth riots just four years previously highlighting the inequalities experienced by the City's large, but predominately self-contained black community. Indeed, in the inquiry into the riots headed by Lord Justice Scarman, the former barrister - who had earlier chaired an inquiry into troubles in Northern Ireland - had called Liverpool a, "uniquely racist city." It is an inconvenient truth that for many black Liverpudlians, their experience of the 1980s was one of exclusion at best and outright racism, often violent, at worst. Few black faces were to be found working in the city centre for instance, and even fewer were seen at Anfield or Goodison.

Howard Gayle was the only black player to have any impact at Anfield before Barnes' arrival in 1988 and, despite the minor celebrity status afforded the one black Liverpool fan of note at the time – the famous flame-haired 'Jaffa' of the Kop - black footballers and supporters were still a rarity in most football grounds of the day, including Anfield. In September 1985 the game was still a long way from non-white players or fans feeling entirely comfortable pursuing their careers, or supporting their teams, in English grounds.

With hooliganism a very real and very frightening possibility at most matches, and almost anything accepted that would unsettle the away team so as to afford the home side even the slightest advantage, racist abuse of the few black players there were, was commonplace. John Barnes was no exception. During this game Barnes was barracked by the Kop unmercifully due to his colour. The fact he was so obviously and clearly a gifted footballer, and had been instrumental in helping Watford take the lead, only added fuel to an already hostile atmosphere.

An anonymous letter to the Football Echo the following week showed that all hope was not lost however, and that some fans at least found the targeted abuse of black players repellent. "I write to express my disgust at the behaviour of many people on the Kop," wrote 'Red One'. "They still abuse skilful players whose colour they cannot accept." Imploring their fellow supporters to stop such chanting, "childish behaviour," and to, "grow up," the writer advised that it would help their side more if the crowd supported their own side instead of resorting to mindless racial discrimination.

Despite going behind so early, Liverpool dominated the remainder of the game. Craig Johnston went close soon after the opening goal whilst Alan Kennedy, an increasingly common target for some of the more fickle home fans' displeasure, was found unmarked in the area by a perfect through ball from Molby - only to mistime his shot and allow keeper Tony Coton to save comfortably. Despite his heroics for the club in Europe and at home in the recent past, the crowd's audible groan voiced an increasing frustration at Kennedy's erratic form. A loyal servant since 1978, the amiable Geordie was in the twilight of his Liverpool career, a fact not lost on an informed but unsympathetic home crowd.

In the 27th minute Molby, Rush and Nicol combined well outside the Watford penalty area only for the latter, once he was in the box, to be bundled to the ground by Nigel Gibbs. It was perhaps a challenge that happens every few minutes in most games but, in front of a baying Kop, referee M. Peck pointed to the spot and was immediately surrounded by the Watford defenders.

Even the normally reserved Graham Taylor couldn't control his anger at the decision and he leapt from the dug-out to remonstrate with both referee and linesman. Before Phil Neal sent Tony Coton the wrong way to equalise, the likeable Taylor had calmed down enough to discuss the decision in a more rational manner with a number of home fans in the Paddock. Despite the equaliser, Liverpool failed to increase their pressure on an obviously nervous Watford back four and the half ended 1-1.

Such a lack of momentum was soon forgotten once the second half got underway, and the next 45 minutes saw the Reds create chances almost at will. Indeed, if it hadn't been for the athleticism of England candidate Coton, Liverpool could well have reached double figures. The Watford keeper was in inspired form, denying Liverpool three times in quick succession within the opening 10 minutes of the half.

Hansen floated in a long free-kick that was only half-cleared to Whelan and the Irishman sent in a powerful shot from distance that Coton, with Rush lurking, did well to hold on to low down at his right hand post. A snap shot on the turn by the Welshman soon after took a deflection off a defender and again Coton did well to tip the ball around his post for a corner.

Playing, "with determination and skill," Molby, giving, "the midfield that extra fillip that many feel was so sadly lacking last season," was also denied by Coton before Steve Terry was booked for a crude challenge on Rush, who was giving his man-marker a torrid time. Soon after his yellow card Terry was lucky not to be booked again for climbing all over the Liverpool striker and, to the astonishment of the home crowd and the Liverpool manager this time, the referee failed to take further action minutes later when Rush needed attention after again coming off the worst in a challenge between the two. Terry's tussle with Rush only allowed more room for Liverpool's other attack minded players however, with Johnston in particular taking full advantage.

Just after the hour mark the speedy Australian, "burst into the box on the left...before flashing in a shot," that deflected off Coton's shoulder for a corner. Minutes later another deflection, this time off McClelland from another Johnston shot, wrong-footed the keeper and put Liverpool deservedly in front. "Liverpool were now in full flight," and Rush put the result beyond doubt with a little over a quarter of an hour remaining. A high centre from the right by Nicol was headed goalwards by Whelan, and the loose ball fell to, "that deadly goal poacher Rush [who] cashed in from close range."

Despite Liverpool's two Anfield victories in a week moving them up the table, they still trailed in the wake of Manchester United whose seven straight wins from the start of the season had the media purring. Champions Everton - who lost 3-0 to QPR at Loftus Road while Liverpool were beating Watford - would also be concerned with the growing gap between them and Ron Atkinson's runaway leaders.

However, the press's desire to crown media-darlings United as Champions was exposed in a letter from an Everton sympathiser to the Football Echo published that same evening. "Evertonians and Liverpudlians must be amazed at the euphoria created by the tabloids in connection with Manchester United," the unnamed contributor wrote, "Glowing tributes such as, 'magnificent,' 'marauding,' and, 'insatiable,' jump out from every headline. Some even suggest the title is as good as won."

The letters also summed up the shared hostility many on Merseyside felt towards the Old Trafford side - created by the media's apparent willingness to serenade aspirational Manchester United at the expense of proven stayers Everton and Liverpool. The unnamed writer also added that although United's winning start to the season was commendable, the Old Trafford side had yet to meet any of the better sides in the Division.

"Fair enough, they've won six on the trot which is an excellent start to the season. However, lets get a few facts straight. Firstly, they have only played one top team this season – Everton in the Charity Shield. They were completely outclassed by the Blues and deservedly lost. In contrast, Everton's start to the season has included a sound win at Tottenham and a stunning victory at Hillsborough, both feats far advanced to anything yet achieved by United.

"It is obvious the 'Dailys' are going completely overboard on their heroes. I doubt they will be as ecstatic in a few months time when the going gets tougher and Atkinson's 'fancy dans' are overtaken by the true champions."

The Anfield crowd also came in for some criticism of its own in the letters' page of the 'Pink', mainly due to it's increasing hostility towards experienced full-backs Alan Kennedy and Phil Neal. The Watford game had seen Kennedy endure the wrath of the Kop, but Graham Pryer of Broadgreen defended veteran right-back and captain Phil Neal, who had also taken his share of stick from elements within the crowd. Mr Pryer complained,

"I'm sick of the abuse Phil Neal gets. As a regular at Anfield for 25 years I find it very sad to hear the constant verbal attacks on Phil Neal. Phil has been a great servant to the club though he may now be past his best. But at each home game this season, standing on the Kop, the abuse is getting more widespread. Get off his back. Other players in the side have not been exactly 'world beaters' and have made as many if not more errors as Phil."

The increasingly worrying form of Liverpool's experienced full backs was highlighted again in an almost prophetic address from another, "Reds Fan – name and address supplied." Encapsulating the early season thoughts of many supporters regarding Dalglish's best team, they wrote, "The selection of Grobbelaar, Hansen, Lawrenson, Whelan Rush and Dalglish require no explanation, but the others may." The contributor then added the names of "Nicol, Beglin, Johnston, McMahon, Molby and sub Walsh." The names of Neal and Kennedy were conspicuous by their absence.

At pains to stress that, although he had defended Phil Neal, the right-back was nevertheless suffering from an obvious dip in form, Mr Pryer had no such words of encouragement for fellow defender Alan Kennedy. "Neal and Kennedy have served Liverpool so well over the past six years but their loss of form, particularly Kennedy's, has been alarming…The claims of Nicol and Beglin, both current internationals, cannot be ignored. In Beglin, they have their first 'footballing' left back since Alec Lindsay." As the season developed from its embryonic stages, it was almost as if Mr Pryer of Broadgreen was a nom de plume for a Mr Dalglish of Southport.

Away from Anfield and the domestic game, the week also saw the sad death of former-Everton star Alex Stevenson – an event overshadowed by the shocking news that Scotland manager Jock Stein had collapsed and died from a heart attack during the Wales v Scotland World Cup Qualifier at Ninian Park, Cardiff. The death of Dalglish's legendary, former European Cup-winning boss at Celtic reverberated round the footballing world – overshadowing even the interview that Juventus captain Michel Platini gave to French newspaper L'Equipe, in which he argued that UEFA had been wrong to ban English sides, especially Liverpool, from European competition following the Heysel disaster.

Elsewhere, and with barely a ripple of interest at Anfield – where the Kop were fast becoming disillusioned with any references to the national side - England qualified for the World Cup in Mexico with a 1-1 draw with Romania at Wembley.

Oxford United v Liverpool
Saturday 14 September 1985

"Molby is the key. Despite his size he is a tremendously skilful player with enormous vision. He is extremely comfortable on the ball and is perhaps the most natural player in the squad. The arrival of McMahon would be the perfect foil for him, adding a bite that has been missing recently. He would steady the midfield and provide Molby with the platform he needs to become creatively important to the Reds as Hoddle is to Spurs.

Johnston can provide pace and width, offering the ability to take on and beat full-backs while I feel Dalglish will play until after next year's World Cup with Walsh easing into his place. John Wark's goals last season were the main reason Liverpool finished runners-up but I feel there is no place for him because his all-round contribution is not good enough. Gary Gillespie though is too good a footballer for the reserves and would walk into any other team."

Graham Pryer, Broadgreen, Football Echo letters page, 7 September 1985

Members of the Football league for only 24 years – voted in in 1962 – it was no surprise that Liverpool had yet to meet Oxford United in the Football League. Owned by controversial media tycoon Robert Maxwell, who had taken over the ailing club in 1982, United won the Third Division in 1984 under Maurice Evans. The following year, they won the Second Division title and suddenly the 'Boys from up the Hill' – an earlier reference to their existence as Headington United – were in the top flight.

One of the main reasons for their rapid and spectacular double promotions was undoubtedly the 34 goals scored by former South Liverpool striker and self-confessed Liverpool fan John Aldridge. Before the game, the future Anfield favourite had revealed that as a child he had not only stood on the Kop to cheer his heroes on, but had also had hopes of one day playing for his hometown club when he was a teenager. "When I was 14 I actually trained with the Reds a couple of nights a week," he said, "but nothing came of it." Goals alone were not the only reasons journalists and fans were interested in the likeable striker however, and Ken Rogers was not alone when he noted that Aldridge bore not only, "an uncanny resemblance," to Liverpool star Ian Rush, but also possessed the Welsh striker's, "uncanny knack of being in the right place at the right time."

Although an all-ticket crowd of barely 11,500 fans witnessed the first ever league meeting with Liverpool - the clubs had met here in an FA Cup Third round tie back in 1972 - the tiny, almost claustrophobic, Manor Ground was packed to capacity, with around 2,000 Reds' fans making the long trip to witness the debut of Steve McMahon in the number 11 shirt. The Reds' latest signing had played for the reserves in their midweek victory over Newcastle, with Paul Walsh also scoring twice to underline his fitness for a recall to the first team. Together with Sammy Lee, who made way for McMahon - thereby ensuring Dalglish's first change for four games - the Londoner was included in the Reds' 14 man squad and was eventually named as substitute.

With Oxford having lost their last four games - including a 3-0 trouncing at Old Trafford in their previous fixture, Liverpool were unsurprisingly favourites to record what would be their first away win of the season. As early as the 20th minute of this bruising encounter, substitute Walsh found himself in action, replacing Ronnie Whelan who was on the receiving end of the sort of high challenge from defender John Trewick that would likely guarantee a sending off in today's game. Ultimately, the strong-arm defender was only booked, but Whelan left the field clutching his bleeding face – the blow to the side of his head eventually requiring seven stitches.

Five minutes earlier, Aldridge had put the home side in front, displaying, "the kind of scoring touch that earned him goals last season," by heading in full-back David Langan's pinpoint cross at the far post. Langan had been found in space by the sort of defence splitting diagonal pass Oxford's new £125,000 signing from Fulham, Ray Houghton, would later bring to Anfield. Houghton had only signed for Oxford the day before this game.

In a scrappy, entertaining match, both sides carved out a number of chances in the first half. A testing Trevor Hebberd cross was headed over for a corner by Nicol, "setting up a difficult couple of minutes for the visitors." Grobbelaar could only push another cross over the bar and then caught a Charles header at the second attempt. "An outstanding crossfield ball by Molby," then found Johnston bearing down on goal but keeper Steve Hardwick did well to save at the Australian's feet.

With Walsh joining Rush up front, Johnston was moved to midfield and, in a tactical switch that may have puzzled a few visiting fans, Nicol was moved to the left wing. The switch almost paid off immediately however, as Nicol sent a header wide when it seemed easier to hit the target. Seven minutes before half-time, the young Scot had Liverpool's best chance of the game, but his goal bound shot was cleared off the line by Bobby McDonald.

Just before the interval, Molby appeared to have set Walsh free with a delightful through ball but to the dismay of the Liverpool bench and the visiting fans, the nippy striker - who had hitherto had a poor game by his standards - had his heels clipped by Gary Briggs. Although the cynical Briggs was booked for a foul, the move had been stopped in its tracks and the chance had gone.

Liverpool worked hard for an equaliser after the break, with Rush, Nicol and Johnston all going close, but the Reds had to work hard in defence too, with Houghton sending a dipping lob just over the bar after Hansen failed to clear a through ball. The visitor's dogged determination finally paid off in the 62nd minute when Rush latched on to, "a superb through ball from Molby," to scramble the ball into the net from close range.

13 minutes later, Liverpool's dominance saw Nicol find Rush down the left and his cross, "was chested down by Johnston just outside the angle of the box before he unleashed an unstoppable shot that gave Hardwick no chance at all." It was, "a goal fit to win any match," wrote Joe Lovejoy in the Mail on Sunday – a rising volley that every striker would relish. "With Liverpool completely in the driving seat," however, "disaster struck with just three minutes to go." Attempting to steer a routine cross back to his goalkeeper, Alan Kennedy instead diverted the ball past the advancing Bruce Grobbelaar into his own net. It was a farcical way to end the game. Again Liverpool had only themselves to blame for yet another failure to capitalise on their territorial dominance away from home.

An hour after the game Dalglish refused to single out any individuals for the loss of a further two points, instead preferring to focus on alternative reasons for his side's lacklustre start to the game. "We started off badly," the player-manager said, "I am sure it's down to the international matches in midweek." In the privacy of their Manor Ground dressing room immediately after the game however, it was a different story.

"Kenny went crazy in the dressing room afterwards," recalled Kennedy in his autobiography some years later. "He totally blamed me – he had a right go." Kennedy admitted he hadn't had the greatest of games, but in his view other players were perhaps just as culpable – Liverpool again guilty of giving the ball away far too easily, particularly when in their opponents half.

Despite his protestations, it was the final straw for the player-manager. The England left-back's loss of form had been obvious for a while and, together with Phil Neal, the hero of two European Cup finals had been the target of sustained and targeted abuse from sections of the Anfield crowd for some time. It was Kennedy's last game for the Reds. Within a week, and after a deal had firstly been agreed with Newcastle United, the likeable Geordie moved to Second Division Sunderland, managed by Lawrie McMenemy. Kennedy's omission however, was not the only surprise on Liverpool's next team sheet.

Chapter Two
Bring on the Dancing Horses

Liverpool v Southampton
Screen Sport Super Cup: Group Phase
Tuesday 17 September 1985

"Liverpool is now quite literally out of control. Britain's fifth-largest city is like a juggernaut hurtling towards a cliff-edge with a handful of passengers fighting each other to grab hold of the wheel.

Local Government editor Peter Phelps, Liverpool Echo, 17 September 1985

Hastily introduced by the Football League in the aftermath of the Heysel disaster, the Super Cup is perhaps one of the least fondly remembered competitions in which Liverpool have participated. In order to generate some of the revenue lost by those clubs who were now banned from Europe, the Super Cup was a convoluted and - for most fans, managers and even players - as poor a substitute for continental competition as they could have wished. Few held it in any sort of regard. To create a sufficiently competitive number of games - and supposedly some much needed income - the six sides banned from Europe; Everton - as league champions, Manchester United – as FA Cup winners, together with Milk Cup winners Norwich City, and the three teams who qualified via their league position Liverpool, Southampton and Tottenham, were placed into two groups of three.

After playing each other home and away – with three points awarded for a win and one for a draw - the top two sides in each group went through to the semi-finals, also played on a home and away basis. The winners of these games would then play each other, hopefully at Wembley Stadium. Unlike other managers, the chance of yet another appearance under the twin towers was a scenario not readily discounted by Kenny Dalglish. In his programme notes for the opener against Southampton he wrote:

"Liverpool have every incentive to get through to the final. For one thing it could produce another all-Merseyside meeting at Wembley, or a Merseyside-Manchester confrontation. We're taking on crack opposition from our own League and we all want to show who's boss. It may not be the European Cup, but it's still there to be won."

Ultimately however, a Wembley final was discounted and the finalists would play each other on a home and away basis. This decision was more in keeping with the two-legged nature of European football but in truth was more to do with the eventual progression of Liverpool and Everton to the Final, and the bigger priorities for both clubs that emerged as the season wore on. Liverpool found themselves grouped together with Spurs and Southampton, both then in mid-table. Although on paper this provided as easy a group as the Reds could have wished for, their first game in the new competition came just four days before the first local 'derby' of the season.

With Liverpool playing catch-up to the leagues' early pacesetters, Manchester United, they needed as many of their top players fit and ready for the battle between themselves and last season's Champions – a game that could go some way to deciding the destiny of the title. The same could be said of the monetary concerns of those fans lucky enough to attend the fixture at the weekend, and it came as no surprise to find not only Anfield far from full for the visit of the South Coast side, but the team itself much changed from the previous game at Oxford. Indeed, just over 16,000 brave - or foolhardy depending on your outlook - souls paid to see Liverpool's first game for nearly two years without Phil Neal. Neal hadn't missed a game since 5 October 1983 and, though it was tempting to explain his absence here as an opportunity to give him a rest, the presence of Nicol at right-back was an ominous portent.

The shock omission of one of the club's greatest servants was not the only surprise however. "With Dalglish ready to try his two young lions, Nicol and Beglin, at full-back," Alan Kennedy also missed out – Newcastle having already been given permission to talk to the player in anticipation of a move back to his native North-East. Still recovering from his facial injury at Oxford, Ronnie Whelan was also omitted, as was Ian Rush who had left the Manor Ground pitch at full time with a similar injury, and concussion. Sammy Lee replaced Whelan in midfield, with Paul Walsh, "fit again and determined to seize this opportunity," making only his second senior start of the season, upfront alongside Dalglish himself – the player-manager's first start for five games. With two substitutes instead of one also allowed for this competition, the bench also wore an unfamiliar look – Kevin McDonald and a young Gary Ablett being named as numbers 12 and 14 respectively.

Managed by former player and one-time Villa defender Chris Nicholl, Southampton had injury problems of their own, with a number of key players missing. Former Liverpool star Jimmy Case was suspended although notorious hardman Mark Dennis returned in a defence that included emerging centre-back Mark Wright. Although the crowd seems alarmingly small today, it was reported that it was in fact, "slightly larger than expected and about the same as the early season Milk Cup attendances." It was also boosted somewhat by the reduced cost of ticket prices - £2 in the Kop, not the normal £2.50, with a combined Adult and Child ticket in the ground priced at £4.80 instead of £6.00. Stand tickets were priced at £4 and £5.

Despite the changes the new look Liverpool seemed to gel easily and quickly. Within five minutes they found themselves a goal up thanks to a wonderful, "25-yard piledriver," from Jan Molby that left Peter Shilton grasping at thin air. Craig Johnston was equally as eye-catching as the Dane, as was Steve McMahon, "who swept the ball about well," and who could have scored himself in the second half if it wasn't for the alertness of Shilton.

It was at the back however, where Alan Hansen, "was full of class," that Liverpool's future appeared brightest. "Young Eire international Jim Beglin demonstrated [again] that he is ready and waiting to pick up the challenge," of becoming the club's new left-back. Unfortunately for Liverpool, neither Hansen nor Beglin could do little to prevent a Mark Dennis cross from being glanced in by the diminutive but speedy Danny Wallace on 23 minutes.

Three minutes later however, normal service was resumed when Walsh did well to get to the by-line where he centred for his manager to tap in what turned out to be Liverpool's winner. Despite dominating the second half, the Reds failed to score a third. A win was a win however, and with no injuries to concern him, Dalglish could prepare in earnest for what was unarguably the Reds' toughest fixture of the season so far.

The following evening Everton warmed up for the Derby by inflicting Manchester United's first defeat of the season, winning their Super Cup opener 4-2 at Old Trafford. Some may have thought Howard Kendall's teamtalk to have been particularly inspirational ahead of the game as the Blues registered the first goals United had conceded all season, but he was also rumoured to have told his players – as they left the dressing room, "What a waste of time this is – out you go!"

After the game Dalglish was understandably quizzed as to absence of Phil Neal against The Saints. His reply was telling. "Phil is still in contention for a place against Everton. That is another game but I was quite happy with the way the team played tonight." Commenting on his own appearance he added, "It was nice to play again myself...and to score a goal." Despite his surprise omission, Neal remained philosophical and, considering he already knew his time at the club was limited, professional. "I'd like to think I still have something to offer the club," he said, "and I shall be fighting to try and regain my place."

While the first Super Cup fixtures where being screened to miniscule audiences on the sponsor's fledgling cable TV channel, the deadlock in the ongoing row over terrestrial TV coverage between the TV Companies and Football League officials remained unbroken. The continued impasse ensured that even highlights of English games on Match of the Day, The Big Match and the midweek programmes Sportsnight and Midweek Sports Special, were conspicuous by their absence. Such was the level of bad feeling between the two sides that even the screening of 15 minutes of highlights from Celtic's Cup Winners Cup tie against Atletico Madrid the same week caused a minor storm that threatened to derail the talks completely. With World Cup qualification still not confirmed for England, only international games were exempt from the black-out.

Everton v Liverpool
Saturday 21 September 1985

"My only regret about Saturday's derby match was that neither Mrs Thatcher nor her new Minister of Sport was there to see the highly acceptable face of Merseyside football."

Ann Cummings, Liverpool Echo. Monday 23 September

"It was madness before the game. It was absolutely lashing down so our crew from the Yankee sought refuge in the Bierkeller in town. They always had a stripper on, and this girl, making her debut it transpired, made the mistake of coming out wearing, for a while at least, blue knickers. Needless to say, she got swilled with ale by our lot."

A Liverpool fan - who wishes to remain anonymous.

The first Merseyside Derby of the season was not just the signature match of the season for those residing in the environs of Liverpool 4 - it was undoubtedly the biggest game in English football. Everton had denied Liverpool a record-breaking fourth consecutive title in 1985 - winning their eighth league title after a gap of 15 years in the process. For good measure, the Blues also emulated some of Liverpool's best European traits - winning the now defunct Cup Winners' Cup to accompany the Canon League Championship in their greatest ever season. This was the culmination of Everton's rapid rise under Howard Kendall that had seen the Blues transformed from a side watched by crowds as low as 9,000 - against Coventry City in a Milk Cup tie at Goodison - to contest the Milk Cup Final with Liverpool in 1984, before going on to win the FA Cup at the end of the same season.

For the first time in a generation the footballing worm had turned on Merseyside and, with

Liverpool in the early stages of transition under Dalglish, Evertonians had a rightful claim to the City's bragging rights - at least for the time being. They were clearly the two best sides in the country.

The winds of change were being blown through Anfield however, by Dalglish's recognition that advancing years for some were contributing to erratic performances, especially away from home. Although a section of the crowd had been critical of him lately, the dropping of Phil Neal - albeit in a minor competition; the Super Cup in midweek - still raised eyebrows on the red half of Merseyside. Neal was the latest candidate for bench duty at Goodison Park, with Steve Nicol retaining his place at right-back. It was no surprise that Sammy Lee - yet to find consistent form after almost a year out due to numerous injury problems - made way for a fit again Ronnie Whelan.

Paul Walsh, who had enjoyed a rare outing in midweek, made way for the returning Rush, fuelling further speculation that the former Luton man would be forced to look elsewhere for first-team football. There was no doubting Walsh's ability, and his skill and trickery were at times reminiscent of a young Dalglish, but with the player-manager still intent on making periodic appearances, Walsh was struggling to find consistency. It was no secret that he was becoming increasingly frustrated with his bit-part role in the squad.

To the surprise of some scribes - considering he had played the full 90 minutes against Southampton, only his third game of the campaign - Dalglish retained himself up-front. By not naming his side until an hour before kick-off, the Liverpool player-manager kept the press pack, and the 51,509 spectators crammed into a sold-out Goodison Park guessing as to not only his starting line-up, but also the formation his new look side would adopt.

Few could believe their eyes when they saw Danish international midfielder Jan Molby jogging towards his own goal as kick-off approached – to take up a new position in a five-man defence. Watching England manager Bobby Robson was as incredulous as the rest. "Liverpool playing with a sweeper?" he said quizzically to Daily Express football correspondent John Keith. "When did you ever see that?" In Neal's absence the manager awarded the captaincy to his fellow Scot Alan Hansen, whilst Steve McMahon returned to Goodison - this time in red - having graced Goodison Park as a committed Evertonian during the formative years of his career.

Dalglish's team selection, formation and bold tactics were more than vindicated within 20 seconds however, as his new look side went ahead in a sensational start to this 133rd Merseyside league derby.

At a rain lashed Goodison Park, Everton started the game attacking the Stanley Park End. Sheedy attempted a long diagonal ball from left to right straight from the kick-off, but it was capably dealt with by young full-back Beglin. Grobbelaar's first touch of the ball was to pick up the resultant headed back pass and then roll it out to Nicol. The emerging right full-back walked no more than five yards with the ball before sending a long pass forward for Rush to chase. Taking two touches to control the ball, the Welshman laid it back to Dalglish, loitering near the right-hand edge of the penalty area. With just a cursory glance towards goal, the veteran striker suddenly, "unleashed a tremendous shot from 25-yards that soared into the top right hand corner of the net, with Southall comprehensively beaten."

Behind the Gwladys Street goal a few hundred Liverpool fans, including an intrepid group from the infamous Yankee Bar who had deliberately staged an invasion, erupted in celebration as the ball flew into the net. Any thoughts to keeping a low profile on opposition territory went well and truly out of the window with the shock and awe of Dalglish's strike. As many as 15,000 Reds fans were in the ground; present in every part of enemy territory and Liverpool attacks were accompanied by a huge roar.

Including the kick-off, Liverpool had taken just eight touches to score. Everton were a goal behind to Dalglish's spellbinding effort before they had even had time to think. At around 20 seconds, It remains to this day the fastest goal scored in a Merseyside derby.

The bulk of the Liverpool fans, tightly packed into the Park End, together with those in the Enclosure and Paddock at the opposite end to Dalglish's thunderbolt, were ecstatic. They knew however, that given the Reds' previous away form, they could not afford to throw away another lead if they were to steal a march on their neighbours and close the gap on Manchester United. As if to demonstrate the nervousness of players and fans alike, the travelling Red Army breathed a collective sigh of relief minutes later when Lineker, unmarked in the area, managed to stab a shot on goal that Grobbelaar, with a degree of uncertainty in the wet conditions, managed to smother.

Molby at one end and then Pat Van den Hauwe at the other saw decent free-kicks cleared before, on 17 minutes, the expectant Reds' fans found themselves in dreamland as Liverpool extended their advantage. Showing all the defensive instincts that had been a feature of his game since first being given his chance by Bob Paisley, Ian Rush closed down Gary Stevens on the halfway line, dispossessing the defender before exchanging passes with the breaking Ronnie Whelan down the left flank.

No sooner had the Welsh striker played a quick one-two with the Irish midfielder then he was off like a shot into the penalty area. "With the Blues trying desperately to recover and Southall advancing, Whelan slipped the ball through to Rush who netted comfortably." It was a typical, fast flowing Liverpool move, capitalising on errors in the midfield to advance within seconds and, a few sharp, clever passes later, taking advantage of any frailties at the back.

Howard Kendall's decision to give his promising, locally born centre-half Ian Marshall – who had only made his first team debut against Manchester United in midweek - his first taste of league action in a Merseyside Derby, appeared to have backfired badly. The Blues simply had no answer to the speed and guile of Liverpool's attacking play.

As befitted a match between the previous season's top two - when Everton had completed a double over the Reds to win the title easily - the game was being played at a hectic pace. John Keith was moved to note that, "it was the greatest collision between Everton and Liverpool I have seen in almost 30 years…" Bobby Robson was equally beguiled, "I have been in football for 35 years," he later said, "and I don't recall seeing a better game in my life."

Play was sweeping majestically and mesmerically from one end to the other. Dalglish sent Johnston clear down the right only for Marshall to make a desperate challenge as the cross came in with Rush – who had equalled Harry Chambers' record as Liverpool's top derby goalscorer with his side's second of the game - lurking dangerously in the box. Then,

Lineker saw Grobbelaar make a spectacular save to push his curling free-kick around the post. Before the half was over, and despite losing Steve Nicol after 30 minutes through injury – the youngster was replaced by able deputy Phil Neal - the match was to get even better for the Red half of Merseyside.

The visitors were rampant. Liverpool, "were penetrating and ripping Everton's defence apart with ease at times." Four minutes from the interval they appeared to have grabbed all three points with a wonderful goal started and finished by the returning Steve McMahon. Picking the ball up in his own half, the former Everton favourite, "began the build-up himself with a tremendous crossfield ball to Whelan." With Beglin and Dalglish involved, the ball was worked toward the left corner flag before the stretching Liverpool player-manager stabbed the ball back into the path of the unmarked McMahon. The former Evertonian, "thundered in a low 30 yard shot into the right hand corner of the net." It was a spectacular strike.

"Howard Kendall's champions were gasping against a Liverpool side like rapiers in attack and bulldogs in defence", wrote John Keith in the Daily Express. Three-nil up, the Liverpool players left the field at half-time with the ecstatic applause of their rain-soaked fans on all sides of the ground ringing in their ears. Surely the three points – their first away from home this season - were in the bag?
One of Liverpool's Yankee Bar crew in the Everton end then felt sufficiently brave to mount a crush barrier, hold aloft an Everton scarf and set fire to it, which brought a predictably volatile response from the Everton fans who pelted the infiltrators with lighters and other missiles.

Although seemingly out of the game at 3-0, Everton however, were not reigning champions for nothing. With internationals packed throughout their side and an astute a manager as any in the league, they were not to be discounted - even at three goals down. Recognising that his gamble on using Marshall at the back was not working, Kendall used half-time to move Pat Van den Hauwe to centre-half and brought the inventive Adrian Heath – something of a catalyst in Everton's revival since signing from Stoke City – into the attack for his third substitute appearance of the campaign. Kendall admitted later that he had decided, "to throw caution to the wind," by playing three at the back and three up front – whilst three goals down. It almost paid off.

Just as Dalglish's pre-match tactical reshuffle had worked for Liverpool in the first-half, within six minutes of the restart Everton were back in the game courtesy of their carefree second-half approach. Rush had had a goal chalked off for a clear offside barely a minute earlier - his second disallowed goal of the game after another effort was ruled out in the first half - but from the resulting free-kick Everton retained possession well and forced Liverpool onto the back foot with, for the first time in the match, a period of sustained pressure.

On 51 minutes Bracewell tried a shot from inside the area but his strike cannoned off McMahon into the path of Graeme Sharp. The Scottish striker - vying for a place in the national team as the World Cup qualifiers came to their conclusion - made no mistake and lashed the ball into the net off the underside of the bar. "With their fans now urging men forward," Everton began to carve out a number of chances. Heath's speed was causing problems in the hitherto resolute Liverpool defence and, after squeezing between Neal and Molby, the diminutive forward forced a decent save from Grobbelaar as Everton suddenly laid siege to Liverpool's goal.

"With the blue shirts now pouring forward at every opportunity," another fine shot from Sharp was cleared for a corner. The resultant kick from Sheedy was flicked on at the near post by Sharp, and Hansen scrambled the ball clear from under his own bar. Even though a goal-bound shot from McMahon was blocked by Stevens at the other end, Liverpool found themselves under increasing pressure and it took a fantastic tackle by Lawrenson inside a packed area to deny Lineker on the hour.

It was thrilling stuff as the home side pressed, but Liverpool remained dangerous on the counter-attack. Dalglish and Rush combined for a half-chance but Southall saved comfortably. Then Heath made Grobbelaar work much harder to prevent another Everton goal. "The fans were enthralled by a thoroughly gripping encounter," wrote Ken Rogers. Johnston then beat Van den Hauwe for pace and fired in a shot on goal that Southall caught well.

On 69 minutes another Johnston run saw Liverpool force their first corner of the game - a remarkable statistic considering the scoreline and the number of chances they had created up till then. Lineker then found Sharp who chose to shoot rather than pass to the unmarked Heath to his right. This was a lucky break for Liverpool but, with ten minutes remaining, they were even more fortunate.

A hard hit Stevens cross from the right was met by Lineker who, under pressure from Lawrenson, somehow managed to crash a shot against the bar from just four yards out. With six minutes left however, Liverpool's defence was breached for a second time when Sheedy and Sharp exchanged quick passes inside the area to give Lineker the easiest of chances to convert from two yards.

Although Everton were right back in the game - and with the home support roaring them on - it was apparent that all their energies had been spent. Twice in the last five minutes Dalglish could have wrapped things up for Liverpool but, with only Southall to beat, he fired high over the bar with his first attempt, and wide of the far post with his second. The few hundred Liverpool fans who had clambered onto their traditional lofty perch at the back of the Park End terrace - for a better view from one the most dire, shallow Ends in the country - slammed their hands in frustration against the advertising hoardings behind the goal.

From his elevated vantage point at the back of the Park End, Martin Jones from West Derby "couldn't believe Dalglish had missed those two sitters. It was nerve-wracking enough even without Dalglish's misses, and the tension was such that only when the game was over did it register I was wet through from the torrential rain. My derby day rig-out – a sand-coloured Pringle sweater over an adidas polo neck and grey semi-flared cords - was soaked. My bucket hat, turned up at the back of course, would have been more at home on the beach than at miserable Goodison. I went home smelling like a wet dog." Despite Dalglish's misses, anguished expressions soon turned to smiles as referee Shaw signalled the end of a breathless encounter just minutes later.

"It was disgraceful to miss chances like that," Dalglish told the press later, "and I am lucky we got away with it and won…the manager is not too happy about it!" It was an insightful comment from Dalglish, who was always ready with a quip to mask his frustrations at any negative aspects of his team's performance. In his usual self-deprecating manner however, Dalglish also paid tribute to his new look side for contributing to a match his rival Howard

Kendall later called, "a classic." Alluding to his new formation - using Molby as an auxiliary defender - Dalglish explained that, "the players took the biggest decision with their attitude to make it work."

Despite the atrocious wet weather - which may have contributed to the excitement, the match had been played out in an electric atmosphere. Dalglish added, "Two committed teams and sets of supporters as well as the referee made it one of the greatest games I've been involved in, without one bit of nastiness. I find the atmosphere generated by these two clubs quite unbelievable."Gary Lineker, making his first appearance in a Merseyside Derby was disappointed to be on the losing side, but still enjoyed the experience. "I've never played in anything like that before. I've still got a headache from the noise. It was terrific."

Mark Lawrenson who had been at the heart of Liverpool's rearguard action in the second half said, "It was a great goal from Kenny, a hell of a strike, to set us up. We couldn't have had a better start. At half-time we knew everything had to change and it was a back-to-the-wall job at times in the second half but we held on." The final word went to Steve McMahon who described his winning goal, scored against his boyhood club; "Kenny Dalglish had the ball. I went to support him and he laid a nice pass back for me. I struck it just right, fortunately. The game was really end-to-end stuff and with 10 minutes to go we really had to hold on."

For the first time in the season Liverpool had taken three points at an away ground - and at the same time registered a blow to Everton's title hopes. It was the Blues' third defeat of the season. That the Reds had finally found some form away from Anfield was timely as, with Manchester United extending their 100% start to the season to nine games with an emphatic 5-1 victory at West Brom, the Reds still trailed their Mancunian foes by nine points.

Liverpool v Oldham Athletic
League Cup second round, first leg
Tuesday 24 September 1985

"Most Liverpool people feel that their city has not had a fair deal…the way the rate support grant formula operates…does not take into account Liverpool's declining population and industry. But where Councillor Hatton is wrong is to portray that feeling as being support for the tactics of the council…[Our] poll shows that, while most people support the council's efforts to obtain more financial aid, they are against a strike by council workers…We are now at a crucial point in the battle between the council and the government…It seems that suddenly we are at the crunch."

Liverpool Echo Comment, Tuesday Sept 24

Since March 1984, when Liverpool's Labour Council had set an illegal budget – and 50,000 took to the streets to support the council's stance – a confrontation between them and Central Government had been looming. Despite Tory threats to suspend elections and have Liverpool run by commissioners, Labour gained seven more seats in the council elections just a week later – with a 50%+ turnout. This included several gains by Militant supporters.

Two months later Environment Minister Patrick Jenkin was forced to climb down from the Governments stance – there were afterall, bigger fish to fry in the shape of the miners – and extra money for Liverpool was indeed found, although rate rises were also introduced. The feeling at the time however, was that Liverpool's problems had simply been put off until the following year. Derek Hatton recounts being told by Tory MP Teddy Taylor that, "we had to tell Patrick to give you the money. At this stage we want Scargill. He's our priority. But we'll come for you later."

With the miner's defeated and the Council setting another illegal budget in 1985 (again with mass support on the streets of the city) - the stage was set once more. This time however, the Government had no intention of retreating. Unlike 1984 when a number of other left-wing led councils had supported Liverpool and followed their lead, there was to be no such solidarity this time. Originally ten refused to set a legal budget – but by June all but two had relented. Liverpool and Lambeth stood alone.

No additional cash was forthcoming and, as the cash crisis worsened, redundancy notices were issued to Liverpool Council workers – a technical ploy so as to ensure no councillors were surcharged nor the Councils' credit would be lost. Hatton later acknowledged that taking this advice was an enormous mistake, one from which the council never recovered. A way around the problem would be for all workers to go on strike and not to be paid – for around three weeks but possibly until as late as March 1986. Despite a majority in favour of such action in a number of the larger unions however, the motion was defeated - although an all out one-day strike for the Wednesday 25 September was agreed.

Liverpool was now at the brink. Unions marched against the redundancy notices; council buildings were locked; everywhere there was confusion. The Government could have cut the process short at any point, "by getting someone to bring a court case to declare the unbalanced budget illegal, by telling the banks that Liverpool's credit was not good, or simply by stopping central government grant payments," but instead, they did nothing. They didn't have too. "They chose to wait and see... and now they can watch the Liverpool labour movement wound and perhaps tear itself apart." On 8 September the District Auditor had expelled 49 councillors from office and fined them £106,000 – a theoretical loss of interest resulting from the late setting of the rate.

The bewilderment and confusion many felt at the unprecedented events taking place on the city's streets during a day of high political drama were a far cry from a routine night at Anfield that same evening - when Second Division Oldham Athletic were the visitors in the first leg, second round of the Football League Milk Cup.

After treating the competition with disdain –as most of the bigger clubs had done in the trophy's formative years - Liverpool had first won the League Cup in 1981 with a replay victory over West Ham at Villa Park, before winning a further three, high-profile finals in consecutive years between 1982-1984. Their vanquished opponents on each of these showpiece occasions, Tottenham Hotspur, Manchester United and Everton gave the competition's first sponsors, the Milk Marketing Board, the exposure they were seeking, and demonstrated a positive shift in the big clubs' attitude to the traditional poor relation of English football. In Joe Fagan's final season before retirement the Reds' record-breaking run ended with the hiccup of an early exit at Spurs, a game that saw Kenny Dalglish dropped for the first time in his Liverpool career. Fagan admitted later that his decision to omit Dalglish in that game was the daftest thing he had ever done in management.

Just eight weeks prior to the first leg at Anfield the Latics, managed by former Everton legend Joe Royle, had had the temerity to beat the Reds 1-0 at Boundary Park. That was in a pre-season friendly however, an appropriate environment for blooding promising young players, improving the fitness of those who over-indulged during the close-season or, in Liverpool's case in the summer of 1985, a chance to field players who had looked hard at their future and the meaning of the game in the wake of Heysel.

Since their pre-season date at Boundary Park however, Liverpool had taken on a new look; they had a new captain in Alan Hansen; Steve McMahon had been bought to bolster the midfield; and Alan Kennedy, twice a European Cup final hero, had left for Sunderland. More importantly, those who had suffered from the trauma of being involved in a game of football that brought about the deaths of 39 innocent supporters, had been rehabilitated by the familiar routine of a new football season.

Stalwart Phil Neal also appeared to be following Alan Kennedy on his way out of Anfield. The former club captain had held talks with Chairman John Smith and Chief Executive Peter Robinson the day before the game to discuss his future, but although Neal, "would clearly welcome an opening on the coaching staff," the club revealed that even for as cherished a servant as him, no such position existed at the time. It was clear that Liverpool were, "entering a new era under player-manager Dalglish," so, "the vastly experienced defender is now prepared to turn his sights away from Anfield."

The League Cup had become a competition many Reds' fans looked forward to, with the prospect of a trip to Wembley and the weekend away in London that went with it very much part of the average Liverpool fan's social calendar. From a playing perspective, Ken Rogers noted that, "the standards and ambitions [of Liverpool] remain as high as ever and the Reds are keen to make a solid start in a competition they have dominated in recent years.

Although Liverpool entered the game on a high following their pulsating victory over Everton at the weekend, they were not about to take their Second Division opponents likely. Joe Royle's side had not only inflicted the first defeat of the season on Alan Ball's table toppers Portsmouth at the weekend, they also boasted a pair of lively - and unlikely - scouse heroes of their own.

After signing from Stockport County the previous season for just £52,000, burly Liverpool-born striker Mickey Quinn had rattled in 21 goals for the Latics and was unarguably the form striker of the Second Division. So impressive was Quinn's ability to hit the back of the net that he was keeping former Kop favourite David Fairclough on the bench. Following a brief spell with Swiss side Lucerne during the 1984/85 season, 'Supersub' Fairclough - who had scored arguably Anfield's most celebrated goal against St. Etienne in 1977 - found that he had been omitted from the PFA list of available players circulated to clubs at the start of the season.

That oversight meant few clubs were aware he had even returned to England let alone was a free agent and, after unsuccessful trials with both Manchester City and Norwich, the flame-haired frontman jumped at the chance to train with Oldham in the summer as a means of keeping fit. However, he showed enough of his former zest to persuade Royle to add him to his squad at the start of the campaign.

Injury forced Dalglish to rule himself out of contention and - with Nicol also absent with a minor knock and midfielder-cum-sweeper Jan Molby on World Cup qualifying duty with Denmark - the manager re-shuffled his pack. Unlike the modern league cup however, when virtual reserve sides are fielded by most clubs in the top flight, Dalglish's reshaped side did not feature any unfamiliar names.

Football was slower in 1985 when compared to the modern game and players were able to recover faster so as to consistently play twice a week for most of the season. Dalglish therefore named no less than eight of the side that had beaten Everton in the engrossing Merseyside derby at the weekend. Despite being aware his days at Anfield were perhaps numbered, Neal replaced Nicol at right back in one of only three changes; Sammy Lee also started in place of Molby, whilst Paul Walsh replaced the manager to partner Ian Rush in attack.

On paper Oldham had little chance and, in practice, this turned out to be the case. Indeed, they were lucky to keep the score down to just 3-0. Joe Royle's side played, "with pride and determination but they were overwhelmed...by the energy and invention," of a Liverpool side that finally looked like they were beginning to find some fluidity and swagger.

Halfway through a first-half that the home side dominated, Rush let fly from the edge of the area but, although his shot was saved by Andy Goram, the promising young keeper failed to hold onto the ball and it fell to the lurking McMahon who tapped home easily. Ten minutes later, goalscorer turned provider when McMahon fed Rush with an exquisite through ball that sliced through the Oldham defence. Few strikers were as clinical in a one-on-one situation than Rush and the Welshman gave Goram no chance. Allowed the freedom of the left-wing wing usually not afforded him in the top flight, Beglin then found himself in the area only to be upended by Roger Palmer. Neal stepped up to take the spot-kick hoping to register what would have been his 60th goal for the Reds. His low spot-kick beat Goram but, after hitting the left hand post, the referee blew immediately for a free kick to Oldham when Neal instinctively netted the rebound without any other player touching the ball.

Shortly after the break Ron Futcher hit the bar with a fierce header but this was the only time the Liverpool goal found itself under any form of attack. Grobbelaar was a virtual spectator for almost all the game, spending his time whistling, winking and joking with the fans behind his goal. With 14 minutes left, man-of-the-match McMahon, "always ready to mix tenacity with skill," curled his second goal past Goram after latching onto Hansen's superb through ball. 3-0 and the game, and effectively the tie – even with a second leg at Boundary Park to come - was over.

Four minutes later the crowd gave McMahon a standing ovation when he was replaced by Kevin McDonald. His reception paled in comparison to the one David Fairclough had received on the hour mark however, when his appearance produced, "one of the biggest cheers of the night from a crowd who never forget an old friend." Although he showed glimpses of his former energy and sharpness there was no threat of a dramatic 'supersub' impact on a game which Liverpool had controlled easily. With the visit of Spurs at the weekend another big Anfield clash was looming, so the Reds were content to play out time and preserve their three goal advantage.

In a muted atmosphere in front of 16,150 fans, those standing on a sparsely populated Kop took solace in the fact that - if few in the country backed their elected council's entrenched view of the political landscape - then at least they could show support for a side that, amid the social upheaval and depravation faced by so many in the City, still managed to make them feel proud to be Liverpudlians. They realised that the Government were determined not to blink in their high-stakes showdown with the elected council, and many wondered what would happen next as the future of the city remained uncertain. Few would have expected it to be taken to the brink in the manner it subsequently did.

Liverpool v Tottenham Hotspur
Saturday 28 September 1985

"Most people in Britain are fed up with Margaret Thatcher and her politics. That is what the opinion polls and the pundits would have us believe. She is portrayed by her opponents – even by some who pose as her friends – as dictatorial and autocratic, riding roughshod over ordinary working people. This is a distortion of perception over reality. It is exactly the opposite. It has been demonstrated for months, so much so that we are beginning to take Margaret Thatcher's success for granted. She has given back freedom and independence to the workers of Britain. This week in Liverpool they have shown once again that they know how to use it. Her revolution is now their revolution against the tyranny of trade union 'Capos' who have dominated and exploited ordinary unionists for nearly four decades."

Daily Mail Comment, Thursday 26 September

Since 1912, the prospect of a home game against Tottenham Hotspur had filled Kopites of all ages with a warm glow. That was until the 1984/85 season when the North Londoners had the gall to reverse one of the most amazing statistics in English club football and had actually beaten Liverpool at Anfield. It was their first victory there since March 1912 - the same year that the Titanic sank en route to New York.

If Spurs' fans felt they could match that result this season however, they were to be sorely disappointed. Two late penalties may have flattered Liverpool, but the victory was thoroughly deserved and went some way to gaining revenge for the shock result six months previously. In May 1985, Tottenham had ended the season in third place in the First Division – finishing behind Liverpool only on goal difference - and Peter Shreeves's side were fancied by many sports' commentators to mount a serious and strong challenge to the Merseyside clubs for the title this time round. As September drew to a close the North Londoners were tucked away in fifth position and had won their last four games, beating Chelsea and Sheffield Wednesday 5-1 on each occasion, as well as putting four past Newcastle United and winning away at Nottingham Forest.

In fine early autumn sunshine, Liverpool's new captain Alan Hansen - confirmed as skipper before the game despite the return of Phil Neal - lost the toss and the Reds' were forced to attack the Kop end in the first half. For the first half-hour there was little to choose between the teams, with both creating a number of chances. A volley by Paul Allen, the former West Ham midfielder who Liverpool were rumoured to have tried to buy before the season started, had the first shot of the game but his effort flew wide. The lively midfield schemer then tried to beat Beglin but the young Irish international, quickly looking as composed as Kennedy in his pomp - and arguably more threatening in an attacking sense, "slid in with an excellent tackle," to clear the danger.

Beglin's pace and abundant skill going forward was much in evidence in the first half although his dangerous cross on 15 minutes was caught by former Anfield favourite Ray Clemence – given a tremendous reception by the home crowd when he jogged to the Kop to take up his position at the start of the game – after a flick-on by Dalglish. Lawrenson then had a header cleared off the line from a curling corner by the player-manager, before a fierce Molby centre was met by Rush but his spectacular diving header was again well held by Clemence.

At the other end a clever Hoddle through ball gave the speedy John Chiedozie a half-chance but, fast as he was, few attackers in the top flight were able to steal a march on Lawrenson and the Preston-born Eire defender dispossessed the Nigerian international with an excellent, and characteristically composed, tackle. Not only did the cultured centre-half win the ball cleanly, he then proceeded to start another promising Liverpool attacking move, albeit one that came to nothing.

Both McMahon and Neal earned warm applause for crunching tackles on Osvaldo Ardiles and Chris Waddle respectively and, with Spurs just as determined in their challenges, the game became an untidy affair as, "free-kicks erupted like boils across the glazed greensward." In between the frequent stoppages, a long-range Hoddle effort was well held by Grobbelaar - after skidding dangerously across the damp surface - whilst a fierce Whelan volley from a Johnston cross fizzed narrowly wide.

Taking a lead from his combative outfield colleagues, Clemence then gave away an indirect free-kick in his own area after a clumsy challenge on Molby that the referee generously interpreted as obstruction. Dalglish took the kick and slid the ball to Lawrenson but the defender's shot was cleared off the line – a second goalscoring opportunity of the game denied for the Irishman.

"With the Kop in tremendous voice and Liverpool pressing hard for the opener," Molby was brought crashing down by Hughton just outside the box. Clemence punched the resultant free-kick clear from under his crossbar, only to see the ball fall to McMahon whose cheeky lob back into the area caught everyone off-guard, including Mark Falco who appeared to use his hand to clear the danger. With Liverpool's players appealing for a penalty and the Kop spitting their disapproval, the referee, Carlisle's C. Seel, waved play on.

The sheer number of free-kicks awarded, especially after the 30 minute mark, meant that the half was extended by three minutes – commonplace today but almost unheard of in 1985. In the 48th minute yet another free-kick to Liverpool, this time for a Waddle challenge on Rush, was taken by Neal and his deep cross appeared to have eluded everybody until, from the tightest of angles, Lawrenson popped up to beat Clemence at the far post. It was third time lucky for the defender and Liverpool led with almost the last kick of the half.

If Liverpool thought their late, late first-half goal would prove a catalyst for further goals and a psychological blow to their opponents however, they were to be rudely mistaken as within a minute of the restart Spurs were level. Falco's tremendous shot from distance was pushed wide in similarly spectacular fashion by Grobbelaar, but Johnston's half-clearance of the resultant corner fell to Graham Roberts - whose shot struck a defender before falling, almost dead, at the feet of Chiedozie.

The speedy Nigerian winger – whom Dalglish would later say was, "as fast as a hare," - made no mistake from six yards in front of a stunned Kop. Suddenly Liverpool's profligacy in front of goal looked like it would cost them all three points yet again. Forced to make a substitution with MacDonald replacing McMahon at half-time, the Reds, "now faced a major battle against the rejuvenated Londoners."

Liverpool were in determined mood however, and, as they so often did in the 1980s, they slowly but surely went through the gears. Spurs – a, "thoughtful, creative and aggressive team," were, "chewed up and left a torn and crumpled heap of finery on an afternoon fit for kings and heroes", wrote enamoured Observer reporter Derek Hodgson. A long-range effort from Molby looked all the way like a goal-of-the-season contender until Clemence, "saved in equally brilliant fashion," with a potential save-of-the-season himself. The entire ground applauded Molby and the former Anfield hero in the opposition goal.

This came just a minute after the Reds had conceded the equaliser and for the next quarter of an hour the home side dominated proceedings as they visibly cranked up the pressure on the visitors. On 56 minutes Beglin, rampaging forward on the left in the manner of a player modern day managers would pay tens of millions for, found Rush in the area with a pinpoint pass to feet. The Welsh striker controlled the cross deftly with one touch, but he was facing away from goal and with Roberts in close proximity. A twist of the body later however, and Rush had turned, held his marker off, and shot – on target - almost in one movement. Clemence could only watch, as a split-second later the goalscorer supreme was running towards the Kop at the far end to celebrate, the ball nestling nicely in the bottom left-hand corner of the goal.

At 2-1 up the momentum seemed to be with Liverpool, but on the hour mark Spurs almost equalised when Chris Hughton fired wide with only Grobbelaar to beat after a chipped pass from Hoddle caught the Liverpool defence square. "Hughton's agony was increased almost immediately when he conceded a penalty at the other end," for pushing Whelan as the Irishman attempted to reach a Dalglish pass. Despite missing a penalty in the previous game against Oldham, the crowd expected Phil Neal to step up and take the spot-kick, but a-new captain wasn't the only thing Dalglish had changed and it was Danish international Jan Molby who netted from 12-yards, casually caressing the ball wide of Clemence's outstretched right hand.

Just over five minutes later Lawrenson, having a major influence at both ends of the pitch once again, sent Rush running in the box with a clever ball into space. Before he had touched it however, the inform striker was sent sprawling by Roberts and Molby, now known as, "Rambo to the Kop," after the Sylvester Stallone movie character, scored, "as if with a stolen Kalashnikov," his second penalty - in almost identical fashion to his first. MacDonald went close in the dying stages whilst Rush had a goal ruled out for off-side, but there was no mistaking Liverpool's intent.

Unbeaten in nine and with just the one defeat from their first 10 league matches, the Reds of Anfield were doing all they could to hang on the coat tails of the runaway league leaders Manchester United who, in defeating Southampton 1-0 at Old Trafford, had incredibly won their tenth consecutive league game.

The Reds performance had so impressed watching Hodgson, that he was moved to not that, "The Shankly system remains; the defence is as ruthless in denying space, the new midfield could fuel a battlecruiser, while Johnston and Whelan are the defensive wingers fashionable in this decade. Dalglish is still linking while Rush, as his goal proved, remains the lean Lone Ranger and deadly sharp shooter. Even with Nicol temporarily absent, the back four are faster and fiercer. In a phrase, Liverpool are back." Despite such praise, the victory and their impressive record so far, Liverpool were nine points behind the leaders, who they would meet at Old Trafford in just three games time.

On the same afternoon, Everton lost further ground with a goalless draw at Villa Park to slip 13 points behind United with less than a quarter of the season played. It was no time to panic with 32 matches still ahead, but the weekly triumphalism in the media continued as United stretched their 100% record into October.

Queens Park Rangers v Liverpool
Saturday 5 October 1985

"More than one worker in four in Liverpool is now without a job, according to the latest unemployment figures – which have hit a new record nationally of 3,346,198. Swelled by the latest batch of school leavers, male unemployment in the greater Liverpool area rose to 77,698 last month, equivalent to 27 per cent and meaning that three men in every eleven are looking for work."

Liverpool Echo, 3 October 1985.

The news that unemployment in Liverpool had risen to unprecedented levels was announced just days before the opening of the Conservative Party Conference in Blackpool. With political crises and their attendant financial implications a seemingly everyday occurrence for the city, no other English city's population was as politically aware or, paradoxically, as estranged, from mainstream politics as Liverpool.

Despite the efforts of the serious, liberal press, few outside Merseyside fully understood the underlying economic problems and the immediate financial implications faced by the City. But as unions changed sides, redundancy notices were issued then withdrawn, marches were organised both for – and against – the city council's position, and the debate degenerated into a war of words between the local council, the Labour leadership and the TUC, Liverpool's reputation as a trouble spot was only cemented in the eyes of the rest of the country once more.

At the Labour Party conference in Bournemouth earlier in the week, Labour leader Neil Kinnock marked a turning point in the recent history of the party by denouncing those on the left who, by picking ideological battles with central government, he accused of betraying the very people they were elected to represent. "You cannot play politics with people's jobs, with their homes, with their essential services," he told delegates – a speech that has since gone down in Labour party folklore.

Cheered by most of those in attendance, he was barracked and heckled constantly by members of Militant, and Labour MP for Liverpool Walton Eric Heffer – a member of the party's executive committee – famously walked off stage. The Party would never be the same again. A month later Labour would set up an inquiry into the goings on in Liverpool and the councillors – from Lambeth as well as Liverpool - would eventually be expelled from the Party. In May 1986 they would be barred from taking public office by the High Court.

Kinnock's criticism of Liverpool's council leaders was also echoed by David Sheppard and Derek Warlock who, in an open letter to the media, warned that although they, "are concerned that the case for Liverpool and other urban areas does not seem to have been adequately heard by Whitehall," they were, "increasingly anxious about the council's policy of confrontation." "Now the head-on clash has occurred," they said, "a very dangerous moment in the life of our city has been reached." Their 1,000 word letter, almost dripping with sadness and regret, continued, "Before the eyes of the rest of the nation Liverpool is tearing itself to pieces. This is the more tragic in a city which has been renowned for its spirit and solidarity in the face of threat and danger."

The arguments put forward by Kinnock, Sheppard, Warlock and others were also supported by a section of Merseysiders themselves and a 'Militant Out of Liverpool' march organised for Sunday 6 October by local company director Jeff Tinnion (described as, "a loyal Scouser," by the Liverpool Echo) drew - despite the poor weather - around 5,000 to the Pier Head. Although positively supported and promoted by the local newspaper it was short of the 50,000 estimated to have marched in support of the council just a few months previously. While some social commentators often marvelled at Liverpool's inherently political, social and cultural insular attitude, through these latest events its wider image suffered at the hands of a largely right-wing media.

While the political slanging matches raged on, Kenny Dalglish had calmed the waters surrounding Liverpool FC with five wins and two draws in the last seven league games. However, despite pre-match predictions that QPR's infamous plastic pitch would hold no fears for a side that had earned Dalglish a nomination for the coveted manager-of-the-month award Liverpool, after taking the lead on eight minutes through the returning Paul Walsh, lost to the West Londoners for the first time in eight years.

Manchester United, league-leaders and the focus of much of the national sport media's attention after 10 wins from 10 games – including a BBC Football Focus piece that ludicrously dubbed Manchester the, "hotbed of British football" - were also in the South East that same weekend, tackling the First Division's only other plastic pitch - at Luton Town. United's game at Kenilworth Road saw them attempting to equal Tottenham's then First Division record of 11 straight wins.

The press coverage United had received since winning their 10th league game on the bounce was a source of mirth and irritation in equal measure on Merseyside, with many fans expressing the sort of logic and perspective that their counterparts in the media seemed palpably to lack. "Where are all the trophies of the Manchester teams who [supposedly] rule football?" William Brennan of Parlow Road queried on the Football Echo letters page. "In Everton's trophy room!" he answered sarcastically.

Recognising at the same time the daily, political crises that seemed to engulf his city and the potential for United to fall short of media expectation, Mr Brennan encapsulated the feelings of many Mersey football fans. "Come May, United's title challenge will be as strong as our city council's financial position," he added. With talk of, "imminent bankruptcy," for the Council, Liverpudlians consoled themselves with hopes of a similar collapse on the part of Manchester United.

Everton fan Joseph Burke of the Dingle also noted that United had yet to meet, in the league at least, any teams of quality, pointing out that, "six of the teams United have beaten in their so-called record run are presently propping up Division One." Indeed, Mr Burke pointed out that the only side of any real calibre they had met were Everton, in the Super Cup, and – albeit not taken as seriously as other competitions – "we hit the back of the net four times and made United look ordinary."

Even serial-contributor Len Griffiths of Oxton, Wirral - for years seen as the voice of doom wherever Liverpool were concerned - was roused sufficiently to pertinently state that, "No-one would dispute they [Manchester United] have a powerful side. It is the glorified publicity they get...that we object to." He added that, "One dreads the thought of what we would get if they ever won a unique treble, fifteen league titles, six European trophies, or the league for three consecutive seasons!"

Liverpool's hopes of adding another title to their list of honours appeared to rest on not only overcoming United's great, though surprising, start to the season however, but also attempting to outlast an Everton side that had not yet reached the heights of their previous, championship winning campaign.

Despite fans' annoyance with the hyperbole that seemed to engulf United, both Merseyside teams could ill afford to let their North West rivals increase their lead at the top of the table. Liverpool in particular were keen to experience an October every bit as good as the previous month, where four wins and a draw from their five league games had at last forced pundits to acknowledge a potential threat to United's lead.

The season before - in a televised Friday night fixture at Loftus Road - Joe Fagan's side, with a goal apiece from Ian Rush and John Wark, had secured a routine win on the plastic pitch. Before Liverpool's latest trip to Shepherds Bush it was announced that Wark, after a long lay-off through injury, was, "slowly getting himself back into top shape." This was especially good news for Dalglish who, hoping to limit his own appearances and preserve his limbs for the sterner tests ahead, was keen to have more attack minded players in his squad. He was mindful too that Paul Walsh considered himself worthy of a regular start and was unhappy with the bit part role he had played so far.

After a late fitness check on Steve McMahon, Dalglish's only change to the side that had destroyed Spurs the week before was to name himself as substitute, with Walsh taking his place alongside in-form striker Ian Rush - who had netted five goals in five games. Similarly, few midfielders in the top flight had caught the eye more than Jan Molby, especially now the bulk of tackling and tracking back duties had been transferred to McMahon, allowing the Danish international to play the more sublime, expansive game he was originally signed to provide.

Likewise, since replacing Alan Kennedy at left-back just five games previously, Jim Beglin's rampaging, though astute, wing play had also earned rave reviews. His transfer from Shamrock Rovers - the last transfer arranged by Bob Paisley in May 1983 - coupled with subsequent careful nurturing in the reserves - and when the opportunity arose for the first team under Fagan and now Dalglish - appeared another typically masterful Liverpool buy.

Runners-up to Liverpool in 1976 before a rapid decline saw them relegated, Rangers regained their top-flight status in 1983 under Terry Venables. QPR then finished fifth in their first season back in the top division but they regressed again after Venables left to join Barcelona. Should they need him Rangers could call on the services of Michael Robinson, the former Liverpool striker who had been transferred to the West Londoners for £200,000 the previous season. "I regret leaving Liverpool because it is the best football club in the world," Robinson said before the game. "There are so many people there who know so much about football; Ronnie Moran, Roy Evans, Bob Paisley, Kenny Dalglish. Even the tea lady!" The move hadn't worked out well for the likeable, overly self-critical Robinson however, and he was currently on the transfer list at Loftus Road.

Under the newly-appointed Jim Smith, Rangers' immediate target was simply to stay in the First Division. Their cause was more than aided by the artificial pitch at Loftus Road which had been installed in 198/82 and it was their home record that ultimately helped Rangers retain their top flight status.

Even the best teams in the division struggled with the synthetic surface - in September they had beaten league champions Everton 3-0 – so, despite Dalglish's pre-match confidence - gained from Reds' victories at Loftus Road in the past two seasons - the Londoners were not to be discounted easily. This turned out to be the case when, despite going a goal behind in front of a large and noisy travelling contingent from Merseyside, the home side then ran out deserved winners against a lacklustre Liverpool. Gallingly for Dalglish, the Reds failed to gain control of the game even after they took an early lead.

Looking lively and seemingly relishing his rare place in the starting line-up, Walsh appeared more at ease on the artificial surface than his colleague, especially McMahon, who was guilty of several hard challenges that the referee perhaps should have treated more harshly. Similarly, the heavily-built Molby found controlling the ball and then attempting to free his forwards with his trademark intricate passes, extremely difficult.

In contrast, the nimble Walsh found the going much easier and it was the Londoner who broke the deadlock after just eight minutes. Attempting a one-two with Rush in Liverpool's first serious attack of the game, a fortuitous rebound off a defender gave Walsh a clear run at goal but, despite his first effort being blocked by keeper Paul Barron, he made no mistake with his follow-up. If this was a call for Liverpool to turn up the heat, as they had in their previous two league games however, then it went unheeded.

A half-chance for Whelan, after a long, weighted pass by Molby that pierced the Rangers' defence; a shot by Rush that sailed over the cross-bar; and a simple clearance by Fenwick with Rush and Molby closing in, was all Liverpool had to offer in the remainder of the half. By contrast, QPR's tally of half-chances and openings comfortably ran into double figures. David Kerslake and Gary Waddock found they had the running of midfield whilst Leroy Rosenior and in particular Wayne Fereday, were causing havoc on the wings.

Half-way through the half a free-kick on the edge of the Liverpool area, after an uncharacteristically clumsy challenge by Hansen on Rosenior, was the catalyst for a period of home side pressure that didn't let up until the half-time whistle. Fenwick should have equalised on the half-hour mark but blasted his shot over from only seven yards. From a corner, Wicks sent an unmarked header straight at Grobbelaar when a yard either side of the Liverpool keeper would almost certainly have resulted in a goal.

Set-pieces, particularly corners, appeared to be Rangers' greatest threat and it was no surprise, with the Liverpool defence, "looking ragged," that they equalised in exactly this manner with just two minutes of the half remaining. A deep, flighted corner was headed back into the area, where Terry Fenwick drove the ball into the roof of the net. With Liverpool spurning not one but two chances to clear the ball in the build up to the goal, Dalglish's face was a glum one as the teams disappeared down the tunnel at half-time.

The second half started just as the first had ended, with QPR doing most of the attacking. Waddock, Mike Fillery and Gary Bannister all sent shots or headers wide of Grobbelaar's goal and the home side's profligacy looked like costing them all three points until, "an outburst of noise from the large Liverpool contingent in the crowd seemed to lift them," and the visitors created a series of chances culminating in Johnston's long range shot being deflected wide and Barron making a great save from Molby's, "fierce left foot shot."

Unfortunately for Liverpool however, that was the height of their response and Rangers upped the pace once again. Getting the better of Neal, Fereday sent in a great cross that was met by Bannister and the statues in Liverpool's defence could only watch in relief as his free-header fizzed barely a foot wide with Grobbelaar well beaten.

On 60 minutes Johnston thought he had put Liverpool back in front only to find his effort disallowed for off-side. Liverpool's disappointment was compounded when, barely two minutes later, Rosenior found, "the speedy Fereday…who again left Neal for dead," and sent in another great cross for Bannister, who slid along the floor to bundle the ball into the net.

Despite three corners in rapid succession in the last quarter of an hour, Liverpool's attempts to force an undeserved equaliser became increasingly desperate and the visitors rarely looked like scoring until a few minutes from time when Lawrenson forced a great save from Barron. Whelan's effort from the subsequent rebound was cleared by Steve Wicks. These however, "were comparatively isolated chances amid a flood of Rangers' attacks which had Liverpool's defence increasingly at full stretch."

Following the game, Dalglish blamed the pitch for his side's lack of fluency – the first time Liverpool, unlike many other sides - had complained about the artificial surface, but the manager's excuse simply masked his frustration at an opportunity missed. In only drawing at Luton, Manchester United dropped their first points of the season. Had Liverpool capitalised on Paul Walsh's early opener, the gap at the top of the table could have been trimmed to seven points. Instead, United's lead had reached double figures, giving the looming clash - even at this early stage of the season - at Old Trafford in two week's time, added significance.

Everton's win over Oxford at Goodison compounded a bad day at the office for the Reds. The one consolation had been the performance of Walsh on his return to the starting line-up but, with Dalglish rested and ready to return to the fray in the coming weeks, another stiff test of his man-management skills was just around the corner.

Also facing a stiff test of his own in local boxing circles was Liverpool heavyweight prospect Noel Quarless. He faced an uphill battle to revive his career following a seventh round stoppage to Birmingham's Horace Notice at the Liverpool Stadium on 3 October – the British title eliminator was one of the last big boxing shows to be held at the famous city centre arena. It would close before the end of the year however, and was demolished completely in 1987.

Of arguably even more interest to local sports fans was the news that Rainbow Quest, ridden by 'housewives favourite' Pat Eddery, had won the Prix de l'Arc de Triomphe at Longchamp after an objection to the first past the post – the French 'wonder horse' Sagace – had been upheld. It was reported that, "When Rainbow Quest was awarded the race in the Stewards' room, the home supporters showed their feelings by pelting Eddery with shingle, cigarette packets, and fruit."

Oldham Athletic v Liverpool
League Cup second round second leg
Wednesday 9 October 1985

"As the crow flies it is only 30 miles from Blackpool to Liverpool. This week the two places could have been at different ends of the world. In Blackpool the Tory party conference has been discussing unemployment…Lord Young had a good news message. He says that an average of 500 new small firms are starting up every week…Chancellor Nigel Lawson was even more ebullient…inflation is low, investment in industry is booming and the economy is strong and growing fast…But where is all this happening? Certainly not in Tees Street, Birkenhead…We've called Tees Street, Dole Street, because all except two of the adults who live there are unemployed…We wish we could say it is exceptional. But there are many similar streets on Merseyside…"

Liverpool Echo editorial, 10 October 1985.

It was a surprise to many that in the week of the Conservative Party conference, the hitherto fervently anti-Militant Liverpool Echo - which had largely ignored the message communicated by an increased Labour vote in Liverpool just two years previously - suddenly castigated the Tory government for their ignorance of, and disdain for, the plight of a growing minority of their readers. Despite this apparent political about turn by the local paper, it says a lot for the standing and influence of football in this seemingly forgotten provincial city, that what astounded most people more during the week wasn't the number of unemployed, nor the anti-Militant march, nor even the Broadwater Farm riots in Tottenham, London – in which a policeman was killed - but the revelation that Liverpool striker Paul Walsh had slapped in an official transfer request.

Indeed, more letters concerning Walsh's flounce arrived in the newspaper's post box than on any other matter – the vast majority sympathising with the former Luton Town striker, who had been captured by Joe Fagan just 18 months previously. Walsh's surprise request followed his omission from the Liverpool side that had defeated Oldham 5-2 in the second leg of their second round Milk Cup tie at Boundary Park. He had scored in the Reds' 2-1 defeat at QPR at the weekend and, with 14 Liverpool goals from a total of 43 appearances - many as a substitute - he felt he deserved a regular place in the team.

With player-manager Kenny Dalglish using himself sparingly, the Londoner was aggrieved that he hadn't been utilised more often than he had been to date but, after his scoring return at Loftus Road, the £700,000 England international failed to make Dalglish's teamsheet at Oldham. Signed in May 1984, Walsh was under no illusions as to the task ahead of him at the time when he admitted, "The problem is getting into the team and staying there."

His prophetic words were no mere footballing cliche. No less a partnership than Dalglish and Rush were the forward pairing of choice for Joe Fagan in Walsh's first season, with John Wark capable of providing extra goals from midfield. When Walsh signed, Liverpool had just completed a remarkable treble of League title, League Cup and European Cup. To even make a squad of 14, let alone the subs bench or starting XI, would have been quite an achievement no matter who the new striker.

When Dalglish first took over as manager, his occasional absences saw him lean toward the re-born Craig Johnston for a deputy alongside Rush. In the absence of cartilage victim Rush however, Walsh was a regular at the beginning of the 1984/85, but he gradually faded from the scene as the campaign wore on when the Welshman returned to resume his partnership with Dalglish.

Ahead of his time as a manager, Dalglish firmly believed in rotating players – himself included – whenever he could despite the restrictions of just one permitted substitute. Liverpool had played 13 games in the season so far and hadn't yet named the same twelve players for consecutive matches. True, most of the starting line-up remained the same, but Dalglish had named an eye-opening six different players as substitute - including Walsh on two occasions.

Following a pre-season injury, John Wark - top goalscorer from midfield in 1984/85 with 27 goals in all competitions - had yet to return to first team action for the Reds but, with Jan Molby on World Cup duty for Denmark and the tie effectively over following Liverpool's 3-0 win at Anfield in the first leg, Dalglish eased the prolific Scot back into action by giving him the number 10 shirt. He named himself up front in place of Walsh and awarded the subs shirt not to the speedy striker, but to midfielder Kevin McDonald.

To add insult to Walsh's perceived slight, - and further enhance Dalglish's growing reputation as a man who knew almost instinctively what he was doing despite his relative inexperience in the managers' role - both Wark and MacDonald scored as the Reds ran out comfortable winners; 5-2 on the night, 8-2 on aggregate.

Indeed, the away side dominated to such an extent, particularly in midfield, that they could afford to take their foot off the pedal for a period in the second-half – to the extent that former Anfield favourite David Fairclough scored two goals against his former club. His goals were cheered by the small band of Liverpool fans in the 7,719 crowd almost as much as a brace from their own Ronnie Whelan; a snapshot after barely five minutes of action and another three minutes after the restart. Wark's powerful drive on 25 minutes and the almost obligatory Rush strike on 64 minutes added to the rout. Rush's goal came just after Fairclough's second had given the Latics some consolation and was followed by Kevin McDonald's first ever Liverpool goal with just over a quarter of an hour to go.

Although Liverpool netted five times, such was their dominance it could easily have been double that figure with Andy Goram, recently called up to the Scotland squad, "at the wrong end of a coconut shy," for most of the game. MacDonald - a replacement for the injured Hansen at half-time with Wark moved into central defence - Rush, Dalglish and Johnston all should have added to Liverpool's tally.

Despite the Reds' attacking prowess however, post-match plaudits once again came for Liverpool's young Irish left-back Jim Beglin. "Beginning to show what he can do going forward as well as in defence," the 22-year old had an outstanding game and played a part in almost all of Liverpool's best attacking moves, linking well with the midfield, particularly McMahon and McDonald.

With so many chances created in a game he did not participate in however, all the talk after the game centred on Walsh. With Aston Villa reported to be interested in signing him – as they had been during the convoluted sale of Steve McMahon - could he have chosen a worse time to vent his frustration and seek a move away from Anfield? Only time would tell but Dalglish, the ultimate pragmatist in the face of a setback, knew the importance of a squad filled with quality players. Footballers who could step in with no negative impact on team performance to replace those suffering illness, injury or a drop in form, were a valuable commodity and it would require an exceptional bid for Liverpool to countenance Walsh's departure.

Liverpool v Southampton
Saturday 12 October 1985

"The 'Manager of the Month' awards are a complete and utter farce. Despite Liverpool winning six and drawing one of their seven games in September, Kenny Dalglish, in his first season as manager, did not receive the award. Manchester United were well beaten at home by Everton in the Super Cup, yet Ron Atkinson won the honour. One wonders what Liverpool managers have to do to end up as 'manager of the Month.'"

M. Dunne, Halewood. Letter to Football Echo, 12 October 1985.

Under Chris Nicholl, Southampton had finished a commendable fifth in the First Division the previous season. Had it not been for the European ban imposed on English clubs after Heysel, they would have been enjoying the prestige of European football with a coveted place in the UEFA Cup. However, after a tough start to the new domestic season - which had seen them defeated by Arsenal, United, Forest and Chelsea - the South Coast side were languishing in 16th place when they travelled to Anfield for the second time in quick succession. A month earlier they had lost 2-1 to the Reds in the Super Cup Group stage and, as then, the Saints were not expected to pose Kenny Dalglish's side too many problems.

For the second home match running, Liverpool welcomed back a much-loved former player in the shape of veteran midfielder Jimmy Case, captaining the side he had joined from Brighton for £30,000 in March. Case had missed the earlier Super Cup fixture through suspension. Alongside Kevin Bond in central defence was the promising 22-year old England centre-half Mark Wright – a player who would attract Liverpool's attentions a few years later.

Despite the appearance of Case however, there was little love lost between the two sides. No less an authority than Bill Shankly had once called Southampton, "an alehouse team," and the Saints' latest incarnation lived up to the billing. The game was punctuated with a plethora of, at first, niggling fouls, and then, with the intervention of former Manchester United 'hard man' Joe Jordan – "now a veteran but full of dirty tricks" - a series of challenges that saw Crewe referee John Lovett struggle to maintain order. Indeed, it was ironic that Wright and Case were booked for strong but not overly dangerous challenges, whilst Jordan was lucky to stay on the pitch, let alone not receive a caution, after an extremely late challenge on man-of-the-match Jan Molby on the half-hour mark.

"It was unfortunate that what was essentially a good-tempered game should flare up around the person of Joe Jordan," wrote Ian Hargraves. Yet, as scathing as he was about Jordan, Hargraves was equally full of praise for Molby – "a big man, 6ft 2in, and weighing 13½ stone, but with the touch of a magician." Later, the same protagonists squared up to one another, "and traded insults," after another dangerous challenge by the Scotsman, but the great Dane was to have the last laugh when Jordan was forced to retire with knee and ankle injuries - to a crescendo of boos, jeers and insults from the home crowd, on 65 minutes – just after Steve McMahon had scored the game's decisive goal.

Captain Alan Hansen's knee injury - sustained at Oldham in midweek - was causing so much concern for Liverpool's medical team that he was not only forced to miss this game, but also to see a specialist who would ultimately recommend a change to his training and a strict recovery regime.

Few matches of his embryonic reign highlighted Dalglish's managerial skills better than this; utilising the versatility of the squad he had at his disposal whilst also exposing the apparent futility of Paul Walsh's decision to ask for a transfer due to perceived inaction. Hansen's fellow defenders, Steve Nicol and Gary Gillespie, were still out injured, so any decision the player-manager had to make regarding the future of Phil Neal, who was still required as cover for those on the treatment table was, for the time being at least, put on hold.

Despite his seemingly imminent departure to Grimsby Town - who had emerged as favourites to take the four-time European cup winner to Blundell Park - Neal made an incredible 639th appearance for Liverpool here as a vastly experienced deputy for the missing Nicol. Neal had actually travelled to Stoke on the preceding Thursday evening before the Southampton game to meet the Mariners' representatives. Here, he learned that the Second Division side were keen to take him to the East coast as player-manager, but even though a swift move away from Anfield appeared inevitable, the former Reds' captain stated that the meeting was, "just a preliminary talk. I am not going into anything so important without thinking it over carefully."

With just one substitute allowed, Liverpool's injury crisis would perhaps have caused problems for some managers, but this is without factoring in Dalglish's ability to shuffle his pack with apparent and consummate ease. Neal continued to deputise for Nicol at right-back – a straight swap. Having already played - to much acclaim - as a sweeper behind a back three, Molby now replaced Hansen at centre-half. The fit-again John Wark filled the spot vacated by Molby in midfield. Dalglish preferred himself to Walsh up front with Rush, and the versatile Kevin MacDonald was named as substitute. Easy.

Although he agreed to Walsh's request to have his name circulated to other clubs, Dalglish knew that the striker's professionalism - and determination to prove him wrong - would provide exactly the type of cover required for his forward line should injuries take their toll. Simply put, the club's best interests dictated that Walsh stay, which it appeared he would be doing for the foreseeable future as the player-manager was also acutely aware that few clubs could pay what Liverpool required for the striker – nor match his wages.

At the start of the season Arsenal manager Don Howe had dismissed Liverpool's purchase of Walsh as a classic case of a mistaken signing, so the North Londoners appeared to have never been in the 'race' to sign him. Not that such a race seemed likely to materialise however, as reported bidders Aston Villa, with new signing Simon Stainrod up front plus Andy Gray, Gary Shaw and Mark Walters, seemed adequately covered for strikers.

At a minimum cost of the £700,000 Liverpool had paid just 18 months previously, Walsh was too expensive for most clubs in the First Division. Dalglish was all too aware of the barriers that stood in the way of Walsh being transferred – a situation that suited the canny manager down to the ground. Of the clubs who could afford him, Manchester United and Spurs seemed to each have enough forwards of note, whilst Everton had only brought Gary

Lineker to Goodison Park at the start of the season.

At a time when 'player-power' was yet to dominate the game in the manner in which it does today, Liverpool simply placed Walsh on the transfer list and waited for, "reasonable' bids." In the meantime - like Phil Neal - he was still available for selection should Dalglish see fit which, for this game at least, he didn't think Walsh was.

Apart from two chances for Southampton and the, "running feuds," that simmered throughout the first half and threatened to boil over in the early stages of the second, Liverpool were on top for almost all the game. Indeed, the Reds', "completely dominated the first quarter of an hour without being able to get the ball into the net." Beglin, Dalglish, and Wark were playing extremely well. Everything they attempted appeared to come off, but it was the, "quite outstanding," Molby, "delivering some superb passes from the back," who caught the eye and, "it was through him that most of Liverpool's best moves flowed."

Wark nearly scored after just three minutes when sent clear by a stunning long-ball from the Dane - only for his shot to evade Shilton and the post. Another Molby-inspired move saw Dalglish stopped just as he was about to shoot from the edge of the box. Lawrenson then got in on Molby's act, his long ball, "taken brilliantly by Rush and turned inside for McMahon," whose return ball fell invitingly for the Welsh striker.

With the 31,070 crowd expectant however, Shilton touched the curling shot wide for a stunning save that even the home fans applauded. Beglin then linked well with McMahon who, with two deft touches and a precise pass, found Johnston on the edge of the box. The Australian, "held off Dennis well, cut into the box and then pulled a fierce shot just wide of the post." Liverpool continued to press. Shilton saved well from Dalglish then palmed a Rush header over for another corner.

Just before the half-time whistle Dalglish appeared to have set up Rush for another goal-bound shot but his pass was cut out with the merest of touches by Kevin Bond. Then, "a marvellous move involving Molby and Dalglish should have presented Wark with a goal right on half-time but Wark's shot went well wide." Such had been Liverpool's dominance that few inside the ground could believe the game was goalless as the sides left the field for the ten-minute break.

Despite the one-sided nature of the game, the home side's, "lack of punch near goal," almost cost them within just 100 seconds of the restart. Case received the ball in midfield and, waiting for an opening to present itself, showed all his old nouse to hold the ball up well before sending David Puckett clean through with only Grobbelaar to beat. As the crowd held its breath, the fair-haired striker seemed surprised at how long he had to pick his spot beyond the advancing keeper and, to Liverpool's great relief, he sent a fumbled shot just wide of the post.

It was a timely reminder for the Reds not to waste any further chances. With the crowd eerily quiet in almost contemplative shock at Puckett's recent very near-miss, Dalglish and McMahon's vocal exhortations to their team mates to pick up the pace were clearly heard all around the ground, causing the Kop to sing their encouragement in return. Any such impetus the crowd needed to roar their side on was quickly forgotten as, within five minutes, the game burst into life.

Bond was booked for a dangerous tackle on Wark, while Jordan brought Molby crashing to the ground, not once but twice, in quick succession - the first resulting in the Dane lying prostrate for almost a minute, the second seeing both, "come together in the middle of the pitch and start jostling each other like petulant schoolchildren." Such a collision would see at least one red card in today's game but instead the referee merely blew for the foul and gave each player another stern lecture. The official was the next to hit the deck after finding himself amid a ruck of players and, "suddenly the game had come stirringly to life."

Such was the roar of an indignant Kop that the next time the ball found itself in the Southampton area, courtesy of a Dennis back header, the unsettled Shilton failed to control it and conceded a corner. It was to prove a costly mistake. The Southampton defence failed to clear Johnston's cross and the ball eventually found Lawrenson in the area, who tapped it square to McMahon. From 12-yards out the relative newcomer made no mistake to register his first league goal at Anfield.

The goal was just what Liverpool needed, but instead of calming things down, the next incident of note saw Molby and Jordan come together again in the centre of the pitch. To the delight of the Kop however, this time it was the Scotsman who failed to recover from the challenge and he was forced to leave the field with a chorus of disapproval and the now familiar, "Rambo! Rambo!" salute to Molby - his nemesis - ringing in his ears.

There was still time for some of the failings of both sides to manifest themselves again before the end of the game. Several harsh Southampton challenges resulted in a number of bookings and free-kicks in dangerous positions for the Reds, only for clear opportunities to be wasted once more. Steve Baker and Wright were booked, and Rush's first time shot from a fierce low Johnston cross was saved by Shilton at the second attempt.

A hard-fought three points moved Liverpool four clear of Everton who suffered their fourth defeat of the season at Chelsea. The champions now trailed United by a staggering 14 points. Chelsea stood in third, level on 24 points with second-placed Liverpool, whilst Arsenal were fourth, Sheffield Wednesday fifth. The Blues were down in sixth. Next up for the Reds? A vital trip to the cauldron of Old Trafford to take on league leaders Manchester United. If not quite a must-win fixture, it was a game Liverpool couldn't afford to lose if they harboured serious hopes of a 16th title.

Manchester United v Liverpool
Saturday 19 October 1985

"Wasn't Sunday October 6 a superb day in the history of Liverpool? A day when the 'silent majority' were seen and heard. May I congratulate the organisers of the Pier Head rally and the people of Liverpool for showing the motley crew of militants what you think of them. After all that rain they really did look like rats crawling back to the sewers."

C L Edwards, Bebington. Letter to Liverpool Echo, 17 October 1985.

"On the basis of the congestion in the Mersey Tunnels and cars on the Formby-bypass, there are no prizes for guessing where the majority of people came from…if there had been a car sale at the Pier head car park this afternoon we could have found the £30 million we need."

Derek Hatton, Liverpool Echo, 7 October 1985.

At the start of the 1985/86 season Liverpool had won 15 league titles in their history. Manchester United had won seven. Since the Mancunians' last title triumph in 1967, Liverpool had finished top of the pile on eight occasions. Not just in the decade since United were relegated for a season in 1974, but over the course of English football history as a whole, Manchester United's domestic record paled in comparison with Liverpool's.

United had beaten Liverpool and Everton in the semi-final and final of the previous season's FA Cup, but had been unable to replicate this form in the league and they had finished beneath the Merseyside clubs in fourth position.

Despite recent and distant history stating otherwise, at the start of the 1985/86 season Ron Atkinson's side were inexplicably tipped by a small number of pundits to finally end their 18-year wait for the First Division championship. So-called experts' predictions were as arbitrary and disingenuous as they had always been. United were the favoured team of a generation of working journalists who had grown up with the Busby Babes and the subsequent European Cup winning team of Bobby Charlton, Denis Law and George Best. They remained the darlings of the media and, despite not winning a title for almost two decades – nor even mounting a credible challenge - were often still referred to as the, "biggest team in the country."

More reasoned and knowledgeable commentators and football journalists however, had tipped Everton to retain the title they had won so convincingly the previous season. Few were convinced that the Reds, after the horror of Heysel, a change of manager – an inexperienced one at that - and a seemingly ageing and, at times, increasingly injury-prone squad, could mount a serious challenge to their near neighbours.

More in hope than expectation a handful of London-based journalists had picked Tottenham Hotspur to perhaps break Merseyside's monopoly of the league title; six of the last seven champions - on five occasions it was Liverpool - had come from the region. Spurs' commendable third place finish the previous season, a young, talented squad, and regular and recent trophy-winning exploits (FA Cups in 1981, '82 and the UEFA Cup in 1984) had thrust the North Londoners into the so-called 'Big Five', along with United, Don Howe's steady but uninspiring Arsenal side, Liverpool and Everton. All of these sides could realistically be viewed as potential champions and, when TV personalities and the football press corps made their predictions for the coming campaign in August, arguments had been made for each.

After ten wins from their first ten games however, journalist after journalist, commentator after commentator and so called football expert after football expert, lined up to state that Manchester United, as they had 'predicted' prior to the season's start, would win the League with ease. Such a comical and widespread *volte face* on the part of the majority of 'experts' in jumping on United's bandwagon was no surprise to those on Merseyside. Accustomed to broken promises from national and local politicians, and often let down by hair-brained government schemes and initiatives, Scousers were largely sceptical creatures when it came to the thoughts and ideas of outsiders, be they in the world of football or politics.

Few other sectors of the population were as enamoured with the simple, yet seemingly ignored logic of believing the evidence of their own eyes and ears, of ignoring propaganda and formulating their own opinions. True, United had won their first ten games – an exceptional achievement that was not to be ignored – but few on Merseyside, as the constant stream of letters to the Football Echo highlighted, were as convinced of United's apparent invincibility as seen by supposedly more 'knowledgeable' commentators.

Red and Blue alike were quick to point out that United had only met one side of note in the first quarter of the season - Everton in the Super Cup – and that in this game, a 4-2 away victory for the Toffees, albeit in a meaningless competition, they had been well and truly put to the sword by quality opposition. Contributors to the Football Echo letters' pages showed that even in the city's darkest economic hours, they still had the foresight and wit to put most national pressmen to shame. "To win the Championship takes consistency", wrote Joe Burke from the Dingle, "something…United have proved they lack. After all, they have finished fourth in a two-horse race for the last two seasons. This year they might make it a hat-trick!"

As well as their flexible predictions which had United crowned as champions as early as October, most commentators seemed to lack a serious understanding and appreciation of recent football history. Almost all were also badly out of touch with the realities of terrace culture, attitude and expectations. So much so that it came as a surprise to many to learn that most Liverpool fans, rather than being daunted by their visit to Manchester, couldn't in fact wait for their trip to Old Trafford. Indeed, many fully expected a victory over the 'serial upstarts', to both silence the media hype and rub the noses of their Mancunian counterparts in the dirt.

Unlike the sanitised, tourist attraction it is today, Old Trafford in the 1980s was a fearsome place for a Liverpool fan. If there was to be a confrontation between supporters however, many of the travelling Liverpool support, mainly young men, would relish it. A racing heartbeat on the Old Trafford concourse, the adrenalin rush of supporting the Reds from the Scoreboard End, surrounded by the baying United mobs on the United Road terrace to the right, and the hostility of the K stand behind? It was all part of the fun.

If Liverpool fans were looking forward to the game for a variety of reasons however, the same could not be said of other football fans around the country. Much to the bewilderment of the average supporter, the dispute between the Football League and the TV companies had still not been resolved and, laughably, the most eagerly anticipated game outside of the Merseyside Derby was unable to be shown either live or as highlights.

"At a time when the league is in such trouble with gates down by more than 10 per cent," wrote Ian Hargraves, "it is an absolute nonsense for its showpiece games to be conducted in such a way. The match is not even on television because of the league's inability to do a deal with the [TV] companies, so a vast amount of both money and goodwill is being frittered away."

Hooliganism, and perhaps more importantly, the potential for and fear of crowd trouble, at any meeting between these two bitter North West rivals had been an issue for well over a decade whilst the tragedy in Brussels and the subsequent ban on all English clubs had denied United their place in the European Cup Winners' Cup; adding to the tension between the respective sets of fans. Hargraves noted that, "recent meetings of the clubs have generated an explosive atmosphere, and there is no doubt many United fans were infuriated by the knowledge that their team had been banned from Europe because of events at Heysel."

Earlier concerns that the highlight of the season so far – pitting first against second – would not be on TV was only of course, partly true. Over 20 countries around the world were taking the game live, including most of Europe. It was clear that despite the European ban and the TV dispute, the English game was still a massive draw for football fans in Italy, Germany, and Spain and beyond. Such interest of course only fuelled the trepidation. Should any serious trouble occur then UEFA's ban would appear to have been a sound and considered response to years of the 'English disease'. Yet with Liverpool fans slowly rebuilding their pre-Heysel reputation for humour and fair play and the fact that, in seven home games watched by over 350,000 people, United had only ejected eight persons from Old Trafford – and the Police arrested just one – it was also, "the perfect chance to show Europe the highly acceptable face of British soccer."

A number of players from both sides were taking part in key World Cup qualifying matches just days before the game was due to take place. Breaks in the league fixture calendar for international football were unheard of so, with many players absent from their clubs for much of the week before the game, it was difficult to predict the sides that would line-up, let alone the outcome of the game itself. Liverpool fans were relieved to hear that Ian Rush would miss Wales' midweek home game against Hungary through suspension, so he was definitely available for selection and would be fresher than others on duty with their countries that week. Strangely however, in 10 games against United, including seven in the league, the prolific Welshman had yet to score. Remarkably, it was a barren record he would not set straight until the spring of 1992.

The Republic of Ireland were also involved in an important World Cup qualifier in Moscow against the USSR – at the time one of the most arduous journeys in European travel. With Mark Lawrenson, Jim Beglin and Ronnie Whelan all involved, and not expected to return to Anfield until Friday afternoon at the earliest, it was clear the fitness levels of key players may be a problem. It was little consolation for Dalglish that he and Kevin MacDonald were just a short hop away in Glasgow at Scotland's friendly with East Germany. No Liverpool players were on England duty as they thrashed Turkey 5-0 in Istanbul.

"It is a farcical situation," noted Hargraves, "made no better by the fact that United are almost equally handicapped." United also boasted a team full of internationals with the likes of Frank Stapleton and Paul McGrath joining the Liverpool trio away with Eire; Jesper Olsen in Norway with Denmark; Mark Hughes with Wales; and Norman Whiteside playing for Northern Ireland – who could also qualify for Mexico '86 - in Romania.

Despite the number of players on international duty however, Liverpool were able to field one of their strongest sides of the season, the only notable absentee being Dalglish himself. The player-manager had injured a tendon in training during the week and so removed himself from selection. John Wark took Dalglish's place ahead of Walsh - who continued to receive sympathy from his many admirers in the local letters pages despite remaining on the transfer-list. It would be, "a travesty of justice…if the great little player in the Peter Thompson mould," was allowed to leave, wrote one 'Disgruntled Red', whilst H. Kelly noted that, "despite infrequent appearances he has played some great games…and has scored some excellent goals."

After recovering from his recent knee problems, Alan Hansen returned to his usual place at centre-half, whilst Jan Molby, who despite the knocks he received against Southampton had played the second half of Denmark's 5-1 win in Norway in midweek, slotted comfortably into the defensive heart of Dalglish's five-man midfield, just behind McMahon and Wark. With Rush alone up front it appeared that Dalglish was attempting to bolster midfield and retain a somewhat defensive formation. After all Liverpool were visiting their biggest rivals – a side who had won their first ten games, were unbeaten in the league, and had yet to concede a goal at home. Such a view of Liverpool's formation was premature however, as, coupled with some attractive attacking play by Johnston, Nicol and Beglin, and poor team selection by manager-of-the-month Atkinson, Liverpool were unlucky not to end the half at least a goal up.

United's Liverpool-born manager had opted to move Paul McGrath from central defence to midfield, leaving out experienced winger Peter Barnes - who was something of a maverick - in the process. Accident prone Bryan Robson - or 'Captain Marvel' as he was known to a fawning media - missed the game - through injury - as did Gordon Strachan. With Jesper Olsen and Mark Hughes the only other true attacking players in the starting line-up, supporting the sometimes ponderous Stapleton up front, United's side appeared to lack balance. This proved to be the case for almost three quarters of the game.

Amid the usual, white-hot, and rabid atmosphere of a Liverpool – United game, "the match began at a tremendous pace with players going in so fast that combined moves were virtually impossible." Norman Whiteside sent a free-kick over the bar in the game's first chance in the fifth minute, before Beglin screwed a shot wide from distance at the other end. Whiteside and McMahon then came together in one of those tremendous, almost slow-motion 50/50 tackles that have long since disappeared from the English game. Both squared up to each other afterwards to send the crowd into a frenzy, before receiving nothing but a stern lecture from referee Mr A. Saunders of Newcastle-upon-Tyne. McMahon then fired over from 20 yards, before Johnston, "came within inches of converting a brilliant cross ball by Whelan."

Dalglish's formation appeared to be paying dividends. Acting as an extra defensive midfielder Molby's presence ensured Liverpool had plenty of possession, but they failed to convert this into goals. Rush almost broke his United goal drought just before the half hour mark, missing a chance from a curling Beglin cross - if the Welshman had a weakness it was in the air, and he directed his header straight at Gary Bailey. Hansen then showed his short spell out of the side had not diminished his timing and reading of the game when he coolly prevented Whiteside from breaking clear with a perfectly clean tackle, before appearing with the ball to launch another of Liverpool's trademark attacks from the back.

Five minutes later United had their best chance of the game so far when Olsen and Stapleton combined well to create a chance for Whiteside. Like Rush before him at the other end however, the Northern Irishman's header was caught easily by the goalkeeper. "As United fans were applauding [this attack], Liverpool broke away," and, evading Duxbury's clumsy tackle, Johnston, "broke through only to see his close-range shot rebound to safety off Bailey's body."

In spite of his occasional over-enthusiasm, the lively Australian continued to cause problems for United with his energetic running. Frustratingly for his manager and his teammates, many of his runs resulted in offside, but the feeling of most Liverpool fans inside Old Trafford was that should Liverpool score, it would come from a move involving Johnston. Right on half-time however, they were almost cheering a goal from an unlikely source as, unmarked and with time in the area, Beglin could only volley wide from a McMahon cross.

The player-managers affirmation of Liverpool's positive approach during the half-time team talk bore instant fruit at the start of the second half with Johnston, implored by Dalglish to get forward at every opportunity, scoring the opening goal within just 19 seconds of the restart. United kicked-off and, after a number of short passes, sent the ball long down Liverpool's right wing. It was an aimless pass however, and Beglin won possession easily. The Irishman, "immediately set Rush free with a perfect pass…the Welsh striker raced through to the edge of the penalty area and then delivered a perfect cross to the far post where Johnston headed the ball into the net." The near 5,000 visiting fans on the Scoreboard End terrace were delirious. The celebrations alone were worth the price of the £2.60 it had cost for a terrace ticket behind the goal.

Visibly shaken by the first goal the home fans had seen them concede at Old Trafford all season, United almost lost the game in the next five minutes. First Rush had a goal-bound shot charged down after cleverly finding space in the box, then it was Wark's turn, "to find a hole in the United defence," in almost identical circumstances, but he too was thwarted by desperate defending.

In stark contrast to a comparatively cautious first half, chances began to come thick and fast. A couple of United corners resulted in lunging Liverpool clearances by first Whelan, then Grobbelaar, but it was still the Scoreboard End that Liverpool were attacking that saw most of the action. Wark pulled a shot wide when he perhaps could, and should, have done better. Then Johnston almost returned the goalscoring favour for Rush but his cross for the latter's head was caught at the last moment by a full-stretch Bailey.

So dominant were the visitors that even Beglin, "one of the stars of the game," could have scored three within the space of 10 minutes, twice firing wide from good angles and seeing another 25-yard effort well held by the keeper.

Liverpool were forced to rue these missed chances in the 63rd minute when United, through the repositioned McGrath, pulled level. For once full-back Arthur Albiston got the better of Nicol down the Liverpool right and sent in a low, but not especially dangerous cross into the area. Lawrenson could only half-clear the awkwardly bouncing ball and it deflected into the path of the onrushing Irishman McGrath, "who promptly smashed it into the back of the net from less than five yards," via an upright. It was a cruel blow for the Reds who had dominated play and possession for long periods. On 70 minutes both teams made substitutions, MacDonald coming on in the place of Wark, whilst United introduced the inventive Peter Barnes – more famous for his early career exploits at West Brom and Manchester City.

Just before the changes in personnel there was a curious incident that reflected the accepted physical nature of the game during the mid-1980s. With the ball a few yards away, Beglin and Mark Hughes clashed outside the Liverpool penalty area. Instead of awarding a free-kick, or booking both players, the referee stopped the game to lecture them both. After the firm talking to, instead of the ref awarding a nominal bounce of the ball to restart, with one team immediately ceding possession to the other against a backdrop of pavlovian applause from a cardboard cut-out crowd, the game recommenced with a fiercely contested drop-ball fought over by players resembling two bull terriers fighting over a stick. McMahon won the kick for the Reds and, to approving clenched fists and throaty roars from the away section, cleared the danger. It was an incident that the game simply wouldn't tolerate today.

There was still time for more goalmouth action. First Grobbelaar, diving backwards, saved spectacularly from Whiteside's effort from a United corner, only to see Hansen's headed attempt at a clearance hit the bar before the ball bounced to safety. Then, with five minutes remaining, Liverpool's man-of-the-match Johnston, "quick, alert and enterprising," saw a fiercely struck cross-shot whistle just over the bar. It was the last effort of note in what had been a pulsating, thoroughly absorbing game.

Although the Old Trafford deadlock maintained the 10-point gap between the sides, most of the 54,492 in attendance – the biggest crowd of the season to date - knew that there was still a long way to go before the destination of the 1985/86 league title would be decided. Even 'Big Ron' himself conceded he was, "delighted," at salvaging a draw, commenting that, "Liverpool have never ever played better against us in my time here."

With the return fixture at Anfield not until February, both clubs hoped to move on and prepare for their next fixtures in the Canon League. However, another clash between the sides – in a different competition - lay just around the corner. It would prove to be a night when one of Anfield's most famous goals helped Liverpool gain a psychological edge for the long battle ahead.

Southampton v Liverpool
Screen Sport Super Cup group stage
Tuesday 22 October 1985

"I reckon Neil Kinnock very inconsiderate attempting to deprive us Liverpudlians of our left-wingers. After all, we have not had the privilege of being entertained by men in that position since the days of Eglington, Liddell, Thompson and Morrissey."

G. Ormesher, Bowland Drive, letter to Liverpool Echo 12 October.

It took two goals – scored within 90 seconds of each other - in the last ten minutes of the game, to enliven the Screen Sport Super Cup Group Stage tie between Southampton and Liverpool that, up until then, had, "seemed to be dying of apathy."

Results so far in the, "hurriedly arranged," tournament meant the Reds only needed two points from three games to qualify for the knock-out stages – where it was hoped they would meet either Everton or Manchester United and at last generate some genuine interest and decent attendances into a, "curious competition," that severely lacked both. In the first leg of this tie only 16,000 had turned up at Anfield to watch a routine home victory for the Reds but, if this was bad enough for the sponsors, the gate at The Dell was barely above 10,000.

Although the Saints made four changes from the side that had been routed 7-0 by Luton at the weekend, this failed to bring significant improvement and though they were, "hard-working," the South Coast outfit were, "generally uninspired." Similarly, Liverpool made a number of changes to the side that had played so well at Old Trafford just three days before; Walsh replacing Rush, Phil Neal – a move to Grimsby still pending - appearing at right-back, and Steve Nicol playing in midfield in the place of Wark, who was an unused substitute.

Despite the introduction of fresh players – and a number of half chances for Walsh and Johnston early on - Liverpool failed to exhibit any degree of urgency for much of the game, appearing, "content to play out time." There was however, at least some incident to entertain the sparse crowd. Indeed, after slips of control and discipline, by Hansen and Grobbelaar respectively, in the early stages of the game, the Reds were lucky they saw out the first half without conceding a couple of sloppy goals.

In the 15th minute, Armstrong hit the foot of the post from 20-yards, then Phil Neal twice saved the day after the, "erratic Grobbelaar," dropped the ball, before coming to the rescue once more when new captain Hansen slipped on the sodden turf letting in Danny Wallace. Goalless at half-time, "Liverpool owed a considerable debt to their former skipper."

Midway through the second-half, Liverpool's below par performance appeared set to continue when Molby took a knock on the leg and was replaced by McDonald. Although the Scot "brought an infusion of energy into Liverpool's play," their use of the ball did not improve until the 81st minute, by which time they had conceded a controversial penalty. After the game Dalglish called the decision, "one of the worst penalties I've ever seen," Most reporters on the night agreed with the incredulous player-manager and saw nothing but an error on the part of referee Mr R. Lewis.

Banking on his teammate's speed of foot and thought, former Liverpool hero Jimmy Case played a fine ball into space in front of the lightening quick Wallace and, with just the keeper to beat once he controlled the ball, he found himself one-on-one against Grobbelaar. Few stoppers were as quick of their line as the Zimbabwean however, and he made up for his earlier errors by racing from his goal-line to get to the ball first and push it to safety - before Wallace collided with him, and fell over. There were a few half-hearted appeals for a penalty from the Southampton players, but even they were surprised when the decision was given – much to the disgust of Dalglish. "From where I was Bruce appeared to play the ball and Wallace [simply] fell over him." Armstrong converted the penalty but, "before the buzz of surprise had died," Liverpool were on the attack and equalised from their best move of the game.

Nicol - whose consistency in the game saw him named Liverpool's man-of-the-match– broke free on the right wing and his, "perfect by-line centre," was volleyed home by Walsh. It was the very least the transfer-listed forward deserved. "He was working away all the time," Dalglish said "and deserved his goal. It will have done him no harm at all whether he stays with us or goes somewhere else." Many fans hoped that, due to the club's injury problems – Rush and Dalglish had both suffered knocks in recent games – they hadn't seen the last goal by the England striker in a Liverpool shirt.

Chapter Three
Are We Believing?

Liverpool v Luton Town
Saturday 26 October 1985

"Top Liverpool pop star Ian McCulloch has one thing to say to the people of the city; 'You're Scum.' ...The city is not such a nice place either, according to the outspoken lead singer with Echo and the Bunnymen "It's a disgusting place and I hate it," said the spikey-haired 25-year old in an interview with Smash Hits magazine...But his manager Mick Houghton today tried to play down McCulloch's bitter swipe...."The day Ian did the interview he was very upset...he had been burgled...the fourth time this has happened to Ian at the same house."

Front-page headline, Liverpool Echo, 28 October 1985

If those Liverpool fans who had criticised the club's decision to place Paul Walsh on the transfer list – albeit at the striker's request – felt their protests and disgruntled letters to the local press had been worth it following the Londoner's goal scoring return in the midweek game at Southampton, then many will have felt their opinions were had been vindicated following his performance in the Reds' victory over his former club Luton Town at Anfield just four days later.

Two goals, instrumental in creating a third, and a deserved man-of-the-match performance by a striker only selected due to Ian Rush's continued absence, earned the player a rapturous reception from the Kop at the end of the game. This mirrored the response Walsh had received before kick-off, when his selection – during the pre-match reading of the teams over the Anfield tannoy - was, "greeted with prolonged applause."

Whether Walsh would remain at Liverpool in the medium-term was another matter. With speculation he was due to talk to Hamburg dismissed by Peter Robinson at the end of the game; "Nobody has been in touch with us," said the club's Chief Executive, "so nobody can talk to him," he did his cause no harm with a fantastic all-round performance, one that his manager, - through his own return to the starting 11 - witnessed first hand.

After a dearth of striking options in recent games, Dalglish juggled with his players once more to select arguably one of his side's most attacking formations of the season. The visitors may well have only been Luton Town, 12th in the league and with just four wins from 13 games, but they had put seven past Southampton's Peter Shilton the weekend before and Dalglish, practising his mantra of 'taking one game at a time,' wasn't about to underestimate the Bedfordshire side.

To nullify the aerial threat of striker Mick Harford and centre-half Steve Foster - easily visible with his trademark white headband - Molby continued in his new role as an extra defender, but it was Liverpool's attacking options – even without Rush - that paved the way for victory here. "Walsh was quick [and] alert," noted Ian Hargraves, "and combined well with Molby, Dalglish and Johnston to give Liverpool plenty of firepower in the middle."

Nicol returned at right back in place of Neal – who was rated a 75-25 chance to take over at Grimsby by Dudley Ramsden, the Mariners' Chairman – and it was the Scottish right back, together with Walsh and Johnston, who combined well within just 100 seconds of the kick-off to give Liverpool their first chance of the game. Nicol's cross from the right wing was met by an unmarked Whelan at the far post but, with time to pick his spot, the midfielder's first-time volley flew well over Les Sealey's bar. It was a glorious chance to open the scoring.

Soon after, following good work by McMahon and then Dalglish, the same player managed to hit the target with two more fierce shots but Sealey saved well on each occasion, "before Walsh sent yet another screaming shot over the bar from a cross by Dalglish." The player-manager's bold team selection appeared to be working with all of his attack-minded stars playing well, particularly Walsh, Johnston and Nicol. "Liverpool's football won repeated applause from the Kop," but despite the number of chances created, Luton's defence held firm an, due to the close attention he was receiving from the visitor's back four, it was Dalglish who was as frustrated as anybody.

In the 20th minute Luton managed to press forward to win a corner but they were quickly exposed by a rapier counter attack and the home side almost took the lead. The Luton corner kick was cleared to Dalglish who, free of his markers for once, managed to control the ball expertly before sending Molby clean through the middle of the pitch with a sublime pass. With the visitors back-pedalling rapidly, the Dane unleashed a fantastic shot from 25-yards that beat Sealey comfortably but was denied entry to the goal by the despairing dive of a retreating Luton defender. Almost immediately Beglin was unlucky to see another long-range effort also saved well by the future Manchester United number one. The Kop could sense a goal and, on the half-hour mark, they at last were able to celebrate.

Attacking in numbers once more - this time down the left - Molby played a square ball inside to Walsh just outside the box. The blonde-haired striker's first touch took him just inside the penalty area and teed the ball up nicely for a low shot that flew under Sealey's body into the net. Within five minutes Walsh had his second, "a real collector's gem," and the points looked to be Liverpool's. Molby won a 50-50 ball in the centre circle and his pass found Dalglish, who had been consistently dropping deep to evade his markers. With yet another pass of exceptional quality, the player-manager found Johnston in space on the right wing near the touchline and the Australian's first time low cross was met by Walsh to fire, again first time, into the net. It was another familiar, free flowing, sublime Liverpool move.

Amazingly, the transfer-listed Walsh was on a hat-trick, and he should have had it just 60 seconds later when, from the edge of the area, he sent a shot just wide. "I didn't realise how much time I had," he later said. Both Walsh and Johnston, "buzzing about all over the place," were causing Luton all sorts of problems and it was the latter who almost wrapped the game up just a minute before the interval. Molby sent the Aussie clear with a fine 20-yard pass but an excellent tackle by Daniel deprived him a sixth goal of the season.

There was still time for Grobbelaar - who had been a spectator for most of the first half - to save well from an Emeka Nwajiobi snap shot on the turn. The shot had been half-blocked by Lawrenson, but the Zimbabwean keeper was at fault early in the second half when Luton pulled a goal back against the run of play. Barely 20 seconds had elapsed before a fine cross from Stein caught the Liverpool number one unawares and, unable to hold onto the ball, it was cleared for a corner by Lawrenson. To the bewilderment of the crowd, his teammates and his manager, Grobbelaar then failed to hold onto the flighted flag-kick and the loose ball was hammered into the net from close range by Steve Foster.

After creating chance after chance in the first half, and notwithstanding their two-gaol cushion, the home side now appeared vulnerable. "We allowed Liverpool to dictate the first half," Luton manager David Pleat later told reporters, "but we were much more ambitious in the second half." The visitors' ambition was fuelled by the actions of Grobbelaar who, "went through his full repertoire of eccentricities," for the remainder of the game.

Just after Walsh had almost scored a third for Liverpool – a mad scramble in the area that saw Donaghy and Johnston collide with such force that both required lengthy medical treatment – a Preece free kick from just outside the area evaded everyone before scraping the top of the bar. Five minutes later the Hatters wasted another free kick - awarded for an alleged handball by Lawrenson, a decision that so enraged Grobbelaar he was booked for dissent – from almost the exact same spot. "Suddenly Liverpool were in all sorts of trouble." Indeed, when Molby and Grobbelaar collided attempting to clear another curling Luton corner, it was clear the Reds were in serious danger of throwing the points away. Both players were still attempting to get to their feet when Johnston cleared the ball for another corner kick.

A few minutes later, as the pressure increased on the Liverpool goal, the Australian came to the Reds' rescue once more when, again foregoing his usual attacking play, he cleared a loose ball halfway down the pitch – much to the appreciation and relief of the home crowd. On 65 minutes, "Liverpool's nerves were greatly soothed by a third goal." With two goals to his name so high was Walsh's confidence that he attempted to wriggle his way past three Luton defenders just outside the box. Their attempts to stop him doing so were deemed illegal by West Midlands referee L. M. Robinson however, and Molby drove the resultant free-kick, "into the bottom of the net with deadly precision." Walsh, "is so clever at winning free-kicks and penalties," his former manager Pleat said after the game, "he used to do it for us."

Walsh, "continued to torment the Luton defence," and he almost sent Whelan free soon after. But instead of extending their lead further, the lapses of concentration Liverpool had shown in the early stages of the second-half resurfaced and in the 70th minute they had an extraordinary escape when Harford, "probably the tallest striker in the Division," and Foster both hit the woodwork in quick succession – a header and a shot respectively.

Five minutes later Luton's second-half endeavours were rewarded by another goal, when a speculative, looping shot from 30-yards by Foster deceived everyone to hit the inside of a post before dropping into the back of the net. Soon after, Grobbelaar rushed out of his area to meet a through ball only to mistime his run disastrously. With Nwajiobi in hot pursuit he was forced to dribble the ball in comical fashion back into his own area, only diving onto it inside the box at the last moment. Few could see the funny side when the keeper smiled and waved the striker away, but it was to be Luton's last attack of the game. With a few minutes remaining a Whelan header from 10-yards beat a full-stretch Sealey only to smash against the bar – the fifth time the woodwork had been struck during an action packed afternoon.

It wasn't the near misses that would dominate the radio waves after the game however, nor the conversations heard in the pubs and bars around Anfield that evening. It wasn't Grobbelaar's antics, or the stubborn ten-point gap between Liverpool and Manchester United who, despite going down to ten men at Stamford Bridge had held out for a 2-1 win. It wasn't even the volatile local politics.

All the post-match chatter concerned the remarkably good form of Paul Walsh. "He had had an excellent game," said Hargraves, "thoroughly enjoyed by the crowd with whom he is extremely popular." Surely Dalglish – whether he was reading the letters in support of Walsh from the bulging Football Echo postbag or not – dare not drop the little striker again? To do so, one wag was overheard to say, would make him more unpopular even than outspoken Bunnyman, Ian McCulloch.

Liverpool v Brighton & Hove Albion
League Cup - Milk Cup third round
Wednesday 30 October 1985

"Liverpool's big pantomime this year is No Cuts in Jobs or Services, Devised and directed by Derek Hatton, who also takes the leading role. Performed in the round at the Town Hall by the City Council Theatre of Comedy, it is a vigorous updating of last year's production, No Rents or Rates Increases to Compensate for Tory Cuts. Once again the format is a series of specialty acts, often improvised but sometimes brought off through stunningly clever puppetry or remote control."

Joe Riley, Theatre Critic, Liverpool Echo, 30 October 1985

A full-page apology in the Liverpool Echo from local songwriter and musician Ian McCulloch for his previous week's attack on the people of the city dominated the local news as Liverpool prepared to face Brighton in the League Cup Third Round. In a rash outburst in the wake of a fourth recent break-in at his home, an emotional McCulloch also claimed the city was, "disgusting" The controversial, yet revered 26 year old singer and Main Stand season ticket holder's comments to the teenage 'Smash Hits' magazine had been, "taken out of context", he said, but still resonated with a disappointed fan base in his native city.

Despite the local annoyance created by McCulloch's unfortunate public outpouring there was still greater controversy surrounding the ongoing saga of Paul Walsh's future at Anfield – as testified by the respective numbers of letters to the Liverpool Echo on each subject. While McCulloch and his fellow members of the esteemed group Echo and the Bunnymen had some reputation building to do before their upcoming show at Liverpool's Royal Court Theatre, Walsh - who had made known his desire to forsake a career at Liverpool FC in the pursuit of more regular football - remained incredibly popular among the club's fans.

For manager Dalglish, a League Cup tie against one of Liverpool's supposed 'bogey' sides presented an opportunity to curry favour with the crowd and retain Walsh. Not a difficult decision to make due to the striker's brace against Luton at the weekend. It was a decision made even easier by the continued absence of knee victim Ian Rush, who missed his third game in succession. Most Liverpool fans wanted an indication from the player-manager that Walsh had a future at the club. It was clear to all, especially the club's hierarchy – who were busy trying to persuade him to remove his transfer request - that the striker could still play an important role in the club's battle for honours this season.

As 'bogey' sides go, Brighton's recent record - in cup games at least - against Liverpool was impressive. The previous January the sides were drawn together in the fourth round of the FA Cup at the Goldstone Ground. In a game televised live by ITV the South Coast minnows brought off the shock of the round by defeating Joe Fagan's side 2-0 - the only blemish in Liverpool's treble season.

The previous season, a 2-1 victory at Anfield in the fifth round of the same competition was an even bigger disappointment - ending Bob Paisley's last hopes of ending more than 40 years service with Liverpool as an FA Cup winner. "With the sort of record we've got against Liverpool," manager Chris Catlin told reporters before the game, "what have we got to fear?" Much had changed for the South Coast side however. Financial problems ensured there had been a huge turnaround in players since those famous victories, and only three players remained at the club who had played against Liverpool just 19 months previously.

It was no surprise that the Reds were strong favourites to win, but the visitors – even though they had shipped nine goals in their two previous games - were not to be taken lightly. They could boast the likes of Justin Fashanu – a £115,000 buy from Notts County in the summer and once deemed worthy of a £1 million fee by none other than Brian Clough. Fashanu had scored one of the greatest ever volleyed goals against Liverpool in his younger days at Norwich. They also boasted Wigan-born Danny Wilson – with 10 goals the highest scoring midfield player in the country - and a young Welsh forward who, owing to a three-match suspension for Mark Hughes, was expected to earn his first cap in the next Wales squad. His name? Dean Saunders - who would later emulate his father Roy in pulling on the red shirt of Liverpool. Prone to rotating at least one or two members of his team between games, Dalglish surprised many by naming an unchanged 12-man squad for the tie.

Although they had to wait until 1981 before registering their first win in the competition, the League Cup then became Liverpool's personal property until a defeat at Spurs ended a record-breaking run in October 1984. Now they were looking to win the competition for the fifth time in six seasons. Liverpool's League/Milk Cup success from 1981 to 1984 inclusive, remains an English record for consecutive wins in one competition.

For much of the first-half it looked as if the home side would emerge comfortable victors. They created no less than nine clear chances inside the first 20 minutes, but only one of these was converted when, in the 11th minute, who else but man of the moment Walsh popped up unmarked in the area to net a clean header after good work by Nicol. The Scottish full-back, "with a lovely chipped pass," had set Johnston up for an equally clever cross. Whelan and Molby also went close during this period but, after Graham Pearce sent a shot a couple of feet wide of Grobbelaar's goal just before the half-hour mark, Liverpool's, "skilled approach work," fell away and Brighton established a stronger hold in the match.

The first quarter of an hour after the break mirrored the last 15 minutes of the first half and, "as Liverpool became enmeshed in their own over elaborate movements," the standard of play by both sides dropped considerably. Brighton came increasingly into the game after this however, and went close on a number of occasions. First Lawrenson slid in well to deny Fashanu with a great tackle, then Nicol had to clear from inside his own six-yard area after Saunders, who was by far Brighton's most potent attacking threat, had rounded Grobbelaar.

It wasn't until the 72nd minute that Liverpool could breathe more easily and be sure the Brighton hoodoo wouldn't be striking for a third time. Dalglish tackled the muscular Eric Young bravely just outside the box, and the ball spilled into the path of Walsh who, "pounced like lightning." Two touches later he was wheeling away having scored Liverpool's second and, just 60 seconds later the popular striker had his hat-trick, "ramming home a fierce volley from Dalglish's header," to score his seventh goal in just four games. Those on the sparsely populated Kop - among a crowd of just over 15,000 - were beside themselves with glee and they immediately struck up the chant of, "Walshy for

England." Ten minutes from the end, with Liverpool merely going through the motions and the crowd happily cheering each pass to a team mate, Dalglish scored a fourth – converting a precise pass from Whelan.

After the game the player-manager was full of praise for Brighton, but he reserved most of his acclaim for Walsh. "He's breathing goals now," Dalglish said. "It's great for us. He's still on the [transfer] list but obviously its not affecting him in any way with his attitude or commitment."Most fans pondered the upcoming fourth-round draw with a degree of indifference - at least until the identity of their opponents in the last 32 were known. For now however, the burning issue, with Rush set to return from injury, was the make-up of Dalglish's preferred frontline in the weekend's upcoming league game against Leicester.

Liverpool v Leicester City
Saturday 2 November 1985

"We all know that Liverpool produces the best comedians in the country but we don't expect them to be running the place. Nobody has any pride in Liverpool now. The Russians and the IRA have had their greatest successes in Liverpool and the Post Office should endorse letters with a new post mark; 'Liverpool – City of Louts and Layabouts'."

J R Wright, Greasby. Letter to Liverpool Echo, 31 October 1985

With Paul Walsh's, "return to peak form and fitness," and Ian Rush's comeback after injury, the strike force which would sustain Liverpool into early February looked the obvious choice for this home fixture against Leicester City – providing of course Dalglish named them both in his starting line-up. Bowing not so much to fan pressure, but instead, "doing what was best for Liverpool Football Club," - a saying which was fast becoming something of a Dalglish mantra – the manager dropped himself for the game to accommodate the in-form pair who in all competitions so far had scored 16 goals between them; Rush with nine in 15 games and Walsh with seven in nine.

Potential team selection was only one of the main topics of conversation around the corridors of Anfield this week however, with most at the club, if not Merseyside Police, delighted with the news that the draw for the fourth round of the Milk Cup had pitted Liverpool at home – in the undoubted tie of the round - against Manchester United.
Many fans felt the Reds had been decidedly unlucky to get a solitary point in the recent league encounter at Old Trafford, so the tie was an early chance to exact revenge against Ron Atkinson's side and strike a psychological blow which might assist in clawing back the 10 point gap at the top of the table. Equally important in the minds of Liverpool's more embittered fans was the chance to put one over on the national media, and their continual fawning over the Old Trafford pacesetters.

In another complication to an already incident packed season, it was also announced that the forthcoming Scotland versus Australia or New Zealand World Cup play-off would be played on 20 November – resulting in the Liverpool v United game having to be postponed until the following week. Scotland boss Alex Ferguson had already made it known he would be selecting four Liverpool players for the Hampden Park leg of the tie – Dalglish, Nicol, Hansen and a fit again John Wark. All were therefore in contention for a trip to Mexico '86. All Scotland had to do was defeat their Oceania Group opponents. Russia's recent defeat of Norway in Moscow meant that the Republic of Ireland were now eliminated from the World

Cup so Lawrenson, Beglin and Whelan could console themselves with the prospect of a lengthy summer holiday come the end of the season.

With the United cup-tie moving to 26 November, the Super Cup game against Spurs scheduled for the following night was also postponed. This was good news for Tottenham – who were encountering fixture problems of their own due to the Broadwater Farm Riots. "It's most unfortunate," Chief Executive Peter Robinson told reporters when evaluating the knock-on effects of the postponements, "because it means we shall be sitting around all week without a match while the fixtures start to pile up."

Besides fixture congestion, also of interest for Reds' fans was the news that Phil Neal had turned down his proposed move to Grimsby as, "he did not want to move his family across country." Whatever his plans, Liverpool supporters wished the four-time European Cup winner every success and many hoped he would remain at the club – at least in the short-term - as an able deputy to Steve Nicol.

Despite the Rush and Walsh partnership which was feted as, "Liverpool's best hope of regaining former glories," the game against Leicester – Liverpool's original 'bogey' team dating back to the 1960's – turned out to be much tougher than expected. One place above the relegation zone, the Foxes had won only three times all season - although one of these victories came in a 3-1 defeat of reigning champions Everton on the opening day. They had also preceded their visit to Anfield with a win at White Hart Lane. "Clearly," wrote Ian Hargraves, "they are a side for the big occasion."

It was not Leicester's recent record that worried Liverpool fans however, it was their reputation as being a side that - against the odds - always seemed to beat the Reds when it mattered most. "Veteran fans will recall how Gordon Banks and company frustrated Liverpool in the days of Bill Shankly," whilst, "their sons will be equally aware that it was Leicester, on their way to relegation, who ended Liverpool's remarkable Anfield record of 85 games without defeat in 1981."

More recently, the Foxes had drawn 2-2 at Anfield on their return to the top flight in a Christmas fixture in 1983, whilst last season they had gone one better, winning 2-1 with one of the goals scored by Alan Smith, the future Arsenal striker and modern-day pundit. Former Ipswich stalwart Russell Osman in defence was another player of note, whilst a promising midfielder signed from Motherwell – using the proceeds from the sale of Gary Lineker to Everton - was beginning to make a name for himself South of the border at Filbert Street. No-one could have foreseen that youngster Gary McAllister would be an inspired, free signing for Liverpool some 15 years later - at the ripe old age of 35.

While Smith, Osman and McAllister all played their part in Leicester's rearguard action, it was the last line of City's defence who stole the Anfield show. Showing himself, "worthy of the mantle once worn by Gordon Banks and Peter Shilton," 20-year old goalkeeper Ian Andrews, a former England youth international, pulled off save after save - most of breathtaking quality - to deny the Reds the goals that their, "almost constant wave of attacks," warranted.

Johnston and Nicol - as they had done in most games this season - combined well down the right wing once again to produce Liverpool's first attack of note inside the first five minutes. Their good work deserved more than a header over the bar from Whelan, but already the home side's attacking intentions - and the defensive approach of the visitors - were clear. Following a foul on the lively Walsh - whose partnership with Rush steadily improved as the game wore on - Molby fired a free kick against the wall soon after. The Welshman almost created a goal for himself when he cut inside from the right wing on eight minutes and, "lashed a shot only a foot or so wide."

Following a clever free-kick by Johnston, Rush was then denied inside the area by Osman. Although at this stage of the game, "the Leicester defence was hard pressed," there was no indication of the goalkeeping heroics by Andrews to come. Leicester's number one then saved easily from Walsh when the forward shot weakly after a fine defence splitting pass by Rush. He then held onto a stinging McMahon shot from 20 yards that flew straight into his hands.

"Liverpool were moving the ball around beautifully," and Beglin and Johnston then combined well to set up McMahon for a shot that, after Simon Morgan ceded possession, flew over the bar. "Confined almost exclusively to defence," Leicester were happy to soak up the pressure for most of the game and they flooded the final third of the pitch in their attempts to frustrate Liverpool.

On 25 minutes, Liverpool's at times, "spectacular," approach play almost saw a goal when, "Molby burst out of defence into open space and was picked out beautifully with a 30-yard pass." Rounding Morgan by the penalty spot the big Dane had only the goalkeeper to beat but although, "it looked an almost certain goal," Andrews somehow managed to block the shot and it rebounded upfield. It was a top class save in front of the Kop, and the terrace patrons showed their renowned, fair-minded appreciation.

Unbeknown to the crowd however, the save was a sign of things to come. Less than five minutes later, the Leicester number one denied Hansen twice within the space of sixty seconds, firstly pushing a fine header wide of the post after a superb cross from the right touchline by Johnston. Then, after a sublime pass by Molby, Andrews rushed out to smother the elegant Hansen's right-footed chip, at the end of a rare foray into the area. The Liverpool captain wouldn't have a better chance to score a goal all season, something he might rue at the end of proceedings in May. After 45 minutes of almost continuous Liverpool pressure - and to the eye-rubbing disbelief of nearly 32,000 paying spectators - the half ended goalless.

A sunny late autumn day had seen Liverpool lose the toss at 3pm, forcing them to attack the Anfield Road End as darkness fell during the second half. Although, "Leicester showed a more positive approach," and Mark Bright - another future TV pundit - caught Lawrenson napping to steal the ball from the Irish defender and set-up in a half-chance missed by Smith on 50 minutes, the game continued in much the same vein as the first half – with Andrews, "repeating his acts of brilliance," again the star of the show.

Rush shot over the bar from close range and Beglin, always willing to shoot on sight, curled a 25-yarder straight into the keeper's arms. The more spectacular saves were still to come however, and on 70 minutes, from 30-yards out, Molby struck a shot so full of venom that it reminded older fans of the great Billy Liddell, only to see the keeper push it around the post for a corner. A few minutes later Andrews managed to pull off a save, "that will live long in the memories of those of us lucky to witness it," when he pushed a curling free-kick from the same player - that was about to enter the net barely six inches off the ground - over the bar with his left hand.

Colin Wood of the Daily Mail later described the save to have been of such high quality that, "it ranks with the save Gordon Banks made from Pele in the 1970 World Cup finals." Speaking after the game, even the Danish international, "who could have scored a hat-trick against lesser keepers," expressed his amazement; "I couldn't believe it myself," Molby said, "and what about the one from me just before? That was going about 200mph!" From the other end of the pitch, Grobbelaar was in awe, urging the crowd to applaud his opposite number - and continuing to do so for some time after. "It was unbelievable Roy of the Rovers stuff," wrote Hargraves, "but, life being less kind than fiction, young Andrews was beaten in the end."

With just ten minutes to go, "there was a tremendous roar as Dalglish was seen stripping off on the touchline." As the player-manager warmed up, Liverpool had a penalty appeal turned down and Johnston had a shot cleared off the line. When he finally replaced the Australian, Dalglish added some much needed guile to the proceedings and, with just five minutes to go, Liverpool scored a dramatic late winner. Nicol found space on the right to send in a cross that was met by McMahon. His half-hit shot confused everyone but, fortunately for Liverpool, the ball fell invitingly for the poacher supreme, Ian Rush. The returning striker bundled the ball into the net from just five yards, "with one of the softest shots of the game." After 85 minutes of frustration and all Andrews' brilliance, bedlam broke out on the Kop in recognition of a crucial winning goal.

As the Leicester players trudged off the pitch, every Liverpool player shook Andrews' hand and, quite rightly, he was applauded off by the entire 31,718 crowd. "They love good goalkeepers here," said Grobbelaar after the game, "and he has won the hearts of all the spectators." These were three points more than well earned by the Reds, but with Manchester United winning again - 2-0 at home against Coventry City, Liverpool's next opponents – the gap at the top remained at 10 points. United had won 13 and drawn two of their 15 games so far. By contrast, fans of the reigning champions Everton were despondent when, after being a goal up through Trevor Steven, they conspired to lose 2-1 to a Frank McAvennie-inspired West Ham. The result saw the Hammers leapfrog the Blues into sixth place. The Scottish striker had already developed a reputation for liking for the London nightlife but he clearly wasn't suffering from the bright lights with 14 goals in 15 games. Everton were now a staggering 17 points off the top of the table, as Liverpool carried the Merseyside fight to United.

Coventry City v Liverpool
Saturday 9 November 1985

"As the Rolls Royce parked up, out popped ex-Coventry boss Jimmy Hill. The steward holding the guest list suddenly left his post to shepherd him inside and so my Dad, Frank Conchie and me, sneaked into Highfield Road. On the pitch , it was Kenny's Rolls Royces who showed the whole country why, with the finest players assembled, Liverpool Football Club would go on to win the league. This match was crucial; Man Utd were leading the way but this day we delivered a big calling card. Jimmy Hill, the guest of the Sky Blues, nodded his head in appreciation to Frank as we made our way out."

Stephen Conchie, Liverpool fan, Norris Green.

Even accounting for Paul Walsh's continued frustrations at failing to land a guaranteed place in the Reds' starting line-up – in an open and candid interview with local journalist Ann Cummings the striker thanked fans for their recent support and spoke of his disappointment at not starting more games. Walsh stressed his preference to remain at the club however, at least in the short term – but there was no-one more aggravated at Anfield during this week than Chief Executive Peter Robinson. The cause of Robinson's angst was the emergence of Australia, ahead of New Zealand from the Oceania group qualifying matches, as Scotland's opponents in a looming play-off to contest a place at the World Cup finals in Mexico.

Despite the tie's colossal travel implications for the Anglo-Scots playing their trade in Division One, the Football League announced they would not allow the postponement of any weekend fixtures, either side of the return leg - scheduled for Melbourne on 4 December. Scotland's faced a gruelling 22-hour flight to Australia on Wednesday 27 November - the morning after Liverpool's eagerly awaited Milk Cup tie at home against Manchester United. The squad would not return to the UK until the evening of Friday 6 December.

With international breaks still a number of years away, the League's obstinacy in refusing to consider postponements meant that as many as four Liverpool players could miss the First Division match against Chelsea on Saturday 30 November - as well as the rearranged Super Cup tie against Spurs just three days later. The jet-lagged Liverpool players would technically be available for the visit of Aston Villa on 7 December but, with just 24 hours to recover from their flight before the game, few expected them to be in any fit state to play upon their return.

International games - especially World Cup qualifiers - still took precedence over the interests and commitments of Europe's top club sides, so there was nothing Robinson could do besides request that league fixtures be postponed. In typical fashion however, the Football League - historically renowned for their inflexibility - had refused to bend and accommodate Liverpool's plea. Arguing that Liverpool were in a unique position because, as well as a number of players their manager was also expected to travel, Robinson stated that the club, "were happy to postpone [games] aware that the return (leg)…could be one of the most important matches Scotland have ever played."

However, Robinson was quick to point out that the League's ruling meant the Reds, "are now in a ludicrous situation in which Kenny Dalglish will have to pick three teams from the other side of the world." The former Club Secretary - his role now re-branded as Chief Executive - went on to note the contradictory nature of the League's own rules. "On the one hand they state that we must play our strongest team," he said, "[but] where does that leave us if Scotland take two [sic] of our best players?" The Scottish FA, "understand our position and are sympathetic to it," Robinson continued, "but they point out the potential importance of the game."

With all avenues for discussion exhausted, Robinson, one of the most respected administrators in the game, concluded that, "We will do our part and release the players." He was left to hope that Scotland won the Hampden Park leg of the play-off decisively – perhaps by three or four goals – and pray that temporary manager Alex Ferguson, thinking they had secured a winning lead, might restrict his selection to home-based players for the return leg. There were simply too many 'ifs' and buts however, and Liverpool officials already seemed resigned to losing key players for two crucial league fixtures.

While the Scotland controversy raged on Liverpool looked forward to their next fixture at

Highfield Road. Coventry City had been a permanent fixture in the top flight since promotion in 1967, and were always a tough opponent on home soil. Although Liverpool had claimed three on points on their previous visit back in May, a 4-0 thrashing in December 1983 - a rare blight on Joe Fagan's triumphant treble season - was still fresh in the memory.

Firmly entrenched in the lower half of the table, the Sky Blues lay just six points above the relegation zone. At the start of the season few commentators thought of Coventry as relegation candidates but, with just four wins to date, they had so far failed to put a string of results together that would carry them safely to their expected position in mid-table. Of even greater concern to manager Don Mackay was that six first-team players – including giant centre-half Kevin Kilcline, captain Wayne Turner, Cyrille Regis, Terry Gibson and Micky Adams - were carrying injuries ahead of the visit of a Liverpool side that had lost just once in 12 league games.

With Walsh, despite a late injury scare, again set to partner Rush up front for an improving Liverpool it would be a major surprise if Coventry could halt the Reds' momentum. For the third game in a row Dalglish fielded the same starting 11, the only change being on the bench where, in place of himself, he opted for the experience of Phil Neal. Neal was still talking to potential suitors after turning down the player-manager position at Grimsby Town – a role which had now been filled by former Everton defender Mick Lyons, assisted by ex-Goodison colleague Terry Darracott.

With Walsh and Rush picking up where they had left off in the previous game, Liverpool were disciplined in defence, always clinical, occasionally sublime and rampant in their attacking play. "Liverpool's 3-0 win at Coventry was as slick as Brylcreemed hair," wrote John Wragg in the Daily Express. Coventry simply could not cope with the power, pace or precision of Liverpool's football. In terms of the title race however, it was not the quality of Liverpool's football but events elsewhere that drew a, "late roar from the mini-Kop behind Grobbelaar's goal."

In the sixth minute former Anfield custodian Steve Ogrizovic – owner of two European Cup winners' medals as understudy to Ray Clemence in 1978 and 1981 – failed to collect a looping, deflected shot from McMahon on the edge of the area. Beglin, who had peppered opposition goalkeepers all season with his powerful shooting, capitalised on the former Liverpool reserve's error and smashed, "an unstoppable shot into the back of the net," for a deserved first goal of the season. Johnston, "whose running and total effort constantly stretched the home side," then went close before McMahon, "orchestrating things in midfield," found Nicol on the right. The Scot's short pass to Johnston was whipped in by the South-African born Aussie only for Walsh to just fail to connect when any touch would surely have resulted in a second Liverpool goal.

Even this early in the game, "the gulf in class and ability [between the two sides] was as wide as it could possibly be." Indeed, it wasn't until just before the half hour mark that Grobbelaar was seriously threatened, holding onto a snapshot by the diminutive Gibson – who had scored a hat-trick in the aforementioned 4-0 win for Coventry two years previously.

With ever more chances created by the visitors, a comeback by City seemed increasingly unlikely. Molby, Rush and Johnston all went close in the remaining quarter of an hour but it was Walsh, as lively as ever, who almost added another on 40 minutes. "With a piece of real skill," the striker, "tricked his way into the left of the box before letting fly with a real screamer that soared just wide of the target."

Coventry mustered only two forays into the Liverpool half in the time remaining before the interval. Following one of these rare attacks, McMahon was forced to leave the field to receive medical attention following a clash of heads with Lloyd McGrath. Unable to recover during the half-time break, the battling midfielder was replaced by Neal, a change that saw Johnston switched to central midfield - with full-back Nicol pushed up to the right wing.

Such was the versatility of Dalglish's side, and the paucity of attacks by Coventry, that the enforced change did nothing to swing the balance of play and within two minutes of the restart Liverpool scored a second goal. A low Nicol cross from the right ought to have been smothered by Ogrizovic, but the normally reliable keeper made his second key error of the game; under pressure from Walsh, he failed to hold onto the ball and the in-form striker was on hand to virtually pass the rebound into an empty net.

Even with 40 minutes still left to play the goal was enough to signal the end of the match as a contest. In a game that began to resemble a training exercise for Liverpool, Coventry wilted further, and the rampant Reds seemed to create chances every time they ventured into opposition territory. There was a hint of complacency about Liverpool's finishing however, and it wasn't until the last ten minutes, after missed chances for Rush, Johnston and Walsh, that Liverpool registered their third goal. Having broken up yet another Liverpool attack it appeared that Trevor Peake was in control of the ball to the left of the Coventry penalty area, but the alert Walsh, "came snapping round his heals to win the ball," and demonstrated he could make goals as well as score them. With only a few thousand City fans left in the stadium, man-of-the-match Walsh cut into the area to shoot but, seeing Rush ghosting in unmarked, he unselfishly cut the ball back for the Welshman to score easily from an even better position than his own half an hour earlier.

Just three minutes later the visiting fans behind Grobbelaar's goal erupted in joy once again – much to the bewilderment of both the players and the dwindling number of Coventry fans. The almost redundant Liverpool goalkeeper had been conversing with the fans behind the goal and, hearing that Lee Chapman had scored a late goal against Manchester United for Sheffield Wednesday at Hillsborough, "signalled the news with a wave and a beaming smile to his teammates and the bench." News of the first apparent chink in Manchester United's armour caused the buoyant Liverpool fans on the terracing and in the stand on the opposite side of the pitch, to strike up a loud, hope-filled chorus of, "And now you're gonna believe us. We're gonna win the league."

Five minutes later referee Mr D Vickers of Ilford brought proceedings to an end and, with the result from Yorkshire confirmed, Liverpool now found themselves just seven points behind the leaders. United had also lost captain Bryan Robson just 10 minutes into his comeback game with a recurrence of the hamstring injury he had picked up whilst playing for England against Turkey the previous month.

Despite United's loss, Dalglish typically chose to concentrate on his own side's victory at the post-match press conference. It had been an, "outstanding display," by the Reds he said. At a stroke however, the Steel City result transformed the national media's supposed, "one-horse race," into a genuine title battle.

Coventry had lost 2-0 at Old Trafford the previous weekend and the Sky Blues' manager Don Mackay was understandably asked his opinion on the top two. "Who's the best?" he wondered. "That's like asking me to choose between a Rolls Royce and a Bentley. United are the team that takes players on and goes past you [whereas] Liverpool are disciplined and use the ball well." The same question was also put to goalkeeper Steve Ogrizovic. The former Anfield employee was a tad more forthcoming than his manager however, telling reporters that, "anyone who thinks that this championship is a runaway for United is being foolish. Because there has been no television I don't know how well Liverpool have been playing this season, but I was impressed [today]. They were better than United last week."

Elsewhere Everton recovered some of their previous season's title-winning form with a 6-1 demolition of Arsenal at Goodison, courtesy of a brace apiece from Gary Lineker and Adrian Heath. The Blues, still trailing United by 14 points, had much work to do, but for second-placed Liverpool, the chase was very much on.

Liverpool v West Bromwich Albion
Saturday 16 November 1985

"Definite plans to close Liverpool down at the end of next week were announced today by city Labour chiefs. No wages will be paid to 31,000 town hall staff after next Thursday and all main services, including schools, will operate for the last time the following day, November 22. Emergency services to care for the old, the sick and the young in council homes, are scheduled to begin on the Saturday."

Front page Liverpool Echo, 14 November 1985

Although they were still seven points behind the leaders, Dalglish and his players knew that - following last week's win at Coventry and Manchester United's first defeat of the campaign - they were very much in the title race. Similarly, over at Goodison Park, no Everton player was about to throw in the towel – as many in the national media hinted everyone should - even though the Champions remained 14 points adrift of Ron Atkinson's side.

On the International scene the Merseyside-based England hopefuls - Walsh, McMahon, perhaps even Craig Johnston at Liverpool and Everton's Lineker, Reid, Bracewell, Steven, and Stevens - were eyeing selection for the World Cup finals now that England had qualified, whilst the large Scottish presence at Anfield were also expectant ahead of their imminent play-off with Australia. With a 4-1 defeat of the Republic of Ireland at Lansdowne Road in midweek, Denmark had also booked their tickets to Mexico so the Reds could add the likeable Jan Molby - who spoke, "flawless English in an accent wavering between Scandinavian and Scouse," - to their potential World Cup contingent. Although Northern Ireland had also qualified from England's group, no players from Liverpool or Everton were represented.

After spending most of the previous season in the reserves, Molby credited his upturn in form to the new-found confidence the new manager had instilled in him. "Kenny gave me a lot of confidence by telling me he was going to give me a run in the side," he said. "I am a much better player than when I arrived because even playing in the reserves at Liverpool did me a lot of good."

With Eire's Jim Beglin and Mark Lawrenson starring on the opposite side versus Denmark in Dublin the match was watched by Dalglish, not only running the rule over his own men but also former Liverpool target Michel Laudrup who had declined the Reds' advances in favour of a move to Juventus in 1983. Laudrup had been recently quoted as saying he would review his position in Italy at the end of the current season, thus renewing Liverpool's interest.

With no World Cup commitments to distract him, perhaps Bruce Grobbelaar had more time than most to form an opinion with regard to the ongoing local political situation. In his autobiography published in 1986 Grobbelaar - a former soldier in the Rhodesian Army - wrote that, "footballers are supposed to be apolitical...but you just have to live in Liverpool to feel the atmosphere and realise how the city has declined. Even my mother sensed it...She was appalled that, having risked life and limb in the fight against Marxism, I was now living in a city seemingly controlled by it."

The eccentric goalkeeper - who also used his life-story to rail against the rise in crime in the city, hooliganism and the fickle nature of fans who had, in the past, criticised himself and some of his teammates – appealed to politicians on both sides to come to some agreement so the events of 1985 and, in his eyes, the damage they had done to the city, would never be repeated.

It was not just local government funding – or lack of it depending on your political persuasion – that was making headlines at this time, however. Most felt that football itself was on the verge of significant and drastic change. Much to the chagrin of the sport's leading journalists and football fans - who saw scant justification for the clubs' demands for greater influence on the game and more cash from the TV companies - the stand-off between the Football League and the broadcasters had created, like the state of local politics, suspicion and bitterness on all sides.

Faced with a loss of revenue due to falling gates – ironically, a problem exacerbated by a lack of exposure on TV – and no European football, many club chairmen felt the time had come to demand a larger fee from the TV companies for their access to match coverage. For most chairmen the scenario was simple – more money meant they might survive until the UEFA ban was lifted and eventually they would be able to retake their rightful place among the continent's footballing elite.

As the club owners and administrators delved deeper however, they saw that the time was potentially right for them to not only increase their revenue streams, but also to assume greater control of their own destiny. It was an opportunity too good for them to ignore. For those representing the likes of Liverpool, Everton, Manchester United, Arsenal and Spurs, nothing short of a breakaway from the constraints of the Football League would be enough. For them, a 'Super League' in which the big clubs might expect a larger slice of the TV cake was a must if the future of English football - or more pertinently their interests as part of 'The Big Five' - were to be secured.

Proposals for an elite league – preferably reduced to 20 rather than 22 teams - had been around for some years, yet it was only now that they began to be viewed with some degree of legitimacy. However, with gates dropping due to the increasingly perilous state of grounds, persistent hooliganism, and a level of unemployment that saw millions with little, if any, disposable income, there were few incentives for TV companies to plough more money into a sport that many thought was dying on its feet.

Compounding the matter further was the costs of improving ground safety following the Bradford stadium tragedy. Grounds needed to be improved but, with fewer fans, with less money, and sponsors departing in droves due to no TV coverage, it really did seem that the game itself was in its final death throes. Watched almost exclusively by a dwindling number of the working class, football had never been so unfashionable. Unlike club chairmen, national broadcasters realised this, so despite the sport's ever-growing need for exposure and a significant increase in cash, the impasse and the resulting TV black-out of the 1985/86 season continued.

If the rest of the country had well and truly fallen out of love with football however, the level of interest on Merseyside never seemed to wane. Liverpool's good form was reflected in the letters to the Football Echo, few of which questioned team selection, players' form, or tactics. With Dalglish dropping himself in favour of Walsh, who had scored seven goals in four games, the issue of Walsh's transfer had died down, and supporters seemed content that Dalglish had decided, for now at least, to take a back seat.

One sentiment that wouldn't go away - and one held with the same passion by Liverpool and Everton fans alike - was the perception that the media were obsessed with Manchester United. A number of contributors consistently wrote in to point out the error of Fleet Street's ways; "Liverpool are inferior to that team from Old Trafford," wrote W. Dutton sarcastically, from Warrington, "they've got to be." Referring to United's collapse the previous season the contributor continued, "To finish fourth in a two-horse race for the Championship is truly amazing by any standards. Just look at the silverware they have won over the last few seasons – their trophy cupboard must be overflowing."

Likewise, D. Wevill of Higher Bebington asked, "Can United really be a better side than the Reds when the last time they finished above them in the league was in 1968?" Orrell Park's Michael Burgess stated that, "a dose of eye drops are badly needed," if, "[Paul] McGrath is the best centre back in the country."

An eye test was certainly in order for anyone who saw any hope for West Bromwich Albion at Anfield. Having taken over from former manager Johnny Giles, who had quit in late-September, former Manchester United legend and England World Cup winner Nobby Stiles - stepping up from a coaching role for the rest of the season - had seen an instant upturn in form.

Under new management, the Baggies achieved a couple of draws and a first win of the season at home to Birmingham. The honeymoon period didn't last though and, having lost their last three league games, they found themselves bottom of the table with just six points and one league win from 16 games. In contrast, Liverpool had played eight and won eight at home, scoring 21 goals and conceding just four.

With such a formidable record it was no surprise when Dalglish selected the same starting 11 for the fourth game in a row – he also restored himself to the bench. The lowly crowd of just 28,400 who braved a cold, wet November afternoon, and the uncertainty surrounding the city's future, expected nothing less than the cheer of a handsome victory. The home fans were in a state of shock however, when, despite dominating play, creating numerous chances, and hitting the bar twice – first from a Hansen header and then from a deflected Walsh shot – Liverpool found themselves a goal behind when Albion scored with their first attack of the game.

Tony Godden had already saved well from a number of Liverpool players, most notably Beglin, Rush, McMahon and Walsh. Whelan and Johnston had also come close to scoring but, with Grobbelaar a virtual spectator, the visitors scored an easy goal when the diminutive Garth Crooks - signed recently from Spurs - squeezed in front of Lawrenson and glanced a header from a free kick by Gary Robson, younger brother of Bryan, past the Liverpool keeper on 38 minutes.

For a few seconds the Liverpool players, let alone the crowd, were stunned into silence. The shock quickly gave way to a defiant roar from the Kop and the Reds came storming back to equalise just seven minutes later when, "Walsh wriggled free of Martyn Bennett in Dalglish style," to hit a dangerous low cross that was only cleared to Steve Nicol. The right-back made no mistake, blasting his shot into the roof of the net via the fingertips of Godden to level the score. The half-time whistle went soon afterwards.

With the news that Spurs were holding Manchester United at Old Trafford this was no time for the Reds to falter in their pursuit of the First Division summit and, from the restart, the restart the Reds moved to attack West Brom once again. Rush and Whelan combined well down the left only for Walsh to poke the resultant cross just wide. The in-form striker then played in Molby only for the Dane to be thwarted by a Bennett tackle just as he was about to unleash another shot. At this stage, "it was hard to believe that the visitors were on level terms having been so completely outplayed."

Stiles' decision to give anonymous 17-year old Andy Thompson his league debut – the youngster had signed professional forms only five days previously – appeared strange and ill-conceived. Thompson was not the only Albion player to suffer however; the entire squad not good enough to compete with a side playing as well and so full of confidence as Liverpool. "Stronger and more experienced players have been over-awed at Anfield," added Rogers.

Just before the hour mark Albion were lucky not to wilt under the relentless pressure the home side were exerting when, with no-one in front of him to prevent a long run from the back, Beglin brought the ball forward until he found McMahon in the box. "Wearing a plaster down the side of his face to protect the (facial) injury sustained at Coventry last Saturday," man-of-the-match McMahon - impressing the returning Graeme Souness who was in the country on World Cup duty ahead of Scotland's game against Australia - "twisted cleverly before unleashing a low shot that was somehow turned wide by Godden." Seconds later a Rush shot was deflected into the path of Hansen whose side foot effort from inside the six-yard box was cleared off the line by a defender. Surely, the Kop wondered, such incessant pressure would pay-off?

In the 62nd minute Walsh found himself with the ball in the area but with his back to goal. Showing bravado as well as confidence, the impish striker, "pulled a wonder pass out of his box of tricks," and somehow managed to back-heel the ball into the path of Molby who forced it into the net from close range. Liverpool finally had the lead. There was to be no let up for the shell-shocked Godden – whose form had been the only reason the Reds hadn't run up a cricket score. He saved brilliantly again from Johnston soon after before Lawrenson, seeing that Albion were penned in their own half, moved forward to send a decent cross-shot narrowly wide. A few minutes later Godden denied McMahon the goal his performance deserved, saving a vicious shot from 20-yards, but neither he nor his teammates could stave off a third Liverpool goal for long.

On 74 minutes, "Lawrenson raced from half-way past a couple of tired challengers...played a one-two with Walsh and rounded the keeper to score." At 3-1 the points were Liverpool's. With nine minutes to go Dalglish brought himself on for Whelan. Five minutes later he provided a pass for Walsh at the edge of the area who, "slammed a rising shot into the corner," for Liverpool's fourth. The Reds left the field to tumultuous, and thoroughly deserved, applause from the home crowd. Seldom one to overstate things in public the manager added to the acclaim after the game. "I thought we were magnificent," Dalglish said. "In the first half we were unlucky on four or five occasions and then went behind, but when we equalised it was just a procession."

Scorer of yet another goal – his seventh in five games - and having a hand in the other three, Paul Walsh was also excited at the possibilities Liverpool's attacking play afforded him. "I could have had four," he said, "Ian Rush and I were falling over each other at the end trying to get more goals."

It had been another stunning Liverpool performance, made all the sweeter by the news that a Ray Clemence-inspired Tottenham had drawn 0-0 with Manchester United at Old Trafford. Highlighting Liverpool's recent charge the Reds were now the division's top scorers with 39 goals - from just 17 games. More importantly, the gap at the top was now just five points. United's lead at the top had been halved in less than a week. With Everton's 4-3 win at Ipswich putting the Blues back in the title picture - albeit with a further seven points to make up – at least the city's ongoing political chaos wasn't mirrored in the dressing rooms at Anfield and Goodison.

Birmingham City v Liverpool
Saturday 23 November 1985

Mrs. Currie "Does my right hon. Friend agree that the disastrous policies of the current Liverpool city council serve only to make things worse in that sad city by deterring any potential employer from moving there? Will he say why people in South Derbyshire should have to fork out a ton of money to keep that council afloat on the Mersey when the money could be far better spent on our own ratepayers and taxpayers?"

Mr. Jenkin "I entirely agree with my hon. Friend. I hope that members of the Liverpool city council will recognise, from what has been said from the Conservative Benches, that Parliament's patience is running very short. It is high time that they set about putting their house in order instead of continually standing with their hands outstretched, asking for more money."

House of Commons Debates 10 July 1985 vol 82 cc1073-6 Liverpool (Rates)

If life had seemed chaotic – and if the national media were to be believed, almost apocalyptic - for everyone in Liverpool the previous week, events in the city during past seven days appeared – on the surface at least – much more banal. A deal with Swiss banks to borrow the £30 million shortfall had been agreed by the City Council - and then cancelled. Amidst much confusion a legal budget was set on Friday 22 November. The crisis had been diverted. The Liverpool District Labour Party was suspended by the Labour party National Executive five days later.

After a dramatic fortnight in which Liverpool had halved the gap at the top of the table, life in the goldfish bowl that was the local football arena also appeared more serene. The hardly earth-shattering news that the Screen Sport Super Cup final would not now take place at

Wembley was greeted with total apathy - even by the few who had bothered to turn up to games in the competition so far. "The prospect of a confrontation under the twin towers was the proverbial carrot dangled before the fans when this tournament was launched," but with the final, "now likely to be a two-legged affair on a home and away basis," most fans low opinion of the ill-starred tournament was confirmed. To compound the matter further, the authorities couldn't even suggest prospective dates for the eventual home and away final ties, such were the other commitments of the clubs still involved.

Of far more interest than the revised plans for the Super Cup however, was the revelation that Kenny Dalglish had been omitted from the Scotland squad for the return leg of their World Cup qualifying game against Australia. Davie Cooper of Rangers and West Ham's Frank McAvennie - from a Dalglish assist - had scored in midweek at Hampden Park to give the Scots a 2-0 first leg cushion to take to Melbourne. The news was met, first with incredulity, then with anger, by many Liverpudlians. Although his non-selection avoided the prospect of Liverpool losing their manager for more than a week, fans wondered how Alex Ferguson could drop a player as iconic as Dalglish.

One of the finest of a rich generation of Scottish footballers and only one cap short of becoming the first Scot to reach a century of international appearances, it seemed strange that Dalglish would miss such an important game. Ferguson however - who had taken temporary charge in wake of the tragic death of Jock Stein - had a legitimate explanation; that he had agreed with the First Division's top clubs to take a maximum of one player from each English side - so as to lessen the impact of the trip to Australia on the league programme.

Ferguson was also forced to leave behind Manchester United's Gordon Strachan, as well as Steve Archibald of Barcelona, but with Nicol, Wark, Hansen, Dalglish and MacDonald all in the frame for the Scots, it was a tough choice for the manager to select just the one Liverpool player for the second leg against the 'Socceroos'. Ferguson eventually opted for the Red's rapidly improving young right-back, Steve Nicol.

That Nicol agreed to travel to Australia at all was proof of his commitment to the Scottish cause, as it was revealed in the week that his father James had been in a coma for several weeks following a sudden illness. Also included from Merseyside's Scottish contingent was Everton's Graeme Sharp, so the Blues were also deprived of a star player for at least two games.

Despite this blow for the Toffees, Everton were celebrating when they were named as the European Team of the year at a gala UEFA dinner at the Winter Circus in Paris. 1984/85 had been a tremendous season - the best in their history for the blue half of Merseyside; winners of the First Division title, the European Cup Winners Cup and the Charity Shield. Howard Kendall's Manager of the Year Award, the PFA Award for Peter Reid, and Neville Southall's Footballer of the Year gong complemented the team's silverware.

Despite coming from two goals down to win 4-3 at Portman Road the previous weekend however, Everton had yet to sparkle and Blues' fans still needed convincing that new signing Gary Lineker – an £800,000 British transfer record at the time – was the right man to complement Sharp and Adrian Heath up front. Although he already had 13 goals to his name, critics had detected a selfishness to Lineker's play that had seen Everton struggle to maintain last season's attractive passing style - and relentless winning form.

Everton's inconsistency continued with a draw at home to Nottingham Forest this afternoon - while Lineker's former side Leicester City caused arguably the biggest upset of the season so far when they scored twice in the first 15 minutes at home to league leaders Manchester United. Without a home win since September 28, Foxes' fans could scarcely believe their eyes when they scored a third goal before the half hour mark.

In response to his side's draw and a loss in their last two games, Ron Atkinson had told the press before the game, "Don't believe the bubble has burst," but his less than prophetic words were the icing on the cake when news of Leicester's goals quickly spread to the, "large contingent," of travelling Liverpool fans at St. Andrews. Hoping to see a fifth league win in a row and so continue the pressure they had exerted on 'Big Ron's' side in the past week, Liverpool supporters were in fine fettle as they saw Rush and Walsh net once again to take all three points. By contrast, United's strike duo were experiencing a costly downturn of form; Frank Stapleton had not scored since 21 September, whilst Mark Hughes was without a goal in five games – statistics that did not augur well for their assault on a first title in 19 years - or their League Cup visit to Anfield in three days' time.

"Playing with confidence and determination in all departments," Liverpool were simply too good for a Birmingham side that had lost its last seven league games. Whereas Ron Saunders' men were in freefall, the Reds appeared to be playing and scoring for fun. After nine minutes Johnston - a revelation under Dalglish - crossed hard and low from the right for Rush, "to punch his 12th goal of the season from close range." Seconds later the Welshman almost scored his 13th – turning quickly just inside the area to unleash, "an unstoppable shot that beat Seaman and rebounded clear off the left-hand post." With McMahon, "looking the perfect foil for Jan Molby in the centre of midfield," and dictating the play to such an extent that Liverpool, "never looked in danger at any stage of the half," the Reds continued to press for more goals.

On 25 minutes the away side were awarded a free-kick on the edge of the box for a clumsy tackle on Walsh and from Molby's chipped set-piece the athletic striker stepped away from his marker and rose to power an exquisite header past David Seaman. It appeared all so easy for the Reds, whose fans, aware of the remarkable score from Filbert Street and despite the cold damp afternoon, instantly began the chant, "'We're going to win the league."

The second–half continued in much the same vein. Man-of-the-match McMahon burst through the Birmingham defence on 50 minutes only to see his powerful shot brilliantly pushed past the post with one hand by Seaman. The keeper also did well to hold onto a deflected Molby shot soon after. Although Grobbelaar had virtually nothing to deal with all game, he owed some thanks to his defence with Hansen, Beglin and Lawrenson all displaying their powers of concentration and expertly thwarting what few Birmingham attacks there were in the second period.

It was up front however, that Liverpool were most dominant. Rush could have had a hat-trick within the space of ten minutes when Walsh found him inside the six-yard box with a clever pass only for his goal-bound shot to be blocked. A similarly astute pass from Molby was then intercepted and cleared almost off the Welshman's toes - just as he was teeing up his shot. Johnston nearly scored after another tricky run and then it was Nicol's turn to provide a cross for Walsh from the right wing that, although the England candidate was able to steer into the net, was correctly ruled out for off-side. Almost the final act of the game was yet another Liverpool chance, Molby firing in another long-range effort just wide.

The same starting 11 from Dalglish and another facile victory for the Reds which - owing to Manchester United's second defeat in three games - meant the gap between the top two was now just two points. All of a sudden the 'Champions elect' tag used by the press to describe the Old Trafford outfit wasn't being used so liberally. The canny Dalglish was in no hurry to make any outlandish claims however, and thereby satisfy a fickle media's desire to suddenly transfer the mantle of title favouritism to his charges. He refused to discuss his side's championship chances, preferring instead to simply respond with the, "tried and tested Anfield motto of 'taking each game as it comes.'"

Of even greater concern to Atkinson was the injury crisis that was now sorely testing the depth of his squad. A number of key players were out; Mark Hughes and Arthur Albiston both picked up knocks in their defeat to Leicester - and joined Remi Moses and Bryan Robson on the treatment table. Conversely, the quality of Liverpool's squad was there for all to see. The highly respected Birmingham manager, Ron Saunders, made a joke of the visitor's riches in the post-match press conference.

"A group of Liverpool players were fighting," before the game he said, "Wark, McDonald and Neal were at it, and even Kenny Dalglish got involved. Neal got an eye, Kenny an elbow...They nearly ripped the number 12 shirt in half!" Wark ultimately got the nod for a place on the bench from his manager. Although it was just a joke to highlight the difference in resources available to the respective managers, the Birkenhead-born Saunders - who had managed Aston Villa to the league title in 1981 - merely underlined what many already thought – few sides looked as strong at this stage of the season as Liverpool.

With almost perfect timing next up for the Reds was the highly anticipated clash with faltering United – in the fourth round of the Milk Cup. The draw for the quarter-finals had already been made with Ipswich or Fourth Division Swindon Town due to come to Anfield in the New Year - if Liverpool could beat United on Tuesday.

As far as the supporters were concerned however, progression to the last eight was almost incidental – this was a grudge match; one which the Reds could use to strike a savage mental blow in the title race and at the same time ram the words of a tiresome, pro-United media and the annoying boasts of Ron Atkinson firmly down their respective throats. With a history of violent behaviour between the two sets of supporters, the potential for trouble had also not gone unnoticed. "UEFA have been quietly monitoring selected matches...[in England] since the start of the season," wrote Ian Hargraves. "And the United game will be a subject of special interest."

Placing even greater emphasis on fans' behaviour at the match, Peter Robinson issued an appeal to both sets of supporters; "We hope everyone will take special care this time," he told reporters. "Any incidents could have a major bearing on when we are allowed back into Europe. Both United and ourselves are eager to get back into European competition as soon as possible, and it would be a tragedy if a flare-up of any kind delayed our return." Whilst attempting to calm the situation however, Robinson's cause was not helped by the recent political situation in the city – a local postal strike ensuring that, just days before the game was due to take place, thousands of people had yet to receive their tickets.

Also, with plans now cancelled to beam the clash live on big screens at Old Trafford - as had been mooted the week before – United seemed certain to take up their full allocation of 7,200 tickets, so the potential for trouble was arguably enhanced. Indeed, with the gap between the top two in the Division now so slight, the game had all the ingredients for a classic cup-tie. It wouldn't disappoint.

Liverpool v Manchester United
League Cup fourth round
Tuesday 26 November 1985

"The hidden misery of Liverpool's unemployed was revealed today. A survey by city planning chiefs claims that as many as one in three people in Liverpool are out of work…Government figures conceal the true level of unemployment because they only count the 58,000 people claiming benefit in the city, according to a council report. They don't take into account people on job creation or training schemes or married women looking for work…More than 48% of 16 to 19 year old men are out of work, and more than 46% of men aged 20 to 24…Conservative councillor Fred Butler blamed the city rates battle for driving business away. Conservative Tony McVeigh said, "Industrialists won't come to Merseyside while you [Labour] are in office."

Liverpool Echo, 26 November 1985

Few meetings in world, let alone British, football stir the passions quite as much as a Liverpool v Manchester United game. The great North West rivals had enjoyed many classic confrontations over the years but this meeting – although only for a place in the fifth round of the Milk Cup - would go down in Anfield folklore as one of the most thrilling, most memorable and - for fans and one player in particular - one of the most enjoyable ever.

Ten points behind the runaway league leaders just two weeks earlier, Kenny Dalglish's side had brushed past recent opponents as if they were Sunday league sides. The statistics were telling; Liverpool were unbeaten in 10 League and Cup games, they had scored 25 goals, conceded seven, with in-form strikers Rush and Walsh netting 13 times between them. Proven internationals with League and European medals to their name; Wark, Neal, Lee and Dalglish himself, were fighting it out with emerging players Beglin, MacDonald, Walsh and Johnston for a starting berth or the solitary place on the bench.

In contrast, United, after a fantastic start to the season, were struggling. Injuries to key men had revealed the paucity of their squad and a recent lack of goals had resulted in points dropped against supposedly inferior opponents. From being firm favourites to win the title after their faultless opening sequence, United were now scrapping for points with the rest of the league. Victory here, for either side, would be a major psychological boost.

It would also be a timely boost for the English game if the match took place without any significant incidents between the rival sets of supporters. Whether it was the murky prospect of an evening negotiating Anfield's dimly lit back streets - or the recent travails of their creaking team - United's followers surprisingly failed to mop up their full allocation of tickets, leaving the clash just short of a capacity crowd. Those that did take their places on the Anfield Road end however, were as passionate and as noisy as they had always been when visiting the home of the fiercest rivals. Even by Liverpool v United standards – the atmosphere was highly charged.

For Liverpool fan John Joynt of Huyton, the anticipation was almost overwhelming. "It was amazing how much everyone was up for the game," recalls John. "We were all looking forward to it, not only because it was United and the atmosphere that games against them usually brought, but also because we knew they weren't the world-beaters that everyone made them out to be. We knew we were better. They hadn't played anyone decent so far. We knew we would beat them."

Merseyside Police had also stated their intention to ensure the match passed off peacefully. Before the game they pledged to confiscate any banners or flags they deemed obscene, unacceptable, or likely to incite violence. "There will be no place for the disgraceful 'Munich 58' or 'Shankly 81' slogans that have soured previous encounters between the teams," wrote Ken Rogers. It is amazing to think now, but in the early-1980s fans with these slogans adorned on t-shirts had actually been allowed into both Anfield and Old Trafford by police and stewards.

In keeping with their promise to keep a close watch on the biggest games in England, UEFA also had an observer at the match, "weighing up the behaviour of the fans. If the leading English clubs are to win an early reprieve on the European scene, it is crucial that the supporters show a lead."

Like Joynt, most Liverpool fans were expecting their side to take the game to a United side they believed had been hyped up by the media, but 'Joynty' and the rest of the home supporters were in a state of shock when Norman Whiteside's astute pass sent Paul McGrath clear in the seventh minute. Needing no invitation, the Irish international, "lashed an unstoppable shot into the bottom left-hand corner," to send the 5,000 or so visiting fans into a frenzy. With United one-up and showing renewed swagger, Dalglish's decision to play Molby as a sweeper rather than the deep-lying creative midfielder he had grown into in recent games, appeared to have back-fired.

"Its no use surrendering anything to Liverpool," Ron Atkinson had said before the game, "to do any good at all you must go at them." Their manager's words appeared to have been followed to the letter by a depleted United side that caused problems for Liverpool straight from the start. In the absence of the injured Arthur Albiston, Wales-born Clayton Blackmore - who had come through the ranks at Old Trafford - started at left-back. The position was a problem one for United as evidenced by the purchase of Colin Gibson from Aston Villa that same afternoon, although his signing came too late for a start here.

Although United had to make do and mend in several positions, they were much the better team for most of the first half. Indeed, if it wasn't for the imperious form of Mark Lawrenson at the back, then Liverpool may well have found themselves two or even three down at the break.

The early period of the second half also saw more United pressure. The, "unflappable," Lawrenson headed a curling Strachan shot off the line just four minutes after the restart and moments later he, "tracked the powerful McGrath as he set off on a long run towards the box and his challenge was good enough to deny the midfielder what would have been another outstanding goal." Nicol, Rush, Whelan and Johnston all went close for Liverpool however, and with Dalglish having moved Molby forward into his more accustomed central midfield position, Liverpool slowly began to recover.

The tackles were flying in but, "no-one revelled more in the white hot atmosphere than Johnston." The vibrant Australian was a constant threat to an increasingly stretched United defence. "He was always prepared to take his man on – using his pace and skill to expose the visitor's left flank." Just before the hour mark however, instead of man-of-the-match

Johnston's pace and trickery, it was, "the explosive shooting power of Jan Molby [that] ripped the heart out of Manchester United." Indeed, within the space of just 120 seconds, it was the Great Dane at the double as this thunderous tie was turned on its head.

With the TV dispute continuing there were no cameras to record the night's action, no highlights to be shown later that evening on Sportsnight or Midweek Sports Special. Manchester United's coaches had recorded the game for training purposes however, but, for many years the tape's existence remained unknown, ensuring that the game - and Molby's equaliser in particular - would earn its place in Liverpool's glorious history as a rare, magical, almost mythical 'I wish I was there,' moment.

If just over 41,000 fans were there, plenty more over the years claim to have seen first-hand what many argue was the Dane's defining moment in a red shirt. In recent years, grainy images of the goal from the training video has been released, viewed by thousands on the internet - but at the time those not in attendance only had the words of Ken Rogers to describe a goal of stunning ferocity and class;

"United, despite their lead, were beginning to feel the heat and when Molby won the ball off Whiteside on the halfway line after 57 minutes, the stage was set for an amazing equaliser.

"The Dane accelerated away from the left-back Blackmore on a diagonal run and the sheer power of the break stunned the Old Trafford defenders. Molby was suddenly in the box and goalkeeper Gary Bailey couldn't have seen the shot that flashed past him, let alone stop it."

Such was the force of the shot that the South African-born keeper would later state he had broken a finger as the ball flew through his outstretched hand into the top right-hand corner of the net in front of an ecstatic, steaming Kop.

Seen from behind the goal, Molby's incredible strike was a thing of beauty. Joynt recalls;

"I remember him tackling Whiteside and knocking him off the ball to a massive roar from the crowd and, as he ran towards us in the Kop, it was obvious he was going to shoot.

"When the ball flew in we went absolutely off our heads. It was the loudest, maddest, most violent goal celebration I have ever known. I must have jumped the highest and furthest I had ever done. When we eventually stopped screaming I was about 20 feet away from where I was before the goal. The Kop was absolutely bouncing – the whole Kop, even the old fellas - were singing and jumping up and down. As a Liverpool fan on the Kop - you lived for times like this."

With the baying crowd roaring them on, Liverpool pressed for the winner. The game had turned on Molby's wonder strike. It was now United's turn to try and soak up the pressure. Whereas Hansen, Nicol, Lawrenson and Beglin had frustrated the United attack in the first half with cool and composed play at the back, United's defence now began to drop deep, making mistakes, almost inviting Liverpool to take the lead – much to the anger of Ron Atkinson on the bench who pleaded in vain for his side to push forward.

Within a minute of the equaliser, they buckled. A swift exchange of passes on the edge of the United box resulted in the ball striking Kevin Moran on the hand. As one, the Liverpool players and the Kop screamed for a penalty. The linesman on the Main Stand touchline agreed and raised his flag accordingly - much to the United players' disgust and their manager's fury. Referee Mr D Shaw of Cheshire pointed to the spot and, after a few moments to compose himself amidst the continuing United protestations, 'Rambo' stepped up to take the spot-kick. "This time it was Molby's accuracy, not power, that left Bailey helpless," as his well struck low shot to the keeper's left put Liverpool in front. Again the Kop exploded in celebration, with several fans appearing on the pitch from the seats in the Paddock as the emotion of the night got the better of them.

Minutes later - with the United players' discipline gone completely - Liverpool should have had another penalty when Blackmore clumsily sent Johnston crashing to the ground just inside the area. To the home crowd's disbelief however, the referee awarded a free-kick, outside the box - and booked the stand-in full-back.

The match official's leniency continued when, with just minutes to go, Whiteside amazingly escaped a red card after swinging a boot at the grounded McMahon following a thunderous 50/50 challenge that the Liverpool midfielder won in typically determined fashion. "If Ron Atkinson is the man Merseysiders love to hate," said Ken Rogers, "then Whiteside is the player they detest." The Northern Irishman's, "anger and cynical attitude in the face of defeat simply reflected United's total frustration at failing to halt the Anfield surge in both league and Cup."

Amidst a crescendo of whistles and exultant scouse voices, the final whistle went soon after and yet another glorious night had been forged on the fields of Anfield Road. As the sands of time passed by, the legend of Molby's wonderful goal grew with each passing tale from those who witnessed it with their own eyes; ably assisted by Molby's exaggerated, hilarious account during his after-dinner speeches.

Years later the precious footage was discovered gathering dust in his attic but, whilst acknowledging it existed, Molby didn't release it straight away - thus preserving the myth for a while longer. When he finally decided to share the pictures with the rest of the word, they revealed a fantastic individual strike more than worthy of the 20-year wait. For those inside the ground that November 1985 night however, the original memory of one of Anfield's greatest ever goals remains forever imprinted on their eyes.

Liverpool v Chelsea
Saturday 30 November 1985

"Allow me to put forward my cure for unemployment; replace all the working, married women with unemployed males. This will return the woman to her rightful place in the home…"

Mr Robert Evans, Allerton, Letter to Liverpool Echo, 26 November.

"In reply to Mr Evans' letter, his statement that women in work are the real cause of unemployment among males is false. There is in fact only one woman in work who is responsible for putting almost four million people out of work and that woman is Margaret Thatcher."

Mr Peter Flynn, Belmont Drive, Anfield, Letter to Liverpool Echo, 5 December

Since Kenny Dalglish had opted to pair Paul Walsh with Ian Rush at the start of the month against Leicester, Liverpool had won five consecutive games – scoring 12 goals in the process and conceding just two. At the beginning of this encouraging run they had been 10 points behind Manchester United but, should their recent run of good form continue - in this, a rare early kick-off - and they were to beat third-placed Chelsea, themselves unbeaten in seven, then the Reds would go top of the table - for three hours at least.

Owing to Chelsea's disreputable away following, kick-off was scheduled for 12 noon so as to lessen any potential crowd problems. Most London clubs had their own 'firm' whose intention it was to cause havoc at away fixtures and Chelsea were no exception, but only a small number of their following would claim to be card-carrying members of the notoriously violent 'Headhunters' crew.

The Stamford Bridge outfit hadn't won a league game at Anfield since December 1935 but, even though they were without David Speedie, – in Australia with the Scotland squad for their World Cup qualifier – manager John Hollins was optimistic of an upset. "Liverpool set the standard for the rest to match," he said. "I have had some great games at Anfield as a player; we will be having a real go at them." Despite the absence of Speedie, skipper Colin Pates and injured midfielders John Bumstead and Mike Hazard, the Londoners, "gave as good as they got throughout a match that had 38,000 fans captivated from start to finish."

Liverpool's incentive of going top of the table with a victory was matched equally by Chelsea's desire to challenge at the summit of Division One, and the visitor's should have scored within the first ten minutes through Nevin. The tricky Scot found himself with a clear shooting chance inside the box, "but he was guilty of a dreadful miss under pressure from Nicol."

Liverpool's right back had been left out of the Scottish squad that had travelled to Australia on compassionate grounds due to the serious condition of his father, James, who had been in a coma since collapsing in Ayr on 2 November. Nicol jnr. had been playing for Liverpool, then travelling the 200 miles to his father's bedside, ever since. His twin sister Susan had revealed that the family had played radio commentary of Scotland's 2-0 win over Australia on 20 November, "hoping that any mention of Steve's name might get through to him." Although his condition was described as, "stable," James remained in a coma. Describing how selecting Nicol would have been futile and inappropriate, Scotland manager Alex Ferguson had told him of his decision the previous weekend. "In the circumstances we couldn't possibly take Steve," he said. "I really feel for the boy. It would have been pointless having him on the other side of the world with his father so ill."

The early kick-off had failed to deter thousands of Chelsea fans from travelling to Merseyside and, even at just before midday, they were in fine voice, mocking a relatively quiet Kop with chants of, "You're supposed to be at home." The Kopites, many of them not long out of their beds and sensing anti-climax after the midweek dramas, looked on with heavy-eyed bemusement. Young Liverpool fan David Brennan recalls;

"My Dad bought tickets for the Anny Road because he feared Chelsea would bring a mob and cause trouble. I loved being in the Kop but to shield me from swearing and aggression, he got us adult/child seats by the Main Stand. There was a big travelling support in noise and numbers - I don't think he realized we would effectively be in the same stand as Chelsea.

"Missing out on the Kop put me in a bad mood. Worse still the Chelsea fans were very loud right next to us. Owing to their reputation it was a noon start but they still brought huge numbers. Their songs

81

Ian Ross in the Daily Post noticed that, when the match started, Chelsea, "refused to be intimidated by the infamous Anfield aura which so often lulls visitors into a false sense of despondency. They refused to play the sacrificial lamb; their application was near-faultless and their attitude brave and commendable." Indeed, it was a full 30 minutes before Liverpool had their first real chance of the game – but it was quickly followed by others as, in the space of five minutes, the Reds could easily have scored four times.

"A curling shot from Whelan clipped the outside of the post, Molby had a free-kick tipped over the bar by Niedzwiecki, McMahon hammered high and wide [when well placed] and then the Welsh keeper showed his quality by twisting to hold another effort from the midfielder." Chelsea's response was equally as exhilarating with the clearest chance falling to Nevin whose rasping left foot shot beat Grobbelaar all ends up only to rebound off the post, hit the stranded keeper on the shoulder and then bounce out for a corner.

If the fans thought the end to the first-half had been thrilling however, then they were in for a treat as the second period was to provide even more excitement. Chances continued to be created by both sides as the crowd were treated to a fine exhibition of end-to-end football. Frustratingly for Liverpool fans however, almost nothing seemed to go right in front of goal. Ian Rush thought he had scored when a curling shot seemed to have beaten Niedzwiecki but, "with a desperate one-handed save," the keeper beat it away with the entire ground applauding in appreciation. After a fine move involving four players, Kerry Dixon then rounded Grobbelaar only to see his effort cleared off the line by man-of-the-match Lawrenson. It was breathtaking stuff.

Just as the game, "seemed destined to be one of the season's more intriguing goalless draws…a suitably dramatic climax materialised out of thin air." With just four minutes remaining, "Mark Lawrenson strode forward manfully before punching the ball forward to the bounding figure of Ian Rush." Finding himself inside the area at the Kop end, the Welshman attempt to control the precise pass only to go down under a challenge from Joe McLaughlin.

It seemed that little contact was made; for a split second there was silence, followed by a huge roar as the Kop beseeched the officials and Chester referee Neville Ashley, who duly pointed to the spot. The consternation of the Chelsea players was all too evident, with most running to the official in disbelief. Ashley waved their appeals away however, and Molby stepped up, "to send the keeper the wrong way with the Kop saluting what looked to be a certain winner."

Chelsea fans, angered by the decision were in a frenzy. 'Liver-pool, Liver-pool, who the f***ing hell are you'?" sneered the Londoners as they contemplated an unjust defeat. At the opposite end, giddy at the table-topping position they now found themselves in, the home crowd were also in full-voice as their autumn title challenge, and 18-match winning home run stretching back to the previous March, appeared to have been maintained. Chelsea were not disheartened though, and, barely two minutes later, they claimed they had scored when a Doug Rougvie header was cleared off the line by Walsh. Although a number of visiting players again converged on the referee screaming that the ball was over the line, play was waved on – much to the relief of Reds' fans. Second later however, relief turned to despair for Liverpool as a goalmouth scramble resulted in Pat Nevin smashing the ball into the net from close range, "after Grobbelaar had gone walkabout in his six-yard area." The large Chelsea contingent behind the goal went ballistic. Liverpool's long Anfield-winning run was finally at an end as Chelsea claimed a deserved point.

From his exile in the Anfield Road seats Dave Brennan recalls that the Chelsea fans were kept behind for an inordinately long time at the final whistle. "My dad and I also waited until most of the Liverpool fans had dispersed. At moments like this you really appreciated Anfield – the floodlights brightening a cold November day, the green turf like a billiard table, the gaudy plastic seats of the "Anny" in stark contrast to the battleship grey seats of the Kemlyn." Leaving the ground at the same time as the Chelsea fans, Dave and his Dad found themselves hemmed in by police horses.

"I remember the roar that went up to this day which left me feeling fearful and excited at the same time as I saw a bunch of Chelsea getting 'lamped' by around ten or so Reds. Chelsea's lads were no mugs though and gave as good as they got. As a 12 year-old, I had no idea what was going on really, and my Dad pulled me into a garden on Anfield Road for safety. I wondered to myself if what had happened at Heysel meant that crews up and down the country wanted to have a go at us, to knock us off some kind of inglorious pedestal.

"I got the impression the police allowed fighting to continue up to a point, but then closed ranks and brought things under control. We just stood there in the garden waiting for the trouble to subside. When it did we ventured outside. On the bus back to Old Swan, two lads were boasting about what they did to the Cockneys. Although my Dad was fuming, I was hooked. The Anny Road it was for me from now on!"

In Anfield's corridors after the game, McLaughlin was adamant he had never touched Rush. "I was probably wrong to challenge him in that position," he told reporters, "but having said that, I didn't make contact." Revealing once again how the Kop could have a bearing on the referee's thinking, the defender said that, "No-one seemed to make a decision, but then the crowd erupted and the penalty was given."

Despite the controversy over the spot-kick– and the header that was cleared off the line by Walsh - Chelsea manager John Hollins was impressed with his side. "It is the first time I have been here and gone away believing that we actually deserved to win. Everyone played well." It was not just the never say die attitude of his players that impressed Hollins, the manner of their play also drew his praise. "It was the best passing performance I have seen from us," he added.

In contrast, Hollins' Anfield counterpart could scarcely conceal his frustration at a result that prevented his side from going top of the table. "Having scored so late on, we are a bit disappointed not to get three points," said Dalglish. "But over the 90 minutes a draw was a fair result."

Fortunately this home draw did not see Liverpool lose any ground at the top. Despite not fielding their best side, Manchester United led Watford at Old Trafford until the last minute, but were denied all three points by a late Colin West equaliser. The principal beneficiaries of Liverpool and United's late concessions were Everton, who also left it late against Southampton at the Dell. Despite twice being behind, an 85th minute Trevor Steven shot from 25-yards saw them win 3-2. The victory moved the Blues up to sixth place – and back within shouting distance of the leading duo. They lay seven points off Liverpool, who remained two points behind Manchester United at the top.

Liverpool v Tottenham Hotspur
Screen Sport Super Cup group stage
Tuesday 3 December 1985

"'Pure Marxist theology' is the reported reaction of one senior member of the Government to the Church of England's report on the state of the inner cities. Other critics have spoken of 'naïve clerics'.

"Such emotional outbursts – before the report has even been officially published – show the sensitivity of the Government to any criticism of its policy towards the inner cities. Could it reflect a sense of guilt that it has not done enough and still has no adequate plans to tackle the huge problems which have built up over many years?

"...Church leaders are right to express their concern at the fragmentation of the nation into haves and have-nots and to put forward their ideas for solutions...[but the report] should produce more from Mrs Thatcher than irritation. It should lead to much more vigorous action."

Liverpool Echo, Comment, 2 December 1985

The Archbishop of Canterbury's Commission on Urban Priority Areas, in which Liverpool's much-loved Bishop David Sheppard played a significant role, had spent two years compiling its 400-page report into the state of the inner cities under Thatcherism. Together with Sir Richard O'Brien, Chairman of the commission, Sheppard dismissed its critics - principally Conservative MPs – who claimed the report, entitled Faith in the City: A Call to Action by Church and Nation, had, "Marxist overtones."

"I find it impossible to serve as a Christian in Merseyside," said Sheppard, "without concerning myself with the human issues which are affecting so many people's lives." Such a commendable, compassionate view wasn't shared by the Government however, with one Tory MP saying the report's authors were, "Communist clerics." Adding only sneering, dismissive comment to the debate, Thatcher herself called the bishops, "cuckoos."

Environment Secretary Mr Kenneth Baker, MP for Mole Valley - a rural seat in Surrey - was particularly scathing. He suggested that the reasons offered for the perceived problems quoted in the report - such as poor estate design; institutional racism; poor quality housing; and a chronic lack of investment in educational and social services – were without foundation. The report's proposed solutions had already been tried in the 1960s and 1970s he said, and had created, "hideous problems." By virtue of their subsequent silence however, it was clear the Government wasn't especially motivated to offer any alternative remedies.

In a meeting in defense of Liverpool's Labour councillors - held at the city's Polytechnic on Friday 6 December - renowned Labour MP Tony Benn compared the situation the report's authors now found themselves in with that also experienced by the local council. Benn told an audience of 600, including the city's Labour MPs Eric Heffer, Terry Fields, Bob Wareing and Eddie Loyden, that, "These councillors are under attack because anyone who dares to criticise capitalism or stands up to this government will be described as extremists, as church leaders are now learning following their report of the inner cities." The report had first been commissioned by the Archbishop of Canterbury as an investigation into the state of the inner cities after the riots of 1981. With Liverpool hosting Spurs in the Super Cup it was ironic that it was published just weeks after the latest riots had occurred - in Liverpool and Tottenham. Clearly the problems highlighted in the report still existed.

Boosted by their first win in six games at Villa Park on Saturday, Spurs were unchanged for Liverpool's penultimate Super Cup group match. Although still seen as a minor competition by many, a win here would guarantee the Reds a place in the tournament's two-legged semi-finals.

Clive Allen, who had been out for a year through injury, had scored in the 2-1 weekend win over Aston Villa, but his very recent return and absence of match-fitness hadn't stopped the marksman dreaming of making the England squad for the upcoming World Cup. "I've had a disastrous spell because of injury," he said, "but if I can maintain my consistency I can pressure the current England strikers." For Kopites at least, Allen's words were nonsensical - even Paul Walsh, who had scored nine goals in eight games for the Reds, wasn't certain of an England call up for Mexico. Together with West Ham and Scotland's Frank McAvennie, Walsh had been in-form striker of the late autumn; his goals catapulting Liverpool to within touching distance of Manchester United in the league.

With Steve McMahon suffering from a hamstring strain, the belligerent midfielder was left out by Dalglish – the first match he had missed since joining from Aston Villa 18 games ago – and Kevin Macdonald started his first game of the season in his place. With Dalglish choosing not to select himself yet again, even for the one of the two available places on the bench – which went to John Wark and Ronnie Whelan – Liverpool's midfield wore an unfamiliar look. Despite experimenting with Johnston in Whelan's usual place on the left, Sammy Lee on the right, and MacDonald alongside Molby – Dalglish's changes had no negative impact on Liverpool's recent good form and they "cut Spurs' defence to pieces with some superb football." Indeed, the home side could, "have had half a dozen goals with more accurate finishing."

With his outstanding form sparking speculation that international honours beckoned, Craig Johnston was, "playing with a fire and fury that suggested he had not given up hope of a last-second call to play in Australia's World Cup eliminator with Scotland." Johnston continued his recent excellence, covering almost every blade of grass to close players down or and using the ball perceptively from which to instigate another Liverpool attack. In the 20th minute the lively Australian linked up well with Beglin and Molby on the right side of midfield. After keeping the ball in play acrobatically on the touchline, he chipped, "a delicate pass forward for McDonald to beat both the offside trap and goalkeeper Clemence."

Even with the Kop, Kemlyn Road stand and the Paddock accepting cash at the turnstiles on the night, the 14,855 crowd was a low one and the opening goal was met with a subdued reaction from the sparse gathering of spectators. The attendance was dwarfed by the 41,000 who had attended the league meeting of the teams on the same ground in September. With the first candle already lit on the advent calendar, for the majority of locals there were clearly more pressing financial concerns than finding spare cash to watch this tournament. "Despite the number of star players in their ranks," Spurs threatened only briefly, their best efforts coming soon after the opening goal when, "after an ambitious run," Waddle hit a post. Clive Allen, doing his supposed England prospects no good at all, fired the rebound two feet wide of the post when well placed to level the scores.

Eight minutes into the second half Wark replaced Molby after the Dane took a kick on the calf. "Subsequently the standard of play deteriorated," said the Liverpool Echo, "although that was not the Scotsman's fault." Despite the local paper's unenthusiastic view of the second period, both Molby and Rush missed further chances for Liverpool before Walsh headed his 10th goal in nine games from Hansen's right wing cross just after the hour mark. The game was effectively over at this juncture and thus Liverpool's place in the semi-final's assured – although there was still one group game - at Spurs - still to play in January.

Liverpool remained on top for the remainder of the game but failed to add to the score. Such was their dominance that they could, "have reached double figures had Rush demonstrated the finishing power for which he is famous." On another off night for the Welshman he, "barely reached Clemence with one shot from well inside the penalty area," before heading a pinpoint cross by Walsh, who was always lively, "high into the Kop," soon after.

Liverpool's experimental midfield formation had, "looked most impressive," with MacDonald's goalscoring return, Lee's contribution and Johnston's performance - on the left - all "giving their manager food for thought." For all the efforts of the occasional performers however, it was another man in form who won the Man-of-the-Match award – for the second game in succession. Mark Lawrenson "completely dominated the middle of the field and was as impressive going forward as he was when keeping Spurs' forwards under control."

With their Super Cup passage assured, Liverpool could now contemplate a packed December programme of league action with five games in 22 days, giving them the chance to exert further pressure on the leaders. Along with his quintet of fellow 'Anglos' Dalglish could also look forward to a fourth consecutive trip to the World Cup Finals when a goalless draw in Melbourne meant Scotland had advanced past Australia to book their tickets to Mexico.

Liverpool v Aston Villa
Saturday 7 December 1985

"As the great championship race enters December Manchester United's title rivals are more determined than ever to make it a black Christmas for the men from Old Trafford. A month ago they were runaway leaders and you could have wall papered every house in Manchester with the headlines that hailed them as champions. It's a wonder Howard Kendall didn't drive down the East Lancashire Road and personally hand over the Canon League trophy to Ron Atkinson. After all, why worry about the remaining 27 matches when it's a one-horse race?"

Ken Rogers, Football Echo, 2 December

Such was Manchester United's complete loss of recent form - two draws and two defeats in four league games - that a victory for Liverpool at home to a Villa side who were in 14th position and just two points off a relegation place, could see the Reds leapfrog their great rivals and go top of the table for the first time all season. In order to do so however, the Reds would also have to be reliant on United slipping up again - at home to Ipswich Town.

Following his fine performance in the midweek win over Spurs, Sammy Lee retained his place at the expense of Ronnie Whelan, whilst Kevin MacDonald continued for Steve McMahon who had yet to recover from his hamstring strain.

In contrast to the home side, Villa's recent form had been poor; without a win in four and with six defeats in their last nine league games. While Liverpool had been securing their place in the Screen Sport Super Cup semi-final, Villa had been bolstering their creaking defence (27 goals conceded in 19 league games) by acquiring Paul Elliott from Luton Town for £400,000. The expensive new signing - and former teenage associate of Paul Walsh - was expected to make his Villa debut at Anfield.

Walsh and Elliott had known each other since they were 12-years old. They had played school and youth football together before they were both snapped up by Charlton Athletic. Moves to Luton Town soon followed and the pair starred in the same Hatters side as they established their credentials in the top flight. Prior to the game Elliott told reporters that there was nothing he didn't know about the in-form Walsh. "I know he's a hell of a good player," he said. "I suppose he and Ian Rush are just about the best pair of strikers playing at the moment," the England Under-21 international added, "and they are guaranteed to keep defenders on their toes for the whole 90 minutes."

With Villains' skipper Alan Evans – Elliott's intended partner in central defence – missing through injury, the debutant's glowing assessment of his friend Walsh was to prove prophetic on a dank December afternoon at Anfield. Evans was replaced by young Dean Glover at centre half, whilst former Everton striker Andy Gray and Simon Stainrod were both passed fit to play up front. Another exciting player returning from a long-term injury was Gary Shaw, who had scored 15 goals in 15 reserve games during his most recent rehabilitation. The former Young Player of the Year - in 1981 when Villa were Champions - was named as substitute. It was not to be a heroes return for Shaw however.

Intriguingly, the encounter also saw two Australian rivals line up against each other – Craig Johnston and Tony Dorigo. Whilst Johnston had made himself available for selection for Australia's second-leg of their World Cup play-off with Scotland the previous week – a 0-0 draw that saw the Socceroos' qualification hopes ended – Dorigo had recently turned down an Australian call-up. As he had yet to receive a full-cap from the country of his birth, Dorigo had instead chosen to represent England – the home of his parents.

Within just 100 seconds of the kick-off Liverpool had the perfect start when a foul on Rush on the edge of the penalty area gave Liverpool's dead ball specialist Jan Molby the opportunity to open the scoring. He didn't need asking twice. Goalkeeper Nigel Spink, "expecting a typical rocket, was fooled completely as the big Dane chipped the ball accurately into the opposite corner."

A goal up with barely two minutes gone, the stage was set for Liverpool – unbeaten in 14 games since early October - to win comfortably but, with Rush continuing to misfire when in front of goal following several missed chances in midweek, this was as good as the scoreline got for the home side in the first half. Rush's, "temporary loss of finishing power made Liverpool work much harder than had seemed likely once they went in front," said Ian Hargraves. "The Welsh star, once so deadly near goal, missed four or five chances in the first half alone," with one in particular – a shot that hit the bar – summing up his last four scoreless games perfectly. Well placed in the area, unmarked, time to control the ball - and even to pick his shot - but still the ball wouldn't go in the net. Rush however, had seen these relatively short barren spells before. When his sights were fractionally out his misses could appear spectacular, but those that had watched him closely knew that once the curse was broken, any drought in front of the net was often followed by a glut of goals. Liverpool wisely continued to feed Rush chances, regardless of this erratic phase.

Villa also showed plenty of spirit and, aided by Liverpool's profligacy in the area and – alarmingly - in possession, they threatened a shock equaliser on a number of occasions. As early as the 11th minute Gray bundled his way past Lawrenson and sent in a fierce shot that Grobbelaar managed to parry but could not hold. Fortunately for Liverpool, Hansen was on hand to clear. "I'll never know how he even saw that one of mine at the near post, let alone clear it," Gray told reporters after the game. "It was a great piece of goalkeeping – incredible reflexes."

The former Everton forward - the Players' Player of the Year in 1977 during his first stint at Villa – was, "pulling out all the stops against his old rivals," but went a bit too far when challenging MacDonald midway through the half. The Liverpool midfielder went down in a heap after a typically clumsy, centre-forward's tackle and Gray was immediately booked. Liverpool continued to press and Molby then forced a good parry from Spink with a fierce left foot shot only for Johnston to volley the rebound over the bar.

Apart from his fine save from Gray, Grobbelaar hadn't had much to do but in 23rd minute he kept Liverpool in front when he, "pulled out a magnificent save to prevent Villa equalising." A long throw by Bradley was touched forward by Gray and a close range shot from Mark Walters looked a certain goal, "before the goalkeeper's intervention."

"Liverpool were playing well in flashes," said Hargraves, "but only rarely managing to put effective passing moves together." When they managed to do so however, few teams could compete and when Johnston and Lee combined well on the left they almost scored, "Rush [eventually] volleying Beglin's centre over."

Debutant Elliott had played well up to now but a slip then gave Rush yet another chance. The Liverpool striker, "in one of those nightmare runs where even the easiest chances somehow slip the wrong side of the post", hit a right foot shot straight at the keeper. Another shot against the bar soon followed - before the Welshman's travails continued when he fired a Nicol cross wide.

As Liverpool continued to cram on the pressure but with no reward, the frustrations of the crowd became all too audible. "A splendid move begun by Johnston and carried on by Beglin," then ended with Macdonald shooting high over the bar when he could have done better. The groans continued and the interval arrived soon after – "with Liverpool wishing they had accepted more of their chances."

Paul Walsh would reveal after the game that - showing a trait hitherto unseen by his players - Dalglish tore into his side at half-time, lambasting them for their failure to capitalise on their fantastic start. "The boss gave us a rollicking at half-time," Walsh said, "and we went out and did the job." The player-manager's words seemed to have struck a chord and Liverpool's play in the second half was much more dynamic; their finishing eventually more clinical.

The second half was just 30 seconds old when Elliott was booked for a crude challenge on Beglin and, "This was the signal for a tremendous offensive during which Rush just failed to connect with a low cross from Macdonald, Stainrod kicked a Johnston shot off the line and Beglin grazed the bar." Somehow however, Villa hung on. Walters then, "caused a minor panic when he swept around Lawrenson and centred to Gray whose shot was scrambled off the line." It was a timely reminder – if any were needed - that for all their second-half possession and pressure, Liverpool held only a slender lead.

"Lee almost did the trick with a splendid through ball to MacDonald who had moved forward intelligently into space," but the bustling midfielder who many on the Kop loved to hate, saw his shot well saved by Spink. Revelling in their own unappealing and unintelligent scapegoating, those who took a perverse pleasure in MacDonald's misfortunes swapped smug smiles and knowing glances – they, and not the manager, obviously knew best.

"Some of Liverpool's approach work was brilliant," with Johnston especially in good form. On 55 minutes he rounded Dorigo easily and crossed high into the area only to find Liverpool player was there to convert. It was another, "typically all-action performance," from the Australian whose frustrations of previous seasons were fast becoming a distant memory. On the bench however, Dalglish's annoyance was evident once more at Liverpool's failure to score another and almost certainly secure the three points. Molby headed down in the box from a Lee corner soon after but again, no Liverpool player was within five yards of the ball and Dalglish threw his arms out wide in exasperation.

Frustration almost turned to despair just after hour mark when Villa broke away and nearly scored. The ball found Hodge who fired in a, "dipping vicious shot from 20-yards which Grobbelaar did well to clutch at full stretch."

Contemplating a change, Dalglish instructed substitute Whelan to warm up. While many on the Kop salivated at the prospect of MacDonald making way, Villa made a change of their own; Gary Shaw replacing Stainrod in a switch that, unfortunately for the visitors, "only had the effect of triggering off a second Liverpool goal." The substitute's first touch was a poor one, sending the ball straight to Sammy Lee. The committed and dedicated scouse midfielder fed Molby whose, "splendid pass," of 40-yards was taken effortlessly in his stride by Walsh. "The nimble striker cut inside [Williams] before beating Spink all ends up with a low shot." The fans' cult hero recorded his 11th goal in eleven games and, "immediately sparked off chants of 'Walshie for England' from the Kop."

His delight evident for all to see, Dalglish signalled for Whelan to return to the bench, before urging his men forward to attack again and again. Spink's performance prevented the Reds from scoring another two or three and the only further reward for their pressure was a third goal from Man-of-the-Match Johnston, "Liverpool's dominant player," nine minutes from the end. "At the heart of so many things," the Australian netted after a fine through pass from Walsh. "Taking the switch from the right side of midfield to the left in his stride, he showed the adaptability of the naturally gifted footballer, and the goal was full reward for his performance."

As the older stand season-ticket holders drifted away apparently uninterested all ears on a youthful Kop were cupped to the soothing tones of George Sephton, but when he announced that United had beaten Ipswich and, as expected, Everton had defeated bottom club WBA 3-0 at the Hawthorns, any hopes they had of seeing the Reds top the table for the first time that season were dashed.

As they melted into the night however, the atmosphere was one of contented anticipation. For a side supposedly, "in the throes of transition," Liverpool were playing well. This was their 19th victory in 27 games - with just two defeats. And yet, "although most of the names were familiar, it is a fact" reported the Echo, "that only four players; Grobbelaar, Hansen, Lawrenson and Rush, are now occupying positions they filled regularly last season."

Liverpool's new-look defence seemed as strong as ever – perhaps even with more to offer when going forward - and their attack, notwithstanding Rush's current blip, was scoring freely. In midfield, where Molby was, "starting to exercise a giant's influence," the aggressive and tough-tackling McMahon was soon due to return from injury. And they still had Dalglish, "almost certainly the best player not actually competing in the first division," to call upon if, and when, he deemed it necessary.

"With so much competition for places," Hargraves said, "Liverpool will take a lot of stopping…its getting quite like old times at Anfield again." Any new-look side would not feature old style players however, with Phil Neal said to be close to taking over at Third Division Bolton. Such optimism was shared by almost all Reds' fans - with United struggling to rediscover their swashbuckling early season form, surely they asked themselves, it was only a matter of time before Dalglish's charges assumed their rightful place at the top of the division?

Chapter Four
When it All Comes Down

Arsenal v Liverpool
Saturday 14 December 1985

"England's football clubs will be allowed to play friendly matches against clubs from other countries next season. FIFA, world soccer's ruling body, announced today it was satisfied, 'adequate measures,' had been taken against hooliganism. FIFA's decision is not unexpected. Their blanket ban was imposed in haste and without serious consideration, and it involved a number of ridiculous anomalies, like the prevention of games between English and Scottish clubs. European clubs in particular have made it clear they want to play teams like Liverpool, Everton and Manchester United..."

Liverpool Echo, Saturday 7 December 1985

The news that FIFA would allow English teams to play lucrative friendly matches against foreign opposition from next season may have been greeted with relief and rubbing of hands by club chairmen elsewhere, but for Liverpool directors and fans the announcement was also tinged with frustration. The ban on English sides as a result of Heysel had been imposed for an indefinite period - but no matter the subsequent length in years, an extra season had been added to Liverpool's exile. Even if they would soon be allowed to participate in lucrative friendlies in Scandinavia, Ireland or Germany – where most of their widespread continental support lay - there would be no immediate prospect of a return to European competition for the Reds.

Kopites therefore, had already resigned themselves to concentrating on domestic matters only and, as the festive season approached, they cheered themselves by looking ahead to a run of games over Christmas that promised a potential takeover at the top of the League for their in-form side. Nearing the half-way point of the campaign Liverpool were handily placed in second, just two points behind the faltering leaders, Manchester United.

Unbeaten since defeat at QPR in early October - a run of nine league games - the Reds' next engagement was a trip to Highbury to face Arsenal. The Gunners had been easily despatched on the opening day of the season and their away form since then had been poor. They trailed the leading pack and, in eighth place, were 12 points behind Liverpool.

Arsenal manger and England coach Don Howe was resisting a growing clamour to see him replaced. Never shy to jump on any bandwagon so long as it helped sell newspapers, the London press corps had thrown the name of Barcelona manager, Terry Venables, into the mix and, persuaded by their machinations some Arsenal fans warmed to the idea of an approach for the flamboyant Londoner - a potentially more glamorous appointment than their often derided, Wolverhampton-born current manager.

Although under pressure, Howe was renowned for an organised and defensive approach to the game. Up front however, his ideas failed to sparkle and Arsenal had scored just 22 goals in their 20 league games to date – a smaller tally than scored by each of the bottom five. Their uninspiring, inconsistent form had also seen their attendances drop alarmingly, to as low as 16,673 in their previous home game - a dour goalless draw with Birmingham.

Not too many Arsenal supporters would be paying the extortionate £19.99 for Mirror

Vision's Soccer 85 video cassette which was advertised in the day's match programme. The tape offered unseen coverage of 16 Canon League matches televised abroad during the continuing English TV blackout, and may even have appealed to Liverpool followers - but not at approximately eight-times the price of admission to a live game. Using the same arbitrary scale this would equate to around £320 today.

Arsenal fans were becoming, "increasingly critical of a side full of expensive players like Tony Woodcock, Charlie Nicholas, Kenny Samson and Viv Anderson," said the Echo. "They have consistently failed to live up to expectations and the feeling is that if matters do not improve rapidly Howe will be for the chop." After a short winter break in Trinidad however, their beleaguered manager was hopeful that the recall of Graham Rix in midfield, and the surprising selection of debutant Niall Quinn – in place of Woodcock - would mark a turning point in their season.

Howe freely admitted that he hadn't been taking too much of an interest in Liverpool's form of late. "I haven't seen Liverpool since they beat us at Anfield some time ago," he said, "but they have been going well and it should be a great game." Arsenal also dropped Kirkby-born Tommy Caton in favour of the emerging young centre-half, Martin Keown.

Despite Liverpool's recent form Dalglish opted to change a winning side and recalled Steve McMahon, recovered from a hamstring injury, at the expense of Kevin MacDonald, who was relegated to the bench. If anything however, the return of McMahon - perhaps playing within himself to prevent a further strain - had a negative influence as Liverpool endured a difficult afternoon in North London.

A coach with England who would be travelling to Mexico with Bobby Robson and the World Cup squad, Howe had his critics. In an age when more ostentatious, media-savvy managers such as Venables and Ron Atkinson were coming to the fore, many saw the Arsenal boss as dull and uninspiring. In reality however, Howe was a pragmatic, yet free-thinking coach, but his persistent realism was a source of annoyance to disenchanted Arsenal fans. Here though, he was to achieve some respite from his critics as his refreshed, new-look side found themselves a goal up within five minutes of the kick-off.

There seemed little danger when Molby and Lawrenson broke up an early Arsenal attack but the normally dependable centre-half – arguably Liverpool's outstanding player of the season so far – aimed a, "suicidal pass," towards right back Nicol who was caught in possession by Rix. The loose ball fell to a surprisingly alert Nicholas, "who beat Grobbelaar with a fine left-foot shot from just inside the box." There was a half-hearted appeal for offside from the Reds' keeper but the referee waved him away.

The shock of the early goal threw Liverpool out of their stride and Paul Davis almost increased the lead, "with a dangerous looking shot from 25-yards," soon after the opener. Although Liverpool tried to fight back, "they never exercised any sort of control and were particularly ineffective in midfield where they were generally second to the ball."

Rush's recent woes continued to trouble him – and not just in front of goal. A goal-kick awarded by Oxford referee Dennis Hedges – when it was clearly a corner-kick to the away side – was disputed vigorously by a number of players, none more so than the Welsh striker, who was given a lengthy reprimand by the match official. The same referee had sent off Everton's Kevin Sheedy for dissent a month earlier - in Arsenal's 6-1 reverse at Goodison.

Molby especially, and McMahon on his return to the side, tried to get the Reds back into the game, "and one of their combined efforts set Johnston free on the left." Although he was able to reach the by-line, the winger's cross was just too deep for Walsh. As combative as ever, and relishing his selection for a third consecutive game, Sammy Lee then won a tackle just outside the Arsenal penalty area and his neat pass found Rush whose shot was charged down. Guilty of ball watching however, Liverpool could only stand back as Arsenal immediately broke away through Kenny Sansom - who was faring better against Nicol than he had when the teams met in August. The England left back ran almost the length of the pitch before feeding Nicholas whose shot this time was well held by Grobbelaar.

Slowly however, Liverpool began to get back into the game, and Walsh, "won applause for a brilliant dribble past three opponents," which although exciting the away fans, ultimately came to nothing. Molby then had a powerful drive deflected for a corner before Nicol, "sent an even more powerful shot just wide of an upright."All this effort was to prove futile in the 25th minute however, when a goal by Quinn, "once again owed a good deal to Liverpool error."

Ambling forward from midfield, the unchallenged Davis suddenly found himself in space at the edge of the area where he tried his luck with another long-range shot. His earlier shot had been easily dealt with by the Liverpool keeper, but there was considerably more venom in this one and the ball, moving through the air, "rebounded from Grobbelaar's chest straight to Quinn who hammered it into the net from close range."

The 6' 4" former Gaelic footballer and hurler had been told he was playing just an hour and a half before kick-off, but with an, "admirable temperament and 18 reserve (team) goals," his immediate impact caused considerable problems for Liverpool's normally formidable defence. His manager's faith in him had been repaid handsomely. "I just had to toss him in and hope he was ready," Don Howe said after the game.

Showing all the youthful energy and eagerness expected of a young player relishing the opportunity afforded him, Quinn was having an outstanding game and most of Arsenal's attacks, either in the air or on the ground, involved the lanky debutant. Just a few minutes after scoring, he was unlucky to see a fine header from a Rix cross pushed around the post by Grobbelaar.

Soon after, Liverpool did manage to pressure the home side when, "a superb pass by McMahon enabled Johnston to lay the ball back for Molby but the Dane's shot flew just wide." Then, a few minutes before the interval, "Liverpool came within inches of halving the deficit when Lee pinged a corner kick to McMahon whose powerful shot seemed certain to ripple the net until Lukic intervened to tip it past the post."

The half-time break was an opportunity for a glum-faced Dalglish – visibly gathering his thoughts on his way from the dug-out - to read the riot act to his players. The Liverpool player-manager was particularly scathing in the dressing room at his side's inability, especially in midfield, to compete as he expected.

The second half - though scrappy - saw a much better Liverpool performance, but without the goal their improved efforts warranted. At times their approach was chaotic, with players "in each others way through over-eagerness." This was apparent in the 58th minute when, "Rush and Walsh almost collided," after an attack started by Lawrenson.

Liverpool's, "basic problems seemed to be in midfield where Arsenal were both quicker to the ball and more inventive." Few tried harder to improve and improvise more than Sammy Lee however, and when the Anfield-born firebrand and McMahon managed to combine well, Lee fed Rush for a half-chance but his snap shot flew well wide. Player of the moment Mark Lawrenson – and Liverpool's man-of-the-match again here - then went on a tremendous run beginning from inside his own half. "The centre back burst down the middle, played a one-two with Rush and narrowly failed to beat goalkeeper Lukic to the return ball." Under such Liverpool pressure, "Arsenal showed signs of fallibility," but the Reds' defensive frailties almost allowed the home side to add to their lead just after the hour mark when, "a bad ball by Beglin out of defence almost set up another goal for Quinn."

MacDonald had replaced Lee moments before this chance, but Liverpool's overall performance remained erratic with the midfielders the main culprits. "Molby seemed unusually slow," wrote Hargraves, "McMahon understandably rusty and Lee simply uninspired. Their passes were intercepted with frightening regularity and Walsh had few chances to show how he has averaged a goal a game." While the criticism was justified, Liverpool had managed to create some chances but poor finishing let them down once more. With ten minutes to go Hansen made a rare foray upfield and his accurate header from a Johnston cross found the Welshman unmarked in the area. "Rush seemed to have plenty of time but unaccountably pulled his shot wide." It was easily Liverpool's best chance of the game. Minutes later Nicol's rising shot struck an upright. Then MacDonald headed wide from an awkward angle.

At times Liverpool had played well enough to score, especially in the second half, "but luck was a stranger." Their frustrations at such a patchy performance were exemplified just two minutes from the end of the game when, in quick succession, first Beglin – on the advice of a linesman – and then Nicol, were booked for clumsy challenges.

After the game Dalglish could barely conceal his disappointment – and anger - at seeing his side throw away their 14-match unbeaten run. "I'm disappointed more with their attitude than their play," said the player-manager. "If they had applied themselves a bit more we could have had a better result today [but] the first goal was a direct result of our approach." Dalglish dismissed suggestions that Arsenal's first goal was offside, preferring instead to concentrate on the inadequacies of his own side rather than any favourable decision afforded to his opponents. "If you don't compete," he said succinctly, "you don't deserve the referee to favour you."

For Arsenal, as well as some much needed points easing the pressure on their manager, the game also pleased the board of directors, as the crowd of 35,048 was their second highest of the season. Victory moved the Gunners up a place to seventh in the table but more significantly, the gap between Manchester United and their closest pursuers was restored to five points. Their 3-1 win at Villa Park saw Mark Hughes score his first goal in nine games.

The season had now reached its halfway point with the leading teams having played 21 games. West Ham's 2-0 win over Birmingham saw the Hammers move to third, level on 44 points with Liverpool, with Chelsea fourth and Sheffield Wednesday fifth. Reigning Champions Everton lost 2-1 at home to Leicester - for whom Gary McAllister scored the equaliser and set up the winner – and they languished in sixth place, 12 points off top spot with much work to do if they were to re-enter the title race.

As Christmas approached, United held sway and appeared favourites at this stage of the season, but experienced observers were reluctant to make lavish predictions as to the League Championship's eventual outcome.

Back in Liverpool, a new TV comedy show was also the subject of much discussion, with filming of Carla Lane's Bread taking place in the Dingle area of the city. Some saw the story of a family of scouse benefit cheats as little more than harmless fun, but others were less welcoming of yet another opportunity to stereotype the city and its people. "Mike Bell of Merseyside Welfare Rights Centre claimed the programme will be doing a disservice to the city. 'I think there is enough bad publicity about Merseyside without someone misrepresenting the people up here.'" The series was a national hit - and ran until 1991.

Liverpool v Newcastle United
Saturday 21 December 1985

"Sanity returned to soccer when the 92 football league clubs bowed to the inevitable and resumed their partnership with television. The five-month black out was planned to pull back the fans to see in the flesh what was being denied them from the comfort of their armchairs. Instead it turned out to be the most disastrous public relations exercise in the history of sport.

"Advertising hoardings disappeared from grounds, sponsors shirked from pumping money into an invisible product and, as the blackout bill ran into millions, spectators deserted the game in droves. Small wonder then that the clubs dashed back to the negotiating table.

"The television companies who originally offered a staggering £19.2million over four years, and then almost £4million for a single season, have come away with a bargain – the better half of the season for a cut-price £1.3million."

Liverpool Echo 20 December 1985

Just days before Christmas it seemed that the dispute that had prevented football from being shown on TV all season was finally coming to end. Viewed at first as a petty spat between two sides who seldom had the best interests of the match-going supporter uppermost in their minds, the quarrel had quickly become a prevalent topic for the media, scrutinised by the broadsheets, and discussed by contributors to late-night magazine TV shows. The general consensus among social commentators was that football was destroying itself from within and, if the predominately middle-class media assessment was anything to go by, few seemed to care.

At first, not many supporters had understood the intractable actions on both sides and, as the issue dragged on and on through early autumn and winter, even the most passionate fans were losing interest in the saga. For those who attended matches however, the absence of the cameras made little difference. Indeed, for some there was even a certain smugness that only those who bothered attending were able to view one of the most exciting seasons in recent memory.

As the winter nights drew in a resolution to the saga seemed an increasingly forlorn hope until the League, realising that the absence of TV coverage, instead of encouraging fans out of their armchairs had in fact marginalised the sport still further, eventually caved in to the demands of the broadcasters. With, "League football now likely to be back on the nation's screens in the New Year," casual supporters and older fans of the game could at least look forward to seeing what they had hitherto been denied with the renewal of the Match of the Day and The Big Match highlights package, and the occasional live transmission.

"Perhaps the greatest tragedy of all," wrote Hargraves, "was that [post-Heysel] the game made a magnificent effort to put its house in order but lost, in television, its greatest ally. Not only were grounds safer but the football was spectacular. English viewers were denied – United's start, Liverpool's fight back, McAvennie's 19 goals, Molby and Lineker etc." Of the season's early games, footage exists from just a small number that were, ironically, transmitted abroad. The appetite for the English game was, despite the European ban, as huge as ever.

Negotiations between the two sides in the TV dispute had been ongoing for over a year. Originally the League had refused to agree to show more than a handful of live matches, with the TV companies in return refusing to approve the showing of recorded highlights. The result? No football on TV and supporters, already blighted by hooliganism, racism and poor facilities, deserted the game in droves. Almost every club saw a significant drop in attendances.

It seems absurd that fans were denied the chance to see one of the most exciting seasons in recent years, with – up until Christmas at least – five or six sides in with a real chance of title glory, but the root of all these problems was money, and the pursuit of it, by over-eager and over-reaching chairman who had failed to understand the importance of wide TV exposure and the attendant media coverage necessary to advance and increase the profile of the sport.

Both parties had in fact managed to reach agreement earlier in the year, "only for the clubs to throw out their negotiators' recommendations on the advice of Oxford chairman Robert Maxwell." There was hushed talk about a new breakaway 'super league', free of Football League control, and maybe even a British Cup competition, but for now at least, none of these ideas came to fruition. It would be another seven years before the clubs were powerful enough to leave the League behind and form the Premier League.

Resolving the dispute owed much to the efforts of Everton Chairman Phillip Carter. He and BBC Head of Sport Jonathan Martin had, "found fresh ground to explore," during a private meeting in early December. Here, the outlines of a compromise had been reached. The League agreed to show six live matches from January plus live screening of both Milk Cup semi-finals – in return the TV companies were prepared to increase the number of recorded highlights from the original 14 matches.

The new money from the TV deal, although significantly less than what was first offered at the start of the season, was a welcome addition to the revenues of clubs who had been hard hit by the downturn in attendances, but it was to little too late for fans of Third Division Swansea City who were in danger of seeing their club wound up in the High Court. On the day Liverpool faced Newcastle, the Swans failed to fulfil their fixture against Walsall and, with £146,000 owed to the Inland Revenue, their hopes were pinned on finding a late, late saviour to come to their rescue and prevent them flirting with closure – an experience familiar to followers of Charlton Athletic, Derby County and Bristol City in recent years.

Another saga that had intrigued Merseysiders over the course of the football season also came to a conclusion during the week – the jailing of local crime figure Tommy 'Tacker' Comerford for 14 years, later extended to 20 for drug trafficking, at the Old Bailey. One of the first criminals in the country to establish an international drug trafficking network, Comerford became known – and respected - in Liverpool crime circles courtesy of rumours that he had forced the London-based, murderous Kray twins from the city in the 1960s.

He then hit the headlines in 1971 when he was jailed for 10 years for his part in a raid on the old District Bank in Water Street. Comerford and his gang spent two days tunnelling into the strong room and, after breaking through the steel doors with thermal lances, they made off with an estimated £140,000. Only when Comerford's QC gave a senior policeman a light from a cigarette lighter that was part of the haul - during a boxing show at the Adelphi Hotel - was the crime eventually traced back to Comerford. With more than a hint of irony the lighter had been a gift from 'Tacker' to his lawyer.

On his release Comerford organized a gang to pick up a consignment of cannabis from North Africa but, after local Drugs Squad and customs officers discovered the plot, he was arrested again. Never one to shy away from publicity, Comerford cemented his place in Mersey folklore by holding daily 'press conferences' for reporters during each day of his trial at Liverpool crown court. He was eventually jailed for seven years - reduced to four on appeal.

Finally, in the summer of 1984 the regional crime squad was tipped off that Comerford would be flying from Stuttgart to Heathrow. After walking through the 'nothing to declare' exit, he and an accomplice were arrested and found with a suitcase containing half a kilo of heroin.

The façade of a man with a council flat in Lee Vale Road, Belle Vale who used a rent rebate and further benefits to decorate it and buy a cooker, was at an end. He had masterminded an international drugs operation that stretched from Colombia to Pakistan. As he was sentenced and sent down, Tacker looked at the judge and wished him 'Happy Christmas.' It was the stuff of a Hollywood crime biopic.

If the TV dispute and Comerford's trial had appalled and enthralled onlookers in equal measure, Liverpool's game with ninth placed Newcastle United was another intriguing encounter, captivating a crowd of 30,746 to the same degree.

Shorn of the use of Phil Neal as an able deputy should Steve Nicol be injured or unavailable – the right-back signed as player-manager with Bolton Wanderers the same afternoon - Dalglish had delayed naming his side even later than usual, mainly due to doubts over the fitness of Grobbelaar. The keeper retained his place however, although Jan Molby was granted a well-earned rest - John Wark taking his place. MacDonald also missed out as the player-manager named himself on the bench for the first time since his substitute appearance against West Brom in mid-November.

Perhaps as a result of shuffling his pack Dalglish, and the supporters who witnessed the Arsenal defeat, expected Liverpool to show a much more positive attitude than that displayed when losing at Highbury. Instead, Kopites were treated to almost the worst possible start when, inside the first 60 seconds Newcastle advanced into penalty area and, "Lawrenson dropped Paul Gascoigne with a flying tackle from behind."

With home fans dreading the concession of another early goal referee Keith Hackett, "immediately thrust a finger towards the penalty spot." On the touchline however, a linesman had failed to grab his attention immediately but on seeing a raised flag, the referee blew up and ambled across to consult with his colleague. To the relief of the Kop, young Gascoigne had strayed offside before Lawrenson's tackle and, thanks to the intervention of the man with the red flag, the decision was reversed and play restarted with a Liverpool free-kick. The linesman's name? Mr Everton. Crisis averted – for now.

Four minutes later it appeared that normal service was resumed when, "a bewildering move by Liverpool ended with a side-footer from Ian Rush," which rebounded off Martin Thomas without the keeper knowing too much about it. Home fans readied themselves for more of the same, but the Red's midfield and attack gradually fell into the same stupor that had afflicted them in North London and, as possession was wasted and attacks became increasingly rare, Newcastle began to dominate. After the recent departures of both Kevin Keegan and Chris Waddle, the visitors were short on experienced star players but they had a great work ethic and, in Peter Beardsley, "a young man on the fringe of great things." The tricky, diminutive number 10 was, "the No 1 menace to the home defence," all afternoon.

Newcastle's defence - marshalled by former Everton full-back John Bailey – was resolute and well-organised whilst on their right wing, 17-year old Paul Stephenson, his legs bowed to the extent that they resembled two bananas, looked to have the beating of Beglin all day. In the 15th minute a well-hit cross by the teenager, "brought a juicy header from Billy Whitehurst," that flew just inches over.

Seven minutes later, with the danger signs unheeded, Newcastle took the lead in uncomplicated fashion. "With the sweetest of contacts," Bailey "volleyed an enormous clearance from his own penalty area deep into enemy territory." Shaking off the attentions of Lawrenson, Beardsley – drawing admiring glances from those on the Kop and in the Liverpool dug-out - saw Grobbelaar coming off his line and his subsequent lob, "cunning in flight and pace, just managed to make it home off a post." It may have been a direct move, bordering on route one football, but it was an approach that often unsettled more cultured passing sides like Liverpool, and yet there was no mistaking the invention and precision of Beardsley's finish.

As was the Kop's way, they immediately roared their team on – even as Rush and Walsh stood on the centre spot to restart - but despite the increased vocal encouragement the failings that had been exposed by Arsenal resurfaced once again. The defence was nervous, the midfield strangely quiet, conceding possession cheaply and failing to provide Rush and Walsh with any clear sights of goal.

Even when the forwards managed to create opportunities of their own, luck was again a commodity that appeared to have deserted them. Just two minutes after conceding, "Rush must have felt that he would never score again," when, "having rounded the keeper brilliantly he deliberately angled his shot towards the net and stood back in amazement as John Anderson somehow scraped the ball from under the bar." The Welshman's barren run was, by his own standards, taking on epic proportions – five and a half games without a goal and all manner of misfortune suggested that Rush had mown down more than one black cat on his daily commute through the Mersey Tunnel.

Liverpool's luck finally turned in the 34th minute when McMahon, hitherto, "strangely anonymous," sent a, "magical pass inside to Steve Nicol." Newcastle's defence were well positioned to prevent any cross or pass but, with his options limited, the right-back decided to go it alone – "which meant threading his way across the penalty line, cutting through two tackles and then firing diagonally into the far corner." It was a fantastic strike that the young Scottish international's solid performances – especially considering his personal situation in relation his sick father – thoroughly deserved.

The equaliser galvanized Liverpool and at last they began to play more like a side with title aspirations. Just before the interval Rush wasted yet another, easier chance when Wark's, "20-yard bomber was beaten away by Thomas." The ball dropped perfectly at the Welshman's feet but, with all of Anfield about to celebrate his first goal in six games, the misfiring forward, "struck it over the top from six yards." As the Kop howled, he clutched his face in disbelief - his inner turmoil utterly transparent.

Even a second-half tactical switch by Dalglish – swapping the positions of midfielders Lee and Johnston - "made no difference to the way Newcastle were able to shut players down at tremendous speed." The visitors were further encouraged by a raucous away following which filled the away sections and had spilled over into the Anfield Road and Kemlyn Road stands where they mingled, apparently in harmony, with the seated Liverpool fans.

In, "a marvellously athletic game," the visitors, "allowed their hosts no breathing space," to gain even a minor foothold in the game and it was almost in desperation that the player-manager replaced Wark just after the hour mark. Although Dalglish, "got an enormous ovation", Liverpool's lethargy continued. Indeed, Newcastle were unlucky not to score a winner when Gascoigne eluded Nicol with just ten minutes remaining. "His final chip from the left was flicked away one-handed by Grobbelaar," and Hansen cleared. It was the last meaningful action of another disappointing game for Reds' fans and, as the home crowd faded into the developing early winter darkness, the legions of, "Geordie fans cheekily sang them homeward with a blasting chorus of You'll Never Walk Alone."

Dalglish was as frustrated as he was disappointed after the game, lamenting his side's failure to compete fully for the second game in a row, yet it was up to Ian Rush to put the thoughts of both manager and supporters into words. "We played terribly at Arsenal last week," he said, "and we were not at our best today, but at least we got a point."

On a personal level, Rush remained sanguine concerning his recent run of misfortune in front of goal. "I missed one for sure, and the keeper made a good save from me and I had another effort kicked off the line, but I have to keep going even though the goals have dried up." The Welshman concluded, somewhat presciently, that, "the fight for the title will probably go right to the end of the season."

Although they had dropped points at home for only the second time all season, results elsewhere ensured the Reds actually gained ground on the leaders. The loss at Arsenal the previous week was put in a more favourable light when news came through that Don Howe's resurgent side, including three teenagers, had beaten Manchester United at Old Trafford – Ron Atkinson's sides' first home defeat of the season. The result in Manchester soothed those disappointed Kopites who had stayed behind to await George Sephton's final score summary, and their pre-Christmas cheer was heightened when it was revealed that the United man they loved to hate – Norman Whiteside – had also seen a 20th minute penalty saved by John Lukic.

Fans knew that the dropped points here could be clawed back after the next round of matches, when a Boxing Day dual Merseyside v Manchester confrontation would see Liverpool travel to Maine Road to face a struggling City, while a stuttering United would motor in the opposite direction along the East Lancs Road to face an Everton side who had already beaten them convincingly twice this season, albeit in the Super Cup and Charity Shield. A 3-1 win over Coventry at Highfield Road saw the Blues, on a fine run of form, move to sixth in the league on 40 points. After a goalless draw at Luton, surprise package West Ham remained tied on 45 points with Liverpool in third place.

Manchester City v Liverpool
Thursday 26 December 1985

"A report drawn up by economic development director Geoff North shows nowhere in the peninsular is the jobless rate less than 10 per cent. Highest is in Birkenhead where, apart from the Bidston ward [which has 41.3 per cent], Tranmere has 37.1 per cent of the workforce unemployed and Birkenhead 36.1 per cent. In Wallasey, Leasowe has 28.5 per cent out of work, New Brighton 26.9 per cent and Seacombe 27 per cent.

Even the more affluent areas have their problems. Clatterbridge has an unemployment rate of 10.7 per cent, Heswall 10.8 per cent and Roydon 12.5 per cent. Labour group leader councillor George Clark said,] "these figures are obscene…I don't think the ruling group on Wirral council really appreciate the depth of despair people suffer in these areas of high unemployment. Unless proper representations are made to the government on this desperate situation, I can't see any improvement."

Liverpool Echo, 27 December 1985

The news that local unemployment had now risen to unprecedented levels ensured that the festive period was anything but for a large number of Merseysiders. If these figures weren't bad enough, those for youth and female unemployment were even higher. No wonder that in many households, young men and women were forced into making an unsettling and upsetting Yuletide decision – to leave their homes, families and friends, and travel, mainly South, in search of work. By the end of the year there were only 460,000 people living in the county – a 5% fall in just under four years; Liverpool suffered an 11% drop in the same period. It was estimated that 12,000 – mainly young – people were leaving the area every year.

Sean Doyle from Norris Green was part of the inevitable, soul-destroying drift to London;

"I remember like it was yesterday. I decided to leave after New Year. I knew I was leaving from about August '85 when my YTS at Yew Tree finished. So Christmas came and went and on 2 January 1986 and after a brief conversation with my family I left home on a National Express coach bound for London. I was 19."

Whilst those who travelled South in search for work were left to rue the breaking of links with family, friends and football that such a move demanded, those who remained embraced the sport as a means to escape the monotony of everyday life like never before and – unlike the rest of the country – crowds for both Liverpool and Everton actually increased during the season. Such a rise was no doubt helped by the increasingly intriguing battle both sides were fighting at the top of the table – with few, if any, able to confidently predict who would eventually come out on top. There were many ever-changing factors to consider – not least the recently unpredictable form of Liverpool.

With Dalglish once again opting to start without Jan Molby for the short Boxing Day trip to Maine Road, Reds' fans could be forgiven for worrying that their midfield might be out of sorts for the third game in a row.

Whereas midfield bite was lacking in their last game, in Manchester "through the control of Steve McMahon and the power play of Kevin MacDonald," Liverpool blew away the Christmas Day hangovers and conspired to give as good a midfield display as any that their fans would see all season. At a windswept Maine Road, both contributed greatly to a Reds' display that was as dominant as it was luckless.

Much pre-game talk had centred on the Reds' misfiring midfield and if Molby would return, "to provide the extra drive and inspiration that could take his team to the Championship." Opting to rest the Dane against a side who "look rather ordinary," were struggling to move clear of the relegation zone, and who had won only five of their 22 league games to date, Dalglish shuffled his midfield pack once more with Sammy Lee paying the price for the lacklustre showing against Newcastle. MacDonald came in at the expense of Wark who, like Lee, was dropped completely, whilst Dalglish named himself as substitute.

Alongside McMahon, MacDonald and Johnston the remaining midfield position was filled by Ronnie Whelan who, after four games out following the Anfield draw against Chelsea at the end of November, returned, "to inject fresh drive and imagination into midfield."

Despite having, "the virtue of guaranteed graft and dependability for the full 90 minutes," Lee's omission split fans' opinion with some feeling he had not had a fair crack of the whip in this, his testimonial season. Others however, were more forthright when expressing their opposing views. Never one to shy away from expressing a personal perspective relating to Liverpool's plight and freely dismissive of Dalglish's team selections, the doyen of the poison pens, Oxton's Len Griffiths, told the Football Echo's letters page that, "the return of Lee is a backward step. He belongs to the Paisley era, as did Neal and Kennedy."

Griffiths' criticisms didn't end there. "You never change a winning team," he added – a view that many fans would have agreed with – "and since the manager did, the side has looked unbalanced." Some would also have agreed with his assessment that, "Wark and MacDonald, like (the recently departed) Hodgson and Robinson, are not Liverpool types, and should be sold." However, even the football "mastermind" from Oxton would have found few who agreed in his evaluation of promising young Jim Beglin, who in filling a left-back position which was a problem for most of the title pretenders, the majority predicted would be a mainstay of the future. "Beglin is far too slow," Griffiths said, "and a decent left back must be purchased. Until these facts are accepted, Liverpool will continue to hover around the top, without actually taking over."

However, Griffiths' familiar rant was lent credence by the eventual outcome at Maine Road, and even more so when set in the context of the preceding, disappointing results at Arsenal and at home to Newcastle. "At the very moment when they should be taking over at the top," wrote Hargraves, "Liverpool seem to have lost their sense of direction. As against Newcastle and Arsenal they promised all sorts of exciting achievements…but somehow nothing quite came to fruition.

Despite creating numerous chances, the Reds' recent wastefulness in front of goal resurfaced once again. In previous games, especially against Newcastle, such profligacy, in a lacklustre showing, was countered by at least one effort finding the net – thereby salvaging at least a point. Conversely, Liverpool's lack of a clinical touch had also cost them earlier in the season, for example in the draw at Old Trafford, when they had turned in a good performance but passed up too many chances for the supporters' liking. This time however, "the longer the game lasted the less they looked like scoring," and Liverpool's sloppiness in defence and their creative play in midfield, was balanced neither by decent finishing nor good fortune in front of goal. Indeed, what luck was on offer at Maine Road was lapped up by the home side. With the only shot on target they had all afternoon, City scored. They could barely believe they had their first win against Liverpool since the corresponding Bank holiday fixture in 1981.

Liverpool had created numerous chances against Arsenal and Newcastle, but not even the most biased Red's fan could argue those performances merited three points. They had never looked in the game at Highbury, whilst a Peter Beardsley inspired Newcastle had simply taken advantage of a lack of purpose in Liverpool's midfield to grab a well-deserved point at Anfield.

On a bumpy Maine Road pitch, buffeted by gale-force winds blowing down from the Pennine's however, "it was a case of attack after attack breaking down as shots, centres and passes were blocked or booted to safety." Dalglish's side dominated possession, and, "much of [their] approach work had a slickness about it that one associates with championship teams," but for all their effort and precision, "throughout the whole 90 minutes there were only three occasions when Liverpool looked as if they might get the ball past Eric Nixon."

MacDonald hit a tremendous shot from 30-yards that the future Tranmere Rovers goalkeeping legend just managed to push round a post. McMahon clipped the bar with a delicate chip, and Dalglish volleyed just wide from Johnston's header. Despite over a dozen corners, half a dozen free kicks around the box, and almost 70% possession, this was the sum total of Liverpool's goal-bound efforts. By contrast, City's, "freak statistics," consisted of, "just a single corner, a single shot and a single header in 90 minutes of back-pedalling resistance."

"Quite what has gone wrong," said Hargraves, "is hard to say...[as] there was no lack of effort or commitment." Molby's continued absence was seen as one reason for the Reds' poor showing, but even accounting for this, "there were plenty of excellent combined movements with Johnston and Nicol linking up nicely on the right, MacDonald getting through a tremendous amount of work in the middle and Whelan looking encouragingly lively on his return." Unfortunately for Liverpool, "it all broke down when they reached the penalty area."The subtle Dane was missed however, when Liverpool won free-kicks around the City penalty area; "in Molby's absence dead ball situations were little more than an embarrassment and the corners were not much better."

City's defensive trio of Mick McCarthy, Kenny Clements, and David Phillips, "presented an impenetrable barrier against which strikers Walsh and Rush made no impression at all." Indeed, so well did City marshall Rush - now seven games without a goal - that the Welshman, "did not even have the satisfaction of getting into scoring positions...while Paul Walsh suffered such frustration that he was booked for a wild foul in the second-half and eventually substituted," on 61 minutes.

Dalglish's introduction came just after City unexpectedly scored. Liverpool's defence failed to clear a throw-in on the right, striker Gordon Davies beat Grobbelaar to the ball and his half-hit shot rebounded off the goalkeeper to Clive Wilson who, "brought down Liverpool's might army with a single grenade," to nod home with ease. "All I needed to do was keep my concentration and the header flew in through Steve Nicol's legs," Wilson told reporters after the game.

Such was the away side's dominance that even the home fans in the 35,584 crowd could scarcely believe they were ahead. City manager Billy McNeil conceded to the assembled press, "We had to play a protection game." But their luck held and Liverpool crashed to only their fourth defeat of the campaign – but their second inside three games.

When the game finished, the Liverpool players were as incredulous as anyone and, "the prospective champions tottered off the field as though shell-shocked." Somehow Liverpool had contrived to lose a game they had dominated from start to finish, " and squandered a marvellous chance to close the gap at the top."

"Dalglish must try to find out what had gone wrong," lamented Hargraves, "and get the goals flowing again while there is still time," Liverpool were now faced with a major test if they were to prove critics in the media wrong, assure the increasingly worried fans, and drain the ink from Len Griffith's bottomless well.

With Chelsea and West Ham also both losing their Boxing Day games, Everton were the only side in the top five to win, courtesy of a 3-1 drubbing of Manchester United at Goodison Park. A 30-yard screamer from Gary Stevens and a Gary Lineker brace were more than enough to condemn Ron Atkinson's side to yet another defeat and a miserable end to a year that, at one time, had promised so much. United still led the rest, but they were creaking badly. Finally showing last season's form of champions, the Blues had reduced the gap between them and United from 17 points to just six –in a little over a month.

Nottingham Forest v Liverpool
Saturday 28 December 1985

"Manchester's combined loss in rate support grant and housing support is £181.9 million. The gain is £3.7 million. For Birmingham, the comparable figures are a staggering loss of £214.5 million set against a gain of £3.4 million. Newcastle upon Tyne has had a loss of £101.9 million and a gain of £3.4 million. The record is the same for virtually all city and urban authorities. Liverpool has suffered the largest percentage of reduction in rate support grant of all—a staggering 76.4 per cent. reduction between 1981–82 and 1985–86.
Those authorities have had to cope with such cuts year on year for six consecutive years of Conservative Government. How dare Ministers claim that they are concentrating resources on those communities most in need? Such claims are a deception—frankly, a lie."

Dr Jack Cunningham, Labour MP for Copeland, Cumbria
House of Commons Debates 11 December 1985 vol 88 cc929-1007

Just two days after their unlikely and arguably undeserved defeat at Manchester City, Liverpool's hectic Christmas schedule continued with a trip to Nottingham to face an unpredictable Forest side that lay 10th in Division One. The Reds' were seeking a first league 'double' of the campaign, having won 2-0 at Anfield in September, but nothing could be taken for granted over any side managed by Brian Clough. Although Forest's glory days were seemingly over, enough of the rivalry generated in the late 1970s and early '80s remained to make this a fixture with plenty of needle, both on and off the pitch.

The wintry conditions at the City Ground were as much a barrier to good football as they had been at Maine Road, with persistent rain and cold wind in the first-half resulting in players from both sides slipping at inopportune times – much to the frustration of Dalglish, who had seemingly bowed to recent pressure by naming himself in the starting line up for the first time in two months. Before the game Ian Hargraves had argued that the player-manager faced one of, "the toughest decisions," of his reign when he sat down to select the side facing Clough's men. "He must decide," the reporter said, "whether to bring himself back into the side...or whether to persevere with the men who have temporarily lost their touch."

It was no easy decision for Dalglish to make, as bringing himself back – in his preferred and most effective position up-front – meant that he, "would first have to drop one of his team's joint top scorers – Ian Rush or Paul Walsh." Walsh had been averaging a goal a game up until the Arsenal defeat two weeks previously, so an argument could be made for his continued presence in the side. The same could not be said of Rush – who hadn't scored in seven matches – but, "it would take considerable courage to omit such a potentially dangerous marksman."

Offering versatility as well as skill and commitment, Dalglsih could of course start in midfield, but his, "impact is not as great there as it is up front," said Hargraves. With Molby expected to return to action after a spell out with an, "infected mouth," however, there seemed little chance he would recall himself to play in the centre of the pitch which would mean dropping either McMahon or MacDonald – who had enjoyed a great game against City and whom the boss clearly rated more highly than a significant percentage of the fans.

When the 34-year old Scot did name his side, it was clear he retained most faith in those who had served Liverpool well in recent seasons – despite temporary lapses in either form or fitness. Molby returned in place of McMahon who had a minor injury and Dalglish named himself up front – at the expense of Walsh – who was dropped. Sammy Lee was substitute.

The changes however, "not only failed to solve his side's goalscoring famine but actually added to his selection problems." Playing himself from the start brought, "no noticeable improvement in Liverpool's fire power," and served only to further frustrate and unsettle Walsh who, it was revealed after the game, had been, "on the verge of coming off the transfer list after a splendid run during which he scored 11 goals in as many games." For many fans and commentators alike Dalglish had dropped the wrong man. Rush, "once such an amazing opportunist – made little impression...missing two early chances and never looking like ending his scoreless sequence – now lasting eight games."

It wasn't only up front where Liverpool were having problems, and once again their defence looked fallible, with Birkenhead-born Peter Davenport and veteran Scottish wingman John Robertson creating havoc in and around the Reds' penalty area for most of the game.

In the first ten minutes however, it had been all Liverpool, with Kevin MacDonald in particular unlucky not to open the scoring when his well hit shot from the edge of the area, "cannoned off a red shirt," and out for a corner. Sutton, in the Forest goal then won a lucky rebound off Rush, "when he raced out of his area in response to a searching through ball by Lawrenson." Minutes later, "Dalglish shook his head in dismay when he lobbed an inviting chance tamely into Sutton's arms," but it was the out-of-form but still selected Rush who, "was even more culpable just afterwards when, unmarked to the left of the goal, he put a cross-shot well wide." If he was shaking his head at that miss, Dalglish was looking to the heavens in exasperation seconds later when Forest took the lead with their first attack of the game.

Brian Clough's son Nigel, "looking almost demure in a pair of gloves, sent Neil Webb surging through the centre with a beautifully judged chip," and he in turn fired past Grobbelaar who could only half-block the venomous shot. Molby, "whose bulk was a handicap in the conditions," wrote The Observer's Ronald Atkin, then had a shot saved well by Sutton, before the Reds' keeper answered his growing army of critics by producing two saves within seconds of each other that kept his side in the game.

"Clough uncorked another lovely ball, this time to Davenport," but – clean through - he was thwarted by a superb save by Grobbelaar who made himself big to prevent a certain goal with his body, before following this up immediately by throwing himself at the rebound from Ian Bowyer. The Ellesmere Port-born midfielder's goal-bound effort was deflected wide off the keeper's legs. Grobbelaar, "has had some shaky games this season and was in real danger of being dropped," with young reserve Mike Hooper travelling with the squad to Nottingham but, showing the stubbornness that would become an integral part of his managerial career, Dalglish kept faith with the Zimbabwean and he was rewarded here with arguably the keeper's best display of the season.

Liverpool almost conceded again when Johnny Metgod got away on the right and Davenport's shot from his cross was kicked away by Lawrenson with Grobbelaar beaten. Former Real Madrid defender Metgod was a constant menace to the Reds' defence and it was no surprise when Beglin was booked for a wild tackle on the bald-pated Dutchman mid-way through the half. Davenport's shot from the resultant free-kick was deflected wide for a corner.

MacDonald, "getting through a lot off hard work," then intercepted a poor clearance by Sutton, eventually shooting just wide, before Dalglish's name was added to referee K. Baker's book for dissent. The player-manager's frustrations at Liverpool's poor finishing were plain to see. Clever play by Molby and Dalglish then, "gave Rush his first real chance of the game but the Welshman's shot hit the goalkeeper and Forest almost scored from the breakaway that followed." Davenport found Metgod on the left and his perfect pass to Robertson split the Liverpool rearguard once more. Only, "another great save from Grobbelaar," ensured the Reds' remained just the one goal down at half-time.

"Liverpool attacked with great spirit on the resumption but still could not find the finishing touch." Within five minutes of the restart the Reds created two openings to which their forwards failed to add the required clinical response. Again the fulcrum, MacDonald found Rush on the right but his cross was met with zero attacking presence in the Forest area. More than a few in the packed, open away end cursed the absence of Walsh at this point.

Soon after, an almost identical situation on the right arose when Dalglish found Johnston.

This time Rush was in the area to receive the Australian's cross, but clumsily, he took too long to control it and the chance was lost. Again, Dalglish's decision to drop Walsh was pondered by many of the 4,000 Reds' fans in the 27,141 crowd – Forest's best attendance of the season despite the cold, blustery Christmas weather.

Liverpool's best period of play followed, with MacDonald having another shot blocked; then Dalglish and Rush just failed to convert half-chances that came their way. On 55 minutes however, the visitors' persistence paid off – and it was their man-of-the-match who started and finished it

"MacDonald began it, Whelan and Johnston kept the momentum going and, when Dalglish squared a pass across the face of the penalty area, Macdonald was there again, arriving at full-tilt to strike a low shot into the corner of the goal." It was the reserve midfielder's first goal of the season and just reward for a fine performance. If not all the Liverpool support were entirely convinced of MacDonald's worth they still savoured this equaliser; their celebrations illuminated by the amber glow of the incongruous floodlight stationed among them on the Bridgford End terracing.

10 minutes and two wasted Liverpool corners later, Forest were given a chance to take the lead once again when they were awarded a penalty after Webb's pass found Davenport in the area only to be tackled crudely by Beglin. Already booked for a foul in the first-half the Irishman was lucky not to receive a second yellow card. MacDonald complained so bitterly that he became the third visiting player to be booked, but he needn't have bothered as, throwing himself to his right to turn the ball aside, "Grobbelaar produced one of his other world reactions to the kick."

It was a tremendous save that even some home fans could not help but applaud. The keeper revealed after the game that he had received some welcome pre-match advice from Bob Paisley who told him, "not to commit himself too early on the slippery surface." As the afternoon wore on, temperatures dropped, frost began to gather and players were slipping and sliding on a surface that now resembled a skating rink.

As Liverpool gained the upper hand, supporters of both teams raised the decibel levels, but the Liverpool supporters seemed more intent on winding up the home contingent with vociferous and venomous taunts of 'scabs'. This was a reference to Nottinghamshire miners' perceived role as strike-breakers in the violent miners' dispute which was finally crushed in March 1985. The miners' eventual defeat hugely diluted the political power of the unions and allowed the Conservative government to forge ahead with its monetarist programme. Even the most apolitical among the Liverpool following were aware of the damage Thatcher's policies were continuing to inflict on their fellow citizens.

Buoyed with belief after his goal, MacDonald almost turned creator when he found Rush with as precise and subtle a pass as any seen that afternoon. It, "would have given Rush a goal 12-months ago but this time the striker lacked a yard of speed," and he was foiled by Sutton. "His confidence seems to have gone," said Hargraves and, "he badly needs to get the ball in the net again - even if only against minor opposition."

With 15 minutes to go MacDonald almost grabbed a winner when, following, "a tremendous surge from midfield in which he bypassed at least two players," he fired narrowly wide. It was clear the Scot's confidence was flowing with fine performances in his recent, albeit rare, starting appearances. Lee then replaced Johnston, who had, "covered acres of ground in midfield," but there was no further significant action in what had been, "an incident-packed game." It ended 1-1.

Dalglish's presence on the field hadn't been able to halt the Reds' faltering run or provide them with the missing cutting edge up front. "Liverpool's commitment remains as strong as ever and they are still in touch with the leaders but they will have to do something urgently about their lack of scoring power if they are to actually win anything."

After winning seven out of their previous nine league games – with two draws – the Reds had been imperious as they ground out results and forced their way back into title contention, but December had seen their hitherto magnificent run of form come to a shuddering halt.

Amid the dark nights, snow flurries and falling temperatures, they had played five league games in the final month of the year – and had won just one. They had scored five and conceded five, but in a piece of unwanted symmetry, they had picked up just five points out of a possible 15. It was not the form of championship contenders, let alone league champions.

"It is a real test for Dalglish," to turn his side's fortunes around said the Liverpool Echo, and one, "which the Scottish maestro in unlikely to solve by his own playing skill. Now is the time to find out if he is equally expert as a tactician and motivator." 1985 had been a momentous year for Liverpool and for the football club that bore its name, predominately for the wrong reasons. For both the club and city, the year ahead promised more uncertainty and, on the field of play the scrutiny on tyro manager Dalglish was as intense as ever.

Wednesday 1 January
Liverpool v Sheffield Wednesday

Mr. Alton asked the Paymaster General if he will make a statement on the unemployment situation on Merseyside.

Mr. Lang: On 9 January 1986, the number of unemployed claimants in the Merseyside metropolitan county was 142,696, which corresponds to an unemployment rate of 21.5 per cent.

Hansard: HC Debate, Written Answers, Employment 18 February 1986

As Liverpool prepared to face Sheffield Wednesday at home on New Year's Day, player-manager Kenny Dalglish's main aim was to steer Liverpool's title ship back on course. A worrying run of two draws and two defeats either side of Christmas meant that, although handily placed in third, the Reds appeared to be fading from the title picture. Five points behind leaders Manchester United, Liverpool were tied on 47 points with two other sides – current champions Everton and Chelsea - and were just two points ahead of the surprise package of the season, West Ham United.

Although such a position would have appeased fans of most other clubs, Liverpool's recent record of five titles in seven seasons meant that expectations at Anfield were much higher. Liverpool's fans simply demanded more. Despite starting 1986 still competing on four fronts, there had been growing criticism of Liverpool's performances in general – the defensive and goalkeeping lapses at the back, and the lack of clinical precision upfront. In recent weeks Dalglish's team selections in particular had come under scrutiny - from elements of the media and the more caustic section of the Anfield crowd.

Attempting to divide his time between prolonging his playing career and his new-found managerial duties, Dalglish had purposefully not selected himself to any great extent in the first half of the season. Liverpool's results up until December meant the player-manager had been relatively immune from criticism but a sudden, recent run of poor form saw many people begin to question his selections. Calls for his reinstatement on the pitch by those off it, press and fans alike, grew more vociferous. In truth Liverpool had played fluently only in patches so far. A run of seven wins back-to-back in late October and November had convinced many that they could capitalise on Manchester United's increasingly erratic league form and stage a title challenge of their own, whilst the home victory over United in the Milk Cup meant that they were just two ties away from another Wembley final.

However, that encouraging run had been followed by just one win in six league games with most critics arguing that Liverpool's best performances had come when Dalglish was in the starting line-up. In reality however, Dalglish hadn't always played when Liverpool were winning more regularly in the autumn. What the armchair pundits failed to recognise was that if Liverpool were to grow as a team, and continue to challenge on four fronts, then it was important to integrate the exciting, attacking talents of Paul Walsh and Craig Johnston and add a burst of speed to a squad sadly lacking in pace. Dalglish had no option but to exclude himself if he was to give both young attackers the necessary run of games.

Other critics suggested that Dalglish's absence was also affecting the form of Ian Rush. With the Welshman entering the match against Wednesday without a goal in eight games there had to be some truth in this argument, but Paul Walsh's attitude and commitment when he was on the pitch, ensured he remained both a crowd favourite and a more than able partner - despite his transfer request back in October.

Most crucially for Liverpool in the long term, Dalglish was mindful that his ageing limbs needed longer to recover than in previous seasons. He was nearly 35 years of age and had been a professional footballer for over 18 of them, almost all at the very top level. Dalglish's body simply couldn't play every game at this stage of his career.

Throughout the Shankly and Paisley years, Liverpool fans had grown accustomed to seeing a similar eleven - fitness permitting - picked each week but Dalglish, factoring in his own fitness levels, had recognised a need for change. Football was much more competitive now. Sides who wanted to compete at the top level had to make full use of their squads if they were to succeed and mount any serious challenge. Rotation, even in its infancy - with just one substitute allowed - was already a part of Dalglish's managerial armoury. Indeed, he was not only confident the emerging young talent in his squad could compensate for his early season absences but, as the season progressed and injuries and tiredness took their toll, he was convinced opportunities would arise for himself to figure more frequently as the season moved into its crucial later stages.

Despite the manger's in-depth considerations, some less-optimistic, more judgemental supporters felt that although the old guard such as Phil Neal and Alan Kennedy had been phased out and new blood had been purchased in the shape of Steve McMahon, Dalglish's team changes hadn't significantly improved performances since the end of the previous season when Joe Fagan's side had finished 13 points adrift of Everton. They worried that, with the Blues again threatening to find their best form as the New Year dawned and the title race heated up, the balance of football power on Merseyside - as many pundits and commentators had predicted - was shifting.

With more than half the league matches played, the season was well into mid-winter but temperatures on Merseyside at the turn of the year were unseasonally warm and this milder weather drew a large Bank Holiday crowd of 38,964 to Anfield to see if Liverpool could gain three much-needed points in their quest to keep pace with the leaders.

Promoted as recently as 1984, Sheffield Wednesday had already established themselves in the top-flight as an uncompromising, physical side who played a long-ball game that, although an eyesore to purists, brought results, and the Owls entered the match sitting proudly in sixth place. Memories were still fresh of their 2-0 win at Anfield the previous season, so nothing could be taken for granted by the subdued Kopites who, despite their numbers, seemed more concerned with dealing with hangovers than debating team selection before the game kicked-off.

Owing to the dire unemployment situation on Merseyside, disposable cash was at a premium for many, but the locals still knew how to enjoy a big night out and, if the aroma of stale Higson's ale, Embassy No.1 and the unmistakable noxious fumes of over-indulgence were a guide, it seemed that most of those inside Anfield this New Year's Day had spent the previous evening celebrating with gusto the passing of a tumultuous 1985. With their preference for local performers such as The Farm, China Crisis, and Groundpig however, few on the Kop would have danced the night away to the first number one single of the year - West End Girls by the Pet Shop Boys.

After leaving himself out of the starting line-up since the end of October, Dalglish had returned in the preceding 1-1 draw at Nottingham Forest and the Anfield crowd were delighted to see him take to the pitch against Wednesday alongside the goal-starved Ian Rush. Any notion that the renewal of their favoured strike partnership would quickly see Liverpool back on track however, was shattered after just 44 seconds when, after Ronnie Whelan conceded a corner at the Kop end, Carl Shutt headed in the resultant set-piece after a flick-on by Lawrie Madden.

Reeling from the shock of conceding such an early goal Liverpool, despite Dalglish's cultured presence, struggled to make an impression in their opening forays and Wednesday's strong, physical line of blue and white striped shirts snuffed out a succession of aimless Liverpool balls as the home side laboured in search of an immediate leveller.

Only when the Reds started to play through midfield, with impressive surges from Molby, Lawrenson and Hansen, did the Wednesday defence come under any pressure but, as half-time approached, the home side still hadn't been able to force an equalizer. McMahon was unlucky when hitting a post from the edge of the box, whilst Whelan had a 25th minute header blocked on the line. Rush's frustrations in front of goal continued with one effort blocked by the legs of Martin Hodge and another opportunity being blazed over the Anfield Road goal when in a one-on-one confrontation with the ex-Everton keeper.

Just three minutes after the restart however, the moment Anfield - and Rush - had been waiting for arrived when the Welsh striker ended his goal drought with a precise left-foot finish from a Craig Johnston header. By now the crowd had awoken from its first-half slumbers and, encouraged by Liverpool's own recovery, they roared the home team on. The Kop goal was besieged as Liverpool launched attack after attack.

After 73 minutes Dalglish removed himself from the fray, bringing on Paul Walsh in his place, and it was the man who had replaced the player-manager to such good effect for much of the campaign who put Liverpool in front with just a quarter of an hour left. Latching on to a neat through ball from McMahon, Walsh fired past Hodge to complete Liverpool's comeback.

There was a cruel twist at the end however, when a hopeful long-ball from Morris was touched on by Shutt before Gary Thompson, holding off a challenge from Molby, hooked past Grobbelaar for a last gasp equalizer. As the Wednesday fans celebrated the Kop looked on in shock. To add insult to injury Liverpool had time to create one last chance to win the game - but Hodge again saved with his legs from a visibly frustrated Rush.

On the verge of gaining three crucial points in their quest to keep pace with their title rivals Liverpool's profligacy in front of goal and their inability to keep their opponents from scoring had surfaced once again. It was their fifth league game without a win – a damaging sequence. More through frustration at their wasteful finishing and complacent defending than the overall standard of an otherwise improved performance, the depressed Liverpool players left the field with boos from the Kop ringing in their ears as they reflected on dropping 12 points in five games.

For fans, this wasn't the auspicious start to 1986 they craved. For the manager, there was plenty to contemplate as his attention now switched to the quest for the FA Cup – a competition the Reds had not won since 1974.

Chapter Five
To See the Sun and Walk the Sand

Liverpool v Norwich City
FA Cup third round
Saturday 4 January

"We're on the march with Kenny's Army, We're all going to Wem-ber-ley
And we'll really shake them up when we win the FA Cup
'Cos Liverpool are the greatest football team."

The Kop chant which became the soundtrack to Liverpool's season.

For almost every football fan in the 1980s the third round of the FA Cup - when lower division and those non-league teams who remain in the competition are included in the draw with the hope of meeting one of the 'big boys' of the top two divisions - was one of the highlights of the football calendar. The FA Cup may have lost some of its lustre in recent years but in 1986 it retained its position as the most famous football competition in the world. In terms of glamour it would not be far-fetched to say it was almost the equal of the League Championship itself. With no European football for England's leading clubs the Cup took on added significance. In a season when Liverpool had so far failed to show the consistency required of potential Champions, it was especially important for Kopites as, despite their recent domestic dominance, the Reds had not won the cup for over a decade.

Liverpool had last won the trophy in 1974 when, in the great man's last competitive game as manager, Bill Shankly's second great Anfield side ruthlessly destroyed an over-confident Newcastle 3-0 at Wembley. In stark contrast, Shankly's successor Bob Paisley saw his own, unparalleled success at home and abroad stained only by inexplicable and recurring misfortune in the FA Cup.

Days before being crowned European Cup winners for the first time in 1977 - and already confirmed as League Champions - Liverpool contrived to lose 2-1 in the Final to a hugely inferior Manchester United side, scuppering dreams of an unparalleled European and domestic Treble. Two seasons later, with arguably their greatest ever team - and one which had stormed to the 1978-79 League title with a goal difference of plus 69 - Liverpool's Cup hopes were again denied by United. The Old Trafford side had finished the season in ninth place - with a goal difference of minus three - but in a replayed semi-final at Goodison Park, the Reds lost 1-0 after a 2-2 draw at Maine Road.

The following season Liverpool again reached the semis only to fall in spectacular fashion once more, this time to Arsenal. The Cup was so sacred at the time that the FA had barely considered the concept of penalty shoot-outs to decide drawn any tie, let alone semi-finals and in 1980, after an initial goalless draw at Hillsborough, the tie was replayed twice at Villa Park, both ending 1-1 after extra-time. An unprecedented fourth meeting was required where a 1-0 defeat at Highfield Road, Coventry finally saw the Gunners progress and Liverpool's hopes dashed for yet another season.

Liverpool legends with multiple league and European honours such as Graeme Souness, Jimmy Case, Terry McDermott, Phil Neal and Alan Kennedy, all saw their Liverpool careers end without adding a single FA Cup Winners medal to their names.

Their Cup jinx continued under Joe Fagan's two-year managerial reign. In January 1984 his vastly under-rated treble-winning side somehow managed to lose a fourth round tie at Second Division Brighton and Hove Albion. In his second year as boss Fagan guided Liverpool to yet another semi-final appearance against Manchester United. Driven mainly by the refusal of the London-based press to fully acknowledge their obvious and sustained superiority in the League, not to mention Europe, and the media's tendency to celebrate United's occasional victories over Liverpool in Cup competitions, Reds' fans' loathing for United and their supporters – that had been building steadily since the late 1970s – reached its nadir here.

United's three FA Cup victories since their last championship success in 1967 paled in comparison to Liverpool's eight title wins, two UEFA Cups, and four glorious triumphs in the European Cup in the same period, yet still the Old Trafford club managed to remain the glamour side of English football. Few things annoyed Liverpool fans more and things came to a head in the April 1985 semi-final between the two sides at Goodison Park, when the level of crowd violence at the tie was perhaps unmatched in Liverpool's history. The enmity between both sets of supporters spilled onto the streets of Walton before and after the match, and the atmosphere inside the ground was no less poisonous. With distress flares fired and golf balls embedded with nails launched between rival fans, it was at times difficult to reflect that some exciting football took place on the pitch with Liverpool netting two dramatic late equalizers to snatch a draw.

In the replay at Maine Road just four days later, Liverpool went ahead courtesy an own goal by Paul McGrath, but the Reds were again denied a trip to Wembley by two second half goals from Bryan Robson and Mark Hughes. With United fans celebrating reaching Wembley at the expense of their great rivals once again, more battles between the warring younger factions ensued in the dingy streets surrounding Maine Road after the game. Older supporters dodged the chaos outside the ground and sloped back to Merseyside to lick their wounds, their dreams of making the Final shattered for yet another year.

Such levels of violence had become an accepted part of the match-going experience, and whilst no doubt this added to the excitement for younger fans disaffected by a lack of opportunity, jobs and a coherent voice, flippant attitudes towards hooliganism would be seen in a very different light just weeks later when tragedy unfolded in Brussels.

In the dozen years since 1974, Liverpool's FA Cup history was at odds with their relentless success in other competitions. For elder statesmen at the club such as Alan Hansen and Dalglish himself, who had experienced so many disappointments, glory in the FA Cup had become something of a Holy Grail. For fans too, the desire to see Liverpool's famous red shirts grace Wembley once again in the showpiece event of the season, was genuine and palpable. It says much for the Cup's loss of prestige today, that for fans and players of previous eras it was a genuine dilemma to decide which competition they would rather win; the FA Cup or the League title. However, such talk would never have been countenanced in the mid-1980s Anfield dressing-room, where any chance of adding silverware to the Reds' bulging trophy cabinet was met with equal respect and desire.

The third round draw had paired Dalglish's side with Second Division Norwich City. Although relegated the previous season the Canaries had won the Milk Cup after beating Sunderland (for whom ex-Red Howard Gayle made a substitute appearance) 1-0 and, with most of their players retained, looked likely to return to the top flight at the first time of asking. Unlike Liverpool, Ken Brown's side were in fine form, having won their last seven league games in a row, so confidence was high that they could create the shock of the round and thwart the Reds' dreams of a Wembley FA Cup appearance once again.

Grey skies and biting cold brought flurries of snow to Merseyside on the morning of the tie and fans arriving at the ground after midday found the streets around Anfield covered in a white blanket of snow. With the match looking likely to fall victim to the weather, the pubs and bars around the ground drew an even brisker trade than usual with fans seeking refuge from the snow and slush. Most were content to wait and see if the game would go ahead before paying at the turnstiles, but those who did take a chance and pay at the gate were presented with a voucher to use for a rescheduled fixture if the continuing snowfall forced the referee to postpone or abandon the game.

Anfield's undersoil heating and the gallant efforts of the ground staff in clearing the snow and marking the penalty areas, centre circle and touchlines however, finally allowed referee David Hutchinson – just an hour before the scheduled kick-off time - to signal that the game could go ahead. On hearing the news that the match was definitely 'on' the nearby alehouses emptied and, although the attendance numbered just 29,802 - with plenty of empty seats in the Kemlyn Road and Main Stands - there was a healthy, boisterous crowd on the Kop who greeted the referee's entrance with a distinctly Scouse chant of, "Oh where did you get that ball?" in reference to the bright orange match ball Mr Hutchinson had chosen to be more visible on a snow covered pitch. Carrying a minor injury the player-manager chose to omit himself in favour of Paul Walsh and this was the only change from the team that had drawn with Sheffield Wednesday on New Years Day.

With snow still falling at kick-off and the ball holding up in some areas of the pitch, conditions were far from ideal for good football, but Liverpool sought to restore some confidence after five games without a win by following Dalglish's pre-match advice that the tie was, "not about pretty stuff...but about attitude," and they were the first to adapt. The favourites created three good chances to take the lead in the first quarter of an hour with England international Chris Woods in the Norwich goal saving with his legs from Walsh and then blocking an effort from Whelan at point-blank range. Rush also came close with a shot just wide after Kevin McDonald had knocked down a long ball from Lawrenson.

Liverpool were playing pragmatic football suited to the heavy pitch and they eventually broke the deadlock after 23 minutes. McDonald, who had his critics on the Kop for his laboured, languid style, was having an energetic game in midfield and, on one of his loping forward runs, he found himself on the end of a Walsh through-ball and, first time, drilled low past Woods to put the Reds in front. Barely ten minutes later Walsh again justified his manager's confidence when the diminutive striker evaded several lumbering Norwich defenders to head home Molby's chipped free-kick from the right of the box. With the snow at last easing, Liverpool left the field at half-time 2-0 up with the applause of the Kop ringing in their ears and the tie almost sewn up.

The second-half offered the Reds the chance to score more goals and build some much needed confidence. Attacking the Kop Liverpool treated those supporters who had forsaken their firesides with three more well taken goals. Norwich had briefly rallied at the beginning of the second-half with Barham crossing wastefully from a good position down the right and Grobbelaar had to be alert to smother a well-struck volley from Peter Mendham soon after, but this was as good as it got for the visitors.

Liverpool scored a third and decisive goal on the counter attack in the 73rd minute when man-of-the-match McDonald played an accurate through ball for McMahon to run on to and chip skilfully past Woods. McMahon's momentum saw him slide on his backside in the snow for an unusual and memorable celebration in front of the Kop. Five minutes later a header by Whelan from a Craig Johnston cross made it 4-0 and substitute John Wark, on for Walsh just after the hour mark, rounded off the scoring with nine minutes to go - poking home the fifth after Woods couldn't hold a Johnston header following a Whelan corner.

After the game Dalglish, who had bemoaned Liverpool's bad luck in front of goal during their winless run of five games, was, "delighted to see five of them score," as the Reds' strikers and attacking midfielders shared out the goals on their passage to the fourth round. Confidence in front of goal had been given a timely boost whilst the clean sheet, with no repeat of the avoidable recent errors in defence, was an added bonus.

On Sunday, Everton scraped past Fourth Division side Exeter City, 1-0, at Goodison Park. Now, the manager, players and fans alike could look forward to the draw for the next round which would be broadcast live on Radio 2 during Monday dinner time. Who would emerge as Liverpool's next opponents when the balls were drawn out the old velvet bag amid the mysterious, unseen rooms of the FA at Lancaster Gate?

Watford v Liverpool
Sunday 12 January

"Good afternoon and welcome to Match of the Day from Vicarage Road, home of Watford Football Club for this Canon League First Division match against Liverpool. And while discussions have been taking place recently about a Superleague, it's worth remembering that only eight years ago, this fixture could only have taken place as a possible giant-killing cup-tie. Watford then were a Fourth Division club."

Jimmy Hill sets the scene for viewers of Match of the Day Live as Liverpool appear on TV for the first time this season.

The dubious reward for Liverpool's passage in round four was a trip to Stamford Bridge, the scene of their inglorious exits in 1978 and 1982. The numbered wooden balls drawn from the infamous velvet bag – also ensured there were three other all-First Division ties, but this was undoubtedly the pick of the round. Everton meanwhile were drawn at home against Second Division Blackburn Rovers.Before the Reds could contemplate their difficult assignment however, they travelled to 12th placed Watford in the hope of breaking their five match winless run in the League.

Since their promotion in 1982 trips to Watford had ben viewed with some trepidation by the top sides. Not only did they have to adapt to Graham Taylor's side's, direct, physical approach – a slightly disingenuous label as Liverpool's hard fought victory in early September had proven – but the Vicarage Road playing surface was notoriously poor, a fact that would be highlighted even more by the recent bad weather. The heavy, rutted surface, typical of the times for even the bigger clubs come mid-winter, was not made for Liverpool's pass and move style and a hard fought contest was expected.

Such a potentially stark contrast in styles also attracted the BBC who, having only recently agreed to a new, much delayed, deal with the League ensured that this would be Liverpool's first ever live appearance on a Sunday 'Match of the Day'. Live TV broadcasts in the 1980s however, were not the polished, glitzy, studio-based affairs introduced by the SKY revolution which would engulf the game in later years.

In a contrast as striking as the playing styles of the respective teams on view, the BBC's coverage of the match began just minutes before the scheduled 3.05 kick off, with the 'build-up' consisting of a brief welcome to viewers from veteran presenter Jimmy Hill – who was perched on a hastily assembled, and frankly dangerous looking TV gantry - and the briefest of insights from former Watford boss Bertie Mee (who also managed Arsenal to their Double in 1971) and ex-Liverpool goalkeeper Ray Clemence.

Mee singled out Watford's mercurial young winger John Barnes, who had ran the Liverpool defence half-ragged in the reverse fixture earlier in the season, as a big danger, whilst Clemence attributed the Reds' disappointing recent league form to Ian Rush's frustrations in front of goal. The former Kop idol also stressed the importance to the team of Dalglish's first signing, Steve McMahon.

And then the game began. There was no mention of any 'pressure' on the respective managers, no talk of 'must win fixtures', analysis of the frailties of zonal marking or rotation or any of the hyperbole that accompanies today's coverage. Just a simple, 'over to the commentators' for a much welcomed return to live TV pictures and commentary.
For supporters who followed Liverpool away from home, the fixture also presented additional difficulties. With the usual limited weekend train service Sunday games meant the inconvenience of arriving home late on a Sunday night, or early Monday morning – a problem for those lucky enough to have work. Indeed, with a round trip of approximately 360 miles for Liverpool's fans it was estimated that only about 800 supporters made the trip from Merseyside – a situation that would be unheard of for a club of Liverpool's stature today.

Live televised football had only been introduced on a regular basis in 1983 and was still a novelty for broadcasters. With a lack of ideas on how to market the game in a time of economic hardship, hooliganism and decrepit stadia, attendances were often drastically reduced by the presence of the cameras. So much so that the broadcaster would supplement the home side's gate receipts with a compensation payment so as to reflect the lost revenue at the turnstiles. Again, such a situation is simply not reflected in today's game.

Liverpool were unchanged from their morale-boosting cup win over Norwich, with Kevin McDonald rewarded for his recent run of good form with a place in central midfield and Paul Walsh continuing in favour of Dalglish up front. Although he remained on the transfer list, Dalglish recognised Walsh's worth and his continued selection ahead of the player-manager was a consistent vote of confidence in his abilities. To avoid a clash with Watford's multi-coloured home strip Liverpool took the field resplendent and immaculate in all white as they sought to get back to winning ways and keep pace with the leaders.

There was nothing immaculate about Liverpool's start to the game however. The visitors looked short of confidence and their passing game struggled on the heavy pitch. A dubious first half highlight for Reds' fans watching the live TV coverage at home was hearing an audible obscenity from Ronnie Whelan - aimed at a linesman and picked up by the pitch-side microphones - for incorrectly awarding the Hornets a throw-in on the left touchline. Watford's direct style was arguably more than just the footballing philosophy of their coach, but also an understanding of how to function best on a wretched playing surface – and with a strong wind in your favour. Either way, the home side created the best chances of the first half.

As at Anfield in September, John Barnes added to his growing reputation by stinging Grobbelaar's palms after a powerful run and shot inside the first six minutes, whilst Liverpool were fortunate not to concede when Molby blocked a goal-bound effort from Watford's muscular striker Colin West soon after. The home side's pressure paid off in the 19th minute when they took the lead with a swerving shot from Kenny Jackett that evaded Grobbelaar's despairing dive. Yet just as it looked as though Liverpool would trail at half-time, they summoned their first meaningful attack just a minute before the break to level.

Johnston and Rush exchanged passes on the right edge of the penalty area but the ball bobbled away from them just as it looked like the move may come to something. Fortunately for Liverpool however, the ball ran into the box – straight into the path of Walsh, who lashed a shot from 12-yards high and wide past Tony Coton's left hand. Although just the boost Liverpool needed after another lacklustre first-half, on their performance so far it was a scarcely deserved equalizer.

Dalglish's half-time team talk seemed to galvanise Liverpool and, with the wind at their backs, they began the second half with far greater cohesion and attacking intent. Coton was forced to make a number of saves as Watford were pushed back under increasing Liverpool pressure. The Reds were playing well and, with just a quarter of an hour left, the breakthrough their second half play deserved finally came when Johnston made space for a cross on the right hand side and dinked a cross into the penalty area towards Rush. Although the ball fell slightly behind him and his initial touch took him away from goal, the Welshman managed to turn swiftly past a defender and strike a powerful right foot shot into the top corner of the net. Liverpool's small army of travelling fans behind the goal welcomed Rush's second goal in three games and erupted with joy and relief in equal measure. The goal scorer supreme was back.

There was a distinct London lilt to the accent of the Liverpool support in the celebratory singing that followed the goal - testament to the numbers that had not only latched onto Liverpool in the South of England after years of success at home and abroad but also the absence of a dominant London team. It was a precursor of what would come after the launch of the Premiership in 1992 and the TV revolution that followed; Liverpool's local away support remained loyal, but with the game televised, played on a Sunday afternoon, and with disposable cash in short supply, perhaps only a third of the Reds in attendance were from Merseyside.

Playing with a fluency that hadn't been seen since late-autumn Liverpool refused to sit back and protect their lead and they continued to attack Watford, often overwhelming the home side in the process. The game was sewn up with five minutes to go when the lively and energetic Walsh latched on to an under hit back pass, stabbed the ball through the legs of the advancing Coton, and saw the ball trickle inside the post to make it 3-1. Since putting in his transfer request the striker had scored 15 times in 17 games.

Watford pulled a goal back shortly before the final whistle, Grobbelaar doing his dwindling support no favours by spilling a routine cross from Worrall Sterling at the feet of Jan Lohman. The former Dutch U-21 star tapped in a simple chance to reduce the deficit. Though Liverpool clung on to win three vital points, Watford's late consolation kept the

Reds in third place behind Everton on goal difference, giving further ammunition to Grobbelaar's growing army of critics.

After the game Dalglish deflected questions about his keeper and instead preferred to reflect on Paul Walsh's impressive run of recent form. He believed it was Walsh's best game in the three seasons since he moved to Anfield, adding that Liverpool were, "so satisfied with him that there's no way I can get back in the team." More importantly from a team perspective, Liverpool had turned in an impressive performance in the second half when the first had been far from fluent, though they still trailed leaders Manchester United by five points having played a game more. After a Super Cup engagement in midweek at Tottenham, another stiff test in the league beckoned the following weekend with the visit to Anfield of improving West Ham.

Tottenham Hotspur v Liverpool
Screen Sport Super Cup group phase
14 January 1986

"Things went astray walking up to Seven Sisters Road and we get spotted. A swift sidestep into a newsagents doesn't work as we're followed in by about seven Spurs lads. Words are exchanged, then boxes of crisps, washing powder, jars of jam, anything we could lay our hands on flew all over the shop as we tried to avoid a pounding. Finally the shopkeeper came from behind the counter, brandishing a broom handle shouting with a strong Asian-cockney twang "not af******g again" and sort of helped us get them out the shop and into the street. The Plod then arrived and after another half an hour we left the shop, covered in "Daz" but with no worse an injury than a back pocket hanging off of my Fu's jeans"

'Maca', Liverpool fan, Huyton.

Just two days after victory at Watford, Liverpool journeyed south again to face Spurs at White Hart Lane for their final group match in the heavily criticised, and poorly attended, Screen Sport Super Cup. Although the competition was firmly at the bottom of the list of Liverpool's priorities, Kenny Dalglish travelled with a full complement of first teamers to London. This of course was during an era before large squads of 20 plus players became the norm. Indeed, such was the confidence the manager had in the fitness and attitude of his first team squad, that the selected XI taking the field on a cold London night was not far removed from a side the Reds could send out in the league.

To underline the indifference many fans felt towards the competition in general, and the unimportant nature of the match in particular, barely 10,000 spectators paid for the 'privilege' of watching what turned out to be a routine Reds' win. 'Maca' from Huyton still can't believe he was at the game;

"This was a bit of a bizarre one for me. I was working in Edinburgh at the time but was due some leave. As soon as I found out I had the week off I looked up the fixtures and saw that we were away to Spurs in this Super Cup thing.

"I had to get the Monday overnight mail train from Edinburgh to Preston, then change on to the 6.15am to Euston. I met a blue lad who was the only one of my mates who fancied a bit of a mad one in London so, no, the super cup wasn't popular.

"We planned full day on the ale, starting in the Somers and after that who knows? Up to the ground,

watch the match, with a plan to stop for a couple after and get the train home to Liverpool. But we got into some bother with some Spurs skins and missed the rattler. It was looking like a night trawling round Kings Cross when we got chatting to some student girls. They smuggled us into their accommodation – and although we never married them, it went well. Nice one Kenny."

'Maca' and his Everton mate, Whitey weren't the only Scousers to chance their arm on this cold January night. Dave Hardman had moved to London in October looking for work, so it was short tube ride to White Hart Lane. Dave admits;

"I had a muzzy and big, mad long hair at the back so I blagged into the Directors Lounge claiming that I was Billy Lawrenson, Mark's brother, and that I was doing a Care In The Community course for the two lads with me. Surprisingly we got in, got as much free ale down us as possible, and lasted in the Directors box for at least 20 minutes before being lashed out. I imagine the steward who let us in never worked at White Hart Lane again."

As for the match, despite a convincing victory earning his side a semi-final tie with Norwich City however, Dalglish would be given cause to rue his confidence in, and reliance on, his regular players, with two first-half injuries doing much to restrict the manager's midfield options over the coming weeks.

After he had been incensed by a referee's decision seconds before, in-form Kevin McDonald broke an arm in a rash sliding tackle on Steve Perryman. The Inverness-born midfielder had yet to win over Liverpool fans, many of whom felt uninspired by his combative though laboured style. His simple and compact short passing game was much admired by fellow-Scot Dalglish however, and after the game the manager was keen to stress McDonald's positive attitude. "When he came off the doctor said it was broken," said Dalglish. "If Kevin is showing the effects of an injury then you know it's bad. He would play on with a broken leg if he could."

Of far more concern to Liverpool fans however, was the news that Steve McMahon - whose skill, steel and grit in central midfield had done much to silence those who still felt Graeme Souness' departure had left a hole in Liverpool's midfield - would miss the next five weeks due to a knee ligament injury. McMahon had been in fine form since his early season signing. With league games against surprise title challengers West Ham, Manchester United and Everton in the next few weeks, not to mention a tough trip to Stamford Bridge in the FA Cup, McMahon's loss was potentially a big one.

Indeed, the only positive Dalglish could take from the game apart from the victory, was the fact that Ian Rush scored twice – on 49 and 61 minutes - to maintain his return to goal scoring form. Sandwiched between Rush's brace Mark Lawrenson grabbed the other goal on 56 minutes. Dalglish was delighted to see Rush on the mark. "That first goal of Ian Rush will give him a lot of confidence and he was very sharp off the mark for his second", said the manager. As he boarded the coach back to Liverpool however, Dalglish's thoughts must surely have drifted to his midfield dilemma, and who would take to the field at Anfield to face West Ham on Saturday.

Liverpool v West Ham United
Saturday 18 January

"Throughout my career I'd never been to Liverpool and won but I really felt we had a chance that day. To be fair, we played exceptionally well but didn't take our chances to go in front…After leaving Anfield, we looked back down the Liverpool teamsheet and thought to ourselves, if we can reproduce that kind of performance in our next few games, we'll have a good chance of winning them and continuing our challenge."

West Ham defender Alvin Martin, quoted in Tony McDonald and Danny Francis, Boys of '86, The untold story of West ham's greatest-ever season. Mainstream, 2001.

Due to the dispute between the Football League and the BBC and ITV, televised football in the first half of the season had been conspicuous by its absence. The TV blackout meant that the exploits of free-scoring West Ham new boy Frank McAvennie had been missed by the nation's football followers. With a reputation for the high-life following his move to London from the relative obscurity of St Mirren, McAvennie had even been paraded down a busy London Street by Football Focus - much to the indifference and bewilderment of most passers-by.

There had been a brief glimpse of the blonde-haired striker on BBC's midweek Sportsnight programme scoring, from a Kenny Dalglish pass, for Scotland in the World Cup play-off against Australia at Hampden Park in November, but the man with 20 goals to his name already was recognised more easily on the capital's club-scene than he was on the country's football terraces.

Forming an exciting and formidable striking partnership with the diminutive but fleet-footed Tony Cottee, McAvennie's exploits on the pitch had helped push West Ham to within two points of Liverpool at this stage of the season and before the game there was a genuine feeling amongst Kopites that this was a top-of-the-table clash, albeit one against a surprising opponent.

Long-serving Hammers' boss John Lyall had a reputation for encouraging an aesthetically pleasing passing style on his teams, but the Ilford-born former defender – who had joined the club in 1955 - had also instilled discipline into their game. So much so that the East-Londoners boasted not only two free-scoring forwards but also a miserly defensive record - just 11 goals conceded in 13 away games. West Ham's impressive away record hid an alarming Anfield statistic however, and their last win in front of the Kop had been in September 1963 – just two months prior to the assassination of President John F. Kennedy.

Perhaps their new coach driver was taking this run into account when he took a wrong turn heading for Anfield, instead driving the team towards Goodison Park and the visitors had to rely on the local knowledge of their Liverpool-born defender Alvin Martin to steer them back on course.

The potentially intriguing encounter drew a crowd of 41,056 to Anfield – Liverpool's second biggest home gate in the League this season – and those home fans who packed into the ground on a damp and cool afternoon were delighted to see Liverpool gain three crucial points in the increasingly wide-open race for the title. Without the injured midfield duo of McDonald and McMahon, Dalglish drafted John Wark into midfield. Gary Gillespie started in a five-man defence, whilst Craig Johnston shook off a minor strain to line-up in place of Sammy Lee, who had deputised in midweek.

Liverpool kicked off attacking an Anfield Road End that housed several thousand, very vocal, away fans. With a considerable amount of not-so-good-natured chanting and gesticulating between the Liverpool fans at that end of the ground and West Ham's self-titled Inter-City Firm - the club's notorious hooligan element - the opening forays saw Liverpool win an early corner. From Craig Johnston's flag-kick and Molby's flick on, Gillespie slipped in front of an open goal and the chance went begging. Almost immediately the Hammers responded at the Kop End but Mark Ward's shot from McAvennie's astute pass was smothered by Grobbelaar.

Liverpool went closest to opening the scoring after 15 minutes when Rush nipped in between West Ham's Martin and Walford only to see his clever shot hit the inside of the post. Phil Parkes in the West Ham goal was relieved to see it canon safely back off the woodwork and into his arms.

To test Grobbelaar's handling in the slippery conditions West Ham countered with a number of long balls into the penalty area. From one such centre by Mark Ward the under-pressure Liverpool keeper failed to connect with his initial punch and was forced to shepherd the ball out for a corner to the left of the Kop goal. Grobbelaar later restored his confidence, and received the applause of the Kop, with a smart save from a long-range effort by Hammers' full-back Ray Stewart.

As had been expected in a match between two sides challenging for the title, the game was closely fought, with few clear-cut chances. Hansen, Lawrenson and Gillespie had managed to restrict the supply lines to McAvennie and Cottee whilst at the other end, although Rush looked sharp throughout, Walsh had struggled to escape the close attentions of the under-rated Alvin Martin and the first-half ended goalless.

Now attacking their favoured end, the second-half began with the Kop roaring Liverpool towards goal. Despite the encouragement however, West Ham stuck to Lyall's defensive disciplines and the Reds were restricted to hopeful efforts from long-range with West ham content to try and release Cottee and McAvennie on the break. More than one Kopite wondered if the outcome of a tense encounter would be settled by a mistake, a piece of individual skill or a controversial decision.

Just before the hour mark this is exactly what happened. In pursuit of Paul Walsh, who had broken free of his marker at last, Alvin Martin appeared to throw an arm into Walsh's back just inside the box. Walsh went down and, in unison, the Kop bayed for a penalty. Referee George Tyson duly obliged by pointing to the spot. Almost all the West Ham players surrounded the referee to protest vehemently at the decision, arguing long and hard that Martin's intervention had been accidental.

Ignoring the protests Jan Molby calmly place the ball on the spot and awaited the referee's whistle. After a short delay the Dane hammered the penalty low and hard to Parkes' right to send the Kop wild in celebration. Although the goal stood and the Dane accepted the back slaps and hand shakes of his teammates on their way back to the centre circle, the Hammers continued their complaints. Ray Stewart was sufficiently argumentative to receive first a yellow, and then a red card from Mr Tyson, before the game resumed.

Commenting on the decision that put Liverpool in front after the match, Dalglish later told reporters, "From where I was sitting Martin looked a bit unlucky." The Kop didn't care however, taking a sadistic pleasure in the part they had played in persuading Mr Tyson to award the spot-kick with their co-ordinated and concerted shout for a penalty.

Down to 10 men and with the Kop's victory songs ringing loud in their ears, a previously unflustered and well-disciplined West Ham fell apart. Molby nearly grabbed a second before Rush made it 2-0 with his 100th League goal for Liverpool on 67 minutes - converting a clever inside pass from Johnston on the right wing. Just three minutes later the home side rammed home their superiority with a third goal, this time from the prolific Walsh who, skilfully manoeuvring his way into the box, unleashed an unstoppable shot past Parkes for an emphatic third. In the space of barely a dozen minutes West Ham's title aspirations had been cruelly exposed as a distant London dream.

Self-proclaimed world champions at taunting beleaguered opposition, the Kop rubbed it in with chants aimed at West Ham's support of, "Where's your famous ICF?" This was a popular refrain that for young fans was best sung from the safety of the length of a football pitch, even if the greatest fear for some was that they would be subconsciously influenced by the Londoners' questionable, colourful attire. The exasperated Londoners took the bait and motioned back with some barely audible response only to be taunted further by the slightly surreal jibe of, "There's only one Ice Cream Factory." The jovial mood was rudely interrupted, albeit briefly, when the Hammers scored a consolation goal through Alan Dickens eight minutes from time.

The giddiness on the terraces was excusable as Liverpool, in a match that was bordering on stalemate, had torn West Ham to shreds in the space of 12 second-half minutes. In the process they had laid down a marker for the rest of the season against a major player in the title race. The Reds looked set to put together a run of wins which would turn up the heat on Manchester United and Everton.

So much for West Ham's deadly striking duo. For Liverpool, Rush was back in form and alongside him Walsh, with an avalanche of goals and assists, was pressing his claims for a spot in the England squad for the forthcoming World Cup. The perfect day was complete for Liverpool fans when they learned from George Sephton over the tannoy that a last-minute winner for Nottingham Forest at Old Trafford had cut the gap at the top to just two points. The race for the title was on and the jubilant fans poured out of Anfield for a celebratory pint or two before heading home to pick up a Football Echo and enjoy United's demise on that evening's Match of the Day.

Liverpool v Ipswich Town
Milk Cup Fifth Round
Tuesday 21 January

"It was in the early stages of my Scotland career that I started to room with Kenny and I have to say it was an education. The very first time it happened I was in for a shock when we returned to the room in the afternoon of an evening game. We had been for lunch and then jock Stein wanted a meeting with everyone. After that it was free-time until the pre-match meal at about 5pm, so I was looking forward to watching a movie on the box. When I got into the room the first thing I did was switch the TV on. But Kenny had other ideas and began to issue his instructions. 'Telly off, Warky, and close the curtains. We're going to sleep,' he said, and at first I though he was joking. Not a bit of it. He quickly added: 'Take the phone off the hook as well. We don't want to be disturbed'."

Wark On, the autobiography of John Wark, 2009

Liverpool's reward for their dramatic Jan Molby-inspired comeback against Manchester United in the previous round of the League Cup was a home quarter-final tie against Ipswich Town – whom the Reds had beaten 5-0 at Anfield earlier in the season. With a potential Wembley final just two months away, Dalglish was keen to land his first silverware as Liverpool player-manager and he again named a strong side to take on Bobby Ferguson's men. Whilst Dalglish was treating the tournament as seriously as anyone, the same could not be said of many Liverpool fans.

Perhaps sated by recent success in the least significant competition in English football (until the arrival of the Super Cup), or arguably uninspired by the opposition, or maybe just put off by the cold weather or the cost of a ticket in the harsh economic climate, most fans chose to stay at home and a crowd of just 19,762 watched Liverpool take their place in the semi-finals - for the seventh time in nine seasons.

Prior to the tie Ipswich's commanding centre-half Terry Butcher - buoyed by a recent call-up to the England squad by his previous manager Bobby Robson - had spoken of his desire to tame the newly resurgent Ian Rush. Like most sports however, football has a habit of making fools of players who make extravagant claims in the press. In 1974 Newcastle's Malcolm MacDonald had famously boasted of the damage he would inflict on Bill Shankly's Liverpool prior to that season's FA Cup Final. The rest was history. Liverpool romped home 4-0, the biggest winning margin for 14 years, and MacDonald barely touched the ball. Asked what their motivation had been after the game, skipper Emlyn Hughes uttered just two words, "Malcolm MacDonald."

Rush appeared to have taken the attitude of the Reds' former captain to heart as he led the lumbering, bumbling Butcher a merry dance throughout the match. Despite his barren spell either side of Christmas, Rush had continued to work tirelessly as Liverpool's first line of defence. He was a perfect exponent of Bob Paisley's, 'pressing game.' Snapping at his opponent's heels, high up the pitch, with tireless bursts of speed that often panicked defenders into hasty long balls to surrender possession, Rush's team ethic alongside his metronomic finishing and assured link-up play made him indispensible to Liverpool. Forget big battering rams up front, players who were the target for long, 'alehouse' balls played in their general direction, who simply bullied their way through opposing defenders and goalkeepers. With his deft touch, sharp brain and clinical finishing Rush was the complete centre-forward of the day.

Ipswich's resistance to Liverpool's - and Rush's - excellent all-round play lasted just 17 minutes. Attempting a back-pass to goalkeeper Paul Cooper, Butcher blundered and a lurking Rush intercepted. The Welshman unselfishly turned the ball square for an unmarked Paul Walsh in the area and the Londoner rolled the ball into the net as the Ipswich defence and Butcher looked on red-faced. Had England manager Robson been in attendance he may have consoled himself at Butcher's embarrassment and ineptitude by instead considering the England claims of Walsh who, in his burgeoning partnership with Rush, had added goals to his undoubted skill and trickery.

Rush's unselfish harrying of Butcher paid dividends again just 11 minutes later when he chased down and dispossessed the panic-stricken Ipswich centre-half once more. Jan Molby accepted the loose ball and, in one move, played it wide to Ronnie Whelan. The Irishman, back in midfield after a short stint at left-back, cut inside and curled a perfect 20-yard effort beyond Cooper to put Liverpool two up. Recognising Butcher's torment at the hands of the effervescent Rush, those few who had congregated on the Kop warmed themselves with a cruel taunt of, "Give it to Butcher," every time Ipswich managed to gain possession.

With the visitors rarely threatening the game was already effectively over at half-time and Liverpool were able to ease up in the second-half ahead of Sunday's big FA Cup tie at Chelsea, although Gary Gillespie's departure with a thigh injury after 50 minutes was a cause for concern, especially with McMahon and MacDonald already ruled out long-term.

The night however, belonged to the rampant Rush who finally got a well-deserved reward for his tireless display in the 66th minute when, collecting a clever Walsh pass on the edge of the box, he rounded the keeper before stroking his sixth goal in six games to finish off the scoring. Through to the last four, Liverpool were just a two-legged tie away from Wembley in Dalglish's first season as player manager.

A much more anticipated cup tie lay ahead however, with a trip to Stamford Bridge in the fourth round of the FA Cup just five days away. With McMahon and MacDonald out injured and Gillespie doubtful, the manager would need all his remaining top players to perform, none more so than Rush, his striker supreme.

Chelsea v Liverpool
FA Cup fourth round
Sunday 26 January

"It doesn't matter if you're left or to the right.
Don't try to hide behind the cause for what you fight.
There'll be no prisoners taken when the day is done.
No flag or uniform ever stopped the bullet from a gun."

Phil Lynott and Gary Moore, Out in the Fields, 1985

The Thin Lizzy frontman had collapsed at his home in Kew on Christmas Day and died in Salisbury hospital 10 days later. He was 36-years old.

Twice, in the third round in 1978 (4-2) and a fifth round tie in 1982 (2-0) - when Chelsea were a Second Division side – the Reds had been unexpectedly bundled out of the FA Cup at Stamford Bridge. With this fourth round clash giving Liverpool a third cup visit to Chelsea in nine seasons, Reds' fans wondered justifiably if the omens were against them in their quest to lay an FA Cup bogey stretching back to Bill Shankly's last competitive match at Wembley in the 1974 Final.

After yo-yoing between the top divisions during the late-1970s and early-80s the West London side were enjoying a surprisingly good 1985-86 season and their home record of 11 wins from 12 games saw them level on points with the Reds.

Chelsea's vast, open stadium - unlike many of England's major grounds in that the stands were far removed from the pitch - was an inhospitable place at best. Add the tight streets around the ground, the exposed, open terracing arcing behind each goal, and their fans' reputation for unruly behaviour home and away, and the scene was set for an epic cup-tie on alien territory.

Chelsea fans' actions had even been noted at Government level, to the extent that their Thatcher-admiring Chairman Ken Bates had controversially installed electric fencing (which was never actually switched on due to understandable health and safety objections from the Greater London Council) to discourage supporters from attempting to invade the Stamford Bridge pitch. Indeed, a Milk Cup semi-final defeat at home to Sunderland the previous season had seen a mass pitch invasion with mounted police charging up and down the pitch attempting to restore order. That game was held up for a full 20 minutes.

Stamford Bridge therefore had become synonymous with ugly terrace battles rather than classic football encounters. For Liverpool's players and fans an uncertain afternoon lay ahead. Chelsea's emerging young side had a superb home record, Liverpool's recent form at Stamford Bridge was poor to say the least and the shared, uncovered North Terrace allocated to Reds' fans had seen fighting during both of Liverpool's previous visits in the Cup.

Despite such misgivings, the match was undoubtedly the tie of the round and it was an obvious pick for ITV's live Sunday afternoon coverage – the channel's first live cup-tie under the newly agreed television deal. Given the financial issues facing many supporters, there was again much debate in the local press as to how this would affect the numbers of Liverpool fans travelling from Merseyside.

FA Cup ties would generally see several thousand make the trip to support the Reds, but Ian Hargraves suggested during the lead-up to the fixture that live transmission of the game would restrict the amount travelling from Liverpool to, "just a handful of supporters," to swell, "the thousands who travel from the Midlands and South." Like many football writers before and since however, Hargraves' views were badly out of sync with Liverpool's grass-roots support. In an age before internet forums and fanzines, the only platform for such views was the Saturday night Football Echo letters page and, following his sweeping assumption, fans let loose with their feelings.

B.Watson of Lower Lane, Fazakerley sent in one such angry response. Under the headline, "Anfield Army on the march," the letter countered that at least, "12 coaches from Liverpool, a special train and numerous fans in cars," would make the trip to London and therefore outnumber the out-of-town supporters that Liverpool drew from elsewhere. Hargraves had clearly underestimated not just the loyalty of Liverpool's away support but also the significance of the game to those who yearned to see the Reds end 12 seasons of FA Cup frustration.

As was customary, several hundred supporters also opted to travel on the 'ordinary' train services to the capital so as to escape the attention the heavy police presence that greeted the arrival of the, 'Football Specials.' The extra freedom of the scheduled train would not only afford fans the chance to suss out any welcoming committees among Chelsea's notorious following, but also exercise the option of 'browsing' the richer shops en route to Fulham Broadway tube station. The fare on the 'Special' – calling only at Runcorn - was £10 for a train leaving Lime Street at 8.55am and due to arrive at Euston at 12.34pm. There were no 2 hours 15 minute trips to London in 1986 and fares on trains, whether on or off the radar of the Metropolitan police, were significantly higher than the required few pounds to pay at the turnstiles and see the match.

Liverpool's run of five consecutive victories in league and cup had temporarily silenced those critics who pointed to Dalglish's tendency to change his team according to the opposition. He had recently deployed a five-man defence with Molby alongside Hansen and Gillespie (or Lawrenson) in the centre to cope with a perceived aerial threat in certain fixtures, principally away from home.

Despite Paul Walsh's outstanding form there were many observers who would have preferred to see the manager take a more active playing part. The inclusion of the recently-injured MacDonald, the alternating of Whelan and Jim Begin at left back and even the persistence with the occasionally erratic Bruce Grobbelaar, had drawn dissenting voices from fans who believed in choosing a traditional 4-4-2 formation and the same XI each week, regardless of the opponent. Concerned only with results however, Dalglish was never a manager to pick his team based on what press and public were saying.

Chelsea's league position owed much to the goal scoring form of Kerry Dixon - whose 21 goals to date had helped force his way into the England squad - and the smaller, combative David Speedie (16 goals) up front. Dalglish, conscious of the threat posed by Dixon's ability in the air and Speedie's ability to feed off his strike partner, opted once again for a three-man central defence of Gillespie - fit after recovering from a thigh strain - Molby and Hansen. Player of the season so far, Mark Lawrenson, was pushed forward into midfield. Liverpool kicked-off in bright sunshine attacking nearly 3,000 travelling fans on the open North Terrace. The away support stood opposite the Shed End and to the left of some of Chelsea's most vocal and unruly fans in the seated West Stand.

Studio guests for ITV's Big Match Live, Everton's Gary Lineker - making his first appearance as a TV pundit - and former Chelsea and Spurs legend Jimmy Greaves, had briefly run the rule over the respective scoring prowess of Rush and Dixon, referencing Rush's recent return to goalscoring form and Dixon's emergence as a potential partner for Lineker at Mexico '86.

The first significant incident of the game involved Chelsea's leading scorer but only in the sense that it curtailed his involvement in the match. Chasing an agricultural clearance from uncompromising centre-half Doug Rougvie, Dixon pulled up sharply with a groin injury that saw him clatter to the turf after just six minutes. To the delight and amusement of the Liverpool following, a stretcher was called and the Chelsea striker was carted off the pitch to strains of, "Dixon is dead, Dixon is dead," from the gloating Liverpool contingent behind the goal. This incensed the Chelsea supporters and one intrepid, eccentrically-clad individual attempted to scale a fence dividing the rival followers. He was beaten back with relish by the Liverpool fans and was eventually arrested for his own safety, but not before he had taken something of a hiding from some of the Reds' followers nearby.

Chelsea's fans in a crowd of 33,625 were then briefly encouraged by two instances of defensive carelessness by Liverpool. First, Grobbelaar spilled a 15th minute, inswinging Jerry Murphy corner only to be rescued by Whelan's timely clearance. Then Lawrenson's attempted pass back to his goalkeeper was a little too lofted and the fleet-footed Pat Nevin almost capitalized. Despite these two minor scares however, Liverpool were controlling possession and Molby had been able to augment the numbers in midfield by moving forward at times in his now unsurprising sweeper role.

Dixon was replaced by substitute Paul Cannoville but his absence was a major blow to Chelsea morale and their task became doubly difficult when experienced defender Colin

Lee also departed five minutes before half-time with a strained hamstring. With just one substitute allowed, the Blues faced the prospect of playing the remainder of the tie with just 10 men. To compound Chelsea's misery, Liverpool opened the scoring in the three resulting minutes of injury time added by the referee due to the injuries at the end of the half.

Initially Lawrenson, finding his new role in midfield granted him rare opportunities around the Chelsea box, shot across the face of goal. Keith Dublin failed to clear decisively and, after the ball struck Craig Johnston, it fell to Rush who expertly shaped to the right to make an angle for a precise finish from about eight yards. It was another clinical strike by the Welshman. With Chelsea a man down and Liverpool a goal up, it seemed the sting had been taken out of the tie as the teams headed for the dressing rooms at half-time.

Straight after the interval, Liverpool immediately doubled their advantage. Lawrenson, as adept in midfield as in defence, made a perfectly timed jog forward to collect Walsh's lay off from Steve Nicol's pass from deep. He gathered the ball expertly in his path and took a couple more strides before unleashing his shot - straight at Eddie Niedzwiecki in the Chelsea goal. The Chelsea keeper ought to have saved 'Lawro's' shot easily but he managed to the let the ball squeeze beneath his grasp and over the line.

The Liverpool fans, distant at the opposite end of the ground, took a couple of seconds to register the fact that the ball had entered the net but the celebrations and taunting of their Chelsea counterparts afterwards more than made up for a restricted view of Liverpool's second goal. It seemed that the Reds' passage to the fifth round was assured. Chelsea however, had other ideas, and they managed to turn the game on its head after 67 minutes when they pulled a goal back when David Speedie arched his body to hook past Grobbelaar after Gillespie had only partially cleared. The home crowd suddenly came to life as they sensed an unlikely replay might be on the cards.

The atmosphere seemed to affect Liverpool and, instead of pushing forward to exploit their extra man, they sat back and invited more pressure from Chelsea. The three-man central defensive rearguard of Hansen, Gillespie and Molby were forced to deal with a succession of high balls and Liverpool prepared to be penned in for a difficult final quarter. Roared on by those in The Shed and the West Stand, Chelsea came close to equalising seven minutes from time when the dangerous Speedie was allowed to turn in the box. Grobbelaar was forced to make a reflex save with his legs from the resultant low shot and this save proved to be a match winner for Liverpool. Chelsea's pressure finally petered out but Liverpool fans watching at home and those who had travelled to Stamford Bridge wondered how a match that had seen them two goals up with a numerical advantage on the field had ended so tensely.

Former Liverpool striker Ian St John voiced his concerns over Dalglish and Liverpool's perceived negative tactics in his role as ITV match summariser. He stated that Chelsea had been unlucky to lose and that he felt sorry for the Londoners and Chelsea boss John Hollins. At a time when Liverpudlians were sensitive to the national media's portrayal of themselves, their City and their team, it felt strange that a much loved ex-player could be so critical of Liverpool in achieving a result that could go a long way towards clearing a path to Wembley.

Despite Chelsea's rousing finish, Liverpool had secured their spot in the draw for the fifth round and laid some particularly nasty FA Cup ghosts in the process. They had hung on near the end but would undoubtedly have settled for this result before kick-off. Ultimately, Dalglish's tactic of employing three centre-backs had been crucial in quelling Chelsea's late aerial bombardment.

Jubilant at their victory, Liverpool's travelling army of fans filed out onto the streets of West London to be met with a relatively passive throng of Chelsea supporters thereby ensuring a largely trouble free passage back to Euston station. After a near four and a half hour train journey home, many enjoyed a late drink in the city centre - and wondered who would be paired with the Reds in the following day's draw for the quarter-finals.

Having already booked their place in the fifth round courtesy of a 3-1 win over Blackburn at Goodison the day before, the chances of an all-Merseyside Cup Final appeared to be increasing with each round – until Everton were drawn away at Tottenham (should Spurs defeat Notts County in a replay). Due to postponements because of the weather, this tie would not be played until early March. Reward for the Reds' victory at Chelsea was a return trip to Bootham Crescent and a repeat of the previous season's clash with Third Division York City. Few fans saw the tie being the problem it would later become.

Chapter Six
Dont Give Up and Dont Give In

Ipswich Town v Liverpool
Saturday 1 February

"The American space shuttle, Challenger, has exploded killing all seven astronauts on board. The five men and two women - including the first teacher in space - were just over a minute into their flight from Cape Canaveral in Florida when the Challenger blew up. The astronauts' families, at the airbase, and millions of Americans witnessed the world's worst space disaster live on TV."

BBC News 28 January 1986

After a storming January that had seen them progress to the last sixteen of the FA Cup and win seven points from nine in the League, Liverpool travelled to Ipswich confident that they could continue a run which had more than consolidated their position in the title race.

Despite criticism for meddling with Liverpool's traditional style of play; his use of a sweeper system and a more pragmatic, changeable approach to tactics than had been seen in previous seasons, Dalglish had been an obvious choice for the Manager of the Month award - an accolade accepted with his usual humility. The prize was viewed as something of a poisoned chalice however, with a reputation - not without foundation - for its recipients coming unstuck in their very next game.

Champions Everton, with five wins and a draw in their last six league games had also cemented their place in the title picture in recent weeks but, perhaps feeling the pressure of a 19-year wait for a league championship, Manchester United, after their remarkable start to the season, had begun to haemorrhage points. Everton hadn't yet reached the standards of the previous season when they had strolled to the title but, sustained by a steady stream of goals from Gary Lineker, they had begun to grind out results and they loomed ominously in the upper reaches of the table. United by contrast, after Ron Atkinson's early-season Manager of the Month awards, were feeling the pressure.

It was still a wide-open title race however. So much so that the claims of West Ham, despite their recent reverses at Anfield and Stamford Bridge, could not be ignored as they prepared to face Manchester United at Upton Park. Chelsea, with two games in hand and level on points with Liverpool, were also a major threat. If the Reds had any real aspirations to the title then they had to maintain their recent run of good form.

Having beaten Ipswich at Anfield in August (5-0), and again in the recent Milk Cup fixture (3-0), the trip to Portman Road seemed the ideal fixture to extend the Reds' winning run. As a club, Ipswich had fallen a long way from the heights they occupied under Bobby Robson during the late-70s and early-80s when the FA Cup (1978) and UEFA Cup (1981) had taken pride of place in the Portman Road trophy room. In recent years top players had been sold to 'bigger' clubs and, although they retained a family feel in the Boardroom under the ultra-Conservative Cobbold family, new manager Bobby Ferguson had been charged with retaining their top flight status with an increasingly youthful, inexperienced squad.

Dalglish's preparations for the game had been marred by a thigh injury to the in-form Ian

Rush, whose goals had underpinned Liverpool's unbeaten January run. With Rush forced to miss the trip, the player-manager's decision not to step in and instead pair Craig Johnston with Paul Walsh was understandable - given the similarities between himself and Walsh. Johnston's energy, pace and direct running style made him, at least in the eyes of Liverpool fans, an obvious choice to partner the more subtle style of Walsh.

However, the growing clamour from the press for Dalglish to include himself in the starting eleven, regardless of Walsh's quality and Liverpool's recent free-scoring, winning form, was approaching farcical proportions. National journalists who saw a fraction of Liverpool's matches, in most cases only when the Reds visited the capital, were making it an almost personal crusade to disregard what Dalglish viewed as his preferred team. Despite the obvious shortcomings of their argument however, the result here would give Dalglish's London-based critics further ammunition. To compound matters further, Jan Molby's pre-match comment that Ipswich had a, "soft under-belly," would also prove ill-timed and ill-conceived.

Johnston's move up front left a gap in midfield and Sammy Lee dutifully took his place in the centre of the park as Liverpool continued with five at the back - Molby acting as sweeper alongside Hansen and Gillespie.

The first day of February saw conditions far from ideal in East Anglia, with wind and driving rain circling Portman Road as the game kicked off. Despite the awful weather Liverpool were quick to settle and they proceeded to zip the ball around on the lush, wet surface. Ipswich prided themselves on having one of the finest playing surfaces in the country and, even in the depths of winter when pitches were notoriously heavy, they could rely on a surface which encouraged a creative, passing style that was easy on the eye.

The visitors were the first to threaten after just a few minutes play, when a well-constructed move ended with a Steve McCall tackle denying Ronnie Whelan just as the Irishman was in the act of shooting. Ipswich responded by winning a throw-in on the right – 15 yards inside the Liverpool half. From Ian Cranson's long delivery Grobbelaar made a trademark venture from his line to collect, but was forced to gather at the second attempt after initially spilling the greasy ball. Grobbelaar then saved easily from Jason Dozzell's 20-yard shot, and the Zimbabwean was at his brilliant best minutes later when he was forced to save at the same player's feet after the young striker had been put clean through on goal.

The strength of the wind was restricting Liverpool's attempts to venture forward and for a while it appeared they were content to contain Ipswich and wait for the second half so as to take advantage of the conditions. On the half hour mark however, Walsh managed to evade several tackles and wriggle through on the left side of the box before he was denied by a Frank Yallop tackle. The Londoner featured again just six minutes later when Liverpool took the lead. Ipswich were having trouble containing the fleet-footed striker and McCall resorted to fouling the striker on the right hand side rather than risk another tricky run in the box. The free-kick was Molby's chance to step forward and he placed an expert chip onto the head of Whelan, who skilfully directed a looping header into the far corner of the net.

Making light of the wind and rain, and passing with confidence having taken the lead, Liverpool began to play some superb football. So good was it that even the home fans applauded after Johnston's run down the left and turn inside ended with Walsh hooking a first-time shot narrowly wide. As the half-time whistle blew Liverpool were in complete control and, with the prospect of the wind behind them in the second half, those Reds fans who were huddled under the roof of the South Stand after their six-hour train journey, were confident that yet another three points beckoned.

Such optimism was ill-placed however, and the game was turned on its head after just eight minutes of the second half. Frank Yallop, who up till then had enjoyed a fine match in a defensive role, was forced to depart with an injury but substitute, Michael Cole, described in the Liverpool Echo as a, "19 years-old coloured teenager of unusual pace," was not an obvious replacement and he went straight into attack as Ipswich began to ask questions of Liverpool's five-man defence with an extra man up front. The tactical switch worked and Bobby Ferguson's team were level almost immediately. Cranson's pass down the right caught the Liverpool defence half asleep and, from Putney's cross, Ipswich's big centre-forward Mitch D'Avray managed to get to the ball a fraction of a second before Grobbelaar and scramble home the equalizer.

At 1-1, the game - and Liverpool's first half dominance - had turned round completely. Ipswich nearly went in front when young Cole found himself in possession on the edge of the box with Grobbelaar out of position. Crucially however, the novice striker hesitated, delaying his shot just long enough for Gillespie to get back and clear. Liverpool rallied with Steve Nicol almost latching onto a header from Lee, but Ipswich again threatened when Cole's well-struck shot forced Grobbelaar to dive full length to palm the ball away for a corner. The match had developed into a real contest and it was apparent either side could win it. Although visibly rocked by Ipswich's determined second-half response, the Reds continued to try and play some intricate close passing and, at the end of a move involving several players, Johnston glanced a header wide from Walsh's cross.

Sensing that Ipswich had maybe given their best, Liverpool pressed for the winner. Johnston was unlucky to see another header find Cooper's positioning perfect and Lawrenson, again operating in midfield, had a powerful strike beaten away by the Ipswich keeper. Portman Road's biggest crowd of the season, 20,551 were enjoying an end-to-end game, with chances for both teams as the players made light of the persistent heavy rain. It seemed that both sides would have to settle for a point but Liverpool's early season defensive sloppiness resurfaced and, with ten minutes remaining, it cost them the game.

There seemed little danger when Ipswich pumped a long ball into the penalty area on 79 minutes, but Steve Nicol miscued his attempted clearance and the ball fell to Kevin Wilson who watched it drop before unleashing an unstoppable left-foot volley from an acute angle over Grobbelaar. It was a fitting winning goal for an exciting game of football that could have gone either way. "We got what we deserved" said Dalglish after the match. "The two goals they scored were down to ourselves."

Addressing journalists' questions about his persistence with a five-man defence the manger explained that, "Sometimes changes works for you and sometimes against you. You want players who are adaptable and have ability to play [in] different positions. You can give it a try. It doesn't mean you have to stay like that."

While the manager cited defensive errors as the reason for this untimely defeat, an inevitable conclusion was drawn by the national media. "I still believe the biggest mistake Liverpool made," wrote Steve Curry in the Daily Express, "came from Dalglish himself when he decided to keep on his double breasted suit and sit in the stand after Ian Rush had been ruled unfit." The self-appointed football expert added, "I can't see why Dalglish needs to tamper with a central defence of Mark Lawrenson and Alan Hansen which has served the club so ably over such a long period of time and are certainly far from old men." The debate over formation, team selection and Dalglish's non-inclusion was set to rumble on.

An ecstatic Bobby Ferguson emphasized the importance of a win over Liverpool to his young team. "Success against sides like Liverpool, Arsenal and West Ham will help our crowd to believe in the young lads," he said. "Make no mistake, they are babies I have out there. You are seeing teenagers, 18 and 19 years old a lot of them. Winning matches like this puts the club and the players back on the map again."

Whatever the reasons, defeat here was a major bow to Liverpool's title hopes. On the same afternoon, a Peter Reid goal put Everton top of the pile for the first time courtesy of a 1-0 win over Spurs at Goodison Park. Manchester United's latest defeat at Upton Park signalled the growing threat from West Ham, tucked away in fifth with games in hand. Liverpool were now fourth in the table – their lowest position of the season - three points behind Everton, and trailing United – their next League opponents - and Chelsea by two points and one point respectively.

Norwich City v Liverpool
Screen Sport Super Cup, semi-final first Leg
Wednesday 5 February

"Again, I persuaded my (pale) blue mate 'Whitey' to go with me to Carrow Road. We travelled via Euston and stopped in London for a few. When he realised on the train that they were playing Tottenham (at Tottenham) on the same night, he persuaded me - after a few ales, and with Norwich getting further and further away as the day wore on - to go to White Hart Lane instead. It was a bit tasty after the game, more so than the calm at Norwich. I still get stick about this from Blues today. Ha! – the Ordinary to Spurs for the Super Cup. Just about sums them up."

Maca, Liverpool fan, Huyton.

The disappointing defeat at Ipswich had brought Liverpool's unbeaten run in 1986 to an untimely end and perhaps the last thing the Reds' needed was a return trip to East Anglia just five days later. Although a Cup Final berth was up for grabs, this semi-final first leg tie against Second Division Norwich City in the Screen Sport Super Cup was an unnecessary complication ahead of the weekend's upcoming clash with Manchester United. With Ian Rush still struggling with the injury that kept him out at Portman Road however, Dalglish saw an opportunity to give himself a first start since New Year's Day and in so doing gain some valuable match-fitness should he be required to re-enter the fray on a more regular basis later in the season.

Norwich had felt aggrieved by the margin of defeat in their five goal drubbing in January's FA Cup tie at Anfield and, with the taste of last season's Milk Cup win against Sunderland at Wembley which qualified them for this competition still fresh in their minds, the prospect of another Cup Final was more than additional motivation.

Affording respect to the opposition, and in keeping with the times, Dalglish included himself in a strong line-up that saw Liverpool revert to traditional 4-4-2 formation. Alan

Hansen's creaking knees were rested, and Jan Molby was restored to midfield leaving Mark Lawrenson to partner Gary Gillespie in a more traditional – and national media pleasing - central defence. Up front, Paul Walsh partnered the player-manager for only the fourth time of the season. Remarkably, on the three previous occasions they had played together, and challenging the commonly held view that they were too similar, they had scored seven goals between them. Dalglish was on the mark in the Super Cup versus Southampton and Walsh bagged five goals in consecutive games against Luton and Brighton (Milk Cup) with the boss, also scoring versus the latter, at his side.

Keenly contested in the first half Liverpool enjoyed the lion's share of possession, but Norwich came closest to scoring when Peter Mendham's shot from the edge of the box deceived Grobbelaar and bounced off the goalkeeper's chest before being scrambled away to safety. The Reds played some neat football through midfield, but for all their territorial dominance the combative Norwich defensive pairing of Steve Bruce and former Liverpool reserve Dave Watson managed to effectively shackle the deft touches of Dalglish and the mesmeric dribbling of Walsh. Under-rated young defenders at the time, Bruce and Watson would later win League Championship honours with Manchester United and Everton respectively.

With confidence gained from a goalless first half, and in search of an advantage to take to Anfield for the second leg, Norwich carried the attack to Liverpool after the break. Such positivity was rewarded in the 49th minute when Kevin Drinkell took advantage of a slip by Mark Lawrenson to slot past Grobbelaar. Encouraged by a decent-sized home crowd of 15,330 the Canaries immediately sought a second. Pacy winger Mark Barham had given the Reds problems all night down the right flank, but the closest Norwich came to extending their lead was when Wayne Biggins forced Grobbelaar to palm his rasping shot onto a post.

After an excellent second-half performance that hinted at their inevitable promotion to the top flight at the end of the season, the Canaries began to tire and the last word on the night was left to the returning Liverpool player-manager. Throughout his career Dalglish had earned a reputation for producing the unexpected with a catalogue of trademark goals leaving defenders flat-footed and goalkeepers rooted to the spot. Tonight was no exception.

With ten minutes remaining Dalglish received a pass from Molby just outside the penalty area. He turned in an instant and unleashed a shot past a disbelieving Chris Woods in the Norwich goal. In the blink of an eye Liverpool were on equal terms with one of Dalglish's finest goals; recalled today only by the small travelling contingent or the even smaller TV audience watching the Screen Sport satellite TV coverage.

Despite a successful return to the field, Liverpool's manager drew more satisfaction from a solid, if not spectacular, performance. There were no further injuries to complicate his selection for the looming clash with United and the scoreline would see Liverpool start favourites for the second-leg on a date still to be decided. No one could have foreseen on the five-hour return journey however, what was to make the return leg - when it was eventually staged in May - such a memorable night for Dalglish and his team.

Liverpool v Manchester United
Sunday 9 February

*"A United player went down injured only to be implored by the Kop to 'Die you b*****d die'. Then, Atkinson was taunted with 'he's fat, he's bent – his a**e is up for rent'. Wark, not Kenny, replaced Walshy but as the half wore on, we were pushing the Mancs back and the noise of the crowd got louder and louder.*

Eventually Wark equalized and the ground exploded. Mayhem everywhere. The Kop shook to a really nasty rendition of 'Give a dog a bone – Man United f**k off home'. Teenagers and lads in their twenties were up on the barriers, loads of whom seemed to be wearing green jumpers, bouncing up and down like lunatics and appearing to orchestrate the crowd."

David Brennan, Liverpool fan, Old Swan.

By February 1986 relations between the followers of Liverpool and Manchester United were at an all-time low. As hooliganism intensified in the 1970s there had been a gradual and visible increase in animosity at matches involving the clubs. United's 'Red Army', a notorious mob that caused havoc all over the country, especially in the 1974-75 Season after their side had been relegated, clashed frequently with members of Liverpool's intrepid crew of young followers from the Anfield Road End, and the rivalry off the pitch only intensified as the decade drew to a close.

The mutual loathing was a symptom of a violent era and a far cry from earlier in the century when the two Clubs shared no more than normal, geographic footballing rivalry as the signature football teams of the North West's two finest industrial centres. On the West coast was Liverpool, famed for being the world's most pre-eminent Port, whilst 35 miles inland, built on the great wealth generated by the textile industry stood 'Cottonopolis' itself, Manchester.

Before the Second World War, Liverpool's tally of League Championships was four; United's two. In 1945, seeking a future career in management, retiring Liverpool captain Matt Busby was offered only a coach's role at Anfield and controversially, though understandably, he declined this in favour of the manager's role at Old Trafford. The decision arguably changed the course of history for both clubs. When League football recommenced after the War, Liverpool immediately won a fifth league title. Busby's first season in charge at Old Trafford won nothing more than gentle approval, but later, his visionary managerial qualities saw Manchester United become a dominant domestic and European force.

The 1950s was a golden decade for United and they were crowned League Champions in 1952, '56 and '57. Liverpool meanwhile, under poor leadership in the boardroom, were relegated in 1954 and they slipped, readily into obscurity as United's 'Busby Babes' won the hearts of a football nation. When the club tragically lost eight players in the 1958 Munich air disaster, the outpouring of sympathy saw them cement their position as England's most popular club. With Liverpool languishing in the Second Division and no prevailing rivalry or bitterness between the clubs, the reaction to the disaster in Liverpool was the same as in any other British city – genuine shock and horror at the loss of eight gifted and talented young footballers.

Busby, who cheated death at Munich to the extent that he was twice given the Last Rites, was eventually able to rebuild United into a force in English football again, but by this time

Liverpool had begun a recovery of their own under the guidance of Busby's lifelong friend and fellow, inspirational Scot, Bill Shankly.

Champions in 1964 and 1966 and FA Cup Winners in 1965, Shankly's Liverpool – as well as neighbours Everton - challenged United's North West supremacy throughout the 'Merseybeat' decade. The avuncular Busby had the last word however, when his side became the first English team to win the European Cup in 1968 - to the delight of most of the country's football fans.

Remarkably, United's pioneering European triumph signalled the end of their success. Busby retired a year later and the Manchester club endured a scarcely believable wait of 26 years for another League title. Thirty-one years elapsed before they would claim a second European Cup. The nadir came in 1974 when relegation saw them subjected to an embarrassing season in the Second Division. By contrast, during United's barren period Liverpool, led by Shankly and his line of succession from the 'Boot Room'; Paisley then Fagan, amassed 11 League titles and four European Cups. Undoubtedly, Liverpool had superseded Manchester United as England's most successful football club.

Liverpool fans had always enjoyed a passionate, yet relatively cordial, rivalry with neighbours Everton, aided no doubt by the Blues gradual demise from their own period of success in the mid-60s. Instead, Reds' fans saved their loathing for Don Revie's gifted, but cynical 'Dirty Leeds' of the late-60s and early-70s. When Leeds suffered rapid decline in the late '70s, the Kop switched its principal hatred towards the East Midlands. The emergence of Nottingham Forest under the outspoken self-publicist Brain Clough saw them, very briefly, threaten Liverpool's unparalleled European and domestic superiority. Forest's consecutive European Cups in 1979 and 1980 stood comparison with Manchester United's European tally until 2008.

Liverpudlian thoughts were naturally occupied by rivalries with those clubs competing with them for honours, both at home and abroad and, as the 1980's dawned it was Ipswich, Aston Villa and then Spurs who carried the greatest threat. Apart from a heart breaking defeat to United at Wembley in the 1977 FA Cup Final which denied Liverpool an historic treble, the Mancunians were such a footballing irrelevance that they barely registered in the average Liverpool fan's consciousness.

In terms of domestic dominance Liverpool's three consecutive League titles from 1982 onwards, culminating in a League, Milk Cup and European Cup treble in 1984, was threatening the competitive nature of English football. During these Championship winning years, supposedly unfashionable teams such as Ipswich Town, Watford and Southampton had been runners-up to Liverpool whilst, much to the chagrin of the national media, United failed to register a single, credible title assault.

In their elusive search for a manager who would challenge Liverpool's superiority United appointed the Liverpool-born, media-friendly, former WBA boss Ron Atkinson in 1982. Despite his birthplace, Atkinson was the complete antithesis to Liverpool's quiet conservatism under Bob Paisley and later, Joe Fagan. Always ready with a quote for the press and a lover of the TV cameras, the perma-tanned Atkinson, with his penchant for outlandish gold jewellery, was a reporter's dream, filling column inch after column inch with colourful quotes in the build-up and aftermath of every United fixture.

Atkinson's openness and willingness to brief the newspapers, combined with Liverpool's long-held desire to do their talking on the pitch, saw stories concerning United dominate the back pages. This came at a time when the Reds' command of the English and European game was almost unchallenged. When Atkinson crowned his first season at Old Trafford with FA Cup success in a replayed final at Wembley against already relegated Brighton & Hove Albion in May 1983, the media lapped it up. By contrast, Liverpool's 14th League title went almost unnoticed.

Earlier that season, Liverpool managed to beat United 2-1 in the Milk Cup Final, a result which Atkinson, fast becoming a hate figure on Merseyside, claimed was achieved with the help of some dubious refereeing decisions. He chose to ignore his side's second half collapse in the face of a determined Liverpool fightback. A sense of anger at his actions and words in the city of his birth was growing fast, accompanied by United supporters' ongoing resentment of Liverpool's relentless annexation of the big prizes.

When Liverpool fans travelled to Brussels for the ill-fated European Cup Final in May 1985, shortly after losing to an improving United in a replayed FA Cup semi-final – which had seen numerous violent clashes between warring factions - the banners that bedecked the Liverpool end told their own story. Long before the clever, often poetic, flags that accompanied Reds supporters' pilgrimages to Istanbul and Athens, some of the Liverpool flags that night targeted Manchester United, and Ron Atkinson in particular.

Four years prior to Liverpool fans' awful experiences at Hillsborough, and with a generation of supporters that scarcely remembered the 'Busby Babes', several home-made efforts draped over the fencing at the Heysel Stadium bore slogans cruelly referencing 'Munich '58'. Similar, unthinking messages were worn on T-shirts and daubed on sun-hats. For their part, United supporters retaliated by mocking the death of Liverpool's greatest icon – Shankly.

At Heysel, in more personal attacks on the United boss, unsophisticated messages in black paint daubed on white bed sheets proffered 'Atkinson's Tart is a Slut', 'Atkinson's got Aids', and a more cryptic 'Atkinson's Long Leather'. Probably the least offensive banner read, 'Man United, This is the Big Cup', in reference to United's latest FA Cup triumph days earlier. At an event where Liverpool stood on the verge of claiming a fifth European crown and the right to keep forever the most prestigious trophy in club football, an all encompassing, spiteful domestic feud was writ large on the terraces. All this came before the ensuing tragedy which claimed 39 lives and saw the name Liverpool swap fame for infamy.

At the start of the 1985/86 season, as Liverpool contemplated the ramifications of their European ban following Heysel, United put together a record-equalling run of 10 consecutive wins that left title rivals trailing in their wake. At that stage of the season Liverpool were their closest pursuers but had still conceded a nine-point lead. The prospect of United and Atkinson ending the club's long wait for a League title loomed large - and it didn't sit easily with the Kop.

Reds' fans loathing for United wasn't restricted to their manager however, and Kopites had an equally-low opinion of their Welsh striker Mark Hughes, perennially-injured captain of England Bryan Robson and Northern Ireland midfield hard-man Norman Whiteside. Whiteside had fanned the flames ahead of the match in midweek when commenting that, "at United we refuse to lie down when Liverpool attempt to intimidate us."

By mid-autumn, United's early season form had begun to desert them and they were shipping points badly. Liverpool had scored a timely psychological blow by removing them from the Milk Cup in October and by the time they were due to visit Anfield in the League, United's wobbles had allowed Everton to assume top spot in the table whilst Liverpool had closed the gap between themselves and their foes from down the East Lancs Road to just two points. United though, still had a game in hand on the Reds.

Despite the anticipation between supporters and the pivotal importance of the result in the title race, the presence of the BBC cameras for live TV coverage meant that Liverpool were still advertising seats and ground tickets for the game on the Friday evening before the match. Once again the harsh realities of the economic situation on Merseyside were illustrated with Liverpool's biggest match of the Anfield season so far threatening to draw a crowd well short of capacity.

Professionally divorced from such matters, Kenny Dalglish was more concerned with monitoring the fitness of Ian Rush who had missed the last two games through injury. Atkinson meanwhile was considering giving a start to diminutive, newly-signed striker Terry Gibson - who had scored a hat-trick against the Reds for his previous club Coventry back in December 1983.

Although Merseyside Police were on full alert to deal with potential clashes between supporters inside and outside Anfield, no-one could have foreseen that the match would be overshadowed by yet another ugly act of hooliganism. The furore following the opening day service of remembrance for the Juventus fans who died at Heysel, and the subsequent press backlash that followed, had died down but the events of Sunday's meeting ensured that the front pages of the following days' papers would be awash with more bad publicity for Liverpool.

Such virulent hatred was despite a 'From Manchester With Love' gig in support of Militant, staged at the Royal Court theatre on the eve of the fixture. Compered by Derek Hatton; popular Manchester acts The Smiths, The Fall and New Order, performing a debut cover version of Joy Division's Love 'Will Tear Us Apart', appeared together for the first time. In light of events that were to unfold at Anfield the next day, perhaps New Order would have been better covering another Joy Division song - 'No Love Lost'.

As the United team bus drove into the Main Stand car park off Anfield Road it was hit by a barrage bricks and stones. As bad as this was however, things turned nastier when the team began to disembark the coach. Amid chants referencing the Munich air disaster, someone in the large crowd that surrounded the players' entrance fired a canister filled with a gas-like substance in the direction of the United players.

Rumoured to have been ammonia or tear gas, the toxic spray temporarily affected the vision some of the visiting squad and caused panic among those straining for a close-up view of the players. Although the incident passed very quickly, a number of Liverpool supporters were also hurt by the noxious substance that lingered in the air for several minutes.

The worst affected supporters, including children, were ushered inside the security barrier to receive treatment in the visitors' dressing room and the United players were shepherded straight onto the Anfield pitch to get some fresh air and clear their vision. Through the actions of one irresponsible individual, a huge fall-out to the incident would be played out in the press in the coming days. It was yet another opportunity to castigate the behaviour of Liverpool as a city and their fans in particular.

Despite the presence of a fully-equipped outside broadcast crew to cover the match there were no live BBC cameras trained on the players to capture the incident as they made their way off the team bus. Such a scenario is difficult to imagine in the current era, when meaningless footage of detached players ambling into dressing rooms listening to i-Pods so as not to converse with fans and media alike, provides a visual backdrop to inane pre-match punditry. In the absence of such coverage - and the inevitable modern day relay of the controversy via mobile phones - news of the attack on the United squad didn't filter through to those gathering on the terraces in anticipation of an important top of the table clash. This was perhaps just as well if the afternoon was to pass off without further incident.

With Ian Rush declaring himself fit to resume his burgeoning partnership with Paul Walsh, Dalglish resumed his purely managerial role. The Scot was forced into another defensive reshuffle however, when Steve Nicol was found to have a broken jaw sustained during the midweek trip to Norwich – an incident rumoured to have occurred during a 'disagreement' on the return coach journey. The ever-versatile Mark Lawrenson filled the void at right back. McMahon and McDonald were still missing for the Reds so Sammy Lee continued in midfield.

Manchester United had their own injury problems with the flaky Robson (predictably) missing – his absence not enough to quell the Kop's wild assertions about his sex life - along with Gordon Strachan and goalkeeper Gary Bailey who was replaced by the inexperienced Chris Turner. Terry Gibson was included for his first start in United colours whilst Danish signing John Sivebaek was also given a debut in midfield.

Despite empty seats at either end of the Kemlyn Road stand and some gaps at the edges of the Kop showing that Anfield was clearly well short of capacity, Liverpool ran out to a deafening welcome from their supporters in a crowd of 35,004. The Kop immediately noticed that Paul Walsh's flowing 'scallycut' had been shorn since he had last been on view at Anfield, and serenaded him with a chant of, "Walshie's had a hair cut". Merseyside barbers rubbed their hands in glee at the prospect of a glut of copycat business.

Manchester United received a predictable chorus of boos and shrill whistles as they took the field, and they quickly ran towards the sanctuary of their followers in the South corner of the Anfield Road End. United's three-point advantage with a game in hand over the Reds meant this was a match Liverpool couldn't afford to lose. With the home side attacking the Anfield Road in the first-half the match began with typically robust tackles flying in during the early exchanges. Unbeaten at Anfield since 1979, United started the better and had the Reds on the back foot inside the first quarter of an hour and they made their early pressure tell with the opening goal on 19 minutes.

Colin Gibson, an expensive signing from Aston Villa, played a one-two with Mark Hughes at the edge of the box and, although Grobbelaar was able to parry the new signing's shot on the run, he followed up to force the ball into the Kop goal. As he wheeled away in stunned celebration he was given a volley of predictably volatile gestures from the Kop.

Perhaps mindful of the huge significance of the game to their title ambitions, Liverpool had made a tentative start but United's opener seemed to galvanise them and, for the remainder of the half, they mounted one attack after another in a desperate attempt to find an equalizer. For their part United seemed content to sit on their lead and invite Liverpool to attack. Rush went close with a header just wide of the right hand post on 25 minutes before Gillespie, with another header, grazed the crossbar.

On the half-hour Liverpool's attempts to draw level suffered a severe setback when Paul Walsh lost his balance and went over on an ankle. After receiving lengthy treatment from Roy Evans the in-form striker was forced to limp to the dressing room to the audible groans of the home crowd. Later diagnosed as ruptured ankle ligaments, the injury effectively ended Walsh's season and put paid to any ambitions he had of securing a place in England's squad for the Mexico 1986 World Cup. More significantly for Liverpool, the long-term injury to Walsh would force Kenny Dalglish to reconsider his striking options for the remainder of the season. Seemingly so reliant on the Rush-Walsh partnership which had realised 37 goals so far, who would Dalglish turn to now?

With a full hour of the game left the Reds were forced into making a tactical and positional reshuffle. Substitute John Wark slotted into midfield at the expense of Craig Johnston, who moved forward into attack to partner Rush. Despite this makeshift formation Wark took barely four minutes to turn the game on its head.

Always impressive going forward, Jim Beglin brought the ball out of defence and embarked on a long and determined cross-field run before slipping a diagonal pass to the onrushing Sammy Lee. Lee's low toe-poke beat Turner but instead of nestling in the back of the net as the crowd hoped, the ball cannoned back off the inside of the post with the thousands behind the Anfield Road goal holding their heads in despair. Bouncing agonisingly across the six-yard box however, the ball rolled toward the inrushing Wark who, muscling his way past United's ex-Everton full-back John Gidman, prodded the loose ball home at the far post to send Anfield wild.

The half-time break interrupted Liverpool's momentum but the mood on and off the pitch had turned. Gone was the triumphalist goading by the United fans, replaced instead by the chorus of songs and chants that only a fully committed Anfield can inspire. The Liverpool fans sensed a change and felt, if their side started the second 45 minutes as they had ended the first, that the points would be theirs.

With Lawrenson's remarkable and under-rated speed offering an extra attacking outlet at right-back – the Eire international's third different role in as many games - Liverpool started the half by launching a series of forays down that wing. A small but agile keeper, Turner saved brilliantly, first from Rush and then Whelan, and was later fortunate to have Johnston head straight at him from six yards out after a fine cross by Gillespie. A few minutes later Rush fired uncharacteristically wide with a volley from ten yards.

Liverpool were doing all the attacking and Wark, enjoying his best game of the season, almost caught Turner napping with a rasping left foot shot that flew just wide. Seemingly intent on holding onto the point, United had retreated almost entirely, offering only a sporadic threat. Their best chance of the half fell to Gibson but a last-ditch tackle by Gillespie snuffed this out. It was the visitor's only attack of note of the half.

Liverpool continued to threaten as the clock ticked down but a combination of staunch defending, notably from centre-halves Paul McGrath and Kevin Moran, and safe handling from Turner, meant that the home side would have to settle for a point in a game they had dominated for long periods. Kevin Moran admitted afterwards that United had defended for far too long during the game. "You always expect Liverpool to have a spell on top," the committed Irishman said. "You hope to contain them and then get back yourselves, but we never really managed to do that this time." Refusing to blame the pre-match attack on the United players for their lacklustre display he added, "We were coughing and spluttering and our eyes were running, but I am sure it had no effect on our performance. We had an hour to recover and everyone was OK by the kick-off."

Predictably, the rest of the after-match comment related to the incident in the Main Stand car park. Holding nothing back in an emotive outburst aimed at Liverpool fans, United Chairman Martin Edwards said, "I have never known such abuse. It was frightening. A brick was thrown at the coach but luckily it hit a stanchion first otherwise it would have hit Mark Hughes. If you think about it he could have been killed."

Liverpool responded in kind through their Chief Executive Peter Robinson. Though he admitted the Club regretted the incident, "very much indeed," he shifted some of the blame with his assertion that, "It certainly doesn't help when the United captain Norman Whiteside gives an interview the day before the game in which he talks about refusing to be intimidated." The well respected Chief Executive added, somewhat naively given the experiences that both sets of fans had witnessed for some time that, "for some reason there has been a lot of ill feeling between sections of our supporters and those of United over the last few years."

Kenny Dalglish restricted the bulk of his post-match comments to the action on the field but he attempted to play down the incident and the lack of security. "It is a pity it has all been blown up," he said. "There isn't a lot you can do because the players have got to get into the ground. However, it is up to us to try and rectify it."

As the sun set on a dramatic Sunday afternoon, Liverpool fans reflected more on the two points they had dropped in their attempts to claw back United and keep pace with Everton - who had been without a fixture over the weekend. However, the attention had again fallen on the behaviour of Liverpool supporters whose reputation for fair play, tarnished irrevocably in Brussels, had taken another savage blow. Relations between Liverpool and Manchester United had also taken another knock and there was no hiding from the level of ill-feeling between the two clubs that seemed to permeate all levels of supporters.

The extent to which Manchester United players and officials, without a league title for almost two decades, had managed - with the help of the media - to get under the skin of ordinary Liverpool supporters was highlighted in the following week's Football Echo. 'Worried Red' of Knotty Ash wrote that, "On Sunday, the abuse directed at Manchester United officials in the Main Stand was very frightening and the venom and hatred was unbelievable. The guilty ones were not teenage thugs, but older people, many middle-aged or retired." Unfortunately for the administrators at both clubs, but of no great concern to the hard core of both sets of supporters, the venom showed no signs of abating

Wednesday 12 February
Milk Cup semi final first leg
QPR v Liverpool

"Rangers welcome the BBC here this evening as the Milk Cup semi-final will be televised live to the whole country…We have mixed feelings about our selection for this honour. On the one hand it is a pleasure for us to know that our good-looking stadium will be the stage for such an important occasion and will be seen by millions of viewers who will never be there in the flesh.

On the other hand, it is unfortunately true that, where we could have expected a capacity crowd for this fixture, we shall now be lucky if we see 20,000 persons in the ground. We are not grumbling about the financial aspect of the situation – The Football League Compensation Committee give us very fair reimbursement in such circumstances. But the volume of noise and spectator vocal support will not be as great as it should be and this may detract just a little from the glamour of the occasion."

Bush Telegraph, QPR programme v Liverpool, 12 February 1986

Though perceived as a poor relation to the more illustrious FA Cup, the Football League Cup (sponsored by the Milk Marketing Board since 1982) had, by the mid-1980s, established its own importance in the domestic calendar. The brainchild of Football League Secretary Alan Hardaker*, the competition was first introduced in the 1960-61 season in response to most clubs installing floodlights during the 1950's.

*Alan Hardaker's name lives on through the trophy instigated in his name in 1990. Awarded to the Man of the Match in the League Cup Final the honour has been won by two Liverpool players, Steve McManaman (1995 v Bolton Wanderers) and Jerzy Dudek (2003 v Manchester United).

After its introduction the new midweek knockout tournament faced difficulties establishing itself, with the bigger clubs of the time passing up the invitation to compete in its formative years. Indeed, Liverpool, the competition's most prolific winners, who had first entered the inaugural tournament in 1960 as a Second Division side, were subsequently absent for the next seven years. The final was originally settled over two legs – home and away – until 1967 when, as an incentive to persuade the big clubs to enter, the Football League were invited to use Wembley as the venue for future finals. Eventually, the winners were granted entrance to the UEFA Cup and so full participation from the Football League membership was ensured.

Throughout the golden years of the 1960s and '70s, the League Cup had been the only missing link in the Anfield trophy room but, as a host of League Championships, regular European trophies and a couple of FA Cups made the position of Anfield cleaning lady the most secure employment on Merseyside, their frequent League Cup exits were passed off by supporters as insignificant. Though Shankly and then Paisley usually picked full strength sides for the competition, motivation for League Cup ties often proved difficult, especially if crucial League and European fixtures lay ahead.

Liverpool's attitude towards the League Cup altered in the late 1970s however, when an appearance in a high profile, lucrative Wembley final meant additional revenue for a club; finance which could be invested in the best available players and their attendant salaries. The Reds reached the Final for the first time in 1978, eventually succumbing to fierce rivals of the time Nottingham Forest in an Old Trafford replay. Then, from 1981 to 1984, Liverpool emphatically put their past failings in the competition behind them, reeling off four consecutive successes with West Ham United, Tottenham Hotspur, Manchester United and Everton the beaten finalists. To this day, a run of four consecutive wins in an English domestic football tournament is unmatched. With their recent history of success in the competition, the absence of European football and the financial compensations of reaching Wembley, Liverpool had every incentive to beat Queens Park Rangers and contest yet another final.

For Kenny Dalglish it was also an early opportunity to claim silverware as a newly appointed player-manager. There was no talk of the competition being a distraction, or insignificant, or meaningless and, with the, 'take each game as it comes,' mentality ingrained in the psyche of Dalglish and his Liverpool players, the first leg of the semi-final at Loftus Road assumed great importance. In the aftermath of Sunday's controversy, the national media had once again jumped at the chance to sully the reputation of Liverpool fans. An underrated side to Dalglish's management was his ability to protect himself and his players from non-football matters. Questions from the press were played with an emphatic straight bat and Dalglish made an art-form out of answering questions politely without actually saying a great deal.

The written media, frustrated by the Liverpool boss's refusal to give them flavoursome copy, painted him as dour and unhelpful but Dalglish wasn't concerned with his public image. He had little respect for reporters who had never played the game and, though his media responsibilities were fulfilled out of a sense of professional duty, Dalglish regularly made fun of the hacks even if many of his dry witticisms seemed to go over the heads of the assembled press corps.

Complicating matters for Dalglish was the prospect of facing Rangers on their controversial Omniturf artificial pitch. Installed in 1981, Liverpool had long been critics of the perceived advantage offered to clubs using such pitches; the ball skidded off the surface no matter the weather, it bounced extravagantly, and slide tackles were useless unless a defender was prepared to suffer a nasty burn. Prior to the game, Dalglish summed up his thoughts on the surface in his usual dry, succinct manner. "Artificial pitches make artificial games," he said "My opinion about their pitch will not change whether we win, lose or draw."

What didn't emanate from the Boot Room however was that the artificial surface encouraged short, accurate passing and clever movement off the ball – all qualities which Liverpool had in abundance. Nevertheless, over-preoccupation with the pitch was itself a psychological barrier and it would make Liverpool's task in this first leg all the harder.

Concerning Dalglish most in the lead-up to the match was the ankle ligament damage sustained by Paul Walsh three days previously. Initially the manger confirmed that the injury would rule Walsh out of the first leg but it soon became clear that Walsh's ankle problem would effectively end his campaign. With Walsh missing in Shepherds Bush, Craig Johnston resumed his place as partner to Ian Rush. Gary Gillespie had also fallen foul of injury so a shock debut was awarded to locally born, reserve centre-half Mark Seagraves, who lined up alongside Alan Hansen. Jan Molby was again stationed in the libero role that had been created for him by Dalglish; designed to add extra presence at the back but afford Molby the opportunity to bring the ball out of defence and supply intelligent passing into midfield and beyond. The system - contrary to what the national media and ill-informed pundits said - had been welcomed by most Liverpool fans and tellingly, the players, whilst the Reds' form so far this season had more than proved its effectiveness.

Mark Lawrenson continued where he left off against United at right back whilst Sammy Lee and John Wark, who had combined well for the equalizer on Sunday, kept their places in the starting XI. "The lads who finished the game against United were playing well," said Dalglish, who named himself as substitute. "In fact we looked as good as we have all season."

A freezing cold night and the live BBC cameras kept the Loftus Road attendance down to a miserable 15,051 which included around 3,000 Liverpool fans stood behind Bruce Grobbelaar's goal on the School End Terrace. Again the make-up of the away following was swelled by those who had been displaced from Merseyside and London-based Reds joining the several hundred hardy souls who had travelled on the coaches and a football special from Liverpool earlier that afternoon.

In what was fast becoming one of the harshest winters of recent times, the cold weather gave the plastic playing surface a white, even more intensely artificial look and in the opening minutes, players on both sides struggled to keep their feet on the unforgiving, icy deck. The slipperiness of the pitch added to Liverpool's mistrust and they made only the occasional foray forward. The visitors seemed content to concede possession to Rangers' and to soak up the concomitant pressure. The pitch, temperature and lack of atmosphere helped create an eerie atmosphere at odds with that of an important semi-final. The players seemed similarly underwhelmed and their voices could clearly be heard throughout the ground.

The match duly provided little of note and Liverpool were undone with the only goal of the game in the 25th minute. Rangers won a throw-in on the right, ten yards from the corner flag and the taker, Martin Allen, received a return pass down the line from full-back Warren Neil. Evading the challenge of Jim Beglin, Allen cut inside to deliver a dangerous cross into the penalty area. Rangers' captain Terry Fenwick threw himself acrobatically in front of Mark Lawrenson at the far post and he managed to stab a speculative volley past the tracksuit-bottomed Grobbelaar from six yards. Thereafter the Reds seemed content to restrict Rangers to their one-goal lead. Such was their dislike of the artificial pitch, it appeared that Liverpool would gladly take a defeat and look forward to overturning the deficit in the return leg.

The Reds lived dangerously on occasions and were relieved to see referee George Courtney, who hadn't always been Liverpool's friend over the years, rule out two dubious Rangers efforts in the second-half. Seagraves looked comfortable on his debut, although he was less adroit on the ball than his partner Hansen who glided effortlessly through the evening, making several key blocks as Rangers pressed for a second goal. Liverpool's limited ambition going forward was perhaps emphasized by Dalglish's decision to remain on the bench as the match petered out to its becalmed, almost surreal conclusion; Rangers happy to have won a low key affair but concerned with the slenderness of their lead and Liverpool content to take a defeat and resume the tie on the Anfield grass in three weeks time.

Rangers' 1-0 victory had set the tie up nicely for the second leg, although most pundits acclaimed Liverpool's professionalism in restricting the home side's lead and predicted a routine passage to Wembley for the Reds when the teams met again in front of the Kop.

Saturday 15 February
FA Cup fifth round
York City v Liverpool

"Just as 3,500 Liverpool fans arrive in York for the Cup tie, 25 'Vikings' from the Shetland Isles will parade, horned helmets and all, through the city on their way to meet the Mayor. Lock up your daughters."

The Guardian, Soccer Diary.

Three days on and, with Liverpool expected to turn the tie around in the upcoming League Cup semi-final second leg at Anfield, their midweek defeat at QPR was already a distant memory. On the morning of Saturday 15 February, the only thought on the minds of Liverpudlians everywhere was the fifth round of the FA Cup; the next step on the Road to Wembley, and just three games away from a potential appearance in the season's showpiece occasion - for the first time in nine years.

On paper the tie looked easy enough for Liverpool, and it was a financial godsend for a small club like the Minstermen. Using the voucher system to ensure that those who could apply did not exceed the number available, the generous away allocation of 3,500 terrace spots was quickly snapped up. For those who followed Liverpool away from home this meant scurrying round to season ticket holders' houses in search of the spare vouchers ending in the randomly selected serial number that qualified the holder for a ticket. While the system was far from perfect, it generally rewarded those who knew the most season ticket holders. With most of these at the time living either close to or within Liverpool, the system meant the vast majority of away tickets stayed on Merseyside.

Whatever the efforts and dedication of Reds fans to follow their team to this crucial Cup tie, the light-hearted piece in the Guardian's irreverent, weekly Diary on the morning of the match was a reminder of the nation's skewed perception of Liverpool's travelling support. The media's perception of football supporters in general, and Liverpool fans in particular, as unruly, unsophisticated hordes went unchallenged. The wider view of the authorities regarding the predominantly working-class, football follower of the day would have tragic repercussions in later years.

So as to ensure the tie would go ahead on the scheduled date and with the cold spell continuing to blight the fixture list, York invested £3,000 in a plastic covering for the pitch. The sides' fifth round meeting the previous season had been played on a bone-hard pitch and, with Liverpool labouring to a 1-1 draw that afternoon, there was understandable apprehension at another difficult encounter on another awkward surface. In the modern era there may have been talk of York giving up home advantage and playing the match at Anfield to secure a bigger pay-day at the turnstiles. Such a scenario would effectively concede the tie however, and the idea was never countenanced by the City Board.

Instead, and despite their lowly league status, there was genuine belief among the home fans that their side, conquerors of Arsenal on their run to the same stage of the competition the previous year, could make the most of their cramped home surroundings and cause an upset to rank among the most celebrated in a competition renowned for its knack of standing the football world on its head.

With the full extent of Paul Walsh's injury now depressingly confirmed, Dalglish had to decide whether to continue pushing Craig Johnston up in support of Ian Rush, or -

reluctantly - draft himself back into the starting line-up on a more regular basis. Although as energetic and as committed as ever, Johnston had been short of goals in recent games and most observers felt that Rush benefitted more from having a genuine front man for company rather than a winger-cum-striker.

Realising the importance and potential difficulty of the game, Dalglish included himself in the team whilst a second start was granted to young Seagraves alongside Hansen at the back. Molby continued in the sweeper role to add extra aerial presence to thwart York's anticipated long-ball tactics. Good news for Liverpool was the return to fitness of Steve McMahon, who was named as substitute.

Although the plastic covering had taken the edge off the severe frost which had settled over Yorkshire during the week of the game, the pitch was still hard, heavily sanded and described later by Dalglish as, "dangerous and full of holes and ruts." It would undoubtedly act as a leveller of the teams' respective talents, negating Liverpool's passing game and encouraging a more direct approach from the home side. The stud-less training shoes the Reds had worn on the impenetrable plastic at Loftus Road in midweek were duly given their second run-out inside three days.

Despite a crowd limited to 12,443 by the confines of the small, homely ground York, in red shirts and blue shorts, and Liverpool in all yellow, were greeted by a fantastic, traditional FA Cup atmosphere. Liverpool's large travelling contingent stood at the uncovered Boothen End trying their utmost to make themselves heard above the deceptively loud and excited home support. Spurred on by the crowd York made a remarkable start to the game considering the gulf between the two sides – they lay 13th in the Third Division, some 52 league places below Liverpool – and they put the visitors under tremendous pressure in the opening period.

Tony Canham, who had signed for York the previous season from non-league Harrogate Railway, showed electric pace down the left, forcing Grobbelaar to save well from a stinging left-foot shot inside the first four minutes. Seconds later his pace worried first Molby and then Lawrenson, himself no slouch, with the covering Johnston forced to concede a corner which the Liverpool defence were relieved to clear at the first attempt. There was no respite however, and the best chance of the game so far came when, with Liverpool vainly appealing for offside, Gary Ford played in Dale Banton only for the Londoner to shoot wide with just Grobbelaar to beat. The Liverpool fans behind the goal breathed a collective, barely concealed sigh of relief as they jeered Banton's miss.

Visibly shaken by York's attacking play, and surprised by the pace of Canham and Banton on the slippery surface, Liverpool slowly recovered their composure as the half wore on. On 25 minutes Dalglish's persistence on the right won a corner and, when Mark Seagraves flicked on Sammy Lee's centre, Andy Leaning in the York goal was forced to punch clear.

Gradually coming to terms with the icy conditions, the visitors started to play some lovely one-touch football, much to the delight of the away fans. However, when one such move saw Rush threaten, fed by John Wark's precise through-ball, the Welsh striker lost his footing in the act of shooting and the chance had gone. York's simple tactic of lobbing balls over the Liverpool defence to exploit the pace of their forwards almost paid off when Canham found Banton again but Molby, expertly covering as sweeper, was alert to the danger and made a perfectly-timed tackle from which Lawrenson was able to clear.

As the action swung from one end to the other, Dalglish back-heeled to Rush, received a return pass and, holding off the attentions of York defender John McPhail, shot first time, forcing Leaning to save low to his left. It was the best move of the game so far. In Liverpool's next attack Leaning was again in action, saving Wark's header from Lawrenson's cross.

With just a few minutes remaining before half-time the crowd witnessed an outstanding, trademark piece of goalkeeping brilliance from Bruce Grobbelaar. York won a free-kick on the right and, when Steve Senior's centre was knocked down by City's angular centre-forward Keith Walwyn, the ball fell perfectly to the York captain, John McPhail. The Scot's perfectly struck half-volley from 12 yards was heading for the roof of the net until it was spectacularly clawed away at the last possible moment by Grobbelaar's fingertips. The instant, emphatic applause from the Liverpool fans behind the goal was testament to the wondrous nature of the save they had just seen, evidence again that for all the criticism his eccentricity elicited, there was no more athletic keeper in the game than the Zimbabwean. Here, his brilliance kept Liverpool on terms at the break.

Liverpool began the second-half in lively fashion. Jim Beglin's long-range shot was turned away for a corner and, from the resultant kick, Lee played a one-two with Lawrenson before crossing high into the box. Seagraves climbed well but was unable to keep his header down and the ball sailed just over the crossbar, much to his frustration.

Although York remained dangerous on the counter attack Liverpool, kicking towards their own supporters now, were dominant. On 50 minutes Rush was sent clear on goal but was felled by the advancing Leaning. Despite furious protests from the grounded striker, the away fans and most of the Liverpool side, including Dalglish who ran at the referee with his arms aloft demanding a penalty, Howard Taylor incredulously waved play on. Liverpool's sense of injustice at this decision was magnified on the hour mark when York took a sensational lead. There was little finesse to the goal, with Walwyn again winning a high ball pumped into the box, shielding it from Hansen and Molby, and laying it into the path of Gary Ford to strike home a low shot from 14-yards. Suddenly Liverpool faced heartbreak and humiliation.

As the daylight began to disappear over Bootham Crescent, York supporters danced and swayed across the terraces and rocked the small wooden stands as they celebrated the prospect of the most famous result in their 74 year existence. An old footballing adage says that a team is at its most vulnerable just after it has just scored however, and this proved correct as Liverpool were given a dramatic, almost immediate lifeline. Responding to the desperate urgings of their fans, their response to York's opener was to pour forward in numbers and, when Johnston and Rush challenged for a loose ball in the box, it bounced awkwardly and struck the hand of City full-back Steve Senior.

Perhaps influenced by the loud, piercing shout of, "hand-ball," from the Liverpool fans behind the goal or, maybe thinking his previous decision not to award an even more blatant appeal was the wrong one, referee Taylor immediately pointed to the spot. The York players surrounded the referee, protesting Senior's innocence but the decision was made and the penalty area eventually cleared for Molby to advance forward to take the kick. Silence descended on the ground as he ran up to take the kick, but this was pierced by a throaty and defiant scouse roar as the burly Dane coolly sent Leaning the wrong way to equalize. It was Molby's 12th goal of the season, his sixth from the penalty spot and undoubtedly his most crucial so far.

Liverpool took control of the game during the final quarter, with Dalglish, in only his second start of the year, the fulcrum of the attack. Although they dominated possession the Reds' failed to create clear chances and, as the game headed to a stalemate both sides seemed content to accept a draw. After going behind Liverpool were relieved to be able to take the tie back to Anfield and York savoured the prospect of a replay in front of the Kop.

Predictably the controversial handball decision that gave Liverpool their match-saving penalty was the focus for most of the press after the game. "I couldn't believe it," moaned the distraught Senior. "I didn't know anything about it." Dalglish used his usual and classic diversionary tactics to skirt the penalty controversy in his post-match interviews. In response to suggestions that York felt cheated, he retorted that he felt equally, "cheated," by the referee's decision to allow the game to go ahead on what he considered a dangerous playing surface.

Of more concern to the Liverpool player-manager was Liverpool's frustrating search for top form. The second-half showing against Manchester United the previous weekend had been an indication that his side might be returning to their best, but the week's cup exploits had produced two stuttering performances which left work to be done in the subsequent return ties. However, the player-manager could only have been pleased with his own performance on his return to the side. Perhaps, as many fans argued, there was a growing realization that his influence on the field as leader and talisman could be a key factor as the season rapidly approached its business end.

Tuesday 18 February
FA Cup fifth round replay
Liverpool v York City

"Eight police officers have been injured and 58 people arrested in the worst outbreak of violence yet outside the News International printing plant in Wapping, East London. One officer, a 27-year-old sergeant, was taken to hospital with head injuries.

Police estimated 5,000 demonstrators gathered near the printing works for a mass demonstration. Similar mass protests have taken place regularly outside the Wapping plant ever since the start of a strike three weeks ago over new working conditions and the move from Fleet Street to cheaper premises in East London."

BBC News reports violent clashes in the Wapping dispute, one of the most protracted and bitter in Britain's industrial history. 15 February 1986.

The unexpected draw at Bootham Crescent meant a replay at Anfield just three days later. Ahead of the weekend's crucial derby against Everton – who would travel to Spurs on 4 March for a place in the quarter-finals against the winners of Arsenal v Luton - the game was an additional, troublesome fixture in the build up to what was the Reds' most important game of the season so far. Victory over their neighbours would enhance Liverpool's title credentials and close the gap between the two sides to just two points, whereas defeat would leave them eight behind with their league campaign effectively over for another season. By contrast, Everton had a fixture-free midweek for which to prepare for the 134th League encounter between the sides.

In the modern game, an extra cup engagement against lower league opposition would be viewed as something of an inconvenience, with several key players rested to avoid injury and fatigue ahead of a pivotal six-pointer in the race for the title. In 1986 however, this was far from the case. Alongside the league championship, the FA Cup was an equally important target for Liverpool and, to ensure a place in the last eight despite mediocre opposition, no risks were taken by Dalglish in terms of team selection. If the Reds could defeat York, Monday's draw from the iconic velvet bag at FA Headquarters in Lancaster Gate had offered the reward of a home tie with either Watford or Bury in the quarter-finals.

It was the Minstermen's second fifth round visit to Anfield in 12 months and, with the awkwardness of the Bootham Crescent pitch behind them, the Reds were now hot favourites to progress. The previous season's replay had seen the Reds stick seven goals without reply past their Third Division opponents in front of a bumper 43,000 crowd, but this year's renewal attracted only of 29,362 with many supporters choosing to keep their powder dry for the important local spat at the weekend.

Encouraged by his return to the side at York, Dalglish partnered Ian Rush in attack. Gary Gillespie returned in place of Mark Seagraves whilst John Wark came into the side for Craig Johnston who was relegated to the bench.

With row upon row of empty seats in both the Kemlyn Road and Main Stand, the match began in a strangely muted atmosphere although there was plenty of encouragement for the underdogs from the thousands of York supporters behind the Anfield Road goal. Enjoying the luxury of a pitch vastly superior to the rutted, bumpy surface they had encountered in the first game, the Reds started well and they had created a number of decent half-chances before they eventually broke York's resistance on 18 minutes.

Continuing to deputise for long-term absentee Steve Nicol at right back, Mark Lawrenson galloped upfield and whipped in a precise cross for John Wark who, in trademark fashion, arrived late in the penalty area totally unmarked. His low, side-footed effort was well struck but it was helped into the net by the despairing right hand of Andy Leaning. It was unfortunate for the City goalkeeper whose sure handling had seen the York rearguard grow in confidence as the tie progressed as, up until this point, they had managed to repel the best of Liverpool's many attacks.

Perhaps mindful of the looming clash with Everton, or simply through complacency, Liverpool visibly took their foot off the pedal. As the first-half wore on and without an additional goal, York gradually established a foothold in the game and in the 38th minute the Reds were reminded of the slender nature of their lead when Grobbelaar was forced to parry a fizzing shot from Minstermen skipper John McPhail.

York's pluck and persistence was rewarded just before half-time when they shocked the home crowd with a sloppy equalizer at the Kop end. Tony Canham, whose pace had troubled Liverpool throughout the first match, broke down the left and, after cutting inside Lawrenson, fired in a shot which Grobbelaar appeared to have covered at his near post. Somehow however, the Reds' keeper lost control of the shot in colliding with the post and the ball bobbled over the line. The tie was level once again.

The goal, and its immediate aftermath, presented Dalglish with serious questions at the interval. In attempting the save, Grobbelaar appeared to have injured his arm and, with the whistle going soon after, he left the field on the way to the dressing room clutching his elbow and discussing the injury, and no doubt the nature of the goal, with his manager. The equalizer had transformed the game. What had been a lacklustre, almost lifeless Anfield cup-tie had now developed into a full blooded affair and the second-half saw several desperate near misses at both ends.

Stung by the equalizer, Liverpool enjoyed the lion's share of possession with Jan Molby, back in midfield, orchestrating most of the play. He was ably supported by the industry of Sammy Lee on the right but the Reds lacked a cutting edge in the final third and they were restricted to half-chances in the opening minutes of the half while York remained dangerous on the counter.

Liverpool survived a major scare with 20 minutes to go when Keith Walwyn, a continuous and aggressive presence in the York attack, held off challenges from Gillespie and Beglin to bundle the ball past Grobbelaar in the Anfield Road goal, sending the York fans into dreamland. Although the referee had signaled a foul on Gillespie in the build up to the 'goal' to cut short their celebrations, the ironic cheers from the Kop were tinged with more than a hint of relief and the home crowd exhorted their side to raise their game against the minnows.

With the game locked at one goal apiece and with extra-time looming, the anxiety of the home crowd was palpable. Looking short of match fitness, Dalglish had failed to make any real impression and his lack of sharpness was an obvious worry. The player-manager may have been tempted to remove himself from the action but, with Liverpool seeking to add pace to their attacks, he instead chose to bring on Craig Johnston to replace Wark with just 17 minutes of normal time left. As Liverpool pressed for a winner in the later stages Johnston's introduction caused problems for the York defence but, with the clock running down, the visitors showed remarkable fitness levels for a team ranked two divisions below the Reds and they gamely hung on for extra-time.

With the assistance of coaches Ronnie Moran and Roy Evans, Dalglish gave a pep talk to his huddled players as they prepared for another, crucial 30 minutes. A number of his men looked tired, almost bemused by the fact they had been matched over three hours play by the Yorkshire upstarts but Dalglish, so well-versed and convinced of the importance of Anfield's boot room psychology at such times, conveyed nothing but calm and reassurance. Not everyone on the Kop shared Dalglish's conviction however, and many some supporters worried that Liverpool's participation in the FA Cup was, once again, hanging by a thread.

Grobbelaar continued to look discomforted by the knock he had taken to his arm and York's pace, aggression and growing confidence threatened the most ignominious of exits. Older supporters comforted themselves however, recalling similar encounters in the FA Cup-winning years of 1965 and 1974; when the Reds had struggled against Stockport County and Doncaster Rovers respectively on the path to their glorious triumphs at Wembley. Just three minutes into extra-time however, Liverpool's class finally told when they regained the lead through a fantastic strike from Jan Molby - a goal to rival his already legendary League Cup effort against Manchester United earlier in the season.

Although there was no spectacular run from the half-way line on this occasion, the ferocity of his left-foot volley after an incomplete clearance saw Anfield erupt in relief as it scorched past the diving Leaning from 20-yards. As the players congratulated Molby and retreated to their own half for the restart, the big Dane acknowledged the Kop with a clenched fist salute amid chants of the, by now customary, "Rambo, Rambo," from his devoted followers.

In his second season at the club, Molby's impressive range of passing, fierce shooting and ability to dictate play had won the admiration of knowledgeable Kopites, but this was not the only reason the Dane had impressed. Molby's liking for the Liverpool nightlife and his openness towards locals won him many friends, whilst his exposure to the native tongue had already cultivated in him an endearing Scandinavian-Scouse accent. With his match-saving penalty at York and this spectacular effort the Dane was fast becoming a talismanic figure for the Reds on their march to Wembley.

There was further delight for the Kop when the tie was effectively settled six minutes later with a welcome goal for Dalglish. Liverpool had visibly relaxed after Molby's effort but they extended their advantage when Lee, fast becoming almost indispensable as Liverpool's squad was used to the full at this stage of the season, crossed deep to the far post. From an acute angle the player-manager managed to connect with a right-foot shot which beat Leaning at his near post.

Finally able to legitimately relax Liverpool played out the remainder of extra-time without any further drama. After 210 minutes of nerve-wracking FA Cup football they had finally managed to secure their place in the quarter-finals and a home tie with either Watford or Bury – who were not due to play their tie until 5 March. As the York players deservedly enjoyed a standing ovation from their own supporters, an appreciative Kop and a magnanimous player-manager, Dalglish's thoughts turned from consolation to confrontation, and Saturday's visit of Everton.

Despite only sporadic appearances Dalglish had more than earned his pay with over two hours of football and the pressure of coaxing his players through the tensest of evenings. As he surveyed the scenes of fatigue and injury in the dressing room, he contemplated his selection for the weekend's make-or-break game in the Reds' season. At this stage even he had to wait to be sure of the best line-up to face Everton.

Saturday 22 February
Liverpool v Everton

"Your heart pumping as you slowly neared the entrance, ticket clutched nervously in your hand, pride swelling with every chant heard from inside until you were suddenly on the other side of the wall and racing up the decaying steps at the back of the Kop to get that first blinding view of green as you laid eyes on the pitch. Then, the full-on attack on your senses as amid the din you mingled with the thousands of tightly-packed heads, all with a shared devotion to Dalglish's Liverpool."

Dave McKearney, Liverpool fan, Kirkby.

Two days after Liverpool had dropped two points in their poisonous home match against Manchester United, Everton had extended their lead over the Reds to five points with a 4-0 win over Manchester City at Goodison Park. The recent run of victories that had catapulted Everton to the top of the table had been fuelled by Gary Lineker, their £800,000 pre-season signing from Leicester City, who had scored 29 goals in all competitions.

The Blues were also still in the FA Cup, awaiting their twice-postponed fifth round clash at Spurs and a potential quarter-final clash with Luton or Arsenal – who had drawn 2-2 at Kenilworth Road the week before. As the competition had progressed, the routes to the final seen via the glut of postponed games and replays and the two sides had been kept apart, so there remained a possibility that the Merseysiders could face also each other again either in a semi-final or at the Wembley showpiece itself on 10 May.

For now however, such scenarios were mere daydreams and the attentions of both Merseyside clubs were focused on this crucial match at Anfield. Together with Manchester United (in second place on goal difference), and Chelsea and West Ham (both with games in hand), Liverpool and Everton both had realistic chances of landing the title. If the league championship trophy was to be dressed with Liverpool's red and white ribbons however, many felt the Reds had to win the 134th league derby - the 67th at Anfield.

For most fans, to lose to their closest and most enduring rivals here - and slip eight points behind them in the process - would, at this stage of the season, mean they would be effectively waving goodbye to a 16th title. With Manchester United also leading the Reds by two points with a game in hand this was a fixture that Liverpool simply could not afford to lose as the season entered its final third.

Everton's resurgence over the previous two seasons - culminating in their first League title for 15 years in 1985 - had elevated the Merseyside derby to the position of the stand-out game in English football. The vagaries of the newly agreed TV contract, with just a small number of games televised live also meant that - as this game wasn't one of them - the scheduled 3pm Saturday afternoon kick-off remained unaltered and as such there was huge pre-match demand for tickets. The economic situation dictated that many fans were forced to pick and choose their games but the derby was an exception – especially one as important as this. It was a game no-one, Red or Blue, wanted to miss.

Reflecting both the team's form and the biting recession, gates at Anfield had fluctuated dramatically, with no sell-out games and an average gate of around only 35,000 – an amazing 9,000 short of capacity. Chief Executive Peter Robinson reported that for this game however, the club saw, "probably the biggest demand for tickets we have had in the last 10 years". Qualifying vouchers for paying customers had been issued at the January home fixture against West Ham and, in the build-up to the game, the derby was declared the first all-ticket sell out of the season.

Following the gruelling win over York, Liverpool's mounting injury crisis threatened to limit Kenny Dalglish's options ahead of the game. In addition to ankle victim Paul Walsh, it was reported that, "Goalkeeper Bruce Grobbelaar, Ian Rush, John Wark, player-manager Kenny Dalglish… [had all been] on the treatment table this week and the Reds reported at least three other niggling injuries, preferring to keep the situation under wraps." Grobbelaar's injury was causing the most concern but the Liverpool echo reported that although, "his chances looked extremely slim at one stage because of an elbow injury he is also responding to treatment. He was trying to prove his fitness to Dalglish this morning." Grobbelaar was, "desperately hoping to maintain his record of nearly 300 consecutive first team appearances."

In recent years the Merseyside derby had been tagged 'the friendly Derby' by local and national media, although Evertonians may not have always agreed with this assessment having seen Liverpool sweep all before them at home and abroad during a period when their own club had fallen into decline. Indeed, until Howard Kendall managed to assemble a team worthy of challenging their neighbours, derby victories for the Blues had been few and far between. The 1984 Milk Cup Final was the first all-Merseyside Wembley occasion and Evertonians, flushed with pride at their emerging team and Liverpool fans perhaps enjoying the novelty value of an Everton side worth beating, travelled harmoniously to and from the Capital aided and abetted by the neutrality of a goalless draw.

This first all-Scouse Wembley pilgrimage inspired 'Home and Away', a Granada TV documentary following an expectant coach load of fans on their way down to London. During interviews with the 27 supporters on board, much of the talk centred on the hopelessness of unemployment and the unique release from such despair offered by football and a trip away from home. On plans to let off steam, one fan - Ronnie Morris - said "We've got a full weekend of letting off what we've been building up and building up. And if we didn't have it to let it off, I'd say God help her down there." It was doubtful he was referring to The Queen.

A number of the men featured – there were no women visible on the coach - also spoke touchingly on how they hoped a weekend in London might transform the nation's negative opinion of Merseysiders. Some felt a show of unity and good behaviour might even make a difference to their economic plight back home and create more jobs if they made a good impression in the capital city. One fan admitted;

"I think if we give a good account of ourselves and show that we are human beings and not like they seem to think we are, a load of scroungers and dogsbodies, it could create jobs. Because the eyes of the world will be on us down there won't they? People seeing Liverpool and Everton Supporters, you know, together. They're gonna say well, they can't be all bad can they?"

Although Liverpool eventually won that Milk Cup Final in a replay at Maine Road, Everton's subsequent 1984 FA Cup win and 1985 League and European Cup Winners Cup double, had raised the local stakes even higher. However, a shared cultural, social – and to a certain extent, political - mentality ensured that rivalry between Gwladys Street Enders and Kopites were, for the time being at least, confined to animated debate on football matters alone.

Although the Heysel Stadium tragedy had deprived Everton of a tilt at the European Cup there was sufficient interest in the battle for domestic supremacy to quell any thought that somehow Liverpool fans had been collectively responsible for ruining their passage to European hegemony. The descent into bitterness between the two sets of fans which blights today's derbies only manifested itself when Everton failed to build on their 1980's success and became perennial relegation candidates in the early 1990's, coinciding with a period when Liverpool fans had to accept their side had also been superseded - by the galling 'rebirth' of Manchester United.

When Dalglish had scored inside the first minute at Goodison Park earlier in the season a large number of Liverpool fans in the Gwladys Street End erupted in celebration. Away fans in the home areas at a Merseyside derby was nothing new, and in recent seasons, it had also become acceptable at the Anfield game for Evertonians to infiltrate the left-hand side of the Kop - although their numbers never exceeded more than a couple of thousand.

The presence of unsegregated rival supporters on the same terrace had helped created an unrivalled atmosphere befitting of the stature and importance of the fixture and had directly led to the media's 'friendly' moniker. Whilst there might have been isolated incidents and scuffles, terrace warfare between Red and Blue amounted mainly to trying to out sing the opposition and expectantly hoping to claim bragging rights when rival fans shared a drink or two in their local pubs following a famous victory on the field.

With such expectancy among the fans, the Kop began to fill up early and by two o'clock on a crisp, sunny February afternoon the noise from those already in the ground filtered outside to those gathering near the ancient turnstiles on Walton Breck Road, Flagpole Corner and Back Rockfield Road. For younger Kopites there was perhaps no feeling of impatience quite like queuing to join your fellow Reds on the standing Kop to spur on Liverpool to victory over the 'enemy' from across Stanley Park.

In the days when Liverpool's official club shop was no more than a small cabin tucked away in the corner of the Main Stand car park, street sellers outside the ground monopolised the pre-match trade in 'colours'. Kopite Chris Maguire from Netherton recalls, "For seasoned match-goers perhaps a derby day would inspire the purchase of a bobble hat, or a discreet new pin badge with the Liverbird clasped to the heart. There was certainly not a Liverworld carrier bag in sight."

Thatcher's Britain and unemployment had done much to douse the fire in some Liverpudlian hearts but on derby day at least the swagger returned and troubles were forgotten for a few hours at least. Maguire added fondly, "No mobile phones, no pre-arranged meetings at the Shankly statue, no 'daytrippers' in replica shirts, just local people with distinctive clothes and haircuts - when we had hair - milling about their well-trodden streets."

Before the announcement of the teams there was a shock for the crowd when Dalglish was presented – belatedly - with his Bells Manager of the Month award for January. The sight of the boss in a suit just 20 minutes before kick-off suggested that he had failed to shake off the knock sustained against York in midweek. When the familiar, dulcet tones of George Sephton announced the Liverpool team in gladiatorial fashion, starting with his traditional, "Number 1, in goal, Bruce Grobbelaar," it was evident that the keeper was deemed sufficiently recovered from his elbow injury to take his place in the line-up. The same reading of the team sheet also confirmed that Dalglish was absent, with Craig Johnston recalled, but there was also a surprise return for the key influence of Steve McMahon in the centre of midfield.

As the game kicked off in bright sunshine Liverpool attacked the Kop end, Alan Hansen having lost the toss to Kevin Ratcliffe. It soon became clear that Dalglish had again shuffled his pack with Ian Rush playing as a lone striker and Jan Molby tucked behind in an – unusual for him - advanced midfield role. Yet again, new tactics and a rotation of players from the player-manager.

With the crowd at fever pitch the game exploded into life straight from the kick-off with Molby winning a header from a deep cross by Jim Beglin, forcing Pat Van den Hauwe to clear. Everton responded by winning a corner on the right and, when Peter Reid laid the ball back to Kevin Richardson on the edge of the penalty area, his rasping volley was saved by Grobbelaar; the Zimbabwean dealing brilliantly with the shot with the sun in his eyes at the Anfield Road End.

Attention switched briefly away from the game when it appeared that the Kop might have been filled to more than its capacity as hundreds of fans came spilling through gates in the fencing at the front of the terrace to escape an apparent crush. Police and stewards were forced to accommodate the overspill by redirecting supporters to the front of the Paddock in front of the Main Stand, with many of them squatting the length of the touchline close to the pitch. They were later accommodated by police back into the Kop on the Kemlyn Road side where the crowd seemed less dense.

Everton nearly opened the scoring in bizarre fashion when a mix up between Grobbelaar and Mark Lawrenson allowed Richardson to capitalise. Lawrenson recovered sufficiently to get in an awkward block challenge on Richardson but, while Evertonians appealed for a penalty, the ball ran towards goal. The Eire international defender, picking himself up and ignoring claims for the spot-kick, ran back to clear the stray ball off the goal line. The visitors were enjoying the better of the game and again went close with both a Graeme Sharp header from a Trevor Steven cross, and from a corner conceded by Lawrenson when Steven headed wide from Richardson's centre.

Due to their new formation, Liverpool were struggling to gain and keep possession. So dominant and effective in recent games, Molby looked leg-weary and was failing to get involved from his position between midfield and attack.

With tackles flying in on both sides - with Reid and McMahon prominent in the more robust exchanges - there were several interruptions to the play as players from both teams received treatment. Molby was one of the players hurt, sustaining a shin injury which saw him withdrawn at half-time to be replaced by the returning Kevin McDonald.

Everton finished the half the stronger with Grobbelaar alert to intercept a mishit Steven cross and turn the ball away for a corner. From the flag kick Gillespie was able to clear and the referee signaled the end of a breathless first half. Given Everton's aggression and domination of possession, Liverpool were perhaps grateful to still be on level terms.

There was no let up in the pace and intensity of the game at the start of the second half. Peter Reid was enjoying a superbly combative match, snapping into tackles but also, in the 50th minute, showing surprising pace when gathering the ball from Alan Harper on half-way to embark on a run down the right touchline. He reached the goal line before pulling the ball back across goal but, fortunately for Liverpool, it fell behind the advancing forwards Sharp and Lineker.

Dalglish's half-time teamtalk appeared to refresh Liverpool and, despite these early Everton attacks, they contested the second half much more competitively. They missed a chance to take the lead when Johnston, played through by Whelan's defence-splitting pass, bore down on Neville Southall's goal but the Everton keeper read the through ball perfectly and was able to challenge the Australian in the act of shooting and clear the Blues' lines.

Lifted by Liverpool's improvement in the second half, the Kop rallied behind their team and, as the game reached the hour mark, the atmosphere was raised a few more notches as both sets of fans in an official crowd of 45,445 tried to outdo each other in the decibel stakes. One particular chant from the Kop at this stage, declaring "We're by far the greatest team, the world has ever seen", almost deafened even those sitting near half-way, with its intensity.

Although the game had bristled superbly so far, chances for leading goal scorers Rush and Lineker had been at a premium. Both struggled to find space and escape the attentions of markers Kevin Ratcliffe and Gary Gillespie respectively and the game's best openings had fallen to midfielders.

After 70 minutes Steven came the closest yet to scoring, only to be denied by the reactive brilliance of Grobbelaar. Turning away from his marker after collecting a Sharp knockdown, the England international pivoted expertly 12-yards from goal and sent a low, arrowing shot toward the bottom right hand corner. With only a split second to react - and wrong-footed by Steven's adroit turn and shot - Grobbelaar launched himself low to his right and somehow managed to get the fingers of his right hand to the ball and turn it away for a corner. Springing to his feet, the much maligned keeper gestured manically at the sight of the ball rolling harmlessly away behind the Kop goal.

Prone to occasional errors, Grobbelaar's performances were scrutinized intensely by fans and journalists alike, but his style of goalkeeping ensured he dominated his penalty area like no other. This hugely reduced the pressure on Liverpool's back four and it is doubtful that he had too many critics in the dressing room. The brilliance of Grobbelaar's save made the incident that followed minutes later all the more frustrating. Collecting the ball 25-yards out, Kevin Ratcliffe scuffed a speculative shot goalwards. The ball was deflected slightly off Lineker on its way and trickled towards Grobbelaar. Inexplicably, and to the horror of his team mates, the keeper allowed the powder-puff shot to wriggle from his grasp as he dived and the ball trickled over the line and into the back of the net.

From behind the Kop goal it looked so innocuous a shot, that the standing supporters didn't bother straining to see if the ball had been saved and it came as a huge shock to see and hear the Evertonians at the far end of the ground – and in the left hand of the Kop - belatedly rise in celebration. Many would leave the ground later none the wiser as to how Grobbelaar had not managed to keep the ball out. After a stellar performance in which he had made at least two world-class saves, Grobbelaar would now be a sorry scapegoat in they eyes of his growing army of media critics. After the match Dalglish revealed that Grobbelaar had played with heavy strapping on his injured elbow so his shocking error could possibly be explained by him diving in such a way as to protect his arm, but the keeper himself was reluctant to use any such excuses.

Now running out of time to avoid a calamitous and potentially title ending defeat, Liverpool almost silenced the mocking Evertonians when Rush, with his first clear sight of goal in the match, collected a through ball, drew Southall from his goal and rounded his international teammate only to see his expert right-foot finish cleared off the line by the retreating Van den Hauwe. Relieved to see their lead preserved, the ecstatic Blues continued to taunt Grobbelaar with their familiar jibe, "Brucie, Brucie You're a Clown, Brucie, You're a Clown."

Liverpool continued to press forward in search of an equaliser but, with just 13 minutes left, they were caught unawares by a long punt behind their back four. Lineker, unmarked and looking suspiciously offside, ran onto the clearance and clipped the ball beyond Grobbelaar's right hand into the bottom corner of the Kop net for his 24th league goal of the season. As he wheeled away in celebration Evertonians spilled out of the Kop onto the pitch to dance a jig with their leading scorer as he reached the 30-goal mark in all competitions. The remaining minutes ticked by without incident until the referee signaled the end of the contest and Liverpool fans left the ground sombrely to contemplate what had turned out to be an awful afternoon.

By contrast, Evertonians stayed behind to dance and sing in tribute to a famous victory. They had been the better side throughout the game but the nature of the goal that broke the deadlock would give Reds' fans nightmares all weekend long.

After the game most of the Liverpool squad attended a function to celebrate Sammy lee's testimonial. For Craig Johnston, a night out with his teammates was the perfect occasion to rekindle team spirit and knuckledown for the long end of season run-in. "The worst thing you can do in Liverpool is appear in public on the evening you have lost a derby match," he said.

"But we were there for a cause and were determined to tough it out. We had a big drink that night and the mood among the lads was one of steely resolve. Again, the ties of team spirit began to forge as tightly as ever. Stung by the ensuing media criticism of our derby display [some newspapers laughably called Dalglish's men 'the worst Liverpool team in 20 years] we drew closer together. We knew what had to be done."

Most significantly the result left Everton eight points clear of Liverpool with just 12 games remaining; they appeared to be well on course to retain their title. Although Dalglish would refuse to rule Liverpool out of the Championship race publicly, the deficit to Everton and a similar gap to Manchester United in second place, left Liverpool fans hoping for a miracle. They could perhaps take solace in two potential routes to Wembley, but as far as most were concerned the quest to regain their crown as the Kings of English football was all but over.

Chapter Seven
On the March with Kenny's Army

Sunday 2 March
Tottenham Hotspur v Liverpool

"It may well have been freezing outside, but the Redmen had pulled off a brilliant late-late win and inside I was glowing. Oh happy days, brethren. The worst of times in some ways, and of course the best."

Kevin Sampson, Liverpool fan

With no midweek fixture following the shattering home defeat to Everton, Liverpool at least had time to take stock and assess the state of their season before the trip to White Hart Lane – yet another Reds' game to be televised live by the BBC cameras. An eight-day break would give time for injuries to heal, confidence to return and for Dalglish to reassess his priorities, personnel and tactical thinking. In the aftermath of the derby defeat the manager had been strongly criticised for the decision to play Jan Molby as support for Ian Rush but in reality, Liverpool's lethargic display owed more to their exertions in the midweek cup-tie against York.

There was also more heated debate in the Football Echo over the form of Bruce Grobbelaar. While he still had his supporters claiming he was merely suffering a crisis of confidence, a vocal majority were calling for him to be dropped. Some went as far as to suggest Dalglish should enter the transfer market and sign a replacement immediately, with Ian Andrews of Leicester - who had shone at Anfield earlier in the season - David Seaman of Birmingham, and Watford's Tony Coton amongst the names put forward. No mention was made of Peter Shilton, who some fans had called for earlier in the season.

Others suggested that Liverpool's problems lay elsewhere; specifically a lack of creativity in midfield and firepower up front, especially with Paul Walsh injured and Dalglish's appearances sporadic.

Liverpool's inconsistency and recent lack of goals was in no small part down to a catalogue of injuries to some of their most consistent performers - Walsh, Nicol, McMahon, and the much maligned but quietly effective Kevin McDonald. The loss of such players made it difficult for Dalglish to select a settled side. His critics argued however, that tinkering with the formation - with Jan Molby occasionally playing as a sweeper and playing others out of position to cover for injuries - had disrupted the fluency and style of Liverpool's play.

In his first season as manager it would have been easy for Dalglish to become downcast, but despite the criticism of their form in the league he knew there were realistic opportunities for Liverpool to reach Wembley. In addition, his single-mindedness, strength of character and experience of previous title challenges with both Liverpool and Celtic, saw him adopt a far more positive view of their league position than his critics.

Privately, Dalglish saw the Everton defeat as a watershed. He reasoned that with 12 games left, Liverpool's chances of title glory were straightforward enough. Rather than dwell on the daunting gap to Everton at the top of the table – the Blues had extended the margin to 11 points with victory over Aston Villa the day before Liverpool travelled to Spurs – he saw a target of 12 wins from 12 games. Win all these and the Reds would have a chance – albeit slight – of winning the title or at least pushing Everton close. Like everything in life of course, this was easier said than done.

Fortunately for Liverpool, Spurs were experiencing problems of their own. During the 1984-85 season they had been the most credible challengers to Everton in the title race until a late collapse saw Liverpool pip them for the runners-up spot on goal difference. This season they were struggling in mid-table with three successive home defeats piling pressure on manger Peter Shreeves. A week of extremely cold weather in London put the match in doubt but, with the arrival of the TV cameras, the home club went to great efforts to ensure the game went ahead as scheduled on a pitch that looked as though permafrost had set in.

With most Liverpool fans accepting a miracle was needed in the title race - and Spurs' supporters equally down – there, "was a weirdly muted atmosphere." Exiled Liverpudlian Kevin Sampson, who negotiated his way to White Hart Lane on the London tube, recalls that there was, "no big match buzz, hardly any Liverpool fans around and a tiny queue for our end." Once inside however, Sampson saw, "a good few Reds there." He added, "It felt like the coldest day on record. Ever. Capital Radio said volunteers were clearing the pitch of snow, but the game may yet be called off. It wasn't as though I was doing anything special anyway, so I wrapped up and set off from my dingy flat."

Anyone who travelled away alone during these times - or was separated from fellow supporters - would sympathise with Sampson's anxieties en route;

"I got the District Line to Victoria, changed to the Victoria line, and went through that horrible sinking feeling where, every stop past the tourist stations, more and more Tottenham ruffians start getting on; Highbury and Islington - twenty or so; Finsbury Park - twenty, thirty more. To me, the Tottenham lads were on the lookout.

"They probably weren't, truth be told. They were probably freezing too, and wondering if their team would ever win at home again but the walk up from Seven Sisters seemed like it went on forever. The snow was beginning to thaw, making me wet as well as cold as I trudged up the never-ending rat run; little pockets of skins and lookouts every few hundred yards."

Another exiled Liverpool fan, Dave Hardman, did encounter some Spurs fans intent on fighting. "It had been absolutely freezing the night before and everywhere was icy as hell. As we walked up to the overland station it all went off by the flats. This big mad cockney skinhead came running up to us waving a hammer, skidded on the ice like Bambi and flew headfirst into an obliging fist – unluckily for him."

In the safety and warmth of the Liverpool dressing room, groin victim Dalglish named Molby - recovered from his own shin injury - to take his place in a more orthodox central midfield role alongside Steve McMahon. Indeed, the team sheet appeared to give Liverpool a much more recognizable shape than in recent games, with Craig Johnston paired up front with Ian Rush.

The first-half however, saw Liverpool put in yet another uninspired, insipid performance and, after another high-profile error just minutes into the game, the spotlight fell on Grobbelaar once more. Although a phlegmatic character at the best of times, the Liverpool goalkeeper was clearly struggling with the mental side of his game. He remained

157

unparalleled as an instinctive shot stopper but during this period his decision-making and judgment of crosses remained suspect and so it was to prove again here.

Hurt in a collision with Spurs winger Chris Waddle in conceding a third minute corner, Grobbelaar completely misjudged the trajectory of Glenn Hoddle's flag-kick, palming the ball up invitingly inside his six-yard box for Waddle to volley home from no more than a yard out. In the Liverpool end, even his greatest supporters were aware of the growing strain on Grobbelaar, as Sampson admits, "All the talk in the papers had been about how it'd be us who would be clear if it hadn't been for Brucie's howlers, and this was up there with the worst of them. A shocking season, generally, for the hero of Rome a couple of years previously."

After the match Grobbelaar suggested that media pressure, during a weekend when BBC's Football Focus claimed he had cost Liverpool 15 points already, was having an effect on his performances. "After all the publicity I've been getting," he lamented, "it was a poor show to make a mistake like that. Fortunately I didn't drop another clanger later in the match but the [press] lads will be on my back again this week. I'm just a character they like to pick on."

Lucky to be only one nil down at the break, Liverpool's season appeared to have hit rock bottom but whether it was an inspired Dalglish team talk at half-time, a Ronnie Moran-sponsored tea-cup and plate smashing exercise or just a certain degree of soul searching and professional pride from the players, Liverpool were transformed in the second half. Up front Rush finally started receiving support as Liverpool's midfield began to function as a unit. In the early stages former Liverpool legend Ray Clemence was forced to save brilliantly from first McMahon and then Johnston before the unlucky and inspired Molby saw a powerful header cannon back off the bar. Liverpool were playing with a fluency not seen since the second-half display at home to Manchester United. The ball-winning presence of McMahon, back to his best after an extended lay off, gave Molby the much needed foil which allowed him to renew supply lines to the attack.

Despite their improved display and mounting pressure on the Spurs goal, Liverpool couldn't force a breakthrough until the 66th minute when the in-form Molby again provided the crucial equalizer. A Johnston corner from the right was only partially cleared to Rush, who laid the ball back to Whelan. His mishit shot rebounded to Molby who beat Clemence with a powerful low drive from 18-yards. After seeing his shot rest in the bottom corner of the net, the Dane peeled away with both arms raised to take the acclaim of Sampson and his fellow freezing Liverpool fans behind the goal.

As the game entered the final quarter, Liverpool pressed for another. McMahon blasted against the bar and Clemence was in inspired form again, saving a further three times from the revitalized Rush, while Whelan wasted what appeared to be Liverpool's last chance when he shot wide from a good position.

As the clock ticked round to the 90 minute mark it seemed Liverpool would have to settle for a point and a much improved performance to build on for the rest of the season but, with just 30 seconds remaining, there came a defining moment of the entire campaign.

Almost in slow motion Whelan controlled a ball dropping in the centre of the pitch before sliding a perfect through ball between the Tottenham centre-halves Steve Perryman and Paul Miller. Timing his run perfectly Rush ran onto the astute pass and, as Clemence advanced to narrow the angle, the Welshman struck the ball with the outside of his right foot into the bottom corner to spark huge celebrations behind the goal. The reaction of the Liverpool players to the dramatic late winner as they mobbed the goalscorer spoke volumes - and hinted that maybe the Championship wasn't a forlorn hope after all.

The timing and significance of the winner wasn't lost on the fans either. "Just as we were resigning ourselves to being out of the title race," said Sampson, "and starting to think about the walk back to Seven Sisters, Rushie popped up in about the fourth minute of injury time to knock in the winner. Jubilation and scenes of unbridled ecstasy." Sampson's celebrations were only tempered by, "the realisation that what was already going to be an iffy walk back to the tube was now going to be loaded with real anger from the locals. They were on a bad run themselves, they'd been whistling for the ref to blow up as we belatedly started launching a wave of attacks and it didn't help relations the way we celebrated the winner."

Dalglish was in bullish form after the match. "We've never been out of touch," he said. "We always feel we need to win every week and we just get on with our business. If others want to worry about us, that's up to them." Referring to Grobbelaar's error at the start of the match he hinted that his keeper would accept responsibility. "Anyone who makes a mistake knows it and is unhappy about it." A relieved Grobbelaar thanked his teammates for saving his blushes and attributed the second half turnaround to some fiery half-time words from Dalglish. "Sometimes a lot of noise works. The manager is a hard man and you've just got to go and out and play for him."

Even if the eight-point gap at the top of the table remained a daunting one, the victory at White Hart Lane was, potentially, a huge turning point for Liverpool. The Reds would need others, notably Everton, Manchester United and West Ham to slip up in the remaining 11 games to have a chance of glory but, with an away win snatched from the jaws of defeat and a performance that finally hinted at their true form, the Reds could at least look to the rest of the season's engagements with renewed confidence. Only 11 League wins to go.

Wednesday 5 March
Milk Cup semi-final second leg
Liverpool v Queens Park Rangers

"It felt weird. There were thousands of them, yet they had never travelled in numbers before or been renowned for causing bother. Here it seemed like they had half of London with them. I'm not sure how many of them were QPR fans to be honest, but they were having a right good go. Of course, some of the Road End boys, while they might have been taken a little by surprise, were ready for a do."

Mike Nevin, co-author and Liverpool fan on Rangers' away support.

Sunday's last gasp victory at Tottenham had maintained Liverpool's interest in the title race. Just. Three days later, a similar victory in the second leg of their Milk Cup semi-final would guarantee Dalglish a Wembley final in his first season as player-manager. As such, the game assumed even greater importance for the majority of Reds' fans, who were firmly behind the novice player-manager.

Contrary to popular opinion not everyone agreed with Dalglish's appointment in 1985 and the more fickle amongst the Anfield faithful continued to voice their opinions in the local press. For Dalglish and his players, the perfect way to answer the small number of vocal critics would be to deliver Liverpool's first silverware since Joe Fagan's treble-winning team of 1984 had lifted the European Cup in Rome. While the League Championship would always take priority, cup successes were valued highly at a time when additional finance was generated by reaching finals and winning trophies – the pursuit of glory and medals ensuring extra cash, instead of the modern-day fiscal nirvana of a top four finish and revenue from TV for Champions League football.

Liverpool's inability to string consecutive wins together in the league was a major cause of concern for most fans, even the most loyal. Lack of firepower up front, creativity in midfield and most alarmingly, consistent errors from their keeper, were all cited as the reasons behind the Reds indifferent and inconsistent form.

Although still competing on three fronts, Liverpool's confidence remained fragile. Ahead of their game against QPR - who had defeated Liverpool twice already this season - Ian Hargreaves wrote that, "if ever a side needed a boost to their morale Liverpool do now, when Wembley is within 90 minutes reach. And if ever a player needed to know that a crowd appreciate his past services, despite recent mistakes, it is surely Grobbelaar, who has become a target of nationwide criticism."

Mindful of the impact live television coverage of the game by ITV could have on the attendance, and the importance of the supporters' backing to Dalglish's team, Peter Robinson made a rather clumsy last-minute plea to fans to turn up at the gate and assist the players in their efforts to reach the Final. "We need our fans in the stands cheering us on," he said, "not sitting at home by their sets. All the compensation in the world [from the Football League for a TV-affected crowd] cannot make up for the lack of direct support, which could easily cost us a place at Wembley."

Dalglish echoed his Chief Executive's words. "I hope all the Liverpool fans will give us their complete backing," he said. "Your support can mean a lot to us tonight."Despite the public efforts of Robinson and Dalglish to generate a large, supportive crowd their pleas fell largely on deaf ears, and just 23,863 apparently paid at the turnstiles. This included unusually large numbers for QPR, believed to be swelled by supporters of other London clubs on the look out for trouble. They got what they came for as local youths eagerly engaged in scuffles down the dark alleys surrounding the Anfield Road end of the ground before and after the game.

While the relatively poor attendance can be largely explained by the presence of the cameras at a time when every penny counted in so many Merseyside households, the lower status of the Milk Cup and the general depression over Liverpool's spluttering season was also to blame. The 20,000 or so loyal Anfield supporters who did decide to give their backing to the team created a sparkling atmosphere on an exciting, dramatic night when fortunes ebbed and flowed constantly - and Lady Luck donned a rather fetching, tight-fitting, blue and white-hooped jersey.

With the huge incentive of a very winnable final in prospect against relegation-threatened Oxford United - featuring future Anfield stars Ray Houghton and John Aldridge - Dalglish picked an unchanged side from the weekend's victory at White Hart Lane. Despite their first-leg loss, most observers predicted that Liverpool's vast experience of winning two-legged ties in Europe, plus home advantage, would see them through with something to spare.

As the game kicked off the noise generated by both those on the Kop and the Rangers fans' in the Anfield Road more than made up for the thousands of empty seats along the touchlines. With both ends behind the goals well crammed with spectators and the Kop in particular well-populated, the size of the crowd did actually appear much larger than the published attendance.

It was a common theory among supporters at the time that clubs would deliberately underestimate the number of paying customers to maximize their TV compensation payment from the League. Tellingly - and unlike other clubs - Liverpool never announced the official attendance to the crowd inside the stadium, with the documented figure discovered only in the press reports that followed the match. This was just as well, as some of the official Anfield attendance figures would have had the crowd in fits of laughter had they been announced during the game.

Inspired by the noisy backing of the Kop, who had affirmed their support for Grobbelaar before the start with a rousing rendition of, "Brucie, Brucie Grobbelaar, Brucie Grobbelaar in our goal," Liverpool tore into the visitors from the start. Penned in by Liverpool's passing, movement and desire to win back the ball when a Rangers player was able to clear, the West Londoners struggled to clear their own half of the pitch in the early part of the game. After repelling the best of Liverpool's initial attacks it seemed the breakthrough had arrived when the Reds won a disputed penalty after 21 minutes. In fantastic form and practically perfect from the spot, Molby stepped forward confidently to take it but, to the horror of the fans behind the goal, his kick was saved by Paul Barron in the Rangers' goal. It was a rare penalty miss for the big Dane.

Molby atoned for his wastefulness from the spot shortly before half-time however, when, advancing from his own half, he spotted an energetic run by Steve McMahon to his right. A precise pass flicked with the outside of his foot arrived perfectly at the feet of the onrushing McMahon, whose momentum took him clear of the Rangers defence. Confronted by the advancing Barron, McMahon opened his stance and expertly lofted the ball beyond the keeper's dive into the roof of the net to send the Kop wild. As the players celebrated with McMahon and repositioned themselves for the restart, the ground rocked to strains of, "We're on the march with Kenny's Army, we're all going to Wem-ber-lee." It was the first time the song had been sung by so many with such utter conviction and became a refrain that was heard at grounds all over the country not just for the rest of the season but for the next five years.

With the aggregate score 1-1 at half-time, Liverpool fans spent the interval anticipating seeing their team clinch a place in the final so they could enjoy yet another visit to the capital. They would have to do so attacking the Anfield Road End in the second half however, but the drama that would eventually settle the tie would occur under the noses of the Kop as Liverpool suffered at the cruel hands of fate.

In the 59th minute a mix up between Sammy Lee and Mark Lawrenson on the Liverpool right allowed Rangers' Mike Fillery to slalom into the box. A deflection saw the ball cannon towards the penalty spot and panic ensued in the overmanned Reds' defence. Jim Beglin blasted his hurried clearance against the shins of Ronnie Whelan with the ball eventually flying past Grobbelaar for the most chaotic of own goals. Rangers were level on the night and back in front on aggregate.

Roared on by the energetic and enthusiastic home crowd, Liverpool picked themselves up and regained the lead on the night, levelling the tie on aggregate for a second time, just eleven minutes later. Lifted by the support of the fans on the Kop Grobbelaar had produced an assured performance - mixing safe handling with accurate clearances. In the 70th minute the goalkeeper's enormous punt downfield was helped on by Rush into the path of Craig Johnston, who bravely beat QPR keeper Barron to the ball.

Although both players clattered into one another - a split second after he reached the ball first - the stand-in striker's slight touch was just powerful enough to see the ball bounce high into the corner of the net. With 20 minutes remaining, and enjoying huge territorial dominance, it looked as though Liverpool would now go on and clinch their place at Wembley on 20 April. A further defensive lapse would prove the Reds' undoing however, only this time it would come too late in the game for another comeback.

Throwing men forward to supplement the attack and win the tie in normal time, Liverpool were caught on the break in the 83rd minute when McMahon's intended pass for Beglin was intercepted in the visitor's half. Rangers cleverly exploited the space vacated by Beglin's charge upfield, and substitute Wayne Fereday eventually received the ball on the left of the penalty area. Alan Hansen was unable to stop Fereday's cross and Gary Gillespie, under pressure from former Liverpool forward Michael Robinson, clumsily let the ball roll off his right foot whilst attempting to clear.

Like the rest of the Kop, a wrong-footed Grobbelaar could only watch in horror as the ball slowly trickled over the line. The looks of disbelief on the faces of the Liverpool players told their own story. They had controlled the game for 90 minutes but had contrived to miss a penalty, wasted several gilt edged chances and had conceded two calamitous own goals to virtually gift-wrap QPR with victory and a rare visit to Wembley.

As the final whistle sounded to leave Rangers' players and supporters to celebrate one of the biggest wins in their history, Liverpool's stars trooped off to contemplate a season that appeared to be fast disintegrating; eight points off the pace in the league and now eliminated from the Milk Cup in the cruellest of circumstances. It seemed that only the lustre of an FA Cup win could salvage their campaign, and with it Dalglish's early credentials as a manager.

Despite still being able to produce intermittent spells of attacking football that were the equal of any of the Liverpool sides of old, an elusive, special ingredient was missing; a lack of conviction that saw them unable to finish off opponents and a rare defensive fragility that left only the most optimistic of supporters thinking the season could ultimately end in glory. Something special was required to galvanise his players, but Dalglish hadn't earned Bob Paisley's acclaim as Liverpool's greatest ever player for nothing. He was about to find the special, missing ingredient on the pitch - and it lay closer to home than perhaps he realized.

Saturday 8 March
Liverpool v Queens Park Rangers

"Peter Shilton's wish to finish his career with one of England's greatest clubs will be granted by Liverpool. The Englishman universally acknowledged as the world's best goalkeeper will be on his way to Anfield after the World Cup Finals this summer…Shilton's four-year contract with Southampton expires this summer and Liverpool, in despair of Bruce Grobbelaar's televised catastrophies, intend to have his transfer signed and sealed before he embarks for Mexico in May."

Jeff Powell - Sports Journalist of the year, Daily Mail, 4 March 1986

With the season six months old and entering its final third, Liverpool had played 31 league games. Of that number, Kenny Dalglish had restricted himself to just nine starts and three appearances as substitute and the player-manager had only the solitary - albeit memorable - strike in the opening seconds at Goodison Park in September to show for his time on the field. Although a groin injury sustained in the FA Cup replay against York had stopped a recent comeback in its tracks, Dalglish had been fit for most of the season and had generally chosen to leave himself out in favour of the more zestful Paul Walsh or the more adaptable Craig Johnston.

With Liverpool now trailing Everton by eight points and Manchester United - who had a game in hand - by two, the league title was a realistic target only in the eyes of the most optimistic supporters. Privately, most fans' honest prediction for the Reds' final position was third, perhaps fourth. Given the Reds' inconsistency, few expected anything better.

A glut of untimely postponements caused by the continuing harsh winter had created a fixture backlog for the London title aspirants, but both Chelsea and West Ham had ample games in hand to overhaul not only Liverpool but also realistically challenge Everton and Manchester United. To emphasise the number of points dropped since December, Liverpool stood only three points clear of the West Londoners - having played four games more. They were six points ahead of West Ham – but the Hammers had a staggering five games in hand on the Reds.

In the aftermath of their Milk Cup exit to QPR there were renewed pleas from fans for Dalglish to return to the starting eleven on a regular basis. This was as much to inspire Liverpool's forthcoming FA Cup engagements – in the eyes of many the only achievable target that remained - as to breath renewed life into their rapidly crumbling title challenge. Paul Walsh's form and partnership with Ian Rush before his unfortunate ankle ligament injury had given the 35-year old Dalglish a valid reason to be sparing with his own time on the pitch, but fans and journalists viewed his absence from the team differently. They cited the talismanic presence he still carried - this despite a gradual waning of his playing powers - a mortal slip of form and effectiveness that could be traced back to a depressed fracture of the cheekbone following a collision with Manchester United defender Kevin Moran in January 1984.

Although he recovered to play his part in the Treble success that followed, Dalglish's level of performance after his facial injury had - to the knowledgeable observer at least – dipped, and he had been substituted by Joe Fagan in the European Cup Final in Rome. For a Milk Cup tie at Spurs in October 1984 he had even been dropped - for the first time in his career - by the avuncular Fagan. Fagan later admitted this had been the, "daftest," decision of his managerial career. However, although Dalglish regained some form as that 1984/85 campaign progressed, it was clear that the sands of time were catching up with the man Paisley and others were already calling Liverpool's greatest ever player.

On a day scheduled for FA Cup sixth round ties, Liverpool found themselves back in league action as their prospective cup opponents Watford or Bury were still trying to resolve their weather hit fourth round tie. After drawing at Watford just three days previously, the Third Division side were confident of an upset over their more illustrious opponents this afternoon and thus set up an intriguing tie with the Reds at Anfield - scheduled for the forthcoming Tuesday evening.

In a twist of the fixture list Liverpool's Canon League opponents were their midweek Milk Cup conquerors – Queens Park Rangers - paying a second visit to Anfield in three days. An air of disappointment and depression still lingered over Anfield following their cruel midweek exit and this was reflected in another poor home crowd. Rangers' following - numbering barely 100 - was a fraction of the London mob that had accompanied them earlier in the week. With many Liverpool supporters having apparently given up on the title race, just 26,219 paid to see if Liverpool could achieve a form of pyrrhic revenge.

With Everton in FA Cup action at Luton – who had emphatically beaten Arsenal 3-0 at home in a second replay just three days before - the game did at least give the Reds the chance to close the gap at the top, and a fit-again Dalglish gave a boost to those gathered on a muted Kop by including himself in the line-up at the expense of Craig Johnston. Despite the tonic of Dalglish's inclusion, QPR compounded Kopites' Wednesday's misery by taking the lead through a suspiciously offside Leroy Rosenior goal after just seven minutes. Their midweek exploits were to catch up with them however, leaving Dalglish to take centre stage as the Londoners tired.

If Dalglish lacked the eye for a goal that had seen him average one every two games during his most prolific years at Celtic - and early seasons at Anfield - he had lost none of his vision and unparalleled ability to bring out the very best in others.

Trailing to Rosenior's early score, Dalglish mustered his players and calmly, efficiently and ruthlessly – like the celebrated Liverpool teams of old – took the visitors apart. Before half-time the Reds had responded with three goals and the points, despite the inauspicious start, were effectively theirs.

The first came after 19 minutes when Steve McMahon swept home past Paul Barron after a one-two with Ronnie Whelan. Liverpool were in front after half an hour courtesy of Rush after a superb flowing move involving Alan Hansen, John Wark and inevitably, Dalglish. The third came two minutes before the break when Molby's surge from deep again found Dalglish, who crossed unerringly for Wark – arriving late and unseen yet again - to put the seal on Liverpool's most fluent 45 minutes of football for some time.

Prompted constantly by Dalglish in the second half, Liverpool continued to exact revenge for their midweek calamity and Paul Barron was forced to pull off a number of fine saves restricting the home side to just one more goal - McMahon rounding off a typically energetic display with a fine header from Jim Beglin's cross on the left in the 75th minute. Subsequent efforts by Rush, Dalglish and Whelan threatened to add to Liverpool's tally in front of the Kop but they were eventually 'forced' to settle for a 4-1 victory.

Although it had been a much-improved all-round team performance, the plaudits – rightly - belonged to Dalglish. On a day when the Anfield crowd had applauded politely at the quality of Liverpool's passing but remained relatively quiet throughout, at full-time the Kop chanted his name in adulation and recognition as he left the field. There was a sense that the Kopites had to remind him of the impact his selection had hah on the team's performance. This was a crowd that yearned to see their beloved boss as a visible heartbeat on the pitch, a channel through which they could inspire the team with their support for the greater challenges that lay ahead. From his position behind Rush, Dalglish had inspired the whole team but had particularly encouraged McMahon's vibrant bursts from midfield and harnessed the sublime supply line offered by Molby.

The Liverpool Echo summed up the player-manager's display, commenting that, "Dalglish was an inspiration, treating the crowd to his own special brand of wizardry, with clever flicks, cheeky one-twos, deft touches and above all speed of thought." Buoyed by his efforts Dalglish suggested in more ebullient fashion than usual that, "If we had taken all our chances we could have had seven or eight. We played very well and I didn't feel my groin at all."

QPR manager Jim Smith acknowledged that two games at Anfield in a week had been too much for his side. "We couldn't have had a worse fixture after the Milk Cup success," the likeable and always honest Smith said. "We were mentally drained. I feared this. Kenny really made them play." Former Reds' striker Michael Robinson attributed Liverpool's transformation to his former teammate's display. "Dalglish made them a super team again. It was like meeting a different side from last week."

With songs of praise from the Kop, tributes from his opponents ringing in his ears, and a clean bill of health on his return to fitness and form, Dalglish could now contemplate leading from the front as the season entered its decisive final quarter. Liverpool's slow recovery had begun, with the six points taken from this game and the win at Spurs reducing the gap - while Everton had been inactive - from 11 points to five. Next up for the newly-confident Reds was the rescheduled FA Cup fifth Round visit of Watford – who on the same afternoon had won 3-0 away at Gigg Lane - and their own mercurial playmaker John Barnes.

Tuesday 11 March
FA Cup fifth round
Liverpool v Watford

"It's Wayward Lad, trying to break his Cheltenham hoodoo, being pressed now by Dawn Run in the centre, Forgive 'n' Forget on the near side. As they race to the line, and the mare's beginning to get up! And as they come to the line, she's made it! Dawn Run has won it!"

Peter O'Sullivan describes the action as Dawn Run, ridden by Jonjo O'Neill, becomes the first horse in history to win the Cheltenham Gold Cup after previously winning the Champion Hurdle. BBC Sport, 13 March 1986.

While Liverpool had been handing out a footballing lesson to QPR in the League at the weekend, Everton had been retrieving a two-goal deficit at Luton to stay in the FA Cup. Intriguingly Monday's semi-final draw - the day before the Reds' delayed sixth round tie with Watford - kept the two Merseyside clubs apart, so a first all-Merseyside FA Cup final was - results pending - still a real and greatly anticipated prospect. If Liverpool and Everton could overcome their respective quarter-final foes, their opponents in the last four would be Southampton (at White Hart Lane) and Sheffield Wednesday (at Villa Park) respectively.

The possibility of Liverpool reaching their first FA Cup Final since 1977 was an exciting one for Reds' fans and the club anticipated a big crowd for the quarter-final visit of Watford. The idea of a midweek trip to Anfield however, didn't seem to appeal to Watford supporters quite as much, and the visitors returned their full allocation of Anfield Road seats for the tie. These were subsequently put on general sale to grateful home fans on the day of the game.

Having established themselves in mid-table, Watford were in little danger of dropping into the relegation battle. They stood 14 points clear of the drop zone, currently occupied by Midlands trio West Brom, Birmingham and Aston Villa. The target for Graham Taylor's side now was a return to Wembley, where they had lost 2-0 to a resurgent Everton in the 1984 Final. Watford's star player was John Barnes whose burgeoning talents were being carefully nurtured by Taylor. Equally effective on either flank or as a striker, and with the ability to hold-up the long passes from defence that were a feature of Watford's style of play, Barnes' performances had made him a regular in the England squad and a certainty for a Mexico World Cup place.

Former Everton midfielder Martin Dobson told the Liverpool Echo the day before the game that not only was Barnes strong and quick, he was also a joy to watch, "unless you are an opposing manager." "He created havoc against us at times," said Bury manager Dobson, "although Liverpool will be a very different proposition."

Tuesday evening's Liverpool Echo also highlighted an additional, curious element surrounding the game. They pointed out that Watford would be looking to, "touch wood, cross fingers and hope a black cat dashes across their path," in the hope they avoided their Anfield penalty curse; since their promotion to the top flight in 1982, the Hornets had conceded four spot-kicks in as many games at Anfield.

The Reds had already been awarded 11 penalties so far this the season, a figure that the same paper said added weight, "to the whispered theory that too many referees buckle under vociferous pressure from the Kop." A visibly annoyed Dalglish baulked at the local newspaper's representative bringing up the statistic at the pre-match press conference earlier in the day. "I just hope the referee hasn't read about it," he said.

Mindful of Watford's long-ball style and the ability in the air of Barnes and centre-forward Colin West, Dalglish again chose to deploy Jan Molby in his sweeper role, so adding extra presence and heading ability in defence. Despite the logic of such a move, this tactic was perceived as negative by the media, suggesting as it did that Dalglish was more concerned with the opposition than he should be.

An often quoted, old-fashioned view was that Liverpool should just turn up and let the opposition worry about them. In reality however, this was more myth than maxim. Most fans, unlike the so-called experts in the media, weren't so dismissive of Dalglish's attention to detail. Recalling the way Bob Paisley had told Sammy Lee to shadow Bayern Munich playmaker Paul Breitner relentlessly in the 1981 European Cup semi-final, they knew that Liverpool managers had always - when required - adjusted their philosophy and tactics according to the strengths of the opposition. Dalglish's decision to play Molby as sweeper also underlined his determination not to be swayed by his critics, to back his own judgment and to opt for the formation that best served Liverpool and no-one else.

Although most commentators and pundits were principally after cheap headlines, the manager did appear to concur with the press (and fans) that he should now remain in the starting line-up. Free of injury again, Dalglish selected himself alongside Ian Rush for the second time in three days. In the only change from the home win over QPR, Gary Gillespie came in for John Wark, with Craig Johnston named as substitute.

Although not all stand seats had been sold, the Kop was packed almost to capacity and Liverpool were welcomed enthusiastically by near 37,000 expectant and hopeful supporters. Just two wins from Wembley, they were in full voice and didn't even seem to mind skipper Alan Hansen losing the toss and watching the Reds attack the Kop in the first half.

Despite Molby's deeper role there was nothing negative about Liverpool's approach at the start of the game. Expecting this early pressure on the Watford rearguard, Graham Taylor had followed Dalglish's lead by fielding Lee Sinnott as an auxiliary defender. The extra man at the back didn't stop Liverpool however, and the home attacks came in waves. The best chance in the opening stages fell to the player-manager himself, but Dalglish could only direct a 10th minute header from Ronnie Whelan's cross firmly into the arms of Watford keeper Tony Coton.

Signed for £300,000 at the start of the season from Birmingham City, Coton had justified his price tag with a string of excellent displays and critics of Bruce Grobbelaar often cited him as a potential replacement for the under-fire Zimbabwean. Coton's positioning was again excellent later in the half when he smothered two threatening headers, both from Rush. The pace was hectic as Liverpool enjoyed almost constant possession but many of their attacks founded on the rock that was Watford's commanding central defensive pair of Steve Terry and John McClelland.

When Liverpool fashioned their best chance of the half it was Mark Lawrenson, in a typical marauding surge from right back, who shrugged off the attentions of Wilf Rostron to fire in a shot that was superbly turned behind by Coton. Despite their best efforts however, Liverpool were frustrated that Watford had restricted them to fewer shots on goal than normal, and the game remained goalless at half-time.

The second half saw Liverpool continue to press with Dalglish, "always involved, his soccer brain working overtime to open up the visitors battling rearguard." Just after the hour mark the home side came closest to breaking the deadlock when Coton produced a remarkable double save.

Supplementing the attack with another trademark burst from full-back, Jim Beglin shot powerfully from 20 yards only to see Coton dive to his right to save. The busy keeper could only push the ball into the path of Rush, but he sprung quickly to his feet to throw himself in the way of the striker's predatory effort and conceded a corner. It was breathless stuff. From the flag-kick Coton saved Watford again, this time from Steve McMahon's speculative shot. Frustratingly for Liverpool, they had been kept at arms length by a determined Watford defence and, when they did get a sight of goal, Coton seemed to deal with it all. As the second half progressed, the visitors became bolder in their approach and the Kop breathed a huge sigh of relief in the 68th minute when defender Sinnott got forward to attempt an acrobatic overhead kick from Barnes' clever cross. With the Liverpool defence looking on, the ball sailed inches past Grobbelaar's post.

As cup-ties enter the closing minutes with the scores still level supporters' nerves are frayed at the thought of the late goal that would leave their side no time to salvage a replay or extra time. Kopite hearts missed another beat in the 78th minute when Grobbelaar was forced to make a crucial save from Brian Talbot's 25-yard shot. Regarded as an FA Cup bogeyman by Reds' fans, Talbot had broken Liverpool hearts at the end of the famous marathon seven-hour footballing duel in 1980 when he scored a winner for Arsenal amid the agony of a semi-final third replay at Highfield Road, Coventry.

With Johnston having replaced Sammy Lee on the right of midfield for the final quarter, Liverpool reasserted themselves towards the end of the game, but it was the player-manager who remained the most likely source of inspiration. With his back to goal in the area, and with Watford defenders backing away in fear of conceding a penalty, the final incident of note saw Dalglish control the ball and slip a cute pass to Beglin. Hit firmly and with conviction, the shot was on target but once again it was saved by the seemingly unbeatable Coton.

As referee Roger Milford blew for full-time shortly afterwards, Liverpool fans sloped away disconsolately whilst Watford's players and small band of supporters celebrated a goalless draw that would see the teams replay at Vicarage Road the following Monday night. Liverpool's hopes of a first FA Cup final in almost a decade had taken a big blow. "That's the first time I've kept a clean sheet in any of my games against Liverpool," admitted Coton after the game. "Everyone likes to play at home. We hope we have done the hard part getting this result. Now we want to capitalise on it at our place."

On a night of ultimate frustration, Liverpool's outstanding performer was once again Dalglish who consoled supporters by saying, "Obviously we would have liked to win but we're still in the Cup. Hopefully we will make it as hard for them there as they did here. When teams defend like that, the attacking side always needs a little break."

Although a league game against potential semi-final opponents Southampton was next, the cup quarter-final replay was seen by many fans as more important. The Reds would have to continue their quest to reach Wembley without the support of the Kop but, as the fans made their way home, plans were already being hatched all over Merseyside that would see remarkable numbers follow them to Vicarage Road.

Saturday 15 March
Southampton v Liverpool

"Eighty Labour Councillors yesterday lost a legal battle against personal financial disaster and a ban from office. The 80 Liverpool and Lambeth rates rebels – among them Derek Hatton and 'Red Ted' Knight – now face disqualification for five years

Disqualification will mean that interim administrations, drawn from remaining members, will take over the two councils temporarily, turning Lambeth Tory and putting Liverpool under Alliance control. By-elections for the 80 seats will follow and all wards in Lambeth and a third of those in Liverpool are…to be contested in the local council elections on May 8."

Anthony Doran, Home Affairs Correspondent, Daily Mail, 6 March 1986

Just two days before Monday night's FA Cup replay against Watford Liverpool faced an awkward away league fixture at The Dell; two crucial games that could either advance or signal the end of their hopes in two competitions in the space of just 48 hours. While Liverpool were achieving confidence-building league wins over Spurs and QPR – and in the process reducing the gap at the top of the First Division to five points - rivals Everton were securing their place in the last four with a 1-0 victory over Luton Town in a sixth round replay at Goodison Park; they had drawn the first game 2-2 at Kenilworth Road.

The Blues however, still had a game in hand over the Reds and they remained odds-on favourites to retain the title with just 10 games left to play. Liverpool's run had seen them overtake Manchester United to move into second place, but United's spare fixtures – if negotiated successfully - and those held by Chelsea and West Ham, could see the Reds drop down to fifth place in the table.

On the eve of the match against Southampton there was a disconcerting story in the press which suggested that Ian Rush wasn't happy with life at Anfield, in particular his role in the team. Although Dalglish had returned to partner Rush up front in the last two games, the Welshman was reported as telling the Daily Mirror, "I'm not happy. I can't play the way Liverpool want. I'm not a target man. And if I'm not happy on the pitch, I'm not happy off it. If it doesn't go well here I suppose I might have to go abroad."

Although the report might have shocked Reds' fans, Liverpool's refusal to allow Rush to consider a huge contract offered by Italian side Napoli in the summer of 1984 still rankled with their prize asset. At the time, the riches on offer in Serie A dwarfed the salaries of the leading British players and it was no secret inside the club that Rush harboured ambitions of joining ex-colleague Graeme Souness in Italy and enjoying the type of earnings that could secure a player's future for life.

Eventually the lure of the Lira would prove too great for both Rush and Liverpool, but at no point could anyone complain about the striker's effort and commitment on the field. However, his transfer value and desire to maximize his earnings finally saw a lucrative move - for both parties - to Juventus announced at the end of the season.

Dalglish could certainly have done without such unsettling speculation before the clash with Southampton. The game had taken on an additional, intriguing significance as a potential dress rehearsal for the FA Cup semi-final – so long as Liverpool could win their replay at Watford. The Saints had beaten south coast rivals Brighton 2-0 at the Goldstone Ground to book their place at White Hart Lane. Liverpool at least received one significant boost before the match on the South coast when it was announced that former Anfield hard man Jimmy Case, who had reinvented himself as a composed playmaker in the centre of the Saints midfield, would be unavailable here due to an ankle injury attributed to, "flaking of the bone."

For the Reds, Dalglish reported that Paul Walsh was continuing to make progress in his recovery from injury but was still some way short of a return to the side. It emerged in later years that Liverpool's diagnosis and treatment of Walsh's injury had been amateurish in the extreme. A decision was taken not to operate and instead the striker was recommended for a period of intensive heat treatment administered by club physiotherapists. It was only after Walsh failed to make any significant progress over several weeks that the equipment being used was checked and found to be faulty.

Aware that ageing limbs might limit his impact ahead of a potential third game in nine days, and still nursing a groin strain, Dalglish chose to rest himself and he restored Craig Johnston as Ian Rush's partner up front. The only other change saw John Wark deputise for Steve McMahon.

A revelation since his own return from injury, McMahon had been a key figure in the recent Reds' revival; in light of his recent lay-off he was one player the manager couldn't afford to risk before Monday night's crucial replay. Under Dalglish, the emergence of Jan Molby and the arrival of McMahon had confined John Wark mainly to the subs bench, but his unerring competence when called upon was testimony to the Scot's ability and professionalism. He was a more than able deputy, a natural goalscorer from midfield and the Reds' leading marksman the previous season with a remarkable 27 goals.

A notoriously difficult place to get a result, the Dell was the most cramped ground in the First Division with the incongruously designed wooden stands rising almost vertically from the touchlines. Spectators could virtually breath down the players' necks. In addition, the view from the uncovered, narrow strip of terracing at the Archers Road End was renowned as one of the worst for visiting supporters. It seemed that the perimeter wall behind the goal was just inches from the net. So much so that fans could practically whisper to the keeper. The close confines of the stadium generated a fantastic atmosphere however, and Southampton's biggest crowd of the season - 19,784 - was in fine voice at kick-off.

To avoid a clash with the Saints' red shirts and black shorts, Liverpool played in their rarely seen second change strip of all yellow. Playing 24 hours ahead of Everton's televised home game with Chelsea, the match was also an opportunity to apply a little pressure on their neighbours and with victory, reduce the gap between them to just two points – albeit for 24 hours.
After an uneventful and goalless first half, the game sprung to life in the 49th minute when Southampton took the lead courtesy of another sloppy piece of goalkeeping from Bruce Grobbelaar.

Liverpool conceded a throw-in level with the edge of the box on the right hand side and, when centre-half Kevin Bond headed down Stuart McManus's long throw, Saints' muscular striker George Lawrence was able to shoot on the turn from six yards. Grobbelaar appeared to have the effort covered but, partially unsighted by Gary Gillespie, the ball ricocheted into the net via the goalkeeper's left ankle. While not of the magnitude of his recent blunders, another perceived mistake gave his army of critics a further opportunity to highlight his inconsistent form. Recognizing the luckless Grobbelaar's fragile confidence, the Liverpool Echo reported that, "He continues to live on his nerves, aware that any slip will get headline treatment."

While Lawrence celebrated by raising a triumphant arm in the air to salute his unexpected opener, and was mobbed by his teammates in the process, Saints' manager Chris Nicholl gestured wildly at his players to keep their concentration. His warning would fall on deaf ears as Liverpool, stung by the goal, suddenly sprung to life.

To the frustration of their supporters the Reds seemed incapable of showing their true form until they had fallen behind. Some blamed this trait on an overly cautious approach in the early stages of games but, whether by accident or design, Liverpool's tendency to start slowly and win matches late in the day - often by coming from behind - would be one of the most enduring, but theatrical features of their season.

To the dismay of the prophetic Nicholl in the home dug-out, Liverpool were level within minutes. The celebrations of the home crowd were still in full swing when Rush popped up on the right side of the penalty area and laid an inch-perfect ball across for Wark, arriving once again with a perfectly timed late run from midfield. His right-foot shot, hammered first-time without breaking stride, beat Peter Shilton's despairing dive to nestle in the back of the net. Ominously for Southampton, the Reds' celebration on the pitch was a muted one – almost as if they knew the job was only half complete.

Smelling blood, and fully aware of the need for three points, Liverpool pressed for a winner. Ten minutes later it arrived - with Wark this time returning the complement for Rush. Johnston's desire to retain possession on the right enabled him to swing in a testing cross that was knocked down by Wark. Although the lay-off fell behind Rush, the striker was able to seize on the ball in an instant, control it and, on the turn, shoot past a helpless Shilton from 10 yards.

As Nicholl bemoaned afterwards, the Reds had produced a classic sucker punch. "Liverpool are at their most dangerous when they are wounded," he said. Recognizing their infuriating inability, or reluctance to function at full pelt until a goal behind, the former Northern Irish international added cryptically that, "The worse thing you can do against them is score."

Liverpool had won their third league game in a row since the derby defeat. In so doing they had narrowed the gap at the top to two points which - assisted by Chelsea taking a point at Goodison Park the following afternoon - subsequently rose to three. An excellent weekend for the Reds was complete when Manchester United lost ground on both Merseyside clubs with yet another defeat, this time to QPR at Loftus Road. It was Ron Atkinson's sides eight loss in 16 games – a collapse which had begun with defeat at Sheffield Wednesday back in November.

While Liverpool remained in the South to prepare for the Cup replay at Watford, the debate over Rush's future rumbled on. His winning goal here was his 22nd of the season but his prowess in the area was not the only reason the Liverpool Echo named him man-of-the-match. "With Paul Walsh still sidelined and Kenny Dalglish in and out with niggling problems," Ken Rogers suggested, "Rush has had to battle on all-too-often this season without a natural partner. It has taken a lot out of the Welsh striker and he will be much happier when the situation is resolved." A place in the FA Cup semi-final would certainly help quieten the growing speculation about Rush's future.

Monday 17 March
FA Cup sixth round replay
Watford v Liverpool

"My son Mike and his mate Macca badgered me all weekend about the driving to the replay. The fact that they would have to bunk off school hadn't even entered their heads. Before I knew it, we had a car-full heading south on a Monday dinner-time. The highlight of the journey was the sight of a clapped-out three-wheeled van bursting with more than a few tipsy Reds, making very slow progress down the motorway. We passed it three times after lengthy stops at services on the M1. Each time we overtook it, it's passengers appeared more and more dishevelled."

Bernard Nevin, Liverpool fan, Crosby.

Ever since it became fashionable for English football supporters to follow their team to away games, generations of Liverpool players have benefitted from the backing offered by travelling Reds' fans in football grounds all over England, Europe and beyond. Beginning with major cup games - mainly finals and semi-finals- in the early part of the 20th century, then, with the help of developing rail networks from the 1950's onwards, for league fixtures at nearby North-West grounds after the Second World War, and at matches all over the country thereafter, Liverpool had always enjoyed the support of one of the most vocal, fanatical and loyal bands of followers, miles from the familiar surroundings of Anfield.

Every so often however, an away fixture captures the imagination of supporters so much that it sees numbers swell way beyond what would be the norm. A game for which fans put personal commitments to one side; when work, college or school play second fiddle to inspiring the Reds to a famous away victory.

There have been countless occasions where Red's fans' fanaticism off the pitch has complemented the footballing brilliance on it; the chaotic scenes at Wolves, in the final league game of Bob Paisley's first season as manager in 1976 when hundreds among the 20,000 fans who travelled, swarmed onto the Molyneux pitch to salute the players at the final whistle as a late comeback clinched the Championship; the following year 27,000 intrepid Liverpudlians journeyed famously over land and sea to the eternal city of Rome to provided the soundtrack, and stunningly visual backdrop, to Liverpool's first European Cup triumph at the Stadio Olimpico; a generation later, over 40,000 devotees of Rafael Benitez, Steven Gerrard et al made the remarkable passage to Istanbul feel more like a pilgrimage than a trip to a football match.

An FA Cup quarter-final replay at Watford may seem like small beer in comparison but, in an age when the FA Cup retained all of its unique magic, when a trip to Wembley still inspired thoughts of a typically Scouse invasion of the capital and, with the trophy representing Dalglish's best chance of silverware in his debut season as manager, the lure of this game was too much for many.

On the eve of the replay, skipper Alan Hansen summed up the importance of the match in the eyes of the players. "It will be a cracking game and one for big hearts." Recalling Watford's dour defence from the first match, he added, "They will have to open up a bit more than they did at Anfield." Ahead of the game Dalglish reiterated the importance of the squad system which saw him exchange players on a regular basis - either to combat the strengths of the opposition or call on those he felt were in the best mental and physical shape. Paying tribute to players who had experienced spells on the sidelines he stressed, "For any club to be successful, they must have strength in depth. It's easy to remain happy when you are in the side. The test comes when you are out, and all of our players have made a contribution."

Due to the fixture backlog the replay had been scheduled for a Monday night, but this didn't stop thousands from sagging school or taking time off work to start their journey South. The significance of an awkward, potentially exciting replay had motivated large numbers of Liverpool fans to make arrangements to support their team, with many leaving the city in the early afternoon to be sure of their place at Vicarage Road for the 7.45pm kick-off.

Under FA rules that allowed the visitors one quarter of the available capacity, Liverpool had been allocated just over 5,000 tickets for the match but, from the number of cars crammed with five (or more) passengers heading South – many weighed down with crates of the cheap, popular 'Ace' lager - it appeared even larger numbers had deemed this particular away match as one not to miss. All afternoon service stations along the M6 and M1 were engulfed by Liverpool supporters; at familiar stop-offs like Keele, Hilton Park and Watford Gap, the general public looked on in disbelief as the Scouse hordes enjoyed the usual horseplay and shenanigans synonymous with 1980's road-trips following the Reds.

Shortly before kick-off, as the travelling thousands made their way over the peculiar, dimly-lit allotments that lead to the Vicarage Road visitors section on the South Terrace, a build-up of people outside the ground saw Liverpool fans also admitted to the whole of the South West Terrace - and pockets of the East Stand. Hundreds of Reds fans with tickets were allowed inside without any check at the turnstiles, a relatively common occurrence at the time. Remarkably, amid the chaos there was time for romance. London-based Scouser, Dave Hardman had met, "a beautiful Irish nurse who decided she wanted to go to the match with me.

"It was Paddy's day, and she was living in Kilburn so we started on the grog about half-eight in the morning. By the time we got to Vicarage Road both of us were totally bladdered. "Half way around the allotment trek I told her to wait as I was knackered. She said to me 'poor baby', hugged me, went to kiss me - then I was sick all over her. She ran off screaming into the night and I never saw her again - which wasn't so bad as I sold her ticket for The Pogues for the next night for £30."

As kick-off drew closer, the Liverpool supporters under the cavernous roof of the South Terrace recognised the wider presence they had in the ground, and the decibel levels were raised even higher. It was clear that as many as 10,000 away supporters had managed to gain entry and the incredible noise they were creating contrasted starkly with the sedate, old-fashioned chants of, "Watford, Watford," from the home supporters. The Scouse contingent had swelled the crowd to a capacity 28,097. It was the Hornet's biggest gate of the season – by a staggering 9,000.

When the teams were revealed it was confirmed that Dalglish and Steve McMahon would return to the starting XI in place of Sammy Lee and John Wark respectively. Dalglish would partner Rush with Craig Johnston dropping back into midfield. Watford named the same side that had forced the goalless draw at Anfield in the first game, with John Barnes again expected to pose the greatest threat. It appeared that Graham Taylor would also employ the same cautious approach with Lee Sinnott again employed to thwart the surges of Mark Lawrenson from full-back.

As the teams appeared and ran to their respective ends of the ground, even the Liverpool players, resplendent in their all-white change strip, appeared taken aback at the raucous welcome offered by the ubiquitous travelling Kop. For those in the stands, an already electric night was enlivened further when a notorious Liverpool fan let loose a tarantula spider as the players warmed up. Rumour has it that the startled arachnid scuttled off and clung to a warm pipe at the back of the stand. No one can vouch for whether the deadly creature, which had been stolen from a pet shop, eventually made it to Wembley.

The Watford pitch had improved slightly since Liverpool's win in the league fixture two months previously but it remained heavily sanded through the middle and not conducive to passing football.

The opening half saw plenty of endeavour from both sides, with Liverpool taking the game to the home side and Watford again happy to rely on getting men behind the ball and attacking on the counter. Graham Taylor's style and tactical approach wasn't pretty, but it was effective - relying on the pace of Barnes up front to give them an outlet for long balls played from defence. With Liverpool enjoying the bulk of possession, Watford's principal hope was that a set piece would allow them to grab the lead, one which they would later defend to the final whistle. It nearly paid off when, from one such award, the aggressive Colin West nodded down Kenny Jackett's free-kick and Grobbelaar saved smartly from Sinnott's snapshot.

In the 26th minute the home fans appealed for a penalty when Gary Gillespie muscled the troublesome West off the ball to win a header, but the pleas were flamboyantly waved away by charismatic referee Roger Milford. Despite Liverpool's more considered and cultured approach on the bumpy pitch, and the constant urging of their noisy fans, they created little in the first half. Again the Hornets held firm with Tony Coton, the hero of the game at Anfield, only called into action on a couple of occasions, the most notable being a straightforward save from a 25-yard Jan Molby shot.

Attacking their own supporters at the Vicarage Road end in the second half Watford remained calm and unhurried. It appeared that Taylor's tactics were, for the time being at least, working. The moment Watford had been waiting for – and Liverpool supporters dreading - arrived just two minutes after the restart. Jim Beglin was forced to hold back pacy winger Worrell Sterling on the edge of the box and referee Milford had no option but to award a free-kick in dangerous territory.

With the dead-ball specialist Barnes shaping to take the kick, Grobbelaar hastily assembled five players into a defensive wall. It was to no avail however, as the Watford man's vicious left foot shot curled round the static Liverpool line and into the bottom right hand corner of the net. It was a sweet moment for Barnes who, like many black players of the time, had been subjected to the racial abuse and chants which plagued English football grounds throughout the 1980s.

Just as in the last round at York, Liverpool faced shock elimination from the Cup and, sensing their hopes for the season were hanging by a thread, they laid siege to the Watford goal in search of the equalizer that would keep them in the competition.

Content to soak up the pressure and hold out for full-time, Watford retreated further and further back inviting wave after wave of Liverpool attacks. Their defence however, was in obdurate mood and headed clearances, desperate tackles and long punts downfield denied the Reds a clear sight of goal time and again. As the pressure mounted so too did the backing from the vast numbers of Liverpool fans on the South Terrace. Sensing the desperate nature of the situation, supporters drew on every last breath to urge their side forward, but each time Liverpool created a shooting chance, the brilliant Coton was equal to their efforts.

Against a backdrop of disbelieving groans from the Liverpool fans behind his goal, the keeper denied Rush brilliantly on at least three occasions. As the clock ticked down it seemed that Liverpool's Cup jinx would strike again. With just three minutes remaining however, the most dramatic moment of Liverpool's season so far had Reds' fans shaking with delight, fear and relief in equal measure.

Spotting another willing run by Rush, Steve McMahon played a ball into space just inside the right hand edge of the Watford penalty area. Sprinting diagonally in chase of the speculative pass Rush was heading away from goal but Coton, fearful of the threat the Welshman had posed throughout the game, came off his line and dived at the strikers feet. In the blink of an eye Rush got a touch on the ball to nick it past the keeper - and fell to the floor.

The throng of Liverpool supporters gathered in the same corner of the ground punctuated the momentary silence with a deafening plea. In this second, Liverpool's season hung in the balance. Everyone looked towards Roger Milford for his reaction to Rush's fall. When the referee jogged nonchalantly towards the incident and, with an outstretched right arm signaled a penalty, Reds' fans danced wildly on the terracing.

The explosion of excitement among the fans instantly turned to panic however, as they contemplated the outcome of the penalty kick which would decide not only their side's cup fate, but potentially their entire season. Unable to deal with the tension, hundreds of fans turned their backs on the pitch whilst scores of others other placed their hands over their eyes.

What made matters worse for the fans was the scene that was unfolding on the pitch. With no-one willing to step forward to take the spot-kick, the Liverpool players were having an animated discussion over the identity of the penalty-taker. Eventually, carrying the ball under his arm, it was Jan Molby who emerged from the group and, as the entire ground fell silent, he placed the ball nervously on the spot.

At home in Tuebrook, co-author Gary Shaw was listening to the Radio City commentary of the game with his father, Les;

"I usually went to games with my cousin Stephen, but even though a lot of tickets were allocated to Liverpool I could only get one and, being just 15 and with Stephen and no-one else from school managing to get one, there was no way I could travel on my own.

"My Dad worked away a lot but he was home for this and we had had our tea and then settled down to listen to the game on the radio – there were few live games on the TV then. We thought it was all over until the penalty award and I remember thinking if Molby scores this we'll win the whole thing."

Molby explained afterwards that following his miss in the League Cup semi-final, "it was decided that Ian Rush or John Wark would take any [future] penalties. When it came to it, I was not expecting to get the job. The only one who looked ready to step-up was Steve McMahon, but Kenny Dalglish told me to have a go."

Belying his nerves, and uncertain how to outwit the seemingly invincible Coton, Molby took several steps back, looked goalwards, then skipped forward to take the kick. Apprehensive Liverpool fans needn't have worried, and the Dane side-footed a perfect penalty into the bottom left hand corner, sending the goalkeeper the wrong way. The reaction in the Liverpool end? Pandemonium and delirium – emotions mirrored in homes across Merseyside; "We both jumped up and cheered as we danced around the kitchen," recalls Shaw.

As the goalscorer ran behind the goal to take the acclaim of the ecstatic fans he was engulfed by Liverpool players. Covered by almost a full team of white shirts only Molby's outstretched arms were visible, his shoulders seemingly holding up five, six or seven players. Amid the emotion of their dramatic late equalizer, Liverpool had to quickly concentrate their minds on the prospect of extra-time but with their fans singing, "We're on the march with Kenny's army," louder than ever, surely there could only be one winner.

The shattered Watford players listened to the consoling words of manager Taylor at full-time, but their abject body language and evident fatigue suggested that their chance of FA Cup glory had gone. Surely now Liverpool would press home the psychological advantage granted by their late, late equalizer, and score again to avoid the prospect of a second replay.

Although they were forced to wait until the second period of extra-time to claim their place in the semi-finals, the inevitable winning goal duly arrived. Once again, Liverpool were indebted to the brilliance of their goalscorer supreme, Ian Rush. Accepting a pass from Dalglish on the edge of the penalty area in the 198th minute of this pulsating FA Cup tie, the Welshman transferred the ball expertly onto his left foot and, almost effortlessly, sent a low shot bobbling along the bumpy surface. The ball skipped over Coton's dive and nestled in the same corner where Molby's penalty had rested earlier.

Once again the Liverpool fans greeted the goal with ecstatic celebrations. For the first time in the tie the Reds were ahead. Rush sprinted to the supporters with his arms raised – a familiar pose they had grown accustomed to over the years but one they never tired of seeing. He was quickly mobbed by the chief architects of the victory; Molby, Dalglish and McMahon.

The resigned Watford supporters began to drift away and the ground resonated to a triumphant chorus of, "You'll Never Walk Alone," from the massed ranks of away fans behind the goal and dotted all over the stadium. There was to be no denying them. Liverpool spent the remaining 12 minutes exercising a familiar exhibition of keep-ball interspersed with passes back to Grobbelaar.

As the final whistle sounded to send Liverpool through to a semi-final encounter against

Southampton - a fifth meeting of the sides that season - the players received the plaudits of the fans and vice versa. They applauded the part these supporters - who had followed them South in such numbers - had played in their success, especially when the tie had seemed lost with just minutes to go. At no point had the supporters stopped willing their team on and, for those who travelled under their own steam by car and minibus, dry throats were lubricated into the early hours as greedy Hertfordshire landlords earned an unexpected Monday night bonus.

After the match Molby, whose nerve and precision from the spot had saved Liverpool in consecutive rounds of the Cup, described the thoughts running through his mind as he stepped up to take the crucial penalty. "I kept thinking that the keeper had probably seen me on TV taking my last kick [v QPR] and so I took a long run to put some doubt in his mind. You could see he was confused because he went the wrong way." Debating the decision of the referee to give the penalty, Molby admitted with refreshing honesty, "We were all joking and telling Ian Rush what a good dive it was, but he said Coton definitely clipped his ankles. He was moving very fast and so many penalties are given in that situation."

An elated Dalglish, who had dismissed worrying reports of his striker being unsettled, saluted Rush's all-round performance. "The longer the game went on," he said, "the better he was looking and the more chances he was getting." Preferring to comment on the overall balance of play instead of the severity of the situation at 0-1 with just four minutes left, the player-manager added, "I felt we were always in control. Coton was their best player." Looking forward to the semi-final, Dalglish dismissed his side's three earlier wins over Southampton. "Those results won't count for anything come April 5. We're just happy to be in a position to play them in the semis."

The evening had proved to be a huge bonding exercise between players and fans and instilled a belief - on both sides - that there was a spirit at the club which would see them all the way to Wembley. While hopes of winning the FA Cup were very much alive, the Championship was another matter. Liverpool were still searching for their best form, and every game in league and cup called on their most attritional, determined qualities.

Their title hopes still rested on the other challengers - Everton in particular - slipping up more than once in their remaining games, but no side was entering the final stages of the season with more confidence that Dalglish's men. The euphoria of their triumph at Vicarage Road had seen to that.

Saturday 22 March
Liverpool v Oxford United

"I was in my usual spec in the Road End. When we heard Everton were losing at Luton, Molby caught the wave of crowd noise and waltzed through to make it 6-0. It made the hairs on the back of your neck stand up if you were in the ground at that moment."

Steven Kelly – Fanzine editor and Liverpool fan, Bootle.

Reflecting on a hectic spell of league and cup engagements in his programme notes ahead of the home league game against struggling Oxford United, Dalglish said, "We've had our hands full…in FA Cup replays, as well as the semi-final legs of the Milk Cup." Referring to the FA Cup replay victory over Watford, the manager added, "I would like to thank our fans who travelled to the game. They were marvellous and their support was greatly appreciated by myself and the players. They certainly spurred us on to victory."

The task for Liverpool now was to try and maintain the confidence and momentum gained from the win at Vicarage Road and put even more pressure on the teams around them in the table. With a game in hand and a goal difference superior by seven, Everton still led Liverpool at the top of the table by three points, so the Reds were as reliant on their rivals slipping up as they were on their own performances. Manchester United were a point and a place behind Liverpool, but like Everton they also still had a game in hand. If they wanted to pressure their rivals into dropping points, then the Reds needed an almost faultless run during their remaining nine league games.

Despite Monday's exertions, the team to face Oxford was unchanged although there was a welcome return to the squad for Steve Nicol, who Dalglish named as substitute. The versatile young Scot had been absent with a broken jaw, sustained allegedly - mysteriously even - on the coach journey back from Norwich in early February. In Nicol's absence, Mark Lawrenson and, to a lesser extent Sammy Lee, had excelled in unfamiliar roles at full-back, but Dalglish was nevertheless delighted to see the effervescent Nicol back in the fold.

In their first-ever season in the top flight, Oxford's glorious path to the Milk Cup Final at Wembley had been a welcome relief from a predictable relegation battle. Manager Maurice Evans' astute purchases including Ray Houghton, John Aldridge and club record £100,000 signing Jeremy Charles from QPR, had given the 'Us' a veneer of quality, but they lacked depth and their record away from the Manor Ground was abysmal. They had won just two games on the road. Few expected their travel sickness to be cured on their first trip to Anfield.

Borne of Liverpool's hard-won place in the FA Cup semi-finals and their dogged pursuit of Everton in the title race, there was a renewed feeling of anticipation for fans walking to the ground that early Spring Saturday afternoon.

By drawing at home to Chelsea the previous weekend, the Blues had dropped points for the first time since New Years Day and, with the gap at the top having shrunk from 11 points to three since 1 March - Liverpool had played two more games than Everton in this period - all Reds' supporters were tantalized by the hope that, in a race that had once looked all but lost, there was still time for another twist.

The combination of the improving weather, raised spirits and another must-win fixture drew a large attendance of 37,861 for a game the Reds were fully expected to win and, as predicted, the big home crowd was treated to an afternoon of renewed Liverpool brilliance as Dalglish's men turned on the style in emphatic fashion. Responding to a buoyant atmosphere in the ground before kick-off Liverpool roared at Oxford from the first whistle and they were rewarded with the lead after just 60 seconds when Ian Rush registered his 24th goal of the season.

A razor-sharp exchange of midfield passes between Ronnie Whelan, Steve McMahon and Craig Johnston culminated in the ball arriving at the feet of Dalglish. Displaying an almost telepathic reading of Rush's movement past the Oxford back line, the veteran sorcerer nonchalantly flicked a pass into the Welshman's path for the striker to lob the ball over the advancing Alan Hardwick - a perfect start for the Reds and one from which Oxford were never able to recover.

Liverpool went close to adding a second goal soon afterwards when they won a free-kick in midfield after Houghton's handball. The play was directed down the right flank but, from Johnston's deep cross, Whelan wasn't quite able to apply the finishing touch with his head. Since the kick-off, Oxford had been virtually penned in at the Anfield Road End and McMahon was next to go close with a volley from the edge of the box. In their first attack after 15 minutes however, Oxford nearly equalized against the run of play when Charles' opportunist strike from distance grazed the bar at the Kop end.

Stung by this half-chance for the men from the Manor Ground, Liverpool increased the pressure once again and they extended their lead just three minutes later with another rapier-like attack down the right. Showing his versatility and continued excellence from full-back, Lawrenson steamed forward and, continuing his run and looking for the one-two, knocked the ball to Dalglish. Accepting his manager's return pass in his stride, and holding off the challenge of a defender, Lawrenson stroked the ball home under Hardwick's despairing dive. The Eire international celebrated with Dalglish and his other team-mates and, as they jogged back to the half-way line, the whole ground applauded - not only for the brilliant simplicity of the goal but also in appreciation of yet another example of Dalglish's unparalleled vision.

Just eight minutes later however, the goalscorer was forced to limp off with an ankle injury and was replaced by the returning Nicol. The loss of Lawrenson was a blow for the Reds as their record signing had been a key attacking outlet from the back in recent games. His versatility meant that, whether at full-back, centre-half or in central midfield, he could shine in any role given to him. Lawrenson had shown hitherto unrecognised pace from full-back, intelligent passing from midfield and smart reading of the game from centre-half. It would be a month before he featured again. Soon after the forced substitution, Oxford were relieved to see a Rush thunderbolt come back off the bar via Hardwick's fingertips.

Such was Liverpool's dominance, the visitors were in danger of being overwhelmed and they were indebted to the woodwork again on the half-hour mark when Dalglish was denied the goal the crowd craved. Good work by Molby and Whelan sent the manager racing into the box with only Hardwick to beat, and although he was able to slip a low shot past the keeper after he had done his best to narrow the angle, the player-manager's shot cannoned back off the foot of the right-hand post.

Liverpool then rounded off what had been a first-half of virtual exhibition football with a third goal. In uncannily routine fashion Dalglish again found Rush, who squared for Whelan just inside the area. The Irishman then threaded a side-footed shot casually through the legs of Oxford captain Malcolm Shotton - and past the shell-shocked goalkeeper Hardwick. As applause for the Reds' outstanding first-half performance abated, supporters on the Kop eagerly awaited news of Everton's trip to Luton and United's involvement in the Manchester derby. There were hopeful cheers from the Kop when George Sephton reported a goalless first half at Kenilworth Road, whilst the fans' positive mood wasn't greatly affected by news of United's 1-0 lead over City at Old Trafford. It was clear which opponent the supporters viewed as the main obstacle in the title race.

Liverpool emerged for the second period to attack their favoured Kop end and, mindful that Everton's vastly superior goal difference could be worth an extra, crucial point, they played the half with an obvious determination to add to their tally. During the interval Oxford manager Maurice Evans moved centre-forward and record buy Charles from the attack, and deployed him at the heart of the Oxford rearguard; a clear sign that Oxford's second-half priority was to avoid the embarrassment of a heavy defeat.

Despite Evans' defensive tactical switch the first opening of the second 45 minutes was fashioned by the visitors; Aldridge's intelligent ball curled behind the home side's back four for the onrushing Houghton. Grobbelaar however, read his future team-mates' attack well, and dashed out of his box in typical fashion to clear before the bustling midfielder could reach the ball. The Oxford breakaway was just a momentary scare for Liverpool and they soon added to their lead with a penalty in the 51st minute.

Alan Hansen's atypical long ball into the penalty area saw the hapless Shotton wrestle Rush to the ground, and referee George Courtney had no alternative but to agree with the Kop's loud appeal for a penalty. In far less nervy circumstances than five days previously, Molby slotted home Liverpool's fourth goal with a low shot from the spot into the left-hand corner.

The Oxford goalkeeper must have rued the recent injury to United's regular keeper Alan Judge. Hardwick had been recalled at short-notice from a loan spell at Crystal Palace and instead of playing in a Second Division London derby against Fulham, he suddenly found himself in the firing line in front of the Kop. He did however, draw sympathetic applause from the crowd when he made a desperate save from a powerful Whelan header.

At this stage Liverpool were rampant but the delight the crowd was taking in their performance was muted to a certain extent when news filtered through - via transistor radios – that Kevin Richardson had scored for Everton at Luton. Unaware of happenings elsewhere however, Liverpool pressed forward in search of more goals.

With the Reds committed upfield, the visitors made a rare foray on the counter attack. Trevor Hebberd wasted an opportunity to shoot from the edge of the box when he chose to go past Hansen, but the ball ran away from the striker and Grobbelaar was able to come off his line and collect easily.

Although Oxford had barely registered as an attacking threat there were signs that the Liverpool goalkeeper's concentration and confidence were returning after a run of poor performances. Impatient fans in the Echo's letters pages and the London-based media had clamoured for him to be dropped, but Dalglish had kept faith in his keeper and would reap the benefit in the crucial matches ahead.

After 71 minutes Liverpool scored a brilliantly worked fifth goal. Rush and Molby were the architects with an exchange of passes that left Rush clean through on goal. Bearing down rapidly on Hardwick in the Kop goal, Rush used his trademark body swerve to round the hapless keeper with ease before slotting home with his left foot. The celebration for the Welshman's second goal of the game, his 25th of the season, would be nothing compared to what was to unfold a quarter of an hour later.

As Liverpool began to saunter through the closing minutes and the first fans began to drift away from their seats in the Kemlyn Road and Main Stand, an unmistakable, growing guttural roar from the Kop alerted the rest of the ground to startling news coming from Everton's match at Luton. As supporters with bulging eyes looked round praying that the commotion was no false alarm, the rumours were quickly confirmed. The Blues had conceded not one, but two late goals at Kenilworth Road.

Luton led 2-1 through goals from Steve Foster and Liverpool fan Mike Newell, and the Kop was now in ferment as chants of, "We shall not be moved," echoed around the ground. Sensing the elation of the fans and smelling blood, Liverpool suddenly upped the pace as the crowd roared them on. Remarkably, with the clock ticking towards the final minute, Dalglish conjured up yet another defence-splitting pass which found Molby bursting past the Oxford defence. There was a momentary lull as the Dane set himself to shoot, then the ground erupted as his left-foot shot burst past Hardwick. The Kop danced as though they had seen a Championship winning goal in the last minute of the season, Liverpool's sixth goal crystallizing not just the Reds' emphatic win but also Everton's dramatic and unexpected demise.

Thousands of supporters waited on the Kop after the final whistle to gloat over confirmation of the final score from Kenilworth Road. There was further jubilation when it was announced that Manchester United had let slip a two-goal lead to draw with Manchester City. Chelsea maintained their outside chances by winning at Southampton, leaving them in fourth place but with games in hand on the top three.

The main feeling for Kopites however, was that for the first time since Gary Lineker's goal had put the seal on Everton's February win at Anfield, Liverpool were realistically back in the title race - and both fans and players knew it. The Merseyside rivals were now tied at the top on 66 points each and, courtesy of a seven-goal swing on a pivotal afternoon, an identical goal difference. Everton remained top by virtue of having scored two more goals than the Reds and they still had a game in hand but, for Liverpool fans, the title momentum had suddenly shifted their way. The revered League and FA Cup double, not won in England since Arsenal achieved the feat in 1971, was now a tantalizing prospect for both Merseyside clubs.

Secretly delighted that Everton's defeat had coincided with a return to his team's best form, Dalglish preferred to comment on the game at Anfield rather than dwell on results elsewhere. "We could have scored a lot more," he said. "But I'm happy that we're spreading the goals around". Mischievously he then added, "If others want to contribute to our success by losing I'll accept it."

Although famously known for his humility and self-deprecation when it came to taking the plaudits for success on the field, the week ahead for Dalglish was laden with personal acclaim. After the match, he travelled north to meet up with the Scotland squad before winning his 100th international cap in a friendly versus Romania. The achievement would see him receive a gift from the Scottish Football Association - a commemorative solid-sliver cap with 9-carat gold braiding, presented by the legendary German international, Franz Beckenbauer.

It was ironic that a player famed for his role as a 'libero' in the German national team should present the award to Dalglish, whose own occasional sweeper system featuring Jan Molby, had drawn stinging criticism from traditionalists and so-called football experts in the English media.

On the Wednesday evening Dalglish captained his country in a 3-0 win, confirming him - by far - as the most capped Scottish player of the time. Such Scottish greats as Danny McGrain on 62 caps, the retired Dennis Law (55) and Billy Bremner (54) all trailed in his wake. To confirm the regard with which Dalglish was held in his home-town, he also attended a luncheon ceremony to receive the Freedom of the City of Glasgow, allowing him such dubious antiquated privileges as being able to graze his cows in public places and hang his washing in the city centre.

Despite some notorious antipathy from sections of the 'Tartan Army' towards the many 'Anglos' who had chosen to ply their trade South of the border, Dalglish's reputation among his countrymen was almost without compare. Over the coming weeks his status in his adopted Liverpool would eclipse even the adulation he already received from his fellow Glaswegians.

Saturday 29 March
Sheffield Wednesday v Liverpool

Mr Fields: Does the Prime Minister recall her words in the Budget debate on 19 April 1961 and her outright condemnation of share speculation? Do not those words ring hollow today in view of the arrogant disregard— [Interruption.]—of the conventions of this House by a Prime Minister abusing that office in her dealings for five years in undisclosed shares? May we have an assurance that when the district auditors have finished investigating honest politicians in Liverpool and Lambeth they will open up the books of the Prime Minister?

Terry Fields, MP for Liverpool Broadgreen
House of Commons Debate 25 March 1986 vol 94 cc781-6

If the results at the weekend had brought contrasting and conflicting fortunes for the Merseyside clubs, then the midweek international friendlies just a few days later brought an incidental yet equally dramatic twist to the title race. While Alex Ferguson was awarding Kenny Dalglish his 100th Scottish cap in the 3-0 win over Romania. Reds' captain Alan Hansen also played 45 minutes, but only as a second-half substitute for Dundee United's David Narey - a worrying portent for teh cultured Liverpool centre-half, with Ferguson's established Aberdeen duo Alex McLeish and Willie Miller already ahead of him in the queue for a boarding pass to Mexico.

Everton manager Howard Kendall was delighted to see Graeme Sharp partner Dalglish on his Hampden Park debut, but would have been less than impressed with Bobby Robson's decision to play Sharp's strike partner Gary Lineker in England's friendly against Russia in Tblisi. Due to a troublesome groin injury, Kendall had asked that Lineker be rested for the game.

With FA Cup semi-finals looming, neither Liverpool nor Everton could afford to see any of their key players injured on international duty. Away from Glasgow and Tblisi however, the most significant incident of the week occurred at Lansdowne Road, Dublin, where Everton and Wales keeper Neville Southall, the protective bedrock of Everton's emergence as a force in the English game, suffered a dislocated ankle. In the same match Ian Rush continued his hot streak in front of goal by scoring the game's only goal but, in landing awkwardly after catching a routine cross, it was his international teammate and club rival who was the focus of the next day's back pages.

Bemoaning his side's ill-fortune in losing Southall for the title and FA Cup run-in, Kendall said, "It is a tremendous blow to us losing the man I consider to be the best in the country – even better than Peter Shilton." To cover Southall's loss, Everton were forced to recall Bobby Mimms from a brief loan spell at Second Division Notts County. Kendall was bullish about the £150,000 pre-season signing from Rotherham United stepping into the breach. "If he does well enough over the next nine games I shall be delighted to campaign for a championship medal on his behalf." Kendall added that Mimms - who had made his Blues debut in October against Manchester City - had been farmed out, "so that he could keep playing regular league football. He's had three games at Notts County and that should have kept him nice and trim."

In contrast, any injury problems the Reds' had were clearing rapidly. Steve Nicol had returned to the fold and improved his fitness by playing for the reserves in a midweek win over Hull City, a match that also saw a scoring cameo for Paul Walsh, finally fit again following his long-term ankle injury.

As Liverpool fans trekked over the Snake Pass on their way to a rainy Easter Saturday visit to Sheffield Wednesday, they hoped Dalglish would be able to continue where he had left off the previous weekend - providing the ammunition for the inform pair of Ian Rush and Jan Molby. Unsure of his ability to play three times inside a week however, and following his midweek exertions for Scotland, Dalglish opted to leave himself out of the line-up and instead recalled Walsh to partner Rush up front.

As ever, Liverpool faced a hectic Easter period with the manager mindful of not only the upcoming Anfield game against Manchester City on Easter Monday, but also the following Saturday's FA Cup semi-final against Southampton.

Managed by dour Yorkshireman Howard Wilkinson, Wednesday had enjoyed an impressive season so far. Seventh in the league they had also reached the FA Cup semi-finals where they would be Everton's opponents at Villa Park the following weekend. Although the Owls had spent a long spell outside the top flight, since their promotion in 1984 they had proved to be difficult opponents for the Reds. Furthermore, Liverpool's last win at Hillsborough dated back to 1968 so the match offered no guarantees that they would secure a fifth consecutive league victory.

Liverpool showed two changes from the team that had trounced Oxford the week before. As well as Walsh coming in for Dalglish, Nicol started for the first time since early February in place of the injured Mark Lawrenson. Bruce Grobbelaar's was selected in his 300th appearance for the club; the ebullient and ever popular Zimbabwean restored to full confidence after recovering his form in recent games.

Skipper Alan Hansen won the toss and elected to attack the Hillsborough Kop in the first half, while Wednesday kicked towards the 5,000 Liverpool fans crammed into the shallow Leppings Lane terrace.

Time–served Liverpool fan David Swift from Litherland recalls;

"My good mate John Bradley and I got to Hillsborough really early. It was raining heavily so we took shelter at the back, where the slight overhang of the upper tier offered some cover. We were immediately confronted by one of South Yorkshire's finest. 'Get down to the front', one policeman

barked. We pointed out that we didn't want to get soaking wet with nearly an hour to kick-off, but he was having none of it. He shoved John's German brother-in-law, Eckhardt - a neutral, a proper gentleman and an FC Cologne supporter - down the steps towards the front.

"It was ridiculous that we felt the need to apologise to him for the behaviour of our police force, and inside we were fuming, but to avoid arrest we reluctantly shuffled down to pitch level and watched the game through those god-awful railings at the front of Leppings Lane."

The game started in difficult conditions. The persistent rain helped make the centre of the pitch muddy and sticky, with only the wings free of congealed mud. The weather hadn't dampened the passion from those inside Hillsborough however, with both sets of supporters in a crowd of 37,946 in fine voice.

Wednesday started the stronger and at every opportunity seemed to be looking for Brian Marwood on the left flank. On one electric burst down the wing - fed by a pass from skipper Nigel Worthington - the tricky, former Hull City winger cut inside and pulled the ball back for Glynn Snodin, but the midfielder's shot sailed wide of Grobbelaar's goal. In response, Liverpool won a corner on the right after good work by Molby and McMahon but, from Craig Johnston's delivery, Whelan was unable to control a volley, firing over into the massed ranks of taunting Sheffield Wednesday fans in the Kop. Rush then found Walsh with a sweeping cross-field ball but, showing an understandable lack of sharpness after his lay-off, the little striker was dispossessed by the challenge of sturdy Owl's centre-back Lawrie Madden.

As the first half progressed there was no let up in the pace of the game. Marwood's cross from the left resulted in a knock for Jim Beglin as he cleared the winger's dangerous cross under a challenge from the muscular Gary Thompson. Encouraged by the applause of the Liverpool fans behind the same goal, Beglin was able to continue after treatment from Ronnie Moran. In the 22nd minute Thompson was booked following another clumsy challenge, this time on Craig Johnston, on the right touchline. Wednesday continued with their physical approach and Worthington had to be spoken to by referee Peter Willis for another late tackle on Rush.

Both sides were guilty of being occasionally over-eager in the tackle however, as passion and commitment outweighed class and quality and the rain continued to sheet down across Hillsborough. Liverpool's best move came on the half-hour when Johnston, showing great skill inside his own half, swivelled away from the attentions of three players before receiving the ball on the overlap from Nicol. The energetic Australian continued down the right before his cross was deflected for a corner - his sterling run acknowledged accordingly by the Liverpool fans.

Johnston's corner was easily caught by ex-Evertonian Martin Hodge in the Wednesday goal but the busy winger was at the centre of another move by Liverpool shortly afterwards when he collected Molby's pass, and his cross bypassed Rush but reached Walsh. Unfortunately for Liverpool, Walsh's first-time shot sailed high and wide. The robust nature of the game continued when Jim Beglin and Gary Megson were cautioned by referee Willis after a clash on the Liverpool left.

Before the break Wednesday went closest to breaking the deadlock when right-back Mel Sterland's low cross escaped the grasp of Grobbelaar. Marwood turned the loose ball goalwards only to see Nicol clear, in desperate fashion, off the line.

The last action of the half saw the home side suffer a blow when Worthington received a heavy knock and had to be taken off. The introduction of England winger Mark Chamberlain meant that the dangerous Marwood was forced to retreat into a more withdrawn position in midfield.

The urgent need for the Reds to up their game in the second-half was confirmed when half-time scores from other matches were read out over the Hillsborough tannoy. Unsurprisingly, Everton led Newcastle at Goodison. The Reds' fans, defiant in the rain, didn't seem too concerned and amused themselves in slightly bizarre fashion by joining in with Cliff Richard's chart-topping single, Living Doll.

When the second-half got underway it was Wednesday who threatened first when the speedy Chamberlain escaped down the right and tested Grobbelaar with a high cross. Despite the increasingly difficult conditions the goalkeeper caught the ball safely. Liverpool responded by nearly taking the lead with their first attack of the half.

Walsh's cross from the right skipped off the muddy pitch causing keeper Hodge to misjudge the flight of the centre. Evading his grasp the ball cannoned back off the near post, much to the surprise of Rush - and the mass of Red's fans watching from the Leppings Lane, who could only watch in disbelief as, from point blank range, the rebound hit the striker's thigh and dropped a foot wide of goal.

Liverpool made a change on the hour bringing on Kevin McDonald for the increasingly leg-weary Walsh. The switch was a positive one, with Johnston moved forward to join Rush in attack. The Reds came close shortly afterwards when McMahon found Molby on the edge of the box but, short of time and space, the Dane was forced to tamely poke his shot goalwards and Hodge smothered without great alarm. As the pressure grew on the Wednesday goal Whelan missed a good chance from Johnston's cross, heading high over the bar.

At the other end Wednesday, with Marwood's influence reduced by his new anchor role in midfield, enjoyed a rare foray when Mel Sterland advanced forward down the right and struck a powerful cross-shot towards goal. The vast crowd on the Hillsborough Kop groaned as the ball swerved narrowly wide of the Grobbelaar's net with the goalkeeper diving at full stretch. A further moment of alarm for Liverpool resulted from a free-kick to the right of the box but when the ball fell in the area, Gillespie was quick to clear as Thompson seemed poised to score. With time ticking down Liverpool appeared content to take a point, despite the likelihood they would lose ground at the top.

Yet again Wednesday had proved to be tough opponents and when the referee signaled the end of the game, the Liverpool players gave a cursory clap to their supporters as they headed to the warm, dry sanctuary of the dressing rooms. Everton's 1-0 victory was confirmed soon after.

With seven league games to play the Blues had re-established a two-point lead over the Reds at the top of the table, and they still had game in hand. Manchester United's challenge continued to falter with another draw, this time at Birmingham. Commenting on his exclusion from the line-up in favour of Walsh after the match, Dalglish said, "I thought it was the right decision to give Paul a game."

With another league fixture at home to Manchester City in just 48 hour's time however, the canny player-manager had taken the decision based on his own inability to play two games in quick succession and the importance of at least some match fitness for Walsh - who could prove a vital weapon for the run-in. Dalglish knew that the upcoming Easter Monday games offered an opportunity make up the ground lost in Yorkshire as, while Liverpool entertained Manchester City, Everton were travelling to Old Trafford in a must-win game for United.

Monday 31 March
Liverpool v Manchester City

"As a 12-year old going to one of my first ever games, even Bank Hall station and the smell of molasses from the nearby factories, seemed cool. As me and my elder brother walked past the unguarded exit of the station, we had an extra spring in our step – we had successfully bunked the train.
We had to leg it to the ground in torrential rain and our Dave lent me 80p to pay in for £2.60 at the adult turnstile so we would avoid massive queues at the kids' turnstile.

The Kop was a thrilling place full of teenage scallies who 'knew the score' and dead funny old fellas. You had to have your wits about you though, not just to keep up with the quips and wisecracks but to withstand the demanding surges of the crowd.

During the game my laces became undone and by full-time they were drenched by what I realised was p*ss. It was always a double knot for me after that. I spent the train journey back to Waterloo repeating the mantra; do the double, do the double, do the double."

Phil Allan, Liverpool fan, Waterloo.

With many past title races taking a twist during the regional derby fixtures - traditionally scheduled on Bank Holidays to negate travel restrictions and thus ensure large crowds - the Easter weekend programme had always played a significant part in the destination of the Football League Championship.

In the wake of Saturday's results Liverpool only trailed Everton by two points with just seven games left to play but, with a game still in hand - a Monday night home clash with West Ham scheduled for 5 May (intriguingly after Liverpool had completed their fixtures) - the Blues remained favourites to clinch the title. Liverpool's run of four wins and a draw from their last six games had seen them firmly cement second place and had, at last, put daylight between themselves and a fast-fading Manchester United.

Intriguingly, owing to a glut of unplayed fixtures which were the legacy of the freezing winter, it was still mathematically possible for the London duo of Chelsea and West Ham to overhaul United and both Merseyside clubs, but this was still a big ask. Chelsea and West Ham - who had five further matches to play than Everton - needed a big points return from their games in hand to overtake the Blues at the top. With the Reds hoping United would take points off Everton at Old Trafford, Liverpool's home game with Manchester City - who occupied a position in the lower half of the table - offered a real opportunity to regain Saturday's lost ground. A win was imperative, as with games fast running out, a defeat - or even a draw – would effectively rule the Reds out of the title picture if Everton won in Manchester.

The Bank Holiday drew a large crowd of 43,316 to Anfield but it was another grey, wet afternoon, with the rain over the weekend giving the pitch a sodden, colourless look with sticky patches in both the centre circle and goalmouth. In light of recent results, Kenny Dalglish predictably recalled himself to the starting line up in place of Paul Walsh - who had looked way short of full match fitness at Hillsborough. John Wark returned as substitute.

City had lost five of their previous seven league games - conceding 18 goals in the process. They also had a debutant in goal, the well-travelled veteran Barry Siddall - a recent loan signing from Stoke City. Managed by Billy McNeill - legendary captain of the Celtic side who were the first British team to lift the European Cup in 1963 - City relied heavily on experienced full-back Paul Power, uncompromising centre-half Mick McCarthy and the creative trickery of Paul Simpson on the wing. The side however, was a far cry from Joe Mercer's or Malcolm Alison's great City teams of the late-1960s and early-70s; a largely ineffective collection of young players and older hands with just enough quality to avoid being dragged into a relegation battle.

With the Kop approaching capacity and a buoyant crowd happy to see Dalglish back on the pitch, Liverpool began the game attacking the Anfield Road End. At first the Reds seemed content to bide their time, with patient, passing football stretching the City defence and midfield across the greasy Anfield pitch.

Chances came throughout the opening half-hour but Liverpool were wasteful in front of goal, with Siddall especially grateful for errant finishing from Steve McMahon, Dalglish, and Ian Rush. The best chance of the half came in the 16th minute when McMahon went close for a second time, his side-footed shot spinning narrowly wide of the far post after a clever, teasing cross from Craig Johnston.

In the 32nd minute, just as the home crowd were beginning to show the first signs of anxiety at Liverpool's inability to convert possession and corners into goals, the hosts took the lead. Blessed with precise delivery from wide areas, Dalglish had seemingly elected himself Liverpool's corner specialist in recent games. Ignoring the jibes and catcalls of the Manchester City fans seated by the corner flag near the away section, the inform player-manager jogged over to deliver another exact, curling centre which was headed away from a packed penalty area by McCarthy. The retreating Jan Molby returned the looping clearance into the box where Rush attempted a spectacular, though ultimately flawed, overhead kick. To City's dismay however, the ball hit a defender and fell to McMahon. The midfielder pounced on the loose ball and lashed a left-foot shot into the roof of the net from eight yards to give Liverpool the crucial breakthrough.

Having calmed the nerves of the crowd, Liverpool continued to press but they were unable to add to their lead before the break. The Kop waited patiently for the half-time score at Old Trafford and when tannoy announcer George Sephton brought news of the proceedings 35 miles away, it was 'so far, so good' with United and Everton scoreless at the interval.

Attacking the Kop, Liverpool increased the intensity of their attacking play in the second half. The patient probing of the opening period was abandoned in favour of the higher tempo, attacking style they often found so easily when spurred on by the sight – and sound - of 20,000 supporters behind the goal.

Despite their positivity, and totally against the run of play, there was an isolated scare for the Reds in the 50th minute when City's young forward Steve Kinsey fastened onto an under-hit back pass from Jim Beglin. Though Grobbelaar advanced from his goal to force Kinsey wide, the striker managed to direct a shot goalwards from the sharpest of angles - only for Gary Gillespie to brilliantly anticipate the play and race back and clear off the line.

With Mark Lawrenson missing because of his shin injury – since diagnosed as a hairline fracture - Gillespie's intelligent defending and elegance on the ball had cemented his place alongside Alan Hansen. At times both players seemed like carbon copies of each other; at ease on the ball, with a good understanding of the play in front of them and both having the ability to bring the ball out gracefully from the back to start an attack.

Some critics argued that the pair could occasionally be roughed-up by an aggressive old-fashioned centre forward, especially when dealing with the long ball, but Hansen and Gillespie - and the missing Lawrenson - had no peers in the art of interception, perfectly-timed tackles, mastery of the offside trap and an often understated grasp of the defensive side of the game.

Beglin's rare error reminded Liverpool of the need for a second goal and they duly delivered a classic in the 58th minute. In typical fashion, Hansen loped forward, carrying the ball nonchalantly into the Manchester City half before playing a firmly struck pass into the feet of Dalglish, who was loitering with his back to the goal. The magical Scot expertly took the pace off the ball with a deft flick into the path of Molby, and the big Dane's diagonal ball found Johnston, again running into space to the right of the City box.

The Australian had given the experienced Power a torrid time all afternoon, and he did so again by drilling his cross hard and low into the penalty area for McMahon to slide in and divert into the roof of the net with an outstretched left boot. It was a fantastic, flowing move, a goal that summed up everything that was good about Liverpool's football; creative play from the back, vision and quality passing in midfield, pace on the flanks, all crowned with an unerring, clinical finish.

For a predominately right-footed player such as McMahon to score the two key goals from midfield with his left foot was testament to his versatility and importance to the team; belying his reputation as Liverpool's hard man in the middle of the park. This performance, and many others during his first season, was indicative of the underrated, former Everton man's all-round football ability. While Liverpool may have been disappointed that the quality of their play didn't warrant another goal before the final whistle, they were happy enough to register a fifth win in six matches.

The quality of performance, with Hansen, Gillespie, Molby and Johnston all in fine form, and Dalglish once again conducting the play from his slightly withdrawn position behind Rush, was encouraging for the crucial – and few - remaining matches of the season.

Liverpool's day was made complete by confirmation that Everton's match at Old Trafford had ended goalless, drawing them level on points with teh Blues. By virtue of their now superior goal difference, the Reds were also elevated to the top of the table, meaning that - for the first time since May 1984 - Kopites could enjoy the sight of Liverpool heading the pack once more.

After the game Billy McNeill, perhaps eager to deflect attention from another City performance as insipid as the pale blue shirts worn by his team, heaped praise on his fellow Glaswegian and managerial counterpart. When asked about the significance of Liverpool's move to the top, McNeil predicted, "With Kenny Dalglish in the team, I think they'll stay there."

West Ham's back-to-back wins over the Easter weekend also kept them in contention, but they had a heavily congested fixture list ahead of them and few outside of London gave them a realistic chance. To all intents and purposes, it was now a 'two-horse race' particularly in the eyes of the press. This irony was not lost on Liverpool fans who had the seen the media's cherished early-season flyer stumble at more than one hurdle, especially when on an unfamiliar track, miles from home. Ron Atkinson's wounded animal limped on for a few more circuits but now, five points behind the leading duo in third place, many of their punters were calling for the screens.

While it was a legitimate and opportune time to gloat over Manchester United's shattering demise, Everton's game in hand meant that further slip-ups were still required if the Reds were to cross the finish line in first place. For the time being however, it was Liverpool - adrift by 11 points on 1 March, who now sat proudly at the top of the First Division.

Just as the title race was reaching boiling point, both Merseyside clubs had to shift their focus from league engagements to the build-up to the upcoming FA Cup semi-finals; in five days time Liverpool were due at White Hart Lane to face Southampton - whilst Everton would take on Sheffield Wednesday at Villa Park. The question on every Scousers' lips? Could Liverpool reach Wembley for the first time in nine years and perhaps take part in a first ever, all-Merseyside FA Cup Final?

Saturday 5 April
FA Cup Semi-Final
Liverpool v Southampton

To win the FA Cup outright

Liverpool, Everton 6/4
Sheff Wed 11/2
Southampton 6/1

Stanley Racing

If local bookmakers strongly fancied the Reds to beat Southampton and meet Everton in the Cup Final there was certainly no complacency in the Reds' camp. Apart from John Wark - who had represented Ipswich Town in 1978 - no-one from the Liverpool squad had even played in an FA Cup Final, let alone earned a winners' medal.

Despite Southampton's comparatively easy passage to the semi-final - they had beaten Middlesbrough, Wigan, Millwall and Brighton to reach the last four - and their dismal run of form heading into the clash with the Reds, Dalglish remained wary of the threat posed by Chris Nicholl's side.

Although Liverpool had beaten the Saints three times already during the season, their most recent win at The Dell had been achieved in the absence of former Liverpool hardman

Jimmy Case - ironically the scorer of the Reds' only goal on their last appearance in the Final. An experienced motivator and now a key player in the centre of Southampton's midfield, Case had become an FA Cup bogeyman for Liverpool since he had left Anfield - under something of a cloud - in 1981 for Brighton & Hove Albion, before switching his South coast allegiances by moving to Southampton four years later.

Fondly remembered by the Kop for his violent shot, commitment and strong tackling, Case had fallen out with manger Bob Paisley over his friendship with Ray Kennedy which had - in the spring of 1980 - seen the two charged with assault after another of their many alleged nights out. Since his departure, Brighton had twice removed Liverpool from the Cup; in 1983 when Case got the winner at Anfield, and again the following season. Having reached Wembley with Brighton in 1983, and Liverpool in 1977, the former South Liverpool player was looking forward to the prospect of reaching his third final with a third different club.

"It will make the Final all the sweeter if we manage to put out Liverpool," Case said in the build up to the game. "I am delighted we have to meet them rather than Watford because we know exactly what we are going to be up against. When you play against them you have to raise your game to stand any chance, and that brings the best out in your ability." Recalling previous encounters against his former club, Case added, "I still remember the marvellous feeling I had when I hit the winner against them at Anfield when playing for Brighton, and even though I was injured I was made up when we beat them again at the Goldstone Ground the following season."

If the former Anfield hero had plenty of motivation to reach the Final, his former team-mates - player-manager Dalglish and skipper Alan Hansen - wanted desperately to put behind them the heartache of semi-final defeats to Manchester United (1979 and '85) and Arsenal (1980) and complete a set of medals that already included five League Championships, two European Cups, and four League Cups. For Reds' fans too, the semi-final was of huge importance. Supporters had followed their team in large numbers to Chelsea, York and Watford, riding a rollercoaster of emotions on the way as Liverpool's cup existence hung by a thread on more than one occasion.

After numerous semi-final disappointments, this was a gilt-edged chance to reach the Cup Final and the prospect of the Scouse weekend to end all weekends on 10 May. Unsurprisingly, Liverpool's 25,000 ticket allocation for White Hart Lane was snapped up by season ticket holders and voucher holders within days, although many more were expected to travel without tickets. With both semi-finals played simultaneously at 3pm on a Saturday afternoon there was no live TV coverage, although ITV were to broadcast highlights of Liverpool's game the following afternoon.

Dalglish had few selection problems in the days leading up to the game, the only thing to consider being Mark Lawrenson's rapid recovery from his hairline shin fracture. With Steve Nicol now fully rehabilitated and playing again at right back following his broken jaw however, there was no need to rush Lawrenson back and Dalglish settled on an unchanged XI with John Wark an attacking option as substitute.

Southampton were optimistic that their diminutive but powerful forward Danny Wallace would shake off a hamstring injury picked up in their sixth round win over Brighton. The Saints' line-up was also expected to include England goalkeeper Peter Shilton, who had denied Liverpool their just desserts on many occasions when he was a Nottingham Forest player and who, contrary to newspaper speculation, was never a serious transfer target for Dalglish; full-back Mark Dennis, notorious for his fiery temper and committed tackling; midfielder David Armstrong, instantly recognisable through his cultured left foot and bald pate; and a talented young centre-back already capped by England - Mark Wright.

As the atmosphere grew in the pubs on the Seven Sisters Road, the weather in North London was changeable, with heavy showers interspersed with periods of sunshine. Although the Saints weren't renowned for having a hooligan element, here they seemed to have a handy mob in tow and there were numerous scuffles with Reds fans on the streets before the game. Liverpool fans appeared to vastly outnumber their Southampton counterparts and, as the ground began to fill up before kick off, the bulk of the travelling Kop were housed in the traditional East Stand 'Shelf' - a vast expanse of standing terrace that spanned the touchline on one side of the ground. They also inhabited the lower tier of the newly-built West Stand opposite, as well as the terracing behind the Park Lane End goal.

As the teams emerged Liverpool, in their familiar all-red and Southampton in their change strip of blue shirts and black shorts, were met with a reverberating wall of sound created by the 44,605 crowd. The familiar jaunty, confident and defiant sound of, "We're on the march with Kenny's Army. We're all going to Wembley," boomed out from Liverpool supporters occupying three sides of the stadium, before giving way to a chorus of, "You'll Never Walk Alone," that wouldn't have been out of place at Anfield. For their part, the Southampton fans packed behind the Paxton Lane goal and in the upper tier of the impressive West Stand were offering equally impressive support for the underdogs.

The game began at breakneck speed, with heavy rain and a slippery pitch causing one or two early challenges to border on the reckless. Mark Wright had to receive early treatment from the physio, while Case received a strong lecture from Tyneside referee Alan Saunders following a rash challenge on Ronnie Whelan. From the resulting free-kick, Molby thumped the greasy ball into the Southampton wall. After the early skirmishes however, the game settled into a familiar pattern, with Liverpool beginning to dominate possession and dictate play.

Craig Johnston was again prominent on the right wing and the Liverpool midfield looked to use his pace as an outlet on numerous occasions. In the tenth minute the speedy Australian escaped down the wing and floated in a cross towards Rush but the Welsh was striker was unable to control his header and the ball sailed over the bar. Then, during a remarkable assault on the Southampton goal midway through the first half, Liverpool nearly opened the scoring three times inside a minute.

First, a Rush snapshot volley was finger-tipped over the crossbar by Shilton. From the resulting corner Nick Holmes scrambled Whelan's header off the line, but the ball was only partially cleared and Molby, pressed for space, forced yet another save from Shilton when he might have been more astute in squaring for Rush who was unmarked. Southampton then responded with their first serious attempt on goal - Glenn Cockerill firing just wide after Case's free-kick rebounded to him off a Liverpool defender. Clever play from Case then saw him resist a challenge from Molby and free Armstrong down the left, only for the Saints' wide-man to overhit his cross. Jim Beglin was able to clear Liverpool's lines easily.

As the half-hour marked passed the game had evened up but although there was plenty of endeavour from both sides, the score remained goalless. Southampton's chances of maintaining a clean sheet were dealt a cruel blow just 10 minutes from the interval however, when Wright was accidentally hurt in a freak, three-man collision.

The lively Johnston hurtled towards goal after a hopeful through-ball, causing Shilton to advance quickly from his line to gather. At the same time Wright, spotting the danger, came across to cover but, with the striker, defender and goalkeeper converging on the ball at the same time they collided in a heap. Wright would later recount how Shilton had called the ball as his whilst it was in flight, causing the future Liverpool captain – who would ironically lift the FA Cup for the Reds six years later - to ease up on his covering run. Both Saints' players were caught out by the pace of Johnston however, and, sensing the danger, Wright attempted to intercept again but it was too late to prevent the horrific impact that followed.

Wright appeared to get the last touch and the referee pointed for a corner to Liverpool, but the Saints' centre-back remained static on the turf. It was clear that he had suffered the brunt of the collision and a stretcher was called for. The reaction of the players closest to the incident suggested Wright's injury was a serious one and he was carried off to sympathetic applause from both sets of fans. A broken leg was later diagnosed and Wright would miss not only the rest of the season, but a definite place in the England squad for the Mexico World Cup.

After the unlucky Wright had been carried out of sight, the contest was renewed and, from the corner conceded, Liverpool nearly took the lead when Rush only just failed to steer home a loose ball in the six-yard box.

Just before half-time Southampton demonstrated their spirit in adversity by creating an opening for George Lawrence only for Grobbelaar to sense the danger and race from his goal to clear. It was the last opportunity of a breathless first 45 minutes.

During the interval cheers went up from a good number of Liverpool fans when it was announced that West Tip had won the Grand National back home at Aintree. Occasionally a fancy for a horse in a big race would sweep round Liverpool like wildfire – 1988 Epsom Derby winner Kahyasi was another example - and here it seemed that if the Reds got to Wembley, the bar bill would be footed by winning jockey Richard Dunwoody.

Some of the hostility outside had spilled into the ground and West Derby's Martin Jones recalls,

"Southampton fans behind the goal were lashing empty whiskey bottles at us. Me and my mates were standing on The Shelf near their end, while most of the Dads who had driven us down, were up above in the seats. The funny thing was that the bottles were being lobbed back full – not with whiskey obviously – and we spotted some daft South coast loon taking a few swigs."

Liverpool picked up the pace again soon after half-time and went on to dominate much of the second period. The introduction of midfielder Andy Townsend for the injured Wright had unbalanced Southampton and they found it increasingly hard to keep Liverpool at bay, relying on goalkeeper Shilton to preserve parity on several occasions. A free-kick from 30-yards saw Molby chip in a dangerous ball which failed to find a Liverpool head before, from a similar position minutes later, he feigned to square a pass to McMahon whose raking right-foot shot whistled just wide of goal. As Liverpool piled on the pressure Shilton was forced to make a routine save from a Whelan volley, but the Irishman came even closer to scoring in the 62nd minute. A fine move featuring a trademark foray from Hansen and an incisive through pass from McMahon, ended with Whelan beating Shilton with a fierce shot only to see the ball arc just wide of the post.

Southampton reminded Liverpool they were still a threat on the counter attack when Lawrence's tame header at Grobbelaar was the anticlimactic end to a rapid thrust down the left but normal service was soon resumed son after when, with Liverpool on the attack again, the omnipresent Whelan was denied yet again by not one, but two gravity defying saves from Shilton in the space of 30 seconds.

The Reds' fans behind the Park Lane goal cascaded up and down the terrace as Liverpool created chance after chance in front of them, the cries of, "Liver-pool, Liver-pool," raining down from the 'Shelf' growing ever louder and more desperate each time their side threatened to break the deadlock. There was no question that Liverpool should have been in front by now, but Southampton remained in the contest through a combination of inspired goalkeeping, doughty defence and no little good fortune.

With nine minutes remaining Dalglish summoned John Wark from the bench to replace McMahon who appeared to be struggling with a thigh injury – one which would cost him his place in the starting line-up for the key games ahead. McMahon had given the team an extra dimension in central midfield. An underrated passer, strong in the tackle and possessing a fierce shot, his partnership with Jan Molby had many pundits admitting that Liverpool had finally replaced Graeme Souness - albeit with two players.

Although their team had enjoyed almost total possession and a host of chances, Liverpool fans' nerves were still frayed. They had seen too many semi-final injustices over the years to rule out being caught by a sucker punch. For any supporter, the last few painful minutes of a cup-tie represent a unique footballing agony as you fearfully contemplate the late goal for the opposition from which there is no comeback.

Whelan had had an outstanding game and he could quite easily have had a hat-trick. The Irishman threatened the Southampton goal again on 85 minutes with a miscued volley from 15 yards. Rush then had another scruffy effort cleared off the line for a corner.

Wallace had made light of his hamstring problems to have a constant battle with Hansen throughout the second-half, and when he finally received a free-kick after another tussle with the Reds' skipper with just a few minutes to go, Liverpool's fans breathed a huge sigh of relief as Cockerill's shot flew just wide. The full-time whistle went soon after.

Liverpool had almost fallen foul of a late, late winner and they were relieved to regroup in the centre circle to receive the encouragement of their supporters as the game headed into extra-time. Dalglish had had a quieter game than of late but he remained a key figure as he barked out instructions and exhorted one last effort from his teammates. The additional 30 minutes of extra-time would finally bring joy and relief for Reds.

After all their efforts to break down the Saints defence it was ironic that a mistake from defender Kevin Bond eventually gifted Liverpool the lead in the 100th minute of the tie. Looking for Rush on the left-hand edge of the box, Molby played a chipped, speculative ball forward. Bond appeared to be in control of the situation, waiting for the bounce and heading back towards Shilton but, quick as a flash, Rush intercepted and with a simple flick of his right foot, he steered the ball past the horrified Shilton. In the blink of an eye Liverpool had one foot in the final. Rush wheeled manically away past the delighted substitute John Wark and Craig Johnston, heading with outstretched arms for the Liverpool supporters celebrating on the 'Shelf'.

Making a mockery of the tension of the extended goalless period, Rush added a second goal just four minutes later to finally clinch the tie and send Liverpool to Wembley. Starting with a mazy dribble, Steve Nicol advanced diagonally towards the left side of the penalty area before the Scot transferred the ball to Rush. With a quick change of feet and a blistering left-foot low drive across Shilton into the far corner, the predatory Welshman had won the game. As the ball nestled in the bottom corner Rush peeled off to celebrate his second goal, with several ecstatic Liverpool fans threatening to scale the low perimeter fence in front of the lower tier of the West Stand.

The victory songs were underway and for the first time that afternoon, thoughts on the terraces turned to Villa Park and Liverpool's prospective opponents at Wembley. News started filtering through that Everton - through a Graeme Sharp goal - had also taken an extra-time lead at Villa Park.

With Southampton now a spent force and Liverpool content not to twist the knife, the second period of extra-time was played out devoid of further incident. The final whistle saw shattered players raise arms aloft on the pitch and scarves hoisted above emotional heads on the terraces as Liverpool embarked on a triumphant lap of honour.

Celebrating with his teammates as they left the field, Craig Johnston was, like the fans on the terraces, keen to hear the result from Villa Park. "A slow, deliberate nod from Ronnie Moran as we tumbled ecstatically in the dressing room, confirmed the answer to the question we didn't have to ask," he recalled.

"Everton had made it too. The unprecedented was primed to happen. By the time both teams and supporters returned to Merseyside on the Saturday night, the town was in carnival mode. We headed out to celebrate and keep the nightclubs open till dawn."

For John Bradley of Waterloo, the moment of joy was ruined somewhat.

"My mate (the co-author's old man) who was next to me – in the old wooden stand above The Shelf - threw his arms up in celebration, knocking my glasses off. They went flying down about 40ft onto the terrace below and I could hardly see a thing. I had to lean over the balcony and signal down to the lad who caught them to meet me outside to get them back."

For all this near loss however, it was still a special moment shared with the thousands of fans who had backed Liverpool so passionately since the third round and who now lit up three sides of White Hart Lane to celebrate Liverpool's long overdue return to Wembley - in Kenny Dalglish's debut season as player-manager. The impromptu bonding session between players and fans was important; not merely to celebrate this victory but also as a brief staging point before both parties contemplated the most dramatic finale to the season imaginable – a nerve shredding run-in for the title and an FA Cup Final. Both against your fiercest local rivals.

In each competition Liverpool's mission was to deny their neighbours and steal glory for themselves. Amazingly for a city that had suffered at the hands of national government, the press and media, and resultantly in the eyes of the rest of the country; the celebrated League and Cup 'Double' - won only twice since the turn of the century - and all the glory that that honour would bestow upon them, was now firmly in the sights of Liverpool and Everton.

After the match a delighted Dalglish typically deflected attention away from himself and his achievement in becoming the first player-manager to reach the FA Cup Final, to emphasise the collective nature and manner in which victory was ultimately achieved. "This was a victory for the whole club," he said. "I have had tremendous support from all the coaching staff, who remained intact when I took over. Bob Paisley has also helped a lot."

Playing up the importance of his squad system and understanding the need to include those who hadn't started the game, Dalglish said of the victory, "It was due to everyone connected with Anfield and especially three or four lads who were not in the side this time. Lads like Sammy Lee, Paul Walsh and Kevin McDonald were all there cheering us on and they've all played a tremendous part in training and other games." Revealing telling empathy with fellow players Dalglish sighed, "The worst decision I have ever made as manager was deciding who to leave out." Although anxious to salute all his players, Dalglish then singled out Ian Rush for special praise - describing him simply as, "the best there is." On the prospect of meeting Everton at Wembley, the player-manager admitted, "Obviously you are most interested in your own club but I am delighted Everton have also got through. The last time we met at Wembley [in the 1984 Milk Cup Final] both sets of fans were a credit to the game and I'm sure it will be the same this time."

During a season when the club and its supporters had been tarnished further by the national media's willingness to project a decidedly negative picture of Liverpool and its fans, the ever perceptive Dalglish was never slow to seize an opportunity to put a positive spin on things happening off the pitch. He was acutely aware that Liverpool's reputation needed every boost it could get in the face of the City's many critics.

Dalglish's job now was to refocus his players on the task ahead. "I'm only thinking about Coventry City next week," he said. "We'll take the games as they come." If Dalglish communicated any degree of personal satisfaction at his side reaching Wembley he saved it for last - a barbed comment aimed at critics who had questioned his team selection at various stages of the season. "When it comes to picking the team I'll always do what I think is best for Liverpool."

Saturday 12 April
Liverpool v Coventry City

"Home-computing pioneer Sir Clive Sinclair has sold the marketing and merchandising rights to his inventions for £5m to computing rival Amstrad. The sale means the withdrawal of Sir Clive from the market in home computers which his products played so great a role in creating. However, the Amstrad deal allows him to keep control of Sinclair Research which has recently been making losses of about £1m per month."

BBC News 7 April 1986

Since the Merseyside clubs were last in league action there had been a number of developments beneath them as their title rivals jostled for position in the hope of mounting a late, but unlikely, end-of-season challenge of their own. After winning at Coventry on FA

Cup semi-final day, Manchester United missed another chance to temporarily regain top spot in midweek when they lost 2-1 at home to Chelsea. Kerry Dixon's first goals of 1986 left Ron Atkinson's team as outsiders, trailing Liverpool and Everton by two points and having played a game more than the Reds - and two more than the Blues. Chelsea's campaign - which had faltered badly over Easter with defeats to West Ham and QPR and a subsequent home draw with Ipswich - was revived slightly by the win at Old Trafford but they still had four points to make up on the leaders with games fast running out.

The most credible threat to Kenny Dalglish and Howard Kendall's title dreams was emerging from East London. West Ham United's narrow midweek win over Southampton consolidated a maximum six-point haul over Easter, seeing the Hammers jump to fourth place on 63 points. The Hammers still trailed top spot by seven but they had three more matches to play than Liverpool.

After netting the winner against a Saints side still licking their FA Cup wounds, Alvin Martin, the Hammers' Bootle-born centre-half predicted,

"The top four are going to start changing around and I think everything will unfold over the next two weeks. It's going to get really frantic. We have still got games in hand but it would be great if we were still up there by the time we play Everton in our last match of the season."

If Everton could hold their nerve and not repeat recent slip-ups, the Goodison Park fixture scheduled for the Monday of Cup Final week – after Liverpool's League programme had been completed - offered, regardless of Liverpool's rampant form, a potential title shoot-out between the Blues and the Hammers. As stated by Dalglish following the FA Cup semi-final win however, Liverpool's philosophy was to concentrate on winning their own games and so pile pressure on their rivals. Next up for the Reds was a home game against a Coventry City side desperate for points to avoid slipping into the relegation zone.

With the Sky Blues having registered just one goal in their last six matches the pressure was also piling up on Coventry manager Don McKay but fans and pundits alike saw little prospect of any respite at Anfield where - since promotion in 1967 - the Midlanders were without a win in 18 seasons.

Steve McMahon's torn thigh muscle consigned him to a treatment room still overseeing Mark Lawrenson's shin injury and Paul Walsh's troublesome ankle. Walsh, who had scored for the reserves at West Brom in midweek, had been instructed by a specialist to carry on training in the hope that the injury would clear up, while Lawrenson was prescribed a swimming programme to maintain fitness and protect his fracture. The stylish, under-rated Lawrenson revealed, "I'll be going to the pool twice a day. I hope that when I go back to the specialist in two weeks, he will just give the all clear, and that gives me just under three weeks before the Cup Final. I'll have to see what happens then."

Dalglish's programme notes for the game against Coventry thanked the fans for their support the previous weekend at White Hart Lane. "Once again, I have to say the support for Liverpool when we played Southampton in the semi-final was tremendously encouraging to all our players," he said. "And I am sure we shall have the same kind of backing at Wembley." Turning his thoughts back to the League the player-manager added,

"but I also know that Everton, like ourselves, will be doing their best to forget about May 10 and

concentrate on the immediate job which is to pick up points as the battle for the Canon League championship enters its final phase. Coventry…. face the prospect of being in real trouble at the bottom…so there is a great deal at stake for them, as well as for Liverpool"

Relishing the enduring battle for the title, the locals turned out in force with 42,729 packing into Anfield for what was the Reds' penultimate home league game of the season. After this match, Liverpool would have four away games in their remaining five fixtures, so the title would have to be won mainly on the road. In an otherwise unchanged line-up, John Wark deputised for the injured McMahon in midfield, whilst Coventry included former Liverpool reserve goalkeeper Steve Ogrizovic, ex-Everton full-back Brian Borrows and up front the experienced, but injury-plagued duo - Cyrille Regis and Alan Brazil.

Liverpool began attacking the Anfield Road End on another grey, overcast afternoon. Although the pitch had taken a lot of rain in recent weeks, the playing surface remained reasonably smooth, allowing Liverpool to pursue their normal style of passing football.

The Reds were first to threaten when captain Alan Hansen played an incisive long ball down the left for Jim Beglin to gather near the corner flag. Ronnie Whelan collected a pass inside, and squared to Molby who cracked a shot just wide of Ogrizovic's right-hand post. Molby tried his luck from distance again moments later, controlling a short pass from Dalglish before seeing his goal-bound shot deflect off Coventry midfielder Lloyd McGrath to spin wide again.

Liverpool were applying constant pressure in the early stages and went close once more when Dalglish's cross was just too high for Wark, making one of his frequent late runs from midfield. Dalglish then missed the goal only marginally with a powerful effort after being supplied by Beglin's square ball, resulting from the in-form Whelan's initial pass. Playing with great freedom, Whelan was then foiled by Ogrizovic's dash from goal when chasing a ball over the top. The Coventry keeper was not afraid to venture from his line; typical of a goalkeeper who had learnt his trade at Anfield under the great Ray Clemence.

It seemed to be only a matter of time before the Coventry defence was breached and, when the opening goal came in the 20th minute, it was the buoyant Whelan recording his seventh league goal of the campaign. Liverpool had already exploited Coventry's high defensive line with a number of accurate long passes and when Nicol spotted Whelan making a run, he played a magnificent ball from his own half to leave the Irishman bearing down on Ogrizovic. Whelan set himself before side-footing calmly and low to the keeper's right to give the home side the lead.

The Sky Blues rallied briefly with a Nick Pickering effort that Grobbelaar dealt with easily, only to fall further behind after 26 minutes to another, almost identical goal from Whelan. This time the long pass was supplied from the left wing by Beglin, leaving Whelan free to draw Ogrizovic and beat him again with another precise side-foot finish to the delight of the crowd.

Those in the Main Stand and Kemlyn Road Stand, including a vocal faction who hadn't always appreciated his work for the team, stood to clap as the scorer accepted the congratulations of his teammates and the plaudits of the Kop. The fans belted out their simple chant of, "Ronnie Whe-lan," in his honour which was met by a salute from Whelan as Coventry prepared to restart the game.

Liverpool's dominance was interrupted on the half-hour when Ian Rush sustained a foot injury that required lengthy treatment from Roy Evans. The knock appeared to affect Rush's mobility and may have contributed to him taking a heavy touch from Molby's through ball and failing to convert from a tight angle soon after. Rush then missed another chance created by Molby, this time denied by the legs of Ogrizovic when clean through. Liverpool's two-nil lead at the break was scant reward for a superb first-half performance bordering on an exhibition, albeit assisted by some woeful Coventry defending.

George Sephton announce that Everton's match against Arsenal at Highbury was goalless at half-time - which brought cheers all around the ground – a reaction that continued as the teams emerged for the second-half and ex-Red Ogrizovic ran towards the Kop goal. The ovation for a man who made just four Liverpool appearances was heartfelt, warm and long.

The cheers died down briefly as the game restarted but less than a minute later they were heard again as Ogrizovic picked the ball out of his net after Liverpool's third goal of the afternoon. Coventry were unfortunate to see Molby's drive from the edge of the penalty area deflect off the leg of defender Greg Downs and skip over their keeper's horizontal, low dive. Soon after, the away side made a rare sortie into Liverpool territory that saw the pacy Dave Bennett shoot straight at Grobbelaar.

Little had been seen of the Coventry front pairing of Regis and Brazil, but on the hour mark Regis managed to escape the Liverpool markers for once only to blast wide of the left-hand post. Brazil had suffered a succession of recent back injuries and looked a pale imitation of the player that first made his name under Bobby Robson at Ipswich before disappointing spells at Tottenham and Manchester United. Mindful of the role goal difference may have to play in the final title reckoning Liverpool, encouraged by the Kop, continued to press for a fourth goal.

Beglin had showed his usual skills when pushing forward from full-back, and he almost set-up Dalglish on the edge of the penalty area in the 63rd minute only to see Andy Peake intercept. Ogrizovic had to be alert minutes later when diving at the feet of Rush who had run on to a typically deft Dalglish through ball.

Liverpool were rampant. Creating chances almost at will. Nicol then centred from the right and the onrushing Wark seemed certain to score only to trip and land on his face right in front of goal. Ogrizovic was able to smother the loose ball and, as Wark lay crestfallen in the penalty area, the Kop mocked him playfully with a chant of, "What the f**king hell was that?" As he rose to his feet the Kop acknowledged another fine move and the Scottish midfielder heard his name chanted in a more complementary fashion by the same fans who had teased him just seconds earlier.

Coventry missed their best chance of the game with 15 minutes remaining when Regis pulled a shot wide from a goalscoring position after good work by full-back Micky Adams and winger Bennett. The muscular striker was off-target again soon after when he blasted over following a fine individual run towards the box. Never slow to mock the opposition, the Kop responded to Regis' missed opportunities with a triumphant chorus of the old terrace classic, "Nice one Cyril, Nice one son, Nice one Cyril, Lets have another one."

If Coventry thought their nightmare afternoon was over however, they were sorely mistaken. In the 78th minute a calamitous back-pass from Peake was intercepted by Rush, who controlled expertly and calmly rounded Ogrizovic before firing right-footed past Brian Kilcline's attempt to handle on the line. Although Rush appeared to have recovered fully from the effects of his earlier knock Dalglish, in consultation with Ronnie Moran and Roy Evans, decided to give him a rest with 10 minutes to go and Kevin McDonald was duly summoned from the bench. There was still time for Liverpool to round off the perfect afternoon with a fifth goal in the 83rd minute – a well-deserved hat-trick for the outstanding Whelan.

The trauma of the constant assault on his goal he had tried unsuccessfully to stem perhaps finally brought pressure to bear on Ogrizovic, who spilled an errant Johnston cross at Whelan's feet. The thankful Irishman swept the loose ball into the roof of the net and celebrated his treble with a jaunty skip in front of the Kop and his trademark rap of forefinger against middle finger. Since signing from Irish club Home Farm and making his debut in March 1981, the versatile Whelan had become a virtual ever-present occupying several positions, most notably on the left side of midfield from where he was a regular contributor of important goals. In the closing seconds Wark's eventful afternoon ended with him being hurt in a tackle and he limped off ominously at full-time as the crowd stood as one to salute Liverpool's superb display.

With some shambolic defensive organisation in the first half and individual errors in the second however, Coventry had contributed significantly to their own downfall. The sheer poverty of their performance caused boss McKay to tender his resignation after the match, leaving the team under the temporary care of George Curtis. The Sky Blues eventually managed to preserve their stay of 19 consecutive seasons in the top flight and, under the joint management of Curtis and John Sillett, achieved something of a turnaround to experience glory of their own at Wembley a year later.

Since the home defeat to Everton in February Liverpool had scored 17 goals in four league outings at Anfield but Adrian Heath's 80th minute winner for Everton over troubled Arsenal at Highbury took the shine off the Reds' fine afternoon.

Although the Blues, with their game in hand, were slight favourites to retain their crown Liverpool remained top of the table - but now with a significantly better goal difference than their nearest rivals. West Ham continued their surge with a 3-1 home win over Oxford. There was to be no let-up in the drama as the Merseyside rivals prepared for tricky midweek tests away from home – Everton at Watford and Liverpool at Luton Town.

Wednesday 16 April
Luton Town v Liverpool

"In the shoot-out, Carrasco's miss put Gothenburg on the verge of the final once again, but Urruti made himself a Barca hero when he not only saved what could have been the winning penalty by the Swedes, but went on to score himself. The Nou Camp exploded with joy as the Barcelona fans celebrated their first final in 25 years and started to plan the short trip to Seville where the final was to be played."

16 April 1986. Barcelona survive a 3-0 first leg deficit to IFK Goteborg - and a second-leg penalty shoot-out - to reach the European Cup Final where they would now meet Steaua Bucharest.

A good week for Everton began with their £800,000 record signing Gary Lineker was named the Football Writers Player of the Year – at the end of March he had also been named Players' Player of the Year. At Watford on Tuesday night the double award winner succumbed to a recurrence of a recent hamstring injury - but not before his 34th goal of the season had set Everton on the road to a 2-0 win which sent them back to the top of the table.

On the same evening West Ham's title charge was stopped in its tracks by a 2-1 home defeat to Chelsea who leapfrogged Manchester United in the process to go third, three points behind Liverpool. United's title hopes had been all but extinguished by a 2-0 defeat by Sheffield Wednesday on Sunday and Ron Atkinson was now coming under intense scrutiny from the Stretford End. Fans of Liverpool and Everton had been infuriated when headlines such as, "Give it to United," and, "The title is United's," appeared after they had won their first ten league fixtures, so here was more than a touch of understandable Scouse schadenfreude when one newspaper ran the headline, "Let me stay, pleads Atkinson," in the wake of United's latest implosion.

Everton's victory at Vicarage Road the previous evening put Liverpool under tremendous pressure to take all three points on Luton's plastic pitch. Bob Paisley, Joe Fagan and Kenny Dalglish had made no secret of their loathing for artificial surfaces so the Reds also had to overcome a significant psychological barrier if they were to regain top spot on goal difference.

Under the astute management of David Pleat, Luton had risen to sixth in the First Division. The likeable, Nottingham-born Hatters' boss had also urged his players to win as many games as they could before the end of the season so as to ensure Luton's best-ever placing in the Football League.

On the eve of the game Dalglish was relieved to hear Ian Rush declare himself fit after the blow he had suffered to his instep at the weekend. News concerning John Wark however, who had limped off at the end of the match against Coventry, was not so good - his leg injury confirmed as a fracture ruling him out for the rest of the season. Although his appearances had been restricted by the consistent form of Kevin McDonald and the arrival of Steve McMahon, Wark had been an important member of Kenny Dalglish's squad, deputising capably either as a substitute or an occasional starter. The Reds' leading scorer the previous season had also not been shy when found in front of goal this season either, weighing in with six important goals from 18 appearances in all competitions.

Since their promotion to the top flight in 1982, Pleat had moulded Luton into an attractive, attacking side. Their line-up featured the skillful, England-capped midfield duo Brian Stein and Ricky Hill. Up front, Liverpool-born striker Mike Newell and his partner Mick Harford were a troublesome pairing for any defence, especially at a cramped Kenilworth Road - where the Hatters had been defeated just twice all season.

Like a host of clubs in the division, Luton welcomed yet another large Liverpool away following, lured by the increasingly warm weather and their side's recent run of form. An estimated 3,000 Reds' fans help swell the gate to 15,390 and Liverpool started the game by attacking the goal behind which the majority of their fans were located. Most of the noise inside the ground however, was generated by the optimistic Luton supporters, housed at the opposite end under the ugly, three-tiered roof of the shallow Oak Road terrace.

In his programme notes, Pleat praised the Reds for their excellent season so far. "We applaud your excellent season in typical fashion," he said, "a magnificent achievement after the sadness of the Heysel tragedy." He added that, "Of all the teams in Division One, Liverpool are the most patient and accurate team players who also have the qualities of selfless individuals and electric pace in the right areas." Pleat however, also referred to the many Red's fans whose patience over Cup Final tickets was rapidly turning to desperation. "Sorry to all those Merseysiders who have written to me for Cup Final tickets," he said, but, "I am not a conjuror."

The opening period saw Liverpool play some excellent passing football, zipping the ball around quickly and accurately on the firm synthetic pitch. The final ball was lacking though, and several cutting passes accelerated rapidly off the surface, running harmlessly through to goalkeeper Les Sealey. Luton's approach was more pragmatic, their excellent approach play through the speedy Stein and scheming Hill shepherding the ball out wide to winger David Preece. Crosses aimed at twin peaks Harford and Newell made life difficult for Liverpool's defence, but the aerial threat was negated by stout jostling and determined heading from Hansen and Gillespie. Grobbelaar also demonstrated a renewed assuredness, always willing to come off his line and catch the ball and relieve the burden on his centre-halves.

On 17 minutes Liverpool grabbed a priceless lead with Craig Johnston' registering his first league goal since scoring against Aston Villa in December. Although expertly taken by the Australian dynamo there was a slice of good fortune about his goal, with defender Roger Johnson carelessly slicing an attempted clearance straight into his path just 15 yards out. The onrushing Johnston showed great reflexes and adjusted his stride quickly to side-foot low into the far corner of Sealey's net.

A goal to the good and with Luton's threat diminished now they were behind, Liverpool appeared content to sit back and protect their lead, preferring to move forward only on the counter-attack. Roared on by the home crowd however, Luton increased the intensity of their play in the second-half, and Liverpool's goal came under increasing pressure.

On the hour mark Luton were just inches from an equaliser when centre-half Steve Foster - unmistakable with his curly, flowing locks and white headband - crashed a header from a Preece corner against the angle of post and bar. Grobbelaar looked on helplessly as the ball bounced back into play before being hacked to safety. Soon afterwards Liverpool were again thanking Lady Luck when Newell blazed wide of the goal when it seemed easier to score.

Dalglish's experience told him that Liverpool would need to ride out the Luton storm and they gradually did so, with Kevin McDonald an effective, hard-working shield in front of the back four. The Reds suffered a blow 18 minutes from time however, when Gillespie, a tower of strength up until then, was forced to limp off with a groin strain. Demonstrating again the versatility of the players at his disposal, Dalglish moved Molby from midfield to centre-half, whilst Sammy Lee appeared from the bench to fill the gap in the middle of the park. Liverpool survived one final scare when Grobbelaar saved superbly from the effervescent Newell but then, in the closing stages, the Reds twice went close to extending their lead.

With Luton running out of steam - and Liverpool exploiting space on the counter-attack - Johnston broke with lightening pace from midfield but wasted the chance with a stray pass intended for the unmarked Rush. Then Dalglish, who had had a quiet game by his recent standards, shot wide when inside the penalty area - albeit from an acute angle.

Despite their brief attacking flurry towards the end of the game, the Liverpool players were clearly relieved to hear the final whistle and, while accepting the applause of the travelling fans, they left the pitch knowing another box had been ticked on their quest for the title. Another game - another much needed away win. It had been a workmanlike display, a far cry from the recent fluid, free scoring exhibitions of football seen at Anfield. In its own right however, it was a brilliantly stubborn performance – one that as well as earning three vital points, was also the type of display any side wishing to win the title needs at some stage of the campaign.

Luton boss Pleat - who had watched Everton's hard-earned victory at Watford the previous evening - saw similarities in the Merseyside title rivals' collective approach. "Both are very well organized," he said, "and both know exactly what they are doing. Quite simply they are the two best teams in the country - and I mean teams in every sense of the word." Pleat also paid tribute to the Reds' technical ability and strong mentality. "You saw how accurately Liverpool passed against us. We felt a bit disappointed at losing but they are a very good side who probably have that little bit extra where it counts."

Aware of the importance of the three points that sent the Reds back to the top a beaming Dalglish admitted, "It was a great result to a very hard match. Luton were as committed as ourselves because they are in the highest position in the league they have ever been. I think that helped bring the best out of our players. We may have made mistakes on and off the field this season but there's never been any problem with our commitment." Echoing a Liverpool maxim which harked back to the days of Shankly and Paisley; one that would become the player-manager's mantra in later years, the player-manager added, "It's not a question of individual performances. Anything we achieve will be achieved as a team."

Dalglish's words summed up the focused mentality and fantastic team spirit that existed in the Liverpool dressing room. As well as skill, talent and fitness, remarkable mental strength would also be required if Liverpool were to achieve a maximum 12 points from their remaining four fixtures. The Reds faced a trip at the weekend to the Hawthorns to meet West Brom, then their final home game against Birmingham City, before further away days at Leicester City and Chelsea.

Title rivals Everton's next game was at Goodison against Ipswich, followed by trips to Oxford and Nottingham Forest, before home games versus Southampton and then, a potential championship decider - with title dark horses West Ham. The scenario was simple enough. If Everton won all their remaining games they would be crowned champions for the second year in a row. Liverpool were waiting patiently for the Blues to drop three more points to step in and possibly steal the championship by virtue of four more wins, but if the Reds slipped up - even just once - the title would surely be Everton's again.

Saturday 19 April
West Bromwich Albion v Liverpool

"Liverpool are a work-machine, adequately oiled, well-balanced, quiet (to a certain degree) and above all, unrelenting in terms of producing results – on the field of play. At the turn of the year the top of the First Division read: Manchester United 52 points, Everton 47 and Liverpool 47. And United had a game in hand. Things have changed a lot since then, and the bookies – or most of them – are backing Liverpool to take the crown in May."

WBA Match programme, 19 April 1986

With both Everton and Liverpool winning their awkward away matches in midweek, the League Championship drama continued to build. Supporters were hanging on every word uttered from Anfield and Goodison and, following the Blues' win at Watford - which was swiftly countered by the Reds taking another three points at Luton - it was the turn of Kenny Dalglish's managerial counterpart from across Stanley Park to assess the state of play. "It looks like we will both be going all the way," Howard Kendall told reporters.

Deliberately underplaying the advantage his team held in terms of their game in hand - plus three outstanding home fixtures to come - the Everton boss moaned, "Home advantage does not always count. That was proved last night when Liverpool won at Luton, and by ourselves when we won at Arsenal and then Watford. Liverpool and ourselves are capable of winning anywhere, so it is no great advantage when a side is playing well and as confident as those at the top of the table." Kendall was clearly trying to avoid complacency in his ranks, but there was a telling hint of negativity in his assessment of the title run-in.

Amid the obvious excitement surrounding the race for the Championship, supporters' minds were never far from the forthcoming Merseyside occasion at Wembley. Sadly however, the week's news of the two clubs' ticket allocations signalled heartbreak for many. Each side had been allocated just 25,000 tickets, sparking the perennial debate - and one which persists to this day - about the Football Association's policy of distributing as many as 50,000 tickets to other clubs and County Associations.

While there was some merit in the argument that the FA Cup Final was a national showpiece and therefore warranted as diverse a live audience as possible, thousands of tickets allocated to non-league clubs, referee's associations, and countless other tenuous affiliated bodies invariably ended up in the hands of the touts. The ultimate victim of a dated and flawed system was the undervalued loyal supporter. While Liverpool and Everton could satisfy the demand of shareholders and season ticket holders, the many thousands who paid at the gate week after week would have to scramble over the - very small - balance of remaining tickets.

As Liverpool had more season-ticket holders than Everton however, only half of their stand season-ticket holders would qualify for a seat at Wembley with the rest housed in the terraced standing enclosures behind the Wembley goals. The price for a Cup Final ground ticket was £6 with the price of seats ranging from £9 to £25 - but their value on the black market would dwarf the legitimate cost.

Fans' anger and frustration at the familiar Wembley ticket farce were summed up in a letter by an anonymous contributor - 'Fairplay' - to the Football Echo on April 12;

"After two near misses we finally have what we deserve, a Merseyside FA Cup Final. Could I appeal openly to the Football Association to see this marvellous occasion as an exclusive affair to our own city and faithful fans of both clubs. This would eliminate the usual farce of invitations to total outsiders such as businessmen, celebrities and the families and relatives etc. who have no interest in the game, only to boast at dinner parties that they were there."

In the same edition of the paper, the dubiously named Ali Ratsafarian - of Rock Ferry - added, "People who are not even interested in football or either club will end up with the best seats while fans who've been going for years will end up watching it on TV. I think it's a disgrace." In reality however, while there would undoubtedly be a neutral presence at the final, the resourcefulness of Merseyside fans would see the majority get into Wembley – through forged and touted tickets or, failing that, an ingenuity or athleticism that would make the world's finest criminals and acrobats proud.

Concerns over tickets for Wembley's May showpiece were temporarily put aside for the 6,000 Liverpool fans who made the journey to the Hawthorns. Victory over West Brom and the three points that came with it were an absolute must for the Reds – especially with Everton at home to relegation-threatened Ipswich on the same afternoon.

The Baggies had experienced a nightmare season - 24 defeats in 38 matches seeing them under their third manager of the season in Ron Saunders. They had disposed of former Leeds United midfield legend Johnny Giles and England World Cup winner Nobby Stiles in February and had been relegated after a 1-0 defeat at QPR just a week earlier. In the corresponding fixture the previous season Liverpool had swept the Baggies aside with a 5-0 victory – the Reds' best win of the campaign, and nine players who won that day were also in action here.

The groin injury sustained by Gary Gillespie at Luton ruled him out of the trip to the West Midlands but this meant a timely return for Mark Lawrenson, finally recovered from the fractured shin that had seen him miss the last five games. Steve McMahon - who had also missed the last two matches through injury - was included in a travelling party of 14. As was usual, Dalglish would not confirm his starting XI until just before kick-off. When the teams emerged from the Hawthorns tunnel there was just one change for the Reds; Lawrenson replacing Gillespie in the back four. With McMahon given an extra week to recover full fitness, Kevin McDonald retained his place in central midfield. Sammy Lee was back on the bench.

Albion's line-up featured experienced left-back Derek Statham, the gangly 20 year-old midfielder Carlton Palmer, and in attack the little and large duo of ex-Bury marksman Craig Madden and beanpole striker George Reilly. Reilly had already proved troublesome for the Reds' defence earlier in the season, scoring Newcastle's winner against Liverpool at St James's Park before moving to the Hawthorns.

With Liverpool defending the Smethwick End terrace where thousands of their fans were gathered, the Reds started the game well. Dalglish had a goal-bound shot blocked in the early stages, before Johnston, Molby and McDonald combined nicely only for the later to be being crowded out by Albion defenders. The first clear chance came after ten minutes when a long ball from Molby found Rush just outside the area. The Welshman advanced towards goal, holding off the challenge of Paul Dyson, but Stuart Naylor in the West Brom goal made a fine save.

The home side responded when towering midfielder Palmer flighted a perfect centre for Reilly, well positioned in the box. Grobbelaar read the situation brilliantly however, and punched the ball off the striker's forehead just as he threatened to score. The loose ball feel to Darren Bradley - who miskicked - and then Robbie Dennison, who fired over the bar.

In the 23rd minute Liverpool took the lead in fortuitous circumstances - Dalglish scoring his first league goal since his stunning effort at Goodison Park back in September. Whelan's hopeful ball forward to the edge of the penalty area offered no real threat as defender Barry Cowdrill came to cover but, in a moment that encapsulated their season, he collapsed in a heap after standing on the ball – whilst a yard away from Dalglish. The player-manager gleefully accepted this gift and casually stroked a left-footed shot under the dive of Naylor.

Liverpool almost doubled their lead in similar fashion soon after. This time it was Statham who erred - leaving Rush in a good position - but the chance was wasted. The Baggies fought back, with Steve Mackenzie's lob following a corner requiring a neat tip over the bar from Grobbelaar.

The relegated side then shocked Liverpool – and both sets of fans – when they grabbed an equaliser five minutes before half-time. McKenzie's chipped free-kick from the edge of the Liverpool area found Reilly who headed across the face of the goal for Madden to apply the finishing touch at the far post. West Brom trailed Liverpool by 51 points in the First Division but they had parity here - at least for now. A shaken Liverpool nearly regained the lead just before half-time when, in succession, Rush, Dalglish and McDonald all failed to force the ball over the line during a frantic scramble in front of goal.

With the Reds only level at half-time and involved in a major scrap against opponents showing unexpected vigour, there was all to play for in the second-half as the tense situation at the Hawthorns was mirrored at Goodison - where Newcastle were holding Everton, and at Vicarage Road - where West Ham were striving for a breakthrough against Watford.

The Reds started the second period in positive style with Hansen escaping upfield and combining with Whelan to send in a low cross that Rush fluffed with a half-hit shot. The Welshman was having a mixed afternoon but continued to be a threat with his astute runs behind the increasingly laboured West Brom defence. On 50 minutes Dyson was forced to intercept a McDonald pass that threatened to set Rush free. Moments later, the striker then went alone, slalomed into the box and saw his shot blocked at the last minute.

News that Everton had taken the lead with a 64th minute Graeme Sharp goal at Goodison filtered through to Reds' fans and the sudden increase in noise from the Smethwick terrace communicated the urgency of the situation to the Liverpool players. This added pressure only served to have a destabilising effect on the Liverpool defence however, and Albion went close to taking an unexpected lead on two occasions. In each case Liverpool were spared embarrassment as Reilly's wayward finishing let him down, twice dragging shots wide after escaping the attentions of Hansen and then Lawrenson.

The game was now more open and chances were coming at both ends, Steve Nicol being next to go close with a shot from 20-yards that went just wide. Soon afterwards, Rush again missed the target after a cross was headed down to him by McDonald. Reilly had caused the Liverpool defence all manner of problems with his ability in the air but also with his deceptive running. On one such raid he went past Beglin on the right, before screwing a shot across the face of goal. Liverpool could easily have been behind by now but they continued to press forward, their attacks led by the energetic pairing of Nicol and Johnston down the right flank. None of the chances created were taken however, but, just as the noisy Reds fans sensed this might be the day and their lingering hopes of winning the title disappeared, Rush popped up with a dramatic winning goal.

Johnston fed Nicol who spotted Rush making a run across the front of the West Brom box. The Scot curled in a clever pass to the striker – who had his back to goal. Initially facing the wrong way Rush, in one movement, turned and dragged the bouncing ball into a shooting position before clipping a low right-foot shot under Naylor at his near post. Bedlam on the terraces behind the goal ensued as the relieved Liverpool fans celebrated yet another crucial Rush strike - his 29th of the season.

There was still time for Liverpool to survive a few scares before they could celebrate victory. First the indefatigable Reilly went close for a fourth time, heading straight at Grobbelaar. Then, in the closing minutes, Nicol survived an appeal for handball in the box when Dennison's shot struck his arm on its path towards goal. The referee waved away the furious - perhaps justified - claims of West Brom's players and sounded his whistle soon after to signal the end of the match.

After a game in which they had been given an almighty scare by a dogged Albion side seeking redemption following an abysmal season, the Liverpool fans celebrated a fortunate victory. While the fans made a fearsome racket by banging on the corrugated steel fencing at the back of the decaying terrace, the players again took time to acknowledge the huge contingent who had encouraged the team throughout an erratic Reds performance.

Though Liverpool had earned maximum points from two away games in four days, there was some concern that the Reds had delivered a tired performance at the Hawthorns - a point acknowledged by Dalglish after the game. "I thought we were a little bit short today in thought and action," the player-manager said. "But when you don't play particularly well but still pick up the points you can't complain." Despite his goal Dalglish was also forced to respond to questions about his own contribution. "No, I don't find it a strain managing and playing," he said. "I don't have anything to do with the administration except pick the teams. And when I get tired I just keep running from memory."

Even if his mere presence on the pitch continued to galvanise his fellow players, Dalglish's form had dipped in recent games. Ian Hargraves wondered if the player-manager's legs would last until the end of the season. "There is no doubting the psychological influence he exerts on colleagues and opponents alike, nor his immense appetite for the game, but these days his actual striking power is distinctly limited."

Hargraves mused over whether Dalglish offered a sufficient goal-threat to start in each of the remaining three league matches - plus the Cup Final. "He was rarely dangerous himself and it remains a matter for debate whether the much quicker and more direct Paul Walsh would not be a more effective striker." Sympathising with the player-manager's ongoing personal selection dilemma, the Liverpool Echo's chief football writer concluded, "The problem of which one to prefer would delight most other managers, but with Dalglish directly concerned himself it can be expected to give him a few sleepless nights."

The opinions of journalists had never been of concern to Dalglish however, and if he was having sleepless nights it was simply because the frustrating status quo at the top of the table had been maintained for yet another week; Everton had beaten Newcastle 1-0 at Goodison Park, whilst a second-half double from West Ham secured them a win at Watford. The Hammers now lay fifth - 10 points behind leaders Liverpool but with three games in hand. Liverpool and Everton fans could also sleep soundly for another year as Manchester United's fading challenge was finally extinguished after a goalless draw at Spurs. Although still mathematically possible, Chelsea's tilt also looked over having been held by Newcastle – and the West London side now trailed the leaders by eight points.

With just a handful of games to go, the Championship race was realistically down to just three teams - the two Mersey giants and the East End upstarts.

Saturday 26 April
Liverpool v Birmingham City

"After three days of virtual news blackout, the Soviet authorities finally admitted last night what Scandinavia had already deduced from radioactive fallout - that the Chernobyl nuclear accident is a 'disaster', that some people have been killed and many thousands more evacuated. Tucked away on the Soviet television news bulletin, rating below the farm reports, the official statement said that two people had died in the accident, but the 'radiation situation' was now stabilised"

The Guardian 30 April 1986.

If Liverpool needed any extra motivation as they and Everton approached their final games, they found it in the shape of their old adversary Brian Clough who, before his side's game against the Goodison outfit at the City Ground told reporters, "Everton are the best team in the League, but I would like to see John Lyall's West Ham win the title." Never a man to shy away from controversy, Clough had become increasingly erratic in his behaviour and public statements as a battle with drink dependency eroded his more appealing character traits. Although a great admirer of his managerial rival Bob Paisley, it could be argued that the self-titled 'Old Bighead bore a lingering resentment towards the club he never quite managed to usurp as the dominant force in English football. Now however, Liverpool were relying on a win for Clough's Forest that could open the door to another League title.

Dark horses West Ham had emphatically underlined their title credentials with an 8-1 thrashing of Newcastle in midweek. The Hammers' remarkable win featured a unique hat-trick from centre-back Alvin Martin - each goal scored past a different goalkeeper; first choice Martin Thomas, then outfield replacement Chris Hedworth - who also had to withdraw injured - and finally another emergency keeper, England schemer and future Liverpool star, Peter Beardsley. With five games still to play however, the East Londoners remained outsiders to win the league. They had a maximum of 87 points to aim for, while Liverpool could muster 88. Everton, with their game in hand, could reach 89.

Ahead of the visit of already relegated Birmingham City for Liverpool's final home league game, Kenny Dalglish faced a number of injury concerns with himself, Alan Hansen, Jan Molby, Mark Lawrenson, Jim Beglin, Gary Gillespie, Steve McMahon and Jan Molby all receiving treatment. Revealing that another player was also doubtful, Dalglish joked, "We've been talking about getting an extension [to the treatment room] added. John Wark's in plaster but we might even have to wheel him out against Birmingham."

Assuming Liverpool would still take care of the Midlanders with ease, Ian Hargraves suggested the player-boss might consider giving himself a rest and draft in fit-again Paul Walsh in his place. "Even if Dalglish plays himself in the big games against Chelsea and Everton, it would seem good sense to make sure such a valuable player is back in the groove again and ready to be called upon if needed."

In his programme notes Dalglish once again paid tribute to Liverpool's fans, particularly those who had travelled in such large numbers in recent away games.

"At the risk of repeating myself, I would like to express, on behalf of all the players, our appreciation for the support you have given to the team. You have backed us up through the season, and in these closing weeks, you have made yourselves heard at places such as White Hart Lane, Kenilworth Road and the Hawthorns. So the backing has not just been at Anfield."

At a time when unemployment on Merseyside had reached unparalleled heights, Liverpool had nevertheless averaged crowds of over 34,983 for league games – one of the highest in the division - and their total aggregate attendance figure for the season in all competitions was set to pass the one million mark. With such fantastic support in mind, Dalglish was at pains to acknowledge the importance of the bond between players and fans when he told them, "I just hope that we can reward you by winning one, if not both of the trophies which are still in our sights."

On a bright, spring afternoon a near full-house crowd of 42,021 packed into Anfield hoping to see the Reds gain all three points so as to not only maintain their interest at the top of the table, but also to finish the season with just the one home defeat – regretfully against Everton.

With players desperate to retain their place at such a vital stage of the season the injury niggles of the past week miraculously cleared and Dalglish made just one change to his starting XI from the Reds' victory over WBA - the fit-again Gillespie coming in at the expense of Mark Lawrenson. To leave a player of Lawrenson's calibre out of the team for a less-celebrated centre-half spoke volumes for both Gillespie's consistent displays and Dalglish's single-minded approach to management – an advantageous idiosyncrasy that had been apparent all season.

Birmingham not only faced the prospect of starting the new season in the Second Division but also the likelihood that they would lose a host of players, such as promising young left-back Julian Dicks, midfielder Stuart Storer and goalkeeper David Seaman. More experienced campaigners Ray Ransom, ex-Evertonian Billy Wright and striker Wayne Clarke had failed to lift City away from trouble and they came to Anfield already resigned to the drop. As a consequence only a small band of Blues' fans had travelled in support of their side, leaving large numbers of green and cream seats in the Anfield Road End the only vacant spaces at a vibrant Anfield. Birmingham won the toss and elected to change ends meaning that Liverpool would attack the Kop in the first half.

Perhaps unable to shake the importance of the game from their thoughts the home side looked edgy in the early exchanges. In stark contrast - and free of their relegation worries - Birmingham played with a sense of freedom and adventure that belied their league position and which saw them earn a number of early corners. Storer stood out for the visitors, playing some intelligent balls into the path of Dicks, who was always willing to break forward from full-back. The early backing of the Kop soon gave way to anxious groans from the Main Stand as passes were misplaced or overhit, and Liverpool struggled to find any rhythm.

Gradually however, the Reds improved, with Molby twice going close to opening the scoring. After controlling a Dalglish pass on his chest the Dane thundered in a right-foot volley from 20-yards that was well held by Seaman, then a vicious left-foot drive curled just the wrong side of the post.

Throughout what was developing into a scrappy first-half however, Birmingham showed plenty of spirit to occasionally trouble the Reds. Dicks continued to get forward and some accurate left foot crosses kept Clarke - brother of Leeds legend Alan Clarke - interested in the Blues attack, his presence causing both Hansen and Gillespie to concede corners at the Anfield Road End. Fortunately Grobbelaar was at his confident best, twice venturing yards off his line to claim the ball and relieve the pressure on his defenders.

Liverpool were finally able to put their early uncertainty behind them when they took the lead in the 26th minute, albeit slightly against the run of play. Johnston, whose speed and directness had been a feature of the Reds' attacking play all season, skipped away from Dicks on the right flank and sent over a long, though slightly over hit cross. There was no-one near the ball as it bounced on the Kemlyn Road side of the penalty area until Whelan appeared from nowhere to volley goalwards. His angled shot across goal was going narrowly wide until the faintest deflection off Rush's outstretched knee diverted it into the net.

The acclaim for the goal was initially attributed by the Kop to Whelan, with few among the thousands behind Seaman's goal realising it was Rush who got the vital touch, but non-one cared as they celebrated the Reds' 54th league goal of the season at Anfield.

Johnston was Liverpool's most energetic first-half performer, tracking back to make tackles and interceptions, and always making runs to give the Reds' midfield an outlet on the right wing. Occasionally the Australian let his enthusiasm get the better of him and he was caught offside on more than one occasion - to the frustration of a hyper-critical element among fans seated in the Main Stand – but his eagerness to do anything for the Liverpool cause was unparalleled.

The edginess in the home crowd wasn't just confined to the stands however, and the Kop was also relieved to hear the half-time whistle with Liverpool ahead at the break. So much so that when George Sephton announced there was no score at either the City Ground or Upton Park, there were only reserved cheers from Kopites craving an Everton slip-up.

Nerves were finally settled within just 200 seconds of the second half starting, when Liverpool scored two goals in three minutes. Within a minute of the kick-off former Everton defender Wright - chided by the Kop for his Goodison roots and burly frame - conceded a needless corner on the Birmingham left. Johnston's lofted, high centre, hung tantalizingly in the air before being met emphatically by the recalled Gillespie, his powerful header arrowing straight into Seaman's net from 10 yards.

Amid the din of the Kop's celebrations the Birmingham defence got in another terrible tangle from the restart and, under pressure from Dalglish and Rush, full-back Brian

Roberts clearly handled in the box. Seaman got a hand to Molby's firmly struck penalty but to no avail, the power of the shot carrying the ball over the line for the Dane's 20th goal of the season.

Under Dalglish's tutelage, Molby had put his uncertain debut season behind him and had blossomed – whether in central midfield or sweeper - into the passing fulcrum of the team, weighing in with a glut of vital goals. He was an iconic, charismatic figure for the fans, whilst to the media he was something of a novelty with his approachable nature and amusing Scando-scouse accent.

In the 55th minute Liverpool went close to making it four when Johnston got clear in the box and cut the ball back for Rush. The Welshman attempted to side-foot past Seaman but, slightly off balance, he could only direct his shot at the goalkeeper. Twenty-two year-old Seaman was increasingly busy as Liverpool, enjoying the triumphant songs from the Kop, began to play with a confidence and authority that had been lacking in the first quarter of the match.

A fourth goal duly arrived after 58 minutes with centre-half Gillespie, revelling in his selection by Dalglish, scoring his second of the afternoon after starting a sweeping move from his own half. Galloping towards goal, Gillespie played a one-two with Rush and, before Seaman could intercept the return pass, slammed the ball gleefully home to score what was one of the goals of the Anfield season.

Liverpool dominated the remainder of the second half. Gillespie went close to a hat-trick with another header from a corner, Dalglish failed by the narrowest of margins to chip Seaman, and several other efforts were either just wide or repelled by the impressive young keeper. It seemed only a matter of time before the Reds would grab another.

In the 83rd minute the pressure finally told when Dicks tripped Rush on the right-side of the box. Referee George Tyson pointed to the spot for the second penalty of the half but, as Molby stepped up to take the kick, the Kop intervened - chanting for Gillespie to take it instead and claim a well-deserved hat-trick. Encouraged by Dalglish, Gillespie reluctantly jogged forward to place the ball on the spot. Cynics in the crowd muttered about the importance of goal difference but the young Scot dispelled their fears, lifting a fine strike high into the net past Seaman's right hand.

The 20,000 or so fans standing on the packed Kop applauded the defender for emulating Alvin Martin's feat for West Ham earlier in the week, as a huge chant of, "Gary Gillespie," filled the Anfield skies. Dalglish immediately introduced Lawrenson from the bench in place of Whelan.

Fans had grown accustomed to celebrating the end of a league season at Anfield with a title-clinching victory or trophy parade but here, fans nervously looked around for people with transistor radios, thirsting for news of Everton's fate in Nottingham. There had been no building crescendo of noise that usually alerts the rest of the ground to a significant score from elsewhere but once it became known that Forest had held Everton to a goalless draw - a result that edged Liverpool two points clear at the top of the table - cheers echoed around the ground, albeit tempered by the understanding that the Reds' fate still lay out of their own hands.

Agonisingly for fans and players, three wins for the Blues over Oxford, Southampton and West Ham would still see Everton crowned Champions - by a single point. West Ham had won 1-0 at home to Coventry to keep their hopes alive and, with a 'six-pointer' at Goodison scheduled for their last game, the Hammers were also reliant on one more slip-up - from Liverpool - if they were to have a chance of stealing the title by winning their final matches and beating Everton.

With the hopes and dreams of players and supporters hanging on the spring breeze, it was strange curtain call for the season at Anfield. The whole team acknowledged the applause and songs of a packed and throbbing Anfield as they lingered briefly before making their way from the field to contemplate the three remaining games that would shape their destiny. The Reds had banged in 22 goals during their final five home league matches but would it be enough? In contrast to the thoughts of Brian Clough, Liverpool's late-season charge and avalanche of goals suggested that - on their day - the Reds were the best team in the country. They would get the chance to prove it in the Cup Final, but the honour of going to Wembley as League Champions still lay beyond their control.

Authors Note: Liverpool finished their Anfield league programme with 16 wins, four draws and a sole defeat from 21 games in which they netted 58 goals, conceding fourteen.

The title bandwagon now rolled on to Filbert Street and the Manor Ground where lowly Leicester and Oxford would attempt to steal points off the big two to stave off the drop and in the process influence the final destination of the League Championship. West Ham, playing catch-up, faced two midweek games starting with the visit of Manchester City on Monday evening.

As Anfield bade its farewells to the League season it was left to unlikely hat-trick hero, the humble Gillespie, to have the final word. In true self-deprecating fashion he admitted, "The gaffer never names his team until shortly before kick-off and I expected to be left out for Mark. That has happened before because he is such a fine player." Offering a revealing insight into Dalglish's man-management skills, Gillespie added, "When he came over and told me I was playing it was a wonderful boost. I don't get many goals. I think I have scored only seven in whole career."

Whatever Dalglish said to Gillespie and the rest of his side - to inspire not only this five goal victory but a ninth win in 10 league games - had had the desired effect. Now the player-manager had to coax two more wins on the road from his squad - and pray for one further slip-up from Howard Kendall's side if Liverpool were to dethrone the reigning Champions. A tumultuous last week of league football lay ahead.

Wednesday 30 April
Leicester City v Liverpool

"At Oxford we had some good battles with Everton too, particularly the game in 1985/86 at the Manor Ground. They were going for the title and we needed a win to help us escape relegation....We had a great celebration afterwards..."

John Aldridge, Alright Aldo Sound as A Pound: On the Road with Everybody's Favourite Irish Scouser, Trinity Mirror Sport Media, 2010

With the intention of applying maximum pressure on Everton's visit to Oxford United the same night, Liverpool travelled to Leicester City looking for their tenth win in 11 games. The Merseyside clubs' lowly opponents, desperate for three vital points in front of their own fans, promised stern tests in their respective efforts to avoid dropping through the relegation trap-door.

Whereas Everton's match had been declared all-ticket, thousands of Reds supporters were forced to leave schools and workplaces early to head down the M6. Entry to the away sections at Filbert Street, accessed through back and side alleys of people's terraced houses, was by payment at the turnstiles - and no-one wanted to be locked out of the latest episode of the most tightly contested League Championship since Liverpool prevailed at Molyneux in the final minutes of the 1975/76 season.

Ticketing arrangements were not the only differences between the two games. Whereas Liverpool's game kicked-off at 7.45pm, Everton's was due to start a quarter of an hour earlier. If the Blues were to drop points and Liverpool's game was level at 9.10pm, then the Reds would have a whole 15 minutes to force a goal that would make them favourites to take the title.

Another home win for West Ham on Monday evening over Manchester City had made the race a genuine three-way affair, and the Hammers now sought a fifth consecutive win with a second game in just 48 hours at Upton Park against Ipswich. A trip to West Brom at the weekend then beckoned, so John Lyall's men were in the midst of four games in eight days - a sequence that would be scarcely believable in today's Premier League. Then they would travel to Goodison on Monday, for a fifth match in ten days with the title possibly at stake.

Before the evening's games Liverpool led the way with 82 points from 40 games, Everton were second with 80 points from 39 matches, and West Ham third with 78 points from 39 played. Liverpool's superior goal difference (+49) versus Everton's (+40) meant that the Reds probably needed the Blues to drop just a point to nip in and steal the title. While Liverpool had been rattling in the goals during their unbeaten run, Tony Cottee and Frank McAvennie continued to lead the Hammers' charge with an astonishing 43 league goals between them so far. By contrast, Everton's twin strike force of Graeme Sharp and Gary Lineker had endured a dry run, with Lineker in particular struggling to replicate his early-season form. Hampered by a suspect hamstring, he had scored just once in eight league games.

Dalglish was able to name an unchanged side to face Leicester with Mark Lawrenson continuing on the bench, fuelling speculation that Liverpool's most versatile and accomplished footballer might not be able to force his way back into the team for the FA Cup final. Although Dalglish had meddled with his formation and personnel throughout the season according to the opposition, he was reluctant to drop players in form so Gary Gillespie remained in situ alongside Alan Hansen at the back.

Still smarting from a 4-0 home defeat to Manchester United at the weekend, Leicester included the talented Ian Andrews in goal, former Ipswich defender Russell Osman, ex-West Bromwich and Real Madrid winger Laurie Cunningham and their top scorer Alan Smith. Tall, angular and locally-born, Smith had taken on Lineker's goalscoring mantle at Filbert Street and had netted 19 goals in all competitions. The Foxes also included their young midfield playmaker, Gary McAllister.

Once again vast numbers followed the Reds to the Midlands; with almost 5,000 Reds' fans packed into the South Stand terracing and the seats in the shallow East Stand. They gave their side a raucous ovation as they took the field. Leicester fans in the 25,799 crowd - their biggest of the season - gave the home side an equally passionate welcome on an evening when vocal backing was vital if City – in nineteenth place - were to shock the visitors.

A Leicester win - or even a draw - could massively boost the home side's survival chances by pulling clear of Everton's opponents on the same night Oxford United – who lay in twentieth place. Amid the dying embers of the season, one team from Leicester, Oxford, Ipswich or Coventry were set to join already relegated Birmingham City and West Brom in Division Two.

Liverpool kicked off attacking their own fans and started with the attacking intent of a side playing with the utmost confidence. In the third minute Andrews, who had brilliantly kept Liverpool at bay until the final moments at Anfield back in November, pulled off a stunning save to push away a typical Jan Molby thunderbolt from 25-yards. Shortly afterwards Nicol, marauding forward from right-back, gathered a through-ball inside the area only to shoot narrowly wide. The Liverpool fans behind the goal roared their support as the Reds threatened to blow Leicester away inside the opening minutes.

After the Reds early chances however, the game settled into a more even contest but in the 15th minute Liverpool were fortunate to remain on level terms after a complacent piece of defending from Alan Hansen. Prone to an occasional lapse in concentration, the centre-half aimed a long-distance back pass towards Bruce Grobbelaar. The alert Alan Smith was quick to react and he intercepted the ball 15-yards from goal but, fortunately for Hansen, the forward panicked in front of goal and dragged his shot wide with just Grobbelaar to beat. The let-off served as a wake-up call for Liverpool and after 20 minutes the Reds took a vital lead.

Dalglish, playing in his now familiar withdrawn striking role, won the ball in a challenge with McAllister in midfield and dribbled towards the penalty area. Spotting Rush's run across the box, the player-manager dinked a pass with the outside of his foot into the Welshman's path. Rush, shielding the ball from two defenders snapping at his heels, transferred the ball onto his right foot and struck a low snap shot towards goal. A vicious deflection off the lunging Osman defeated Andrews' dive to prevent Liverpool going ahead - and the visiting fans behind the goal went berserk. Their joy was mirrored on the pitch with the Liverpool players engulfing Rush. Having well and truly overcome his barren patch either side of Christmas, it was his 31st goal of the season.

Leicester briefly threatened an equaliser in the 26th minute but Grobbelaar spectacularly caught Osman's flicked attempt from a free-kick. It was Liverpool though, sensing Leicester's deflation at going behind in unfortunate circumstances, who continued to dictate the pace and they were rewarded with a second goal in the 28th minute.

Venturing upfield in typical fashion from right-back, Nicol spotted Whelan making a run into the Leicester penalty area. Showing great vision the full-back clipped a perfect ball over the City defence to the galloping Irishman whose deft touch was enough to beat Andrews, the ball looping high over the keeper into the empty net.

The joyous scenes witnessed on the South Stand terrace just eight minutes previously were repeated but, as the Liverpool fans saluted the goal, many spilled on to the cinder track surrounding the pitch, some of whom appeared to need medical attention. A few were briefly led along the touchline by the local St John's Ambulance crew only to miraculously shake off their injuries and disappear into the more comfortable surroundings of the East Stand - and a significantly better view.

With Liverpool enjoying a decisive lead at half-time, news from elsewhere became all important. As the Reds walked off at the break, the second half was just beginning at the Manor Ground with the scoreline still blank - Everton searching desperately for a winner in the second half if they were to remain in the driving seat. West Ham led Ipswich at Upton Park, a score eagerly cheered by the Leicester fans due to the Portman Road side's shared involvement in the battle against the drop. With Liverpool in control and Leicester unable to make much of an impression, the second-half was played out in a surreal atmosphere, with supporters of both sides more concerned with news crackling in from fans with transistor radios dotted around the ground.

Although giving very little away at the back, Liverpool came forward whenever possible and always looked capable of extending their lead. Rush twice, Molby, Whelan and Kevin McDonald all went close to adding a third goal as Liverpool played out the half in a typically and thoroughly assured manner.

Viewed with the hindsight of 25 years, it is easy to imagine that it was difficult for Liverpool's players to concentrate on the task in hand knowing that just 60 miles away, a goal for Everton could negate all their efforts and leave their great rivals just two home wins from the title. Conversely - if Oxford could keep the Blues out - it would leave Liverpool just a win at Stamford Bridge away from snatching their crown. For the fans, the tension was unbearable with countless unconfirmed reports of goals at either end of the Manor Ground sweeping across the terraces like a series of Chinese whispers.

The majority of the Liverpool support, and certainly the players, were only vaguely aware of events in Oxford until, with 15 minutes to go at Filbert Street and full-time approaching in Everton's match, there was a startling roar from the Reds' followers behind Bruce Grobbelaar's goal. At first, unsure if what they were hearing was true, fans simply stared manically at each other with uncertain expressions of hope tempered by an awful trepidation that maybe the radio wires were crossed and what they were hearing was a hoax or worse still - that it was Everton who had scored.

In the space of a few seconds however, the uncertainty turned to unbridled joy as the news was confirmed – Everton were a goal down at Oxford with just minutes to play. Such was the delirium among the supporters that the message was clearly communicated to the players on the pitch and an increasingly animated Liverpool dug-out. Liverpool then won a corner and Dalglish, coming over to take it, cupped his ear as if to request confirmation of the score at the Manor Ground. The player-manager beamed at the crowd and clenched a fist when, "Oxford 1 Everton 0, Hallelujah!" came back as an almost instant reply.

When the result from the Manor Ground was finally confirmed, the action at Filbert Street became an irrelevance and jubilant Reds' fans filled the warm night air with an ear-splitting chorus of, "Now you're gonna believe us, we're gonna win the League." In truth however, for every Liverpool supporter belting out songs in Leicester and the thousands more at home listening nervously to Radio City's Clive Tyldesley's dramatic commentary from the

Manor Ground, it was the first time all season that anyone really knew, or thought they knew, Liverpool were going to win the league. From the fall of the autumn leaves and Manchester United's runaway start to Everton's mid-winter surge which saw them race 11 points clear by 1 March, no one could have sanely argued that it was Liverpool's title. Until now.

As the incredulous celebrations died down with Liverpool denying Leicester even a touch of the ball during the final moments, a majestic rendition of, "You'll Never Walk Alone,' echoed around Filbert Street. Liverpool fans saved their anthem for moments like this; it was their ultimate victory song, rarely sung at lesser battles and hardly ever in defeat. This was the perfect moment for an airing of Gerry Marsden's hymn, to salute not only the men in Red but also their raw, intrepid, dedicated band of followers as the League Championship – for so long out of sight - sailed majestically into view.

As the final whistle blew, hundreds of Reds fans - mainly from the seats in the East Stand - spilled over the perimeter fencing and onto the pitch. The sheer number of invaders forced the Liverpool players to beat a hasty retreat towards the changing rooms and there was no time for any form of communion with the thousands more who remained in the South Stand terrace.

With a difficult match still to be won at Stamford Bridge before they could pronounce themselves Champions, perhaps it was no time for triumphalism, but in the dressing room and in the cars, coaches and minibuses heading North, everyone connected with the club tried to make sense of the dramatic events of the night. It was slowly sinking in that Liverpool were just 90 minutes away from becoming League Champions.

Despite being huge outsiders - having at one stage trailed their rivals by 11 points - the Reds had doggedly and relentlessly chased Everton since mid-February. The autumn pursuit of early runaway leaders Manchester United seemed an irrelevance compared with this startling springtime comeback. Liverpool had brought pressure to bear on a faltering Everton side with an almost flawless run of 10 wins and a draw in eleven games. In the same period Everton had drawn with Chelsea, Manchester United and Nottingham Forest and had suffered disastrous defeats to Luton and Oxford – shipping a total of 12 points and allowing Liverpool to sneak into pole position with just one game to go. Gary Lineker's goalscoring drought, in contrast to the prolific form of Ian Rush, had come to a head at the Manor Ground.

Long before Oxford's late winner from Les Phillips, Lineker had missed three gilt-edged chances that would have sealed an Everton victory – and arguably the title. The Blues' record signing's dour East Midlands accent sounded flatter than ever in a post-match interview with ITV Sport on 'The Midweek Match.'

Lineker revealed that a pair of 'lucky' boots which he had worn all season had accidentally been left behind at Goodison. His snug footwear, showing severe signs of wear and tear, had been repaired by the Goodison kit-man on several occasions. Sounding a like a child moaning about the soreness caused by new school shoes, the England striker blamed his horrific night in front of goal on having to wear an unforgiving new pair of boots. Ian Rush held no such superstitions and, although Lineker had outscored him over the season, Rush's form had arrived at the business end of the year - with eleven goals in league and Cup during Liverpool's unbeaten run.

In the pressroom at Filbert Street Kenny Dalglish rejected claims that Everton had gifted Liverpool the title. "It's always been in our own hands," he said. "We've always had to get results and Saturday will be no different…but we'll gladly take any help we can get." Focusing again on the all-round effort required of his side - clinical attacking and solid defending - even against sides they were expected to beat, Dalglish typically played down Liverpool's performance. "We got two early goals and after that contained Leicester pretty well but it was important that we did not concede anything."

Asked if the players realised Everton were losing the player-manager smiled coyly and said, "We heard the crowd roar near the end and obviously we knew exactly what it meant – and that Everton had lost."

Dalglish however, seemed genuinely disappointed that the pitch invasion by jubilant fans had prevented his team from acknowledging their followers. "My only regret on the night was that we weren't able to applaud our supporters who are simply great," he said. "We were fortunate in bringing a lot of people with us and they were willing us to win. We would have liked to have stayed on the pitch at the afterwards but unfortunately a number of people ran on, so we could not."

On the last evening of April, the Liverpool fans prepared to dust off their old standard – "Here we go gathering cups in May" ditty. All season - and despite the economic situation on Merseyside - Liverpool's away support had been phenomenal, with thousands following their side to midweek games at some of the most cramped, most inaccessible, and downright ugly grounds ever seen in the top flight.

The Kopites and the lads from The Anny Road End now turned their attentions to a more familiar venue in pursuit of the League Championship trophy - and the first leg of a remarkable and historic Double. The numbers that would follow Liverpool to Stamford Bridge would dwarf those seen at any away ground all season. Kenny's army was firmly on the march.

Saturday 3 May
Chelsea v Liverpool

"We went to the Bridge, Needing a win,
When Kenny put the ball in the net.
That's sixteen, It's beautiful, And it's ours"

Liverpool fans' song celebrating a record 16th League Championship.

"Me and our Stephen had seen Liverpool win the league before, but this was different. It wasn't the procession we'd almost come to expect – it was difficult. For the most part we didn't actually think we'd do it – certainly not after the poor run at Christmas, nor when we'd lost at home to Everton. But when we turned it on we did so in style – the last dozen games were unbelievable. But this was what we did then. We were Liverpool. Winning in the manner we did, after a horrendous year, when it seemed that everyone – and I mean everyone – hated us, despised us? It felt like payback. "

Co-author Gary Shaw

Prior to Liverpool's victory and Everton's collapse in midweek, there had been acute frustration that the Reds' avalanche of goals and remarkable sequence of victories on the run-in could still be to no avail, with the Blue's managing to scrape enough points week after week to seemingly deny Kopite's the glory their rampant end to the season warranted. Now however, after two months of applying pressure with a string of victories in a near impeccable charge, Kenny Dalglish and his players were just 90 minutes away from Liverpool's 16th League title - the first to be overseen by a player-manager – and, for the first time that season, the Reds found themselves in control of their own title destiny.

With just their visit to Stamford Bridge remaining Liverpool led the way on 85 points. West Ham were second on 81 with Everton's recent alarming dip in form all too apparent - they lay third on 80 points. Liverpool's vastly superior goal difference meant that a point at Chelsea would be enough to foil the Toffees, but a draw could still gift the title to the Hammers should the Londoners win their last two games - at The Hawthorns and Goodison Park. Only a Liverpool defeat in London would maintain Everton's hopes, providing they won their last two games - home fixtures against Southampton and West Ham. For Liverpool, the calculations equated to just one simple fact - only an 11th win in 12 games would make sure of the title.

Preferring a London team to win the title, Chelsea boss John Hollins insisted that his side could halt Liverpool in their tracks - and in the process assist their East End rivals. "I would like to think the title can come to London," he said.

"It has not been here since 1971 and that is a long time. Upton Park and East London is the nearest we can get to it to us but it is the next best thing. It is obvious that we shall do our very best. I would sincerely hope professional pride will come into it regardless of our wish to see West Ham win the title."

Although realistic about his side's chances Everton manager Howard Kendall also refused to admit defeat. "Let's just say I'm a Chelsea fan now", he joked. "We will be going flat out to win our last two games and you can be sure our players will be in there fighting against Southampton on Saturday. The League is still not lost although we accept that it's not in our hands now, which is disappointing."

Reflecting on the drought of just seven goals in nine games that had ultimately cost Everton dear, Kendall added "It's not all that long ago that we were the leading scorers in the League. We have fallen short of that standard recently and it has added pressure on the defence and the goalkeeper. Bobby Mimms has done brilliantly for us again but if you are not scoring there is always the fear that one slip will prove costly."

The Football League meanwhile had already decided that Liverpool were probable Champions. They contacted the club offering to stage the presentation of the Championship trophy at Wembley before the FA Cup Final against Everton, but Reds' Chief Executive Peter Robinson quickly poured scorn on the idea. "We told them that if we did win the League, and it is far from settled yet, we would prefer the trophy to be handed over at the Super Cup-tie at Anfield next Tuesday." For Robinson the rearranged semi-final second leg against Norwich City would, "be a much more personal occasion and would give our team a perfect Wembley send-off. However, I must stress again that nobody here is taking anything for granted."

It was typical of Liverpool, even through a respected administrator, to douse any flames of footballing complacency. Secretly though, Robinson would have been eyeing the extra shillings that would be added to the Anfield coffers should a title celebration add several thousand to the gate for the rearranged Super Cup fixture.

In the build-up to the trip to Stamford Bridge Dalglish and his players remained tight-lipped, preferring to concentrate on the task in hand and not offer lavish predictions in the press. Liverpool's record at Stamford Bridge - the FA Cup 4th Round victory notwithstanding - was unspectacular at best and their last win there in the League had been way back in August 1974. Chelsea had also come within five minutes of victory at Anfield in November, denied only by a late Jan Molby penalty.

With so little pre-match talk emanating from the Reds' camp, it was left to Chelsea boss Hollins to fill the back pages with more talk of his team's ability to scupper Liverpool's chances. "We still think we should have beaten Liverpool in the League when we met them at Anfield," he said. "They managed a draw but with ground advantage in our favour we believe we can go one better this time." Despite the Chelsea manager's commendable faith in his side, Liverpool were still odds-on favourites to win at Stamford Bridge - the bookies acutely aware of the momentum, determination and confidence the Reds' had slowly built up with their nerveless run of victories. All this was before anyone accounted for the support Liverpool would have in London.

Few people - perhaps even Dalglish himself - had guessed at the sheer number of Liverpool fans who were planning to flood the capital in support of the Reds at Stamford Bridge. Despite British Rail laying on a plethora of special trains priced at £11.50 and the many thousands more planning to make the trip by coach and car, admission to the ground was to be by payment at the turnstiles - with Liverpool allocated the whole of the open North Terrace.

Although the away section could house upwards of 10,000 supporters there were concerns amongst local fans that the strength of Liverpool's support in the Midlands and South of England would see many of those travelling from Merseyside facing the disappointment of being locked out of the game, so early starts were planned from all over the city.

While excited and animated talk of Saturday's game dominated conversations in pubs, schools and workplaces on Merseyside, Dalglish was assessing fitness concerns over Ian Rush - who had been withdrawn towards the end at Leicester still suffering the effects of a back injury. Jan Molby, who had emerged as a consistent and instrumental figure throughout Liverpool's season, had also taken a knock at Filbert Street making his participation doubtful.

Although Dalglish needed all his key players available the injuries offered hope of a return to the side to Mark Lawrenson. Perhaps the most gifted footballer in the squad, the often under-rated Eire international had enjoyed a fantastic season for the Reds, having delivered equally adept displays at right-back, centre-back and in midfield. If anything, Lawrenson had suffered for his versatility; his untimely ankle injury sustained against Oxford in March costing him his normally assured starting place in the side. Now however, Dalglish's policy of retaining a winning team - which was at odds with his rotational selection policy earlier in the season - threatened to deny Lawrenson a berth in the side for the very games that would decide the outcome of the entire, breathtaking campaign.

On the morning of the game Lime Street station was awash with animated Liverpudlians as the Football Specials and ordinary trains bound for London pulled out and headed towards the Edge Hill tunnels. The Liverpool bobble hats of winter had largely given way to lighter, cotton sun-hats - universally turned-up at the back - as the colours of choice for the visit to London. Very few among the masses of Reds' fans wore scarves or Liverpool shirts, the majority of the younger element preferring the homogenous attire of expensive looking polo-shirts and designer tracksuit tops combined with semi-flared jeans and cords.

Despite the early start, cans of lager were eagerly quaffed on the station concourse and small bottles of spirits smuggled onto trains in coats, socks and underpants to enliven the journey South. Fans had learnt to be resourceful in the face of inevitable searches by members of Her Majesty's Constabularies.

A bright spring day in London greeted the travelling hordes as they dispersed in various directions at Euston Station. Mingling briefly with rugby league fans of Castleford and Hull Kingston Rovers - who were in London for the Challenge Cup Final - the majority headed straight for the District line tube routes down to Fulham Broadway.

Despite a heavy police presence to direct supporters straight to the station nearest Chelsea's ground, a select crew headed instead for Edgware Road. For some Liverpool followers, ensuring a place on the terraces before the Stamford Bridge gates closed wasn't quite as important as the desire to bounce off the train and see what was on offer for the fearless opportunist on the streets of London.

Within minutes, police sirens could be heard as an intrepid Liverpool gang raided a local jewellery store. Others targeted clothing outlets, plucking merchandise that could be resold at home and therefore pay for many a future night out - or away trip. Before the police could arrive in sufficient numbers at least a half dozen lads crumpled back on to the tube - the spoils of their adventures openly displayed for all to see.

Others weren't so fortunate - being confronted before they could navigate a safe route back to the train station. When police reinforcements arrived on the scene, the miscreants were hurriedly forced to dispense with their valuable loot, the result being the simultaneous clank of various stolen precious metals bouncing off the London pavements. What followed was reminiscent of a farcical scene from a TV comedy sketch, with the 'Old Bill' inelegantly pursuing the Liverpool urchins just as Benny Hill used to chase pretty girls.

When the majority of fans arrived at the ground, a Metropolitan Police operation that amounted to no more than a team of police horses wading clumsily into supporters led to a worrying - though common - build up of agitated supporters in long, disorganised queues for the turnstiles. With around 45 minutes to kick-off and patience wearing thin, the safety of the Liverpool fans appeared the last thing on the police agenda - a situation made worse by amateurish organisation, the non-decision to opt for 'pay-on-the-gate' at such a vital match, and the unexpectedly large number of away supporters.

It was amid this confusion that famed Liverpool fan Bobby Wilcox stumbled upon a solitary, unmanned turnstile. Bobby squeezed himself inside, sat himself down and began ushering a group of Liverpool supporters into the ground. Fellow Liverpool stalwart Nicky Allt fondly remembers that Wilcox, who was a renowned facilitator of many an intrepid Liverpool excursion, jovially charged him and countless others 15p to get in – an absolute bargain for a title decider. Such scenes of chaos were commonplace at big matches throughout the 1970s and 80s. Policing here was driven by a perception that all fans were a potential threat.

In equal measure, football followers from a spectrum of society downtrodden by poverty and unemployment viewed the police as nothing more than the Government's controlling arm. Many relished the confrontation. Aggression, disaffection and fiery young blood versus perceived and politically fuelled establishment figures in the shape of the police made for an explosive cocktail. The inner-city riots earlier in the season had come as no surprise to most football fans.

As kick-off approached the Liverpool end was rapidly and raucously being filled to capacity, with views atop fencing, pylons and advertising boards the preferred position for many. Not everyone paid for the privilege however, after the wrought iron gates that sat at the bottom of the terracing gave way briefly to admit some frightened, frustrated but mostly angry supporters who had been kept in queues for what seemed like an eternity. Fortunately the vast majority were eventually ushered inside safely, but such incidents were a worrying, unheeded portent for the future.

As they took to the field ahead of the home side, more than 10,000 Liverpool fans gave the Reds a rousing welcome. Chelsea fans in the Shed and West Stand had bought into the intrigue of the occasion and roared the home side on to the pitch for their last game of the season. With a packed house - the crowd of 43,900 was a staggering 10,000 up on the cup-tie at the same ground earlier in the season - the stage was perfectly set for a dramatic and pulsating afternoon although seldom had Liverpool played on a barer pitch all season, the thinnest covering of grass adding to the grey bleakness of Stamford Bridge.

With its incongruous stands, steel blue fences, cars parked in the corners of the stadium and faded track surrounding the pitch, the spartan ground resembled a vast Eastern European, dual-purpose football and athletics arena - like those Liverpool were so familiar with from their former continental travels. As with many grounds of the era, the colour and flavour of he occasion was provided solely by supporters, the most valuable commodity in the game but one that clubs took for granted and the Government sought increasingly to marginalize. Molby's injury had ruled him out so Lawrenson returned to the line-up, slotting straight into the injured Dane's place in the centre of midfield. This was the only change to the Liverpool team.

In the last quarter of the season Dalglish had settled on a consistent selection with Grobbelaar - his mid-season wobbles a distant memory - in goal; thrusting full-backs Steve Nicol and Jim Beglin, with Alan Hansen and Gary Gillespie an established partnership in the centre of a defence that had leaked just four goals in 11 games; Ronnie Whelan in his old left-midfield role alongside the solidity offered by Kevin McDonald; the returning Lawrenson in the middle; and Craig Johnston who offered pace and width on the right. Dalglish, in his slightly withdrawn position behind Rush, was the link between midfield and attack. Not the most memorable of Liverpool sides to ever roll off the tongue – but certainly one of the most effective.

For Chelsea - who started the game fifth in the table - Tony Godden had taken over from Eddie Niedzwiecki in goal since the last meeting between the sides. To provide service for the established pairing of David Speedie and Kerry Dixon, the Londoners fielded exciting winger Paul Cannoville and the slight but inventive Pat Nevin. They would provide a formidable test for the Reds, especially with the home support revelling in their role as potential scouse party-poopers

With the sun threatening to break through on a warm afternoon, the game kicked off with Liverpool attacking their own noisy, nervous and expectant fans on the North Terrace. First Manchester United, then Everton, had been overwhelming favourites to land the crown, while West Ham had mounted a spirited challenge in the second half of the season. As the last scheduled fixtures were played out however, it rested in the hands of Dalglish's blend of old hands and emerging players to close out their rivals with a victory that would confirm them as Champions of the Canon League First Division.

Lifted by their biggest crowd of their season, Chelsea started the game brightly and it was nearly three minutes before the Reds could lay claim to any kind of meaningful possession. Liverpool eventually settled and in the fifth minute Nigel Spackman, a bustling presence in Chelsea's midfield, slipped and missed a cross from Nicol. The ball bounced through to McDonald offering a half-chance, but the Scot's well-struck shot was pushed round the post by Godden.

It seemed that Liverpool were intent to go all-out for the three points, and they continued to come forward at every opportunity. Minutes later Johnston evaded the Chelsea defence to fire in another shot which was again dealt with by Godden. In contrast Chelsea, despite some bright approach play, often resorted to high balls aimed at Dixon. Lawrenson appeared to drop deeper to supplement Hansen and Gillespie in repelling the aerial threat, with full-backs Nicol and Beglin looking to push forward as Liverpool adopted the 3-5-2 formation that had attracted such criticism earlier in the season.

During the course of the season Dalglish's side had developed an adaptable style that countered the strengths of their opponents, an approach that didn't always please the traditionalists but still relied on the long-held Liverpool values of pass-and-move. Employing three centre-halves also placed greater emphasis on the full-backs to augment the attack and the emergence in these positions of the youthful Nicol and Beglin, replacing Neal and Kennedy, had been a key factor in Dalglish's tactics as the season progressed.

Despite Chelsea's huff and puff, Liverpool were playing the more cultured football and in the 23rd minute they secured the vital breakthrough, courtesy of the talismanic Dalglish. From a corner taken by Nicol on the right, Gillespie flicked on towards Beglin in the penalty area. The left-back's header was cleared as far as Whelan, who chested the ball down and attempted a volley from 25-yards only to see his scuffed effort blocked on the edge of the box. When the clearance rebounded to him, Whelan headed goalwards towards the retreating Beglin - who instantly flicked the ball over three Chelsea defenders towards Dalglish.

Reacting with the speed of his younger days, the player-manager raced onto Beglin's imaginative lofted pass, controlled on his chest in an instant, and volleyed with the outside of his right foot past Godden's left hand. It was in. "If there had been no net Kenny's shot would have literally ran straight to us," recalls Gary Shaw. "We had a great view. The celebrations? Magical. "

The equally ecstatic Dalglish sped behind the goal to salute the thousands of jubilant Liverpool supporters before turning to accept the embrace of his teammates. Significantly,

McDonald, Beglin and Johnston - who had all flourished under his management - were first to engulf their manager, closely followed by Whelan and Gillespie. The electronic scoreboard at the back of the terrace where Liverpool fans were celebrating instantly flashed up the scoreline - Chelsea 0 Liverpool 1. It was Dalglish's seventh goal of the season and, following his memorable strike in the Goodison Derby back in September and the opener at West Brom in April, just his third in the League.

At the age of 35, his prowess as a goalscorer had all but left him and his place in the team now owed more to his ability to act as a fulcrum for Liverpool's play and provide leadership on the pitch but, with the most dramatic timing imaginable, he chose the occasion to remind the football world of the vision, control and finishing that had lit up his early years at Anfield. This was a moment to rank alongside his iconic winning goal in the 1978 European Cup Final, with the added personal significance of helping become the first man in history to play in - and manage - a team to the League Championship.

In the Liverpool end, Dalglish's goal merely added to the unbearable tension. This was the supporters' dream scenario. The man they man hero-worshipped potentially putting the seal on a dramatic triumph, snatched from near neighbours, arch rivals and reigning champions, Everton. However, the Blues clearly hadn't given up on their title, as news filtered through that they led Southampton 4-0 after just 34 minutes at Goodison. West Ham were also leading at West Brom so, with absolutely no margin for error, the Reds on the terraces faced an anxious wait before they could celebrate in earnest.

A curious air of apprehension therefore descended on the vast Liverpool support. There was no lack of encouragement for the team but, with the seconds seeming to tick by so slowly, most of the atmosphere they had earlier generated in a party mood on the open North Terrace was lost to the skies.

Liverpool continued to try and get forward in search of a vital second goal and the effervescent Johnston fired narrowly wide of Godden's goal after half an hour. Chelsea had created very little so far but they registered a first attempt on the Liverpool goal shortly before half-time when, from Nevin's free-kick, Spackman's header forced Grobbelaar into a routine save. Liverpool's five-man defence had been resolute throughout and the teams ended the opening half separated only by Dalglish's moment of brilliance. The Reds were just 45 minutes from regaining the Championship.

The second half began in identical fashion as the first, with Chelsea attempting to increase the pressure but still finding no way through the Liverpool rearguard. The Championship run-in had seen Liverpool play some of their most expansive football of the season. They had racked up a glut of goals which had carried them to a total of 89 - the highest tally in the top division for 18 years but, with the title within touching distance, the opening exchanges of the second period saw them retreat and defend their lead.

Liverpool began to rely on long balls towards Rush to relieve the pressure and, from one such clearance, a slip by Chelsea centre-back Doug Rougvie saw Rush bear down on goal only to be upended by John Bumstead. Unfortunately, the resultant free-kick went to waste and the Reds steeled themselves for another Chelsea surge.

In the 52nd minute Liverpudlian hearts missed a beat when Chelsea claimed a penalty after Speedie went down in the area under Lawrenson's challenge. Home supporters and players alike beseeched referee Lester Shapter to award a spot-kick but, to the relief of the away fans, he waved away their claims and Liverpool breathed again. With Speedie clearly looking to influence the referee, a penalty would have been a harsh decision, but the incident served to remind Liverpool of their fragile lead and, much more alarmingly, the consequences of an equalising goal that could cost them the title.

As time dragged on and the stakes grew higher, tempers began to flare and Rush was annoyed when the clumsy Rougvie flung an elbow in his face as they contested a stray ball, but the referee saw no intent from Rougvie, and the centre-half escaped punishment. Mr Shapter was forced to intervene when Craig Johnston and Chelsea's John Millar clashed in midfield soon after however, earning themselves a stern lecture from the match official. Then, Kevin McDonald got himself booked for a wild lunge that left a sprawling Spackman needing treatment.

It was a second caution in successive games for McDonald who, in the absence of McMahon, had assumed the role of midfield 'enforcer'. An occasional scapegoat for sections of the Anfield crowd, the unselfish Scot was quite prepared to do the dirty work in midfield and leave the more flamboyant aspects of the game - and the plaudits - to others.

The greatest threat to Liverpool was the growing influence of Nevin. The Reds' defence had to be on constant alert to track his bursts of pace and incisive passes around the box but in the main, the defensive trio of Hansen, Gillespie and Lawrenson had stopped him - so far - from opening the supply line to Dixon and Speedie. Although Chelsea were being kept at arms length the prospect of an equaliser, either from a mistake or a moment of inspiration such as Dalglish's, was a constant worry for the Liverpool fans behind Grobbelaar's goal.

With a quarter of an hour left, the player-manager wasted an opportunity to finally settle the match when he received the ball in space on the edge of the box. With the tiring Chelsea defenders slow to close, he had time to look up and pick his spot but lifted his shot a couple of feet over the bar to prolong the agony. As Chelsea faded Liverpool were finishing strongly and Dalglish again went close when finding space in the area only to delay crucially and see his effort blocked away for a corner.

As the Liverpool fans began to sense victory the decibel levels from the away end began to rise, and there were cheers rather than groans when Nicol's attempt from the resultant corner kick sailed high over the bar with just two minutes left to play. As the clock ticked down and supporters glanced at their watches every few seconds however, there was one final scare for Liverpool to endure.

The Reds had coped admirably with the aerial threat of Dixon but one last desperate punt from Chelsea saw the Blues' centre-forward rise above the Liverpool defence and nod the ball into the path of Speedie. To the relief of the frantic Liverpool fans, the combative Scot's control let him down - when a sure touch would have left him with just Grobbelaar to beat – and the ball rolled away for a harmless goal kick. Speedie cursed his error, but for the away fans who knew his chance was almost certainly the last action of the game – the clock had ticked past the 90 minute mark as the chance had gone begging - the party on the terrace behind the goal had started. "Hand it over, Hand it over, Hand it over, Ever-ton", bellowed the massed Liverpool ranks.

As Grobbelaar's clearance arrowed away from the Liverpool box towards Dalglish on the half-way line, Lester Shapter's shrill, final whistle sounded to proclaim Liverpool as Champions. Although most fans were acutely aware of the time on the clock, it still came as a shock to see the Liverpool players raise their arms in triumph. The majority among the supporters began to celebrate, almost in a state of suspended disbelief, as the most unlikely of Championship comebacks was complete.

On hearing the whistle Dalglish sprinted excitedly to salute those on the Liverpool bench, before turning back to shake hands briefly with some of the Chelsea players. It wasn't long before a huddle of Liverpool players gathered in the centre of the pitch to embrace, the release of tension palpable as the emotions of a rollercoaster nine-month campaign displayed themselves on their jubilant faces. Hansen broke away to raise a triumphant punch of his right arm towards the fans and then, after each player individually hugged Dalglish, the player-manager led his team towards their supporters to share the triumph.

There had been times when Dalglish's selections, formations and tactics had been questioned by the media - and a more conservative element among the Anfield crowd. However, those that had followed them on the road – and had done so in such large numbers – had universally lent their vocal backing to Dalglish and his side all season long. This was the perfect opportunity to thank the Reds' travelling army. As the Chelsea fans made their way home, some fighting with police as they left the Shed end, Dalglish's Liverpool players lingered behind briefly to enjoy the acclaim of their followers.

There was no choreographed trophy presentation, no MC, no ticker-tape, no interviews with steady-cams on the pitch. It was just 11 footballers and more than 10,000 ecstatic followers happy in the knowledge that Liverpool FC were English Champions – again.

With Reds fans still in a daze, the team left the pitch briefly. A row of Chelsea Pensioners, resplendent in red and black tunics, stood to wave their congratulations towards the huge contingent who had just seen their team create history. Kenny's Army applauded in return before joining in with Queen's 'We are the Champions' that was now being played by the Stamford Bridge equivalent of George Sephton.

The team soon returned to the pitch and were joined briefly by Molby and other key contributors Walsh and McMahon, to take the acclaim of the travelling Kop. Molby's influence in particular could not have been underestimated. His vision and poise had been instrumental in guiding the Reds to an amazing end of season run, yet the likeable Dane was, like his manager, humble to the extreme. "I think the most important thing about that run was that everybody was chipping in with goals," he said.

"I scored in each of our home games against Oxford, Coventry and Birmingham, as we won 6-0, 5-0 and 5-0; Ronnie Whelan notched a hat-trick against Coventry; Gary Gillespie, a defender, managed to get three against Birmingham; and Steve McMahon popped in two against Manchester City. And all the while, Rushie kept knocking them in – 10 in those last 12 games. It was a real team effort."

Whether it was the ingrained sense of normality however – it was Liverpool's fourth title in five seasons - or the impending quest for the Double and a sense of a job only half done, the communion between players and fans lasted only a few minutes before Dalglish's men sloped off to enjoy a more private celebration. The fans slowly emptied from the North Terrace, the title party underway as they went their separate ways to board Amberline coaches parked in the streets nearby, head back to Euston Station or, for those travelling under their own steam, melt into a warm evening in West London, enjoy a drink, a meal and catch a later train home.

Typically, as the players sat quietly in the dressing room and swigged from bottles of champagne, the ebullient Dalglish played down the quality of his winning goal. "Ah, it could easily have gone in the enclosure," he said. Trying to further decry the goal and his own part in the Championship victory, Dalglish, in his usual self-effacing manner claimed that, "Everyone else did more."

Perhaps the player-manager was alluding to Rush, with his 31 goals. Or the crucial influence of Jan Molby. Or the paternal guidance of Bob Paisley and backroom support of Ronnie Moran, Roy Evans and Tom Saunders. Such was Dalglish's humility that he probably considered the contribution of every player and boot room colleague greater than his own. For the more knowledgeable fan or pundit however, Dalglish had got key personnel decisions right all season.

He made the bold move to discard the experienced pair Phil Neal and Alan Kennedy when the defence was shipping goals; he converted Steve Nicol from a midfielder into an attacking full-back; and he gave young left-back Jim Beglin a break mid-season when the young, inexperienced seasonal debutant suffered an understandable dip in form.

He backed Bruce Grobbelaar throughout his alarming crisis of confidence - and was rewarded with 10 clean sheets in the last 11 games; he identified Jan Molby as the man to provide the subtlety Liverpool lacked since the departure of Graeme Souness; then protected him with the purchase of the robust Steve McMahon.

He ignored the terrace jibes aimed at Kevin McDonald when forced to cater for McMahon's absence - recognising the Scot's ability to nullify opponents; Craig Johnston, an inconsistent performer for four seasons under Bob Paisley and Joe Fagan, was taken under Dalglish's wing, providing pace, width and goals either from the right or as an auxiliary striker.

Crucially, Dalglish got the balance perfect when it came to selecting his ageing presence in the starting line-up. Most observers felt he underplayed himself in the first part of the season, but it is hard to argue with the statistics. Paul Walsh recorded 11 league goals in 20 starts until the ankle ligament injury that was the catalyst for Dalglish's return. We can only speculate as to the outcome if Walsh had remained fit, but there is no question that the player-manager's return on 8 March against QPR at Anfield signalled the start of the winning run that landed Liverpool the title. Dalglish ended with just three league goals from 21 league appearances but his influence, experience and the winning goal at Stamford Bridge had been crucially – and utterly - decisive.

There was one final twist to Liverpool's title clinching win at Stamford Bridge. On the trip back North, with the player's celebrating their victory and looking forward to the challenges still to come, the team coach broke down in the Midlands. In his autobiography Mark Lawrenson revealed that, "the replacement vehicle which picked us up outside Coventry happened to be Everton's official coach which was travelling South to London empty when It heard our SOS over the radio link. It still had Everton Football Club's sign on the windscreen when it pulled up to collect us. The irony of it was not lost on us; we had taken the championship from Everton, and now we had their bus too." Now for the Double!

Final Standings

	Played	Won	Drawn	Lost	Goal Diff	Points
Liverpool	42	26	10	6	52	88
Everton	42	26	8	8	46	86
West Ham	42	26	6	10	34	84
Man Utd	42	22	10	10	34	76
Sheff Wed	42	21	10	11	9	73
Chelsea	42	20	11	11	1	71
Arsenal	42	20	9	13	2	69
N.Forest	42	19	11	12	16	68
Luton	42	18	12	12	17	66
Tottenham	42	19	8	15	22	65
Newcastle	42	17	12	13	-5	63
Watford	42	16	11	15	7	59
QPR	42	15	7	20	-11	52
Southampton	42	12	8	20	-11	46
Man City	42	11	12	19	-14	45
Aston Villa	42	10	14	18	-16	44
Coventry	42	11	10	21	-23	43
Oxford	42	10	12	20	-18	42
Leicester	42	10	12	20	-22	42
Ipswich	42	11	8	23	-23	41
Birmingham	42	8	5	29	-43	29
WBA	42	4	12	26	-54	24

This was a sixth League Championship for Dalglish and Alan Hansen.

It was the fourth time that medals had ended up in the pockets of Rush, Whelan, Grobbelaar, Lawrenson, Johnston and Sammy Lee.

It was a second title triumph for Steve Nicol.

First time winners were Beglin, McMahon, Walsh, McDonald, Gillespie and Molby.

The departed Phil Neal also qualified for an eighth League winners medal - a Liverpool record to this day.

On the same day Everton won their penultimate fixture 6-1 at home to Southampton. They still had a game left however, and secured the runners-up spot with a 3-1 won over West Ham United on Monday 5 May.

Tuesday 6 May
Screen Sport Super Cup, semi-final second leg
Liverpool v Norwich City

"After we won the title at Chelsea, on the coach home, the best part was when we drove along Queens Drive after arriving back; loads had climbed onto the roof and the whole coach was bouncing and singing:

'The blue nosed b*******s aren't the champions anymore,
They went to Nottingham Forest, and they only got a draw,
And then they went to Oxford and they couldn't even score
Now the blues nosed b******s aren't the champions anymore.'"

Wilko, Liverpool fan, Skelmersdale.

Just three days after being crowned Champions, Liverpudlian thoughts of the Double were temporarily put on hold for 90 minutes when the Reds hosted Norwich City in a re-arranged Screen Sport Super Cup semi-final second leg. Having drawn the first leg at Carrow Road back in February, a harsh winter and Liverpool's fixture commitments on all fronts – making the FA Cup Final ensured that the Reds had played all the scheduled games they could apart from one – the League Cup Final - had delayed the return leg until after the completion of Liverpool's league programme.

The ill-fated competition had drawn modest attendances at best. In the absence of European football following the post-Heysel ban it had also provided scant financial compensation for competing clubs. The Football League initially flirted with the idea of a one-off Wembley final so as to add lustre to a tournament that became more of an inconvenience the longer the season wore on. When it became apparent that an all-Merseyside Screen Sport final would be dwarfed in importance and kudos by a potential FA Cup Final between the same clubs, they thought better of the idea and decided that the final of the lesser competition would be played over two-legs instead - and deferred until the start of the 1986/87 campaign.

In truth however, the SSSC had never appealed to most fans – who knew a white elephant when they saw it. With no day out at Wembley to look forward to either, they stayed away in their droves. Liverpool's two home games so far - against Southampton and Spurs - had attracted just 16,000 and 14,000 paying spectators respectively.

With the potential for players to pick up an injury that could rule them out at Wembley, scheduling the game just four days before the FA Cup Final wasn't ideal but no matter how trivial people viewed the competition, the potential income of a two-legged match against Everton - who had already beaten Spurs to reach the final - could not be ignored. As such, Dalglish gave no real thought to using reserve team or youth team players and, with a squad of 16 first-team players, it was anticipated that the majority of Liverpool's star names would take to the field just a few days before the biggest game of the season. When Dalglish chose to omit himself, Alan Hansen, Ian Rush and Jan Molby from this game however, it was clear that they would all appear at Wembley. A last chance to impress was awarded to Paul Walsh, Steve McMahon and Sammy Lee.

While the match had its potential pitfalls it also offered the chance for the Reds' fans to salute the newly crowned League Champions. Supporters were rewarded with reduced admission of £2.00 for the Kop and £4.00 for a stand seat. The reduced pricing seemed to do the trick and, despite driving rain, a crowd of 26,696 - crammed mainly into the Kop - turned up to view the trophy presentations and see the Reds off to Wembley in style.

When the Reds' full first-team squad and backroom staff emerged and made their way to the centre-circle they were greeted to a crescendo of cheers and chants while they waved to friends and family in the Main Stand. The Kop had been in buoyant mood before kick-off, with frequent chants of, "Bring on the Champions." President of The Football League Jack Dunnett accompanied the squad onto the pitch. In his hands he carried the 22-inch high gold trophy which was provided by league sponsors Canon; since its inception it was the third season running the trophy had ended up on Merseyside

The presentation was made not to captain Alan Hansen, but to Liverpool's player-manager who, after a brief but warm handshake from Chairman John Smith - the man who had entrusted the leadership of the Club to Dalglish once he knew Joe Fagan wanted to step down - raised the trophy above his head to a great roar from the crowd. With his trademark beaming smile, Dalglish then passed the trophy down the line for each of his fellow players to receive their own personal salute from the Kop.

Dalglish handed the sponsors' uninspiring bauble first to skipper Alan Hansen and then to each player, a throaty roar welcoming each one; Bruce Grobbelaar, Craig Johnston, Steve Nicol, Steve McMahon, Paul Walsh, Mark Lawrenson, Gary Gillespie, Jim Beglin, Ronnie Whelan, Sammy Lee, Ian Rush, Kevin McDonald, Jan Molby, and John Wark – who had hobbled onto the pitch on crutches. Not forgetting the crucial supporting role played by his staff, the fans also reserved a cheer for Roy Evans and Ronnie Moran as Dalglish ensured they too took their momentary turn in the spotlight.

The biggest cheer of the night however, was reserved for a soberly dressed older man who had shuffled, almost unnoticed, through the gloom of the night and attached himself, reluctantly to the end of the line. When the presentation ended with the League trophy in the hands of former manager Bob Paisley, there was an almighty roar from the crowd - with more than the odd tear wiped from many a reminiscent Kopites' eye. In his rookie season as manager, Paisley's knowledge, unobtrusive advice and sympathetic ear had been invaluable to Dalglish. Recalling the difficulties he had experienced a decade earlier - caused by Bill Shankly's continued presence at Melwood after his retirement - Paisley knew his consultancy had to be kept in the background if the transition to Dalglish assuming total control was to be a smooth one.

If anything, Paisley had been too careful not to interfere and, as the season wore on, Dalglish relied on his advice less frequently. However, Dalglish had been at pains to include his former manager in these celebrations and, he hoped, the ones to come at the weekend. The FA Cup had been the one trophy to elude Paisley and it would be fitting if he could be around to lay the Wembley ghosts that haunted his playing and managerial career. After scoring in the semi-final in 1950, Paisley was overlooked for a place in the team that lost in the final to Arsenal. Twenty-seven years later Tommy Docherty's Manchester United denied him an unprecedented League, European Cup and FA Cup treble as a manager - with a freakish winning goal by Lou Macari.

Once the presentation was complete and the Canon League trophy ferried upstairs to join countless others in the Reds' large trophy room in the Main Stand, the Super Cup semi-final - amid understandable anti-climax - kicked-off.

Norwich seized the opportunity to catch Liverpool cold in the second minute when they opened the scoring at the Kop end through midfielder Garry Brooke. Instead of rallying behind the newly-crowned Champions, the Kop spontaneously decided to applaud Norwich's opener and, in a display of typical, ironic triumphalism, playfully sided with the visitors throughout the first-half.

Shows of support for the visitors were usually reserved for opponents on the end of an Anfield hiding, but the chanting for Norwich was an example of the Kop's unpredictable nature and an expression of disinterest in the match itself. Whether mocking the police, the opposition or - on rare occasions - the home side, the Anfield crowd were masters of making their own entertainment, but their brief flirtation with the visiting East Anglians would revert to adulation for the home side soon after the break.

For many, their cheerful, non-conformist response to the action was preferable to watching in silence, especially as Liverpool's performance lacked its usual commitment and intensity but it was understandable to see players pull out or jump over tackles - which might otherwise rule them out of a potentially career-defining match in four days time.

When Liverpool emerged for the second half - trailing 2-1 on aggregate - they received a great welcome and, with the crowd now showing their true colours and the Reds attacking the Kop end, normal service was resumed in the 54th minute. After Norwich failed to clear a trademark Johnston cross into the box from the right hand side, Kevin McDonald - seldom recognised for his surges deep into opposition territory - forced a scrambled equalizer past Chris Woods at the third attempt.

While Liverpool had understandably played with something in reserve, it was hard not to notice Johnston's running and pacy dribbling down the right. The bubbly Australian had been transformed by Dalglish from an inconsistent, almost unthinking performer - not fully trusted by Bob Paisley or Joe Fagan - into Liverpool's wildcard. His searing pace had finally been harnessed in a predominately right-midfield position, allowing him to race past defenders so as to provide plenty of ammunition for his fellow attackers.

Such was the player-manager's faith in him that Dalglish had selected Johnston in 41 out of 42 League games, becoming the first manager to fully embrace the Australian's sometimes unpredictable use of the ball and meandering runs. If his teammates weren't always sure what was going to happen next, it was also true that neither did the opposition, and his work rate, devastating pace, crossing ability and eye for a goal, more than compensated for some of his more idiosyncratic play.

In the 64th minute Whelan was replaced by Molby, who had shaken off the illness that had seen him miss the title clincher at Stamford Bridge. Immediately the tempo of the game increased and it was no surprise when the Reds settled the match with two goals in quick succession with just over a quarter of an hour left.

For anyone familiar with Liverpool's recent play both goals were as predictable as they were straightforward. On 75 minutes a typically speedy burst from Johnston saw him upended in the area by Steve Bruce. Molby nonchalantly tucked away his 21st goal of the season from the penalty spot. A minute later Liverpool grabbed a third courtesy of the ubiquitous Johnston. Paul Walsh - who had shown some skillful touches without suggesting he was fit enough to challenge for a place on the Wembley bench - sent McDonald racing clear on the left and the midfielder's inch-perfect cross was met by the head of the onrushing Johnston for the goal of the night. A 3-1 victory meant a 4-2 aggregate triumph and a place in the following season's two-legged final against Everton.

The Kop was in its element as fans celebrated the final whistle with their passage to yet another cup final secured, particularly as the manner of victory boded well for the 'proper' cup final to come.As was traditional at the time the noisy Kopites invited each section of the ground to join the party, beginning with a chorus of, "Main stand, Main stand, give us a song, Main stand give us a song," before moving on to single out the patrons of the Kemlyn and Anfield Road. They even included the small band of away supporters.

The jubilant atmosphere continued during a triumphant lap of honour that ended with the players lingering on the pitch to take the acclaim of the supporters in front of the Kop. Amid chants of, "Champions, Champions," and, "We're on the march with Kenny's Army," the fans lauded the player-manager revealing a deeper affection for Dalglish than they had ever shown before.

The well-drilled, synchronized clapping and simple chant of, "Dalglish," temporarily gave way to a more personal tribute as the Kop sang, "We Love you Kenny, we do, we love you Kenny we do, we love you Kenny we do, oh Kenny we love you." It was a spontaneous outburst of thanks and appreciation that recognised not just his brilliance in managing his team to the title, but the genius required to do so while still a player. And all accomplished in the wake of the dark days faced by Liverpool – both the city and the club - following Heysel. If Dalglish was already a legend to fans as a player, he was fast becoming the embodiment of the club as a manager.

While newspaper reporters and TV interviewers found him unresponsive and guarded, the supporters were able to identify with his relationship with the players and his obvious love for their club, symbolised by the beaming Dalglish smile which accompanied every Liverpool goal. If he remained misunderstood by the national media, the Liverpool fans and local hacks knew exactly where he was coming from.

Before leaving the pitch Dalglish, faced by BBC TV reporter Tony Gubba, was quizzed about the team's prospects of completing the Double. With the chants of the Kop still booming out behind him, Dalglish, in supremely confident fashion replied, "Well, we're the only team in with a chance of doing it aren't we?" Gubba responded by stating that Liverpool teams had been to Wembley before and failed to clinch the Double. "Not this season we haven't," answered Dalglish.

In the pressroom afterwards, a more relaxed player-manager was keen to convey his appreciation of the reception afforded to him and the team after the match. "The fans were tremendous," he said. "If the Kop had not been so packed I would have been up there with them. They have been great to me ever since I came here."

"There's a few times I have nearly jumped over the railings to join them after I have scored," he added. " But I have not quite made it yet. The lads were proud to have won the title and I think the fans were proud to have come along here tonight." Once again, whether on the field or in the dressing room, in front of the TV cameras or in the presence of the scribes and their notebooks, Dalglish's words hit the perfect note with the players and fans alike. Now? All roads led to Wembley.

Liverpool eventually won the Screen Sport Super Cup with a 7-2 aggregate victory over Everton, played the following season. The first leg at Anfield on 16 September 1986 was played in front of 20,660, Liverpool winning 3-1. Liverpool's goals were scored by Rush (2) and McMahon.

The second leg at Goodison Park, watched by 26,068, took place on 30 September. Liverpool won 4-1. On the mark for the Reds were Rush – with a hat-trick - and Nicol.

Saturday 10 May
Everton v Liverpool
FA Cup Final, Wembley

"No game before or after ever gave me the same feeling of unbridled ecstasy. Everything about it was sheer perfection, from the greatest Liverpool side I ever played for, and possibly the greatest British side in history."

Ian Rush, reflects on his day at Wembley, May 1986

Once Liverpool's Super Cup engagement and Everton's 3-1 Monday night victory over West Ham - that confirmed the Blues as League runners-up - were out of the way, the build-up to the FA Cup Final could begin in earnest. Featuring the Reds' and Blues' top scorers Ian Rush and Gary Lineker, the cover of the BBC's Radio Times illustrated just how much the first all-Merseyside FA Cup Final had seeped into the national consciousness.

To football journalist's and fans alike, Liverpool and Everton were the dominant clubs of the era; the powerful Liverpool dynasty of the 1970's and early-80's challenged by their upstart neighbours from across Stanley Park who, in just two seasons, had already become a far more credible force than the occasional, ephemeral threat posed to Liverpool's supremacy by Manchester United.

On Merseyside the sense of occasion was huge and both clubs profited hugely from souvenir merchandise; from commemorative mugs, key-rings, cheap posters, hats, badges, flags and scarves. If the Milk Cup Final and Charity Shield of 1984 had already seen the clubs appear together on the same Wembley stage, this latest installment was billed as, "the derby to end all derbies."

With the FA Cup arguably the most prestigious trophy in the game at the time - and the small matter of the 'Double' for Liverpool at stake, the history books beckoned for the Red half of the city. For Everton, to deny their rivals the 'Double' - which had been achieved only twice before in the 20th century - would be ample compensation for relinquishing the League title. A second FA Cup in three seasons would also cement the Blues' position as chief pretenders to Liverpool's domestic crown.

If the official numbers of ticket holders from each club totalled just 50,000, it was estimated that more than twice that number would travel from Merseyside in the hope of obtaining a ticket on the black market - or access to the stadium by other means. The exodus began as early as Thursday morning, and by Friday afternoon as many as 40,000 Scousers on the look-out for tickets, sightseeing and drinking, had flooded the capital.

As usual the popular haunts of Covent Garden and Trafalgar Square were thronged with supporters of both teams mixing happily together the day before the game. Elsewhere, the highlight of the Friday afternoon was perhaps the appearance of an enormous red Soviet flag draped over the public gallery in the Houses of Parliament. In the midst of a Conservative administration that intentionally marginalised Liverpool and its people, the sight of a banner featuring the hammer and sickle being unfurled during a Commons debate was a pertinent, and purposeful, statement of Merseyside political sentiment. News of the act spread like wildfire with those culpable being talked of – for a few hours at least – as heroes to rank alongside the players both sets of fans had come to see the following day.

There was nothing contrived about the peaceful revelry displayed between Red and Blue in London, nor any great effort on either part to create a unique atmosphere; one out of place with the usual hostility normally displayed between supporters of different clubs. In reality it was just groups of Liverpool lads enjoying a few days away from the harsh realities of life on Merseyside and, until 3pm on Saturday afternoon, their friendships were to the fore and their football passions and persuasions incidental.

In the days leading up to the game Dalglish and Howard Kendall had concerns of their own to contend with, not least building nerves and niggling injuries. Most notable for Everton was the worry that that goal-scoring centre-half Derek Mountfield would miss Wembley with a recurrence of the cartilage trouble that had seen him undergo a knee operation earlier in the season. Kendall commented, "We will leave it as late as we can [before naming Mountfield]. To say it's a set-back is an understatement. We left him out against West Ham on Monday, anticipating he would be OK by the end of the week."

Liverpool's preparations were also rocked by the news that captain Alan Hansen - one of the finest footballing centre-halves the English game has seen - had been axed from the Scotland squad for the Mexico World Cup. Caretaker manager Alex Ferguson had preferred his old Aberdeen pairing of Willie Miller and Alex McLeish in central defence in recent games, but it was still a shock, even for Evertonians – who knew a good player when they saw one - to see Hansen axed from the party altogether.

That Dalglish's recent form saw him included in the Scottish squad as one of five strikers – together with Graeme Sharp - made Hansen's omission even more awkward. Just 48 hours before the biggest game of the season it was a stern test of Dalglish's man-management skills to be able to console his skipper and close friend in the wake of such huge personal disappointment.

The Merseyside clubs' domination of the race for the top domestic prizes was again signalled two days before the Cup Final when Dalglish was named the Bells' Whiskey Manager of the Year, an honour habitually awarded to the boss of the League Champions. On the same afternoon the Football Writers' Association named Gary Lineker Footballer of the Year, an award to sit alongside his Players' Player of the Year trophy.

Lineker took time off from the Blues' preparations to receive the honour from England's World Cup-winning captain Bobby Moore at a ceremony in London. With 39 goals to his name, it was hard to argue with Lineker's double award but the irony wasn't lost on Dalglish who saw his own award as a reflection of the all-round team contribution that had made his players League Champions.

If Liverpool could complete the 'Double', the efforts of stand-out performers such as Lawrenson, Johnston, Rush, Molby *et al* would be compensated by the most coveted personal honours in the game – League and Cup winners' medals. Away from the hustle and bustle of London - where up to 40,000 fans of the two clubs enjoyed a drunken, sometimes more than boisterous Friday night - Liverpool's players enjoyed an early night at their pre-cup final base at the Hilton Hotel near Watford.

Pubs in the Capital were thronged with excited supporters; the locals reduced to curious bystanders as Red and Blue sang themselves hoarse in attempting to outdo and out-perform each other long into the night. Inevitably, some fell foul of the Metropolitan Police and by Saturday morning there had been 67 arrests for a variety of offences. Groups of fans ran amok in Kentish Town and the West End, with no apparent distinction between Red or Blue. One time-served Reds follower recalls a,

"big mob of LFC in some boozer by Euston, about 5.00pm, including all the usual suspects. One of the lads was trying to chisel the back off a fruit machine with a heavy ashtray. He's got everyone singing to drown out the noise of him beavering away, but somehow the staff got on to him.

"Next thing, the manager comes over with a cosh in one hand and a Rottweiler on a lead in the other - all dramatic like. He smashes a load of glasses with the cosh, starts shouting, and everyone's a bit stunned. Out of nowhere some young lad hops up behind him and just stripes the Rottweiler right down its back with a Stanley knife. Cue a sharp exit."

Suffice to say, Crufts wasn't on a list of tourist attractions for this gang.

With match tickets at a premium many supporters spent the day before the game hoping to pick up an unlikely spare. When this failed they braced themselves for the anger and frustration of the perennial rip-off by London touts. As far back as the 1960s, fans of both Merseyside clubs had taken exception to such profiteering and ganged up on touts near the stadium to relieve them of tickets which they believed to be rightfully theirs. Although most 'spivs' would make a killing at this Final many became fearful of their safety once the scouse invasion was in full swing.

At a dinner attended by a number of known touts at the Regent Palace Hotel in Piccadilly Circus on the eve of the game, one tout told reporters, "I have only a handful of tickets left, but there's no way I'm going to Wembley with all those Scousers outside." As a result - and anxious to shift the remaining tickets before the day of the Final - touts' prices tumbled, with a £6 ground ticket fetching £30 on the black-market whereas previously they had been trading for up to £150.

As the television companies prepared to do battle for viewers, a row that encapsulated the beguilingly misunderstood day-to-day life of those who lived in Liverpool, broke out when actor and Reds fan Ricky Tomlinson claimed he had been excluded from a group of soap stars who had been invited to appear on London Weekend TVs pre-match build-up show.

The programme - featuring the cast of Mersey TV's Brookside - was due to be hosted by exiled Scouser and comedian, Jimmy Tarbuck. Tomlinson said, "Tarbuck has not forgiven me for remarks I made about professional Scousers who make a living out of the city but can't wait to get away from the place. It is also a well-known fact that Tarbuck appears on Maggie Thatcher's political platforms and I am a member of the Labour Party. He's operating a Jimmy Tarbuck blacklist and it is not on."

While it might have been surprising to see a spat between two relatively high-profile local celebrities make it onto the front pages of the papers on the eve of such a huge occasion for the City, Tomlinson's words highlighted the tension caused by increasing social problems on Merseyside compared with the greater opportunities available down South. Although the City's reputation could have done without another public slanging match so readily picked up by the national media, very few natives of Liverpool attending the final would have found much wrong with Tomlinson's statement.

When the big day dawned it was estimated that another 80,000 fans left Liverpool to join those who were already in London. 400 coaches, 19 football special trains, and well over a thousand cars and mini-buses - the vast majority carrying an equal mix of Liverpool and Everton supporters – slowly made their way South. The huge exodus was a chance not just to see their side in the Cup final, but also an opportunity to show a city's solidarity and sense of purpose in the face of an increasingly hostile national media.

By mid-morning London belonged to Merseyside. Long before the escalating bitterness which has soured the most recent clashes between the clubs, there was a mutual respect between supporters of both clubs. Since the heady days of 1986 Everton and Liverpool have gradually taken on different identities – Everton, the parochial, self-styled, "Peoples Club," while Liverpool have retained a global appeal and still cling to their superiority based on the successes of bygone eras.

In May 1986 however, the Reds' dominance of the 1970s and early 1980s was being challenged by their neighbours and Liverpudlians, perhaps jaded by relentless and predictable success, relished the new found competition. Despite Everton's Championship win a year earlier, the Reds had managed to regain their crown and their 16th title had been celebrated with a gusto not seen for a decade. For their part Evertonians were flushed with pride at seeing their team competing for honours after 14 years in the wilderness. They had seen the Blues become Champions, enjoy success in Europe in the Cup Winners' Cup, and here, reach their third consecutive FA Cup Final. The rivalry was fierce, underpinned by football matters alone, and debated long and hard by mates who went to the same schools and drank in the same pubs but who happened to support different teams.

The atmosphere around the old - and increasingly decaying - national stadium grew with each passing hour and by midday Wembley Way swarmed with thousands of people making their way towards the stadium. It was estimated that up to 30,000 had travelled without tickets in the hope of gaining entry - legal or not. Those desperate enough to locate a tout took a financial hit and paid over the odds.

Others laid claim to the significant number of forged tickets in circulation which, although they were watery in colour, still bore a passing similarity to the real thing. In the inevitable chaos at the turnstiles they at least offered a decent chance of admission. Genuine ticket holders relentlessly checked their pockets so often during the afternoon that they resembled sufferers of OCD and when it came to the point of entry at the imposing Wembley gates, tickets were held in fists clenched so tight that knuckles turned white and almost pierced the skin.

For the truly intrepid the arched, open window features in the flaking stadium masonry offered a more challenging and dangerous route of admission. Hundreds queued to climb onto a concrete ledge, reaching out to the arms of their allies inside the stadium. Risking life and limb, they jumped and swung, often one-handed, cheating the 30ft drop beneath them and were hauled inside by their cohorts to secure the most inventive and athletic passage to Wembley imaginable.

Those who remained on Merseyside tried to drink in the atmosphere through their TV screens. With the new TV deal in place, 'armchair supporters' were growing accustomed to the concept of live televised games even if the pre-match coverage amounted to no more than a ten minute run through of the two teams and perhaps a focus on a couple of key players. The FA Cup Final however was a different matter; the climax and showpiece game of the season with extensive television coverage to match.

The BBC's Cup Final Grandstand had started traditionally early - at 12 noon - for three hours of related features, interrupted oddly - but in true BBC fashion - by the Saturday afternoon racing from Newbury. The horse racing aside, there was a plethora of build-up material focusing on the week just gone; features on the players and fans on Merseyside, a look back on the 'Road to Wembley' for both finalists, and the traditional visit to the team hotels as they prepared to leave for the stadium.

Strangely however, there was a comedy sketch with flavour of the month comedians Mel Smith and Griff Rhys Jones – neither with any apparent connection to Merseyside or the competing teams - and an excruciatingly poorly-judged one-man show from Till Death Us Do Part character Alf Garnett. Played by actor Warren Mitchell, the character reinforced many anti-scouse stereotypes, particularly when he referred in an accentuated 'cockney' accent to, "drunken Scousers getting us banned out of Europe." With so much anti-Liverpool sentiment already being pedalled by an unsympathetic media, these were ill-chosen words for the sake of a bit of cheap comedy.

As the build-up to kick-off reached its climax, anchorman Desmond Lynam introduced the traditional Cup Final panel of analysts whose job it was to provide an expert view of the game. Former Liverpool skipper and TV personality Emlyn Hughes was a guest, as was recently departed Everton forward Andy Gray, making his first appearance as a pundit. Making up the trio with a supposedly neutral view was Londoner Terry Venables, whose Barcelona team - after a mind-numbingly dull goalless draw in Seville - had suffered midweek European Cup Final humiliation when they lost to unfancied Romanians Steaua Bucharest on penalties.

Such was the poor quality of the final - in which Barcelona failed even to score a single penalty in the shoot-out – that afterwards Juventus Director of Sport Francesco Morini called for the immediate reinstatement of English clubs, including Liverpool, to UEFA competition. Everton would have been the competing English team in the 1985/86 European Cup competition and, while there was no guarantee they would have reached the final, the majority of their supporters felt only mildly aggrieved that the ban after Heysel had denied them the opportunity to pit their wits against the likes of Juve, Barca and ultimately Steaua Bucharest.

The excitement of the season at home and the thrilling battle for honours with Liverpool was enough to reduce their exile from Europe - for a while at least - to a mere afterthought. Only when Everton's decline - in the years that followed their halcyon days of 1984-87 - accentuated the perceived sense of injustice, did Heysel, the European ban and Liverpool FC in general became the 'reason' behind Everton's inability to compete.

Evertonians were quick to dismiss the club's shoddy administration and shocking management in the 1990's as the real reasons for their failure to jump on the Champions League gravy train. Liverpool themselves fell into relative decline in the 1990's but recovered sufficiently to win the Champions League in 2005 - to the dismay of those Evertonians who clung to Liverpool's misfortunes to mask the failings of their own club.

The feud rages to this day with very few Reds and Blues able to conduct a sensible debate on the matter. To poke fun at Evertonians' obsession with the impact of the European ban on their club, Kopites at the Anfield Derby in February 2010 unfurled a red and white banner that read, "Steaua Bucuresti, European Champions 1986." Suffice to say, relations between Liverpool and Everton supporters were vastly better on Saturday 10 May 1986 than they are today.

By the time the BBC revealed the teams for the 1986 FA Cup Final to the nation at 2.30pm Wembley was approaching capacity. Indeed, it almost certainly housed more than the official capacity of 98,000, but thousands of genuine ticket-holders and 'bunkers' alike remained outside. Unofficial sources later claimed that as many as 120,000 watched the match from inside the ground.

When the teams were announced, Gary Gillespie was missing for Liverpool. The gangly Scottish centre-half would have played but fell foul of a stomach bug just 24 hours before the game and was too weak to participate. Mark Lawrenson, who ill conceivably might have missed out, was restored alongside Alan Hansen at the back. Jan Molby had recovered from the virus that kept him out at Chelsea and returned to midfield alongside Kevin MacDonald, which meant Steve McMahon, after a fine debut season for the Reds, had to be satisfied with the substitute's shirt against his old club. For Everton, Derek Mountfield passed a late fitness test on his troublesome knee and the Blues lined up as expected.

Everton: Mimms, Stevens, Van Den Hauwe, Ratcliffe, Mountfield, Reid, Steven, Lineker, Sharp, Bracewell, Sheedy. Sub: Heath

Liverpool: Grobbelaar, Lawrenson, Beglin, Nicol, Whelan, Hansen, Dalglish, Johnston, Rush, Molby, MacDonald. Sub: McMahon

As the players assembled in the tunnel, a chant of, "Merseyside, Merseyside, Merseyside," started at that end – where most of the Everton fans were stationed. It soon gathered pace and was taken up by the Liverpool fans at the opposite end so that it echoed round Wembley. In a rare display of camaraderie between rival fans, "Are you watching, Manchester?" followed.

Although some tickets had been swapped so that friends and family could watch the game together, the two ends of the stadium were distinctly red at the far end of the stadium and blue at the tunnel end. It was noticeable however, that an enclave of Liverpool flags was fluttering in the breeze in the Lower Standing Enclosure in the Everton end.

At a glance it seemed that the majority of neutral tickets had found their way into Liverpudlian hands, probably at vastly inflated prices and making a nonsense of the governing body's policy of awarding tickets to other clubs and tenuous county associations. If there were any proper neutrals at all in the stadium, they were few and far between.

Inhabited by supporters accustomed to European finals, the Liverpool end wore a continental look with a sprinkling of AS Roma and, poignantly, Juventus flags fluttering among the traditional cup final scarves and home made banners. Summing up the feelings of the massed ranks of the travelling Kop, one slogan simply read, "Kenny's from Heaven," while another gloated, "City of Manchester, Trophy-free Zone," alluding to the enduring underachievement of the Reds' other rivals at the end of the East Lancs. Road.

By the time Kenny Dalglish and Howard Kendall led their teams into an electric Wembley atmosphere the early morning showers had given way to traditional cup final sunshine. The Liverpool team, in grey tracksuit tops with a red and white shoulder stripe and red sleeves, made their way alongside Everton - already stripped to their blue and white shirts - to the centre circle where they were introduced to FA Chairman Bert Millichip and the Royal representative, The Duchess of Kent. The sight of the youthful player-manager Dalglish in his tracksuit and kit made the balding Kendall, wearing a black double-breasted suit, look much older than his 39 years.

At the head of the Liverpool line, Dalglish was the first port of call for the Duchess. Dressed in a neutral green cloak she appeared to dwell for a longer than usual conversation with the Reds' player-manager before being introduced to the rest of the team by captain Alan Hansen. Widely believed to be a Liverpool supporter she appeared to enjoy her brief chats with the players, and had a special word of encouragement for Bruce Grobbelaar who was sporting a distinctive red cap.

As the players broke away from the preliminaries to run towards their own supporters and begin the warm-up there was a vast roar from fans at both ends of the stadium, abating only slightly as they strained to hear the stadium announcer read out the teams. Liverpool's line-up consisted of a Zimbabwean, four Scots, three Irishman, a Welshman and a Dane with sub McMahon the only English qualified player. More significantly, no player in the Reds' line-up had any experience of an FA Cup Final. They faced an Everton side that had featured in the two previous finals.

If there were any concerns at such a lack of Cup Final experience the Reds' fans did their best to dispel them by reminding their heroes they were the new, "Champions, Champions, Champions," before launching into a spontaneous, "You'll Never Walk Alone," which turned the Upper and Lower Standing Enclosure's at the Liverpool end into a vivid sea of red, white and yellow.

As the clock ticked towards three o'clock, Referee Alan Robinson from Waterlooville, Hampshire invited captains Alan Hansen and Kevin Ratcliffe to the middle for the toss. Hansen won the first honours of the day and opted to attack the tunnel end in the first half. Everton's midfield duo Peter Reid and Paul Bracewell kicked off and, to a guttural roar from the expectant crowd, the first ever all-Merseyside FA Cup Final was underway.

The opening minutes were scrappy as both sides struggled to find their feet on a heavier than usual Wembley pitch that was well worn both in the centre-circle and down Liverpool's right flank. It seemed that the groundsman had also left the grass slightly longer than normal in order to give the pitch a cosmetic appearance of lushness. After the frenzied noise in the build-up to kick-off there followed a slight lull in the atmosphere as both sets of supporters contemplated the importance of what was at stake.

After four minutes the first incident of note saw Molby's advance towards the right wing ended by Bracewell's crude challenge from behind. From the resulting free kick, Johnston fed Steve Nicol overlapping on the right but his cross was headed wide by Rush under a challenge from Mountfield. Three minutes later Liverpool threatened again when Nicol's throw was headed back to him by Dalglish and the full-back, spotting a surge by MacDonald, chipped a diagonal ball goalwards. Continuing his run, MacDonald only just failed to connect with the ball ran before it ran through to Everton goalkeeper Bobby Mimms who gathered at full stretch.

After Bracewell's early challenge on Molby, Whelan exacted revenge in kind with a savage trip on Reid that left the Blues' midfielder cursing as he picked himself up from the turf. Nothing came of the free-kick as Hansen rose to head clear from Stevens' high ball.

After 13 minutes Liverpool responded when Johnston forced Van Den Hauwe to concede a corner on the right. Johnston's flag kick flattened Lineker and rebounded for a throw-in from which Nicol crossed into the box. Beglin, arriving late, headed spectacularly wide. The first quarter of an hour had been remarkably dull with neither side creating a clear chance. The most notable moment so far was the appearance of a Liverpool fan who appeared to have claimed the best seat in the house – on the Wembley roof.

On the pitch, nerves were clearly playing their part along with an unhelpful surface and the rhythm of the match was interrupted by a series of cynical tackles, the latest of which grounded Dalglish in the 17th minute. Lawrenson, trying to play constructively out of defence, aimed a pass towards his manager just inside his own half. With his back to goal, Dalglish controlled and turned in an instant - only to be clattered hard from behind by Mountfield. Referee Robinson finally deemed the tackle worthy of a first ticking-off of the afternoon, but Dalglish was soon back on his feet after treatment from Roy Evans' magic sponge and a soothing chorus of, "I'd walk a million miles for one of your goals, Oh Kenny," from the relieved Liverpool fans.

Everton rarely come away from a derby match without a major gripe against the referee and the biggest derby in history was to be no different. On 20 minutes Kevin Sheedy lobbed a hopeful ball over the top that forced Grobbelaar to advance outside his area to clear from the predatory Lineker. The keeper's clearance landed at the feet of Trevor Steven 40-yards from goal who played the ball out wide to full-back Gary Stevens. Stevens turned inside and delivered a perfect cross, bending away from Grobbelaar towards Graeme Sharp. Nicol spotted the danger at the far post and cleverly muscled Sharp away from the inviting cross. Sharp fell theatrically to the floor but was up in an instant to chase after the referee claiming he had been fouled.

Recovering quickly from the penalty scare the Reds then created their best chance of the game so far. Rush won the ball inside the Everton half and gave way to Dalglish who skipped through Reid's tackle and supplied Craig Johnston near the corner flag. The Australian's floated cross found Rush, who had continued his run, unmarked just eight yards from goal but the Welshman was unable to control his header and the ball sailed high over the bar.

Liverpool had generally enjoyed the better of the first half but it was Everton who opened the scoring with the clock ticking towards the half-hour mark. Ironically the goal stemmed from an error from the hitherto talismanic Dalglish.

Deep in Everton territory the player-manager failed to control Molby's short pass to his feet and the loose ball fell to Reid. The Huyton-born midfielder looked up and floated a long, accurate pass over the Liverpool defence towards Lineker. The Footballer of the Year was able to outpace Hansen, and produce a weak left-foot shot which Grobbelaar was unable to hold. Lineker pounced on the rebound to slot home right-footed via the goalkeeper's despairing attempt to save at the second attempt. The ecstatic Reid, a boyhood Liverpudlian who had twice watched the Reds in FA Cup finals from the terraces, sprinted upfield to mob the scorer.

As the game restarted Evertonians rang out their familiar, though somewhat monotone chant of, "Oh, Gary, Gary, Gary, Gary, Gary, Gary, Lineker." It could be heard clearly from the more sombre end of Wembley. Anxious Liverpudlians steeled themselves against the taunts of, "One Nil, One Nil," and a boastful, "We shall not be moved." Many took a deep breath, looked at each other quizzically and shook their heads as a suddenly tired looking Liverpool sought to reach half-time without falling further behind.

The Reds managed to quell Everton's euphoria before the break but only managed a few flurries on the edge of the box in search of an equaliser. As if to underline their frustration Dalglish was spoken to by the referee when he responded to ruining a move with a misplaced pass, by blasting the dead-ball deliberately at a cowering Sheedy.

Half-time: Everton 1 v 0 Liverpool

If Dalglish's frustrations were there for all to see on the field he now had another job to do in front of a group of players who lay slumped and tired on benches in the Wembley dressing room. While fans on the terraces sat on the steep Wembley steps, some with their flags covering their heads in premature despair, Dalglish quietly exhorted one last effort from his side. Despite being one goal down, he reminded them that they were just 45 minutes away from a good season becoming one which would go down in Liverpool – and football - history.

In his autobiography, Dalglish recalled that Bob Paisley's quiet communication skills had been uppermost in his mind when he said to his players,

"We've come a long way this season.

"We've won the League Championship.

"The Cup is there for us if we want it bad enough.

"When we come back in here, I don't want any regrets.

"The FA Cup Final is not a rehearsal.

"This is it. Lets have a real go. Come on."

Rather than rant and rave, Dalglish felt gentle persuasion was the best way to coax one last push from a group of players who had laid themselves bare for him time and again all season.

If the Reds came out for the second-half with renewed belief however, they certainly didn't show it and Everton threatened to take the game away from them in the opening minutes with Sheedy twice going close to adding to Everton's lead, first with a curling right-foot shot that curled wide of Grobbelaar's right-hand post, and then with a low 25-yard free-kick that the keeper squeezed wide of the goal at the expense of a corner.

With the buoyant Everton fans behind the goal the Blues were now attacking, the din at that end of the stadium played its own part in rattling the Liverpool defence as Everton continued to press for a clinching goal. Grobbelaar made another error when he misjudged a looping right-wing cross from Sheedy. Although the loose ball was cleared, Bracewell returned it from the opposite flank for Sharp to head goalwards. Grobbelaar raced to the left edge of his six-yard box to claim the loose ball and signalled for Beglin to stand aside so he could collect. Beglin inadvertently touched the ball however, moving it away from the keeper's grasp and nearly letting Steven cross towards an empty net in the process. Fortunately Grobbelaar was able to grab the ball before Steven could toe-poke it across goal and Liverpool escaped, but not without a fierce exchange of views between goalkeeper and full-back which ended with Grobbelaar pushing Beglin in the chest.

The incident brought howls of derision and laughter from the Everton end and a few minutes later the eccentric Zimbabwean gave them more cause for mirth. After confidently catching and holding a long throw by Stevens he then inexplicably launched a wild clearance straight into touch on the half-way line. Dalglish's frustration at his goalkeeper's loss of concentration was obvious.

As Dalglish looked back on the chaos that was Liverpool's defence in the early stages of the second half, a solitary and isolated figure stood just 20-yards to his left. Save for a missed headed chance in the first-half, Ian Rush had fed on relative scraps all afternoon. At this stage few Reds' fans watching were confident his predatory instincts would turn the game in their favour.

Though Everton were dominant their lead was still a slender one and Dalglish's frustration was borne of the understanding that if Liverpool could get into the game they would surely create a decisive chance for Rush. For all the praise heaped on Lineker by pundits and commentators alike, it was Rush who was the marksman supreme. After the monumental 1983/84 season when his European Cup Final penalty-kick in the Rome shoot-out was his 50th goal of that campaign, Rush had recovered from a cartilage operation to be Liverpool's leading scorer the following season.

Despite not playing alongside his preferred strike partner for much of this season, Rush's goals, teamwork and defending from the front, had spearheaded Liverpool's assault on the 'Double'. Such skills didn't just disappear overnight – or on one May afternoon – and Rush's class and ability when given even a half-chance was about to expose Everton's dominance as a mirage.

With 57 minutes played Everton's England right-back Stevens needlessly gave the ball away inside his own half. Whelan intercepted and played it inside to the advancing Molby who was able to dribble forward, look up and roll a perfectly weighted pass through the legs of Mountfield into the path of Rush, who had ghosted unseen and unmarked through the heart of the Everton defence.

Forced from his line to meet the striker, Mimms could only watch in wonder as Rush expertly took the ball around the keeper with a touch of his right foot - and slotted home with his left. Johnston, who had made a similar run to Rush, chased the ball into the goal and applied a needless touch just after it crossed the line. For a moment this created an illusion of offside but, to Evertonian's despair, it was anything but. The goal stood. 1-1 and mass celebrations in the Liverpool end.

Suddenly, thanks to Molby's vision and Rush's clinical finishing, the Reds were in the ascendancy. As the name, "Ian Rush," boomed out from the terraces, the Everton fans fell silent. The 'Double' was back on. The game was now transformed with Molby, Whelan and MacDonald spraying passes across the midfield to stretch a beleaguered and increasingly tired looking Everton rearguard.

Despite the apparent change in tempo however, it was the Blues who almost regained the lead soon afterwards only to be denied by Grobbelaar at his athletic best. Trying to atone for the error that led to the Reds' equaliser, Steven played a long pass into the left edge of the Liverpool box. The simple ball panicked Hansen who, under pressure from Lineker, hooked an attempted clearance across his own penalty area. Sharp seized on the ball with a looping header from 20-yards that was heading for the roof of the net until the backpedalling Grobbelaar intervened.

With a salmon leap that propelled him miraculously to the height of the crossbar, Grobbelaar flicked the ball over the bar with an outstretched right hand. In a single moment his value to the team was underlined – the former soldier in the Rhodesian army was occasionally erratic and prone to error, but he was also capable of saves almost beyond belief. His confidence restored, Grobbelaar comfortably caught Steven's inswinging corner to signal the end of Liverpool's defensive brainstorms. As different sections of the Liverpool masses sang, "You'll Never Walk Alone," and, "We Shall Not Be Moved," at the same time, Beglin played a long ball down the left side in search of Rush.

Rush gathered, turned inside and fed a precise pass to Molby - loitering with intent on the edge of the box. Molby's control and fleet of foot bamboozled Stevens and Ratcliffe, creating space for a well-hit, low cross aimed towards Johnston at the far post. With a neat side-foot finish past Mimms the ebullient Australian made no mistake and embarked on a gravity-defying scissor kick celebration barely before the ball had crossed the line.

Reds' fans were in raptures as 'Anfield South' reverberated to one word, "Liv-erpool, Liv-erpool, Li-ver-po-ol." The Wembley concrete shook beneath the bouncing Liverpool supporters as an apparently desperate situation had been overturned in the space of five minutes, the second goal encapsulating the season long efforts of star contributors Rush, Molby and Johnston.

If the scoreline wasn't bad enough for the heartbroken Evertonians at the Tunnel End, they also had to witness their counterparts turn one end of the stadium into a sea of red and white as the flagpoles came off the floor and every Liverpool flag, banner and scarf was held high to accompany a spine-tingling rendition of, "You'll Never Walk Alone.' As ever the anthem was sung at its triumphant best with the scent of victory in Red nostrils.

While Liverpool turned the game on its head Kendall had been powerless to act. If Everton were to summon an equalizer he had to gamble and in the 72nd minute he replaced full-back Stevens with Adrian Heath to give extra support to Lineker and Sharp up front. With the Blues reduced to a three-man defence it was a bold move by Kendall but, with Liverpool's veins pumping and confidence flowing, it was a decision that effectively signed their death warrant. Rather than the substitution giving the Blues a greater attacking threat, Liverpool maintained their new found dominance in midfield and they continued to pick holes in Everton's undermanned defence.

With six minutes to go Liverpool clinched the game, the FA Cup and the historic League and Cup Double with a team goal that summed up their season perfectly. Hansen headed Sheedy's chipped pass away from the danger zone for MacDonald, still deep inside his own half, to collect and lay off to Whelan. The Irishman's lofted, square pass was headed on by Johnston to Rush - who controlled and turned inside to find Molby on the half-way line.

The Dane's peripheral vision saw him switch the play to the left where Whelan was breaking into Everton territory. The Irishman surged forward purposefully, looked up to see Rush drifting, unmarked, into the right side of the Everton penalty area and his perfectly flighted pass was gathered in an instant by the Welshman who fired past Mimms' right hand with the cold-blooded precision of a trained killer.

While Rush had been Liverpool's assassin, it was Molby who had supplied the ammunition with a key part in each of the Reds' three goals. Whelan's contribution too, was a significant factor in not only this game, but throughout the season.

Liverpool fans were now in dreamland. The Double was theirs, annexed at the hands of their great neighbours and arch-rivals. The FA Cup had been absent from the Anfield trophy room for 12 long, painful years. It was now heading home for the third time in the club's history. Liverpool were on the verge of joining Preston North End, Aston Villa, Tottenham Hotspur and Arsenal as the only clubs to achieve the feat of being League and Cup winners in the same season.

Only four minutes remained when Dalglish was felled by Bracewell after a surging run down the right. The player-manager lost his boot in the challenge, causing a brief stoppage which gave the travelling Kop the chance to laud their hero once again. "Dalglish," came the chant followed by a pleading, "I'd walk a million miles for one of your goals, Oh Kenny, Oh Kenny." A goal for the boss would have been the icing on the cake but it was Rush who nearly brought the house down when Dalglish and Molby combined to send him clear in the closing seconds.

With the first FA Cup Final hat-trick since Stan Mortensen's treble in 1953 at his mercy, Rush chose to try and chip Mimms when dribbling around him would have led to an almost certain goal. Mimms saved the attempted lob and the Reds' striker had to be satisfied with 'just' two goals in his first FA Cup Final.

When the final whistle sounded - exactly one week since Liverpool became League Champions at Stamford Bridge - Dalglish held centre-stage again, his arms raised to salute another remarkable success. He was embraced first by Johnston, Rush and Whelan before slowly making his way towards the bench and enjoying a heartfelt moment with his mentor Bob Paisley, a man whose unobtrusive guidance had helped steer him through a triumphant first season in management.

Fans were acutely aware of the footballing irony that was Dalglish's capture of the FA Cup in his first season – the only trophy that Paisley had failed to land in his nine glorious seasons as Liverpool manager. There was also a hug for Dalglish from an ecstatic Ronnie Moran who had lent his invaluable experience and helped supply the half-time verbals in the dressing room when Dalglish took a more active playing role.

The unfortunates who had missed out on selection; the unused substitute Steve McMahon; Paul Walsh whose early season form had confined Dalglish to the dug-out; the luckless Gillespie; the ever loyal Sammy Lee; John Wark and reserve keeper Mike Hooper, all joined the party as Liverpool prepared to climb the 39 Wembley steps to receive the cup.

Skipper Hansen led the team, followed by Dalglish, up the steps to the Royal Box. His omission from the Scotland squad for the World Cup now firmly a distant memory, Hansen listened to some kind words of congratulation from the Duchess of Kent while holding the cup in a vice-like grip, before raising it – slowly - towards the ranks of the Liverpool fans at the far end of the stadium. The captain's beaming smile said it all.

The defeated, deflated Everton players followed the Reds up the steps to collect their losers' medals to sympathetic applause and strains of, "Merseyside, Merseyside," from the fans. There was no consolation though for Kevin Sheedy and Graeme Sharp who headed down the tunnel straight after receiving their mementoes, turning their back on the remaining ten Everton players.

On the traditional lap of honour Liverpool players danced their familiar victory jig. Wearing an oversized, red peaked-hat thrown from the crowd Dalglish cut an amusing figure, while Bruce Grobbelaar tried to steal the show again with his traditional cup-final handstands. The majority of Evertonians stayed behind to acknowledge their own dejected players and sportingly applauded the winners, but the hour belonged to the joyous Liverpudlians who had witnessed their team make history. The supporters lapped up every second and sang their victory songs on the Wembley terraces before the players finally disappeared into the dressing rooms for a more private celebration.

In the immediate aftermath, Dalglish paid tribute to his players and staff and he told ITV's Jim Rosenthal,

"I'm not educated enough to put it into words that would explain it sufficiently. All I can say is that I'm very proud and fortunate to be manager of Liverpool Football Club and any credit is due to go to the lads and every single one of the backroom staff who've helped me tremendously.

"Our lads have been absolutely magnificent. Even if we hadn't won today, as I said before the game, they've been absolutely magnificent this season and an absolute credit to the club and themselves."

Captain Alan Hansen modestly attributed the second-half turnaround to the energy levels of the two teams after a gruelling season. "They got more tired than we were, it's as simple as that," he said. "I mean, we were out on our feet and… first ten minutes of the second half I thought they were going to bury us but we came back strong and that's what Liverpool's all about isn't it?" Full-back Steve Nicol highlighted the importance of Grobbelaar's memorable save when the scores were level at 1-1. "Bruce has come in for a lot of criticism this season but really, the save he made today changed the game for us. Obviously getting the equaliser put us on a high but the save really changed it for us."

Man-of-the-Match Ian Rush, whose two goals edged out the influential Molby for the award, was another to extol the team ethic that served the Reds so well. "As long as the team wins I'm really made up," he said. "I thought the lads played brilliantly today. Most of the goals; I don't see them hit the back of the net but happily I scored two and we were on the winning side again."

Whilst the likes of Rush, Molby, Johnston and Grobbelaar rightly took much of the post-match plaudits from pundits and press, Ian Hargreaves identified some of the Reds' unsung heroes; "For all the highly publicised skills of Rush and Dalglish and the power and subtlety of Molby," he said, "one of the most decisive factors in Liverpool's victory was the performance of two or three players who could hardly have dreamed of playing at Wembley earlier in the season."

Ronnie Whelan, "so erratic at one time, was back at his unpredictable best, swift to challenge, and always liable to deliver a telling pass or shot." Beglin, "the Irish successor to Alan Kennedy, who lost his place a few months ago after a hat-trick of bookings, showed pace and determination that reached a climax with a classic tackle on Sharp which stopped bringing Everton back into the game." Of the team's most underrated performer MacDonald, Hargreaves thought the Scot had, "forced his way into the side with sheer endeavour, and demonstrated why he was preferred to the unlucky McMahon, a regular member of the team until sidelined by injury."

In the losers' dressing room there was, naturally, acute disappointment, with Howard Kendall bemoaning Alan Robinson's decision not to award his side a first-half penalty for Nicol's challenge on Graeme Sharp. "A penalty in the FA Cup Final at that time could have made all the difference because we would have gone two-nil up before half-time," he lamented.

Kendall also thought the referee was going to disallow Rush's first goal for offside. "We felt the referee was going to blow for offside but just as he was about to he was knocked over by a player. When he's picked himself up it was too late and he let the goal stand." Without a hint of irony, the Everton manager added, "Don't get me wrong, this is not sour grapes. I congratulate Liverpool on winning the double – it's a tremendous achievement. But these are turning points in the game and I'm only saying what I feel."

With understandable sadness he also had time to spare a thought for the Blue's fans who had added to the occasion, "It's a shattering end to the season when you think who has won the double. That must be hard for the fans to take." If there was any consolation for Everton it had been a tremendous, uplifting occasion for English football and a source of pride to both Merseyside clubs. "The crowd applauded everything that moved with passionate intensity," said Hargraves, "and so far as one could see the police had little to do. It was indeed an occasion of which our great city had every right to be proud."

Even the national press, who had been surprised and then beguiled by Dalglish's appointment and wizardry on and off the pitch, and who had contemptuously lambasted the club's supporters and the city in the immediate aftermath of Heysel, were awestruck. "A year ago Liverpool was to world opinion what Chernobyl is now," wrote Rob Hughes of The Times, but, "Yesterday the true spirit of our premier football city was allowed to drift around the globe, bounced by satellite to upwards of 50 countries and between 200 and 500 million people who, we trust, gained a kinder picture of the English at play."

The pain and shame of Heysel had been partially eased by Liverpool's efforts on the field. Faith in football supporters had been restored, to a degree, by the camaraderie between Liverpool and Everton fans - despite their teams meeting head-on for the highest of stakes. And, although some national figures were loathe to admit it, the all-Merseyside Cup Final had restored pride to the English game, at a time when it needed all the help it could get. Sadly, despite this uplifting event for English football and owing to the continuing vilification, mistrust and abuse of supporters by the authorities in the following years, only further tragedy lay ahead for Liverpool.

10 May 1986 was a day when Liverpool FC and Kenny Dalglish made history. "His contribution, as it had been in that sweep for the championship, was sophisticated, serene and often swift. The scriptwriters could not have done it better." Despite his obvious genius, the Glaswegian who had made Liverpool his home preferred to bestow praise on the players and staff who had helped him be the first, and so far only, player-manager to lead an English League and Cup winning side.

In his hour of glory, the guarded, softly spoken and self-deprecating Dalglish continued to exude class. Summing up his input to the historic season he simply told reporters, "All I did was pick the team."

FA Cup Final footnotes:

Commenting on speculation linking him with Barcelona, Gary Lineker said after the Cup Final, "I know nothing about Barcelona. Nobody has spoken to me. As far as I am concerned, I expect to start next season at Goodison."

Lineker won the Golden Boot with England at the 1986 World Cup in Mexico before returning home to announce a £2.8m transfer to Barcelona. He spent just one season with Everton. His goal in the final was his 40th in 57 games for the Blues.

In the week after the final Ian Rush, who was watched by Juventus officials, present at Wembley as Liverpool's guests, said, "I would like to secure myself so that I can finish at 30. If at Liverpool, that's great – if not I'll have to think about going abroad."

On 1 July 1986 Ian Rush signed for Juventus for a record £3.2m. Juventus loaned him back to Liverpool for the 1986-87 season and Rush spent just one campaign in Italy before re-signing for Liverpool. He played his last game for Liverpool in the 1996 FA Cup Final against Manchester United, aged 34. He scored 346 goals in 660 appearances for the Reds and is the leading goalscorer in the club's history.

Political postscript:

Despite all the chaos of the previous year Labour in Liverpool – on its way to being stripped of its Militant members – increased its vote in the council elections in May 1986 by 10%. The local Conservative vote was obliterated in this period and the last Tory councillor in the city was voted out of office in 1998.

Derek Hatton was expelled from the Labour Party in 1986 and is now a broadcaster, businessman and after-dinner speaker.

Epilogue

Bruce Grobbelaar

Early 1986 had seen an uncharacteristic crisis of confidence for the Zimbabwe-born goalkeeper which had tested Dalglish's embryonic man-management skills to the limit, but he kept faith with Grobbelaar and was rewarded with a string of assured performances capped by a memorable, match-winning save at Wembley.

Grobbelaar eventually won six titles and three FA Cups in Reds' colours, playing a total of 628 games under five Liverpool managers, before finally leaving to join Southampton in mid-1994 after a short loan spell at Stoke City the previous year. He went on to appear in League football for Plymouth Argyle, Oldham Athletic, Lincoln City and Bury before finally hanging up his gloves as a professional in 2002 when he made one appearance for South African side Hellenic.

In November 1994 Grobbelaar was accused by The Sun newspaper of match fixing during his time at Liverpool to benefit a betting syndicate. Together with Wimbledon goalkeeper Hans Segers, Aston Villa striker John Fashanu, and a Malaysian businessman, Heng Suan Lim he was charged with conspiracy to corrupt. Eventually cleared, Grobbelaar sued the newspaper for libel but was ultimately awarded the lowest damages possible under English law - £1 – and ordered to pay the paper's legal costs.

After retirement, Bruce had a spell coaching Zimbabwe and also managed in South Africa. He now lives in Newfoundland, Canada. He is an active after-dinner speaker, occasional media contributor and is involved with the ex-players' Liverpool Legends team. In April 2007 – when he was 49-years old - Grobbelaar came out of retirement to play in a one-off game for non-league Wakefield side Glasshoughton Welfare to help them in their fight for survival. They beat Maltby Main 2–1.

1985/86 stats: League: Games 42 Goals 0, Cups: Games 21 Goals 0

Mike Hooper

Dalglish's second investment in the transfer market, reserve goalkeeper Hooper was signed from Wrexham for £40,000 in October 1985. Hooper had the unenviable task of shifting Bruce Grobbelaar from his position as Liverpool's number 1 but, due to the League restricting club's to only one substitute at the time, rarely got the opportunity. Was included in the travelling party to the FA Cup Final - and was present on the celebratory team group photographs at Wembley - but again missed out on selection

Made his Liverpool first-team debut in August 1986 but didn't get a proper run in the side until September 1988 – when he played 24 consecutive games due to Grobbelaar having meningitis. Loaned out to Leicester City in 1990 before playing another 15 times for the Reds between November 1992 and January 1993 under Graeme Souness. Left for Newcastle United in May the same year before another loan move to Sunderland. Recently thought to be working as a bouncer in a Newcastle nightclub.

1985/86 stats: League: Games 0 Goals 0, Cups: Games 0 Goals 0

Phil Neal

Owner of a Liverpool record eight league title winners' medals, the distinguished full-back, affectionately nicknamed 'Zico' by the fans in his later years, was a penalty expert and recorded 59 goals for Liverpool in his mammoth 650 games.

After becoming player-manager of Bolton Wanderers (where he scored three goals in 64 games) in December 1985, Neal also managed at Coventry, Cardiff and Manchester City - in a caretaker capacity – and was Graham Taylor's Assistant manager at England in the early-1990s.

His controversial second autobiography 'Life at the Kop', published while Dalglish was still in charge at Anfield – he had published 'Attack From The Back' in 1981 - communicated his pain at not being considered for the position of manager after Heysel. With the passage of time however, Neal is a respected ex-player and deserving of his legendary Liverpool status. Now an occasional media pundit, player and coach of the Liverpool FC masters side and contributor to Liverpool FC's official TV channel.

1985/86 stats: League: Games 13 Goals 1 Cups: Games 3 Goals 0

Steve Nicol

In an Anfield career spanning 12 years 'Chico', the butt of much dressing room humour but hugely popular among his teammates, amassed 468 Liverpool appearances. In 1988/89 he was a deserved Football Writers' Footballer of the Year; personal recognition to accompany a European Cup Winners' medal, four league titles and three FA Cups. His sound footballing techniques; a deft touch, accurate passing, well-timed tackles and precise shooting were the antithesis of attributes boasted by some of the less-gifted players who flourish in the modern game.

After leaving Liverpool for Notts County in 1995 - where he briefly tasted management for the first time – Nicol also played for Sheffield Wednesday, West Brom (on loan) and Doncaster Rovers. Now lives in Massachusetts, USA, where he has forged a successful managerial career; initially with Boston Bulldogs, and more recently with New England Revolution who he led to runners-up spots in MLS in 2002 (when he was also named Coach of the Year), 2005, 2006 and 2007. Left the revolution in 2011. Won the US Open Cup in 2007 and the North American Superliga title in 2008.

A respected coach and manager and one of the few players from the Double winning season yet to release an autobiography although he co-authored a coaching manual 'Coaching Dynamics' in 1994.

1985/86 stats: League: Games 34 Goals 4, Cups: Games 13 Goals 0

Alan Kennedy

An early victim of Dalglish's managerial ruthlessness, Kennedy was blamed for his part in the defensive sloppiness that saw the Reds draw 2-2 at Oxford in September 1985 - he never featured in a Red shirt again - and was sold to Sunderland soon after.

Kennedy left the Reds with a proud record of 359 appearances, 20 Liverpool goals to his name and a reputation for scoring in the biggest games – he famously scored the winning goals in two European Cup Finals. Continued his playing career for a further five years, featuring in League football for Hartlepool and Wigan before reviving his career in non-League football through his association with Colne Dynamoes. Also had brief spells in Sweden (Husqvarna), Belgium (Beerschot) and Denmark (Club 1903). Kennedy eventually settled on Merseyside where he works as a matchday entertainer at Anfield and is a regular guest on LFC TV and local radio as well as continuing to play for the Liverpool FC Masters side.

1985/86 stats: League: Games 8 Goals 0, Cups: Games 0 Goals 0

Jim Beglin

Beglin's blossoming Liverpool career met an abrupt, tragic end in a League Cup quarter-final in January 1987 - when he was the victim of a tackle by Everton's Gary Stevens that broke his leg. Described by Bob Paisley as the worst break he had ever seen, Beglin never played for the Reds again.
Recovered sufficiently to briefly play for Leeds United – whom he helped to the Division Two title, Plymouth Argyle and Blackburn Rovers, but was forced to retire completely in 1991 when he was just 27. His curtailed Liverpool career of 98 games saw him score three goals.

Now a respected match summariser for ITV sport - often doubling up with commentator Clive Tyldesley who brought many of Liverpool's matches to life during 1985/86 as the voice of Radio City Sport. Another ex-Liverpool player who has yet to pen an autobiography.

1985/86 stats: League: Games 34 Goals 1, Cups: Games 19 Goals 0

Alan Hansen

Although 'Jocky' went on to win another FA Cup and two more league titles as a Liverpool player, lifting the Red's first FA Cup for 12 years as club captain in May 1986 - illuminating Wembley with a beaming smile - was the personal highlight of Hansen's career. Throughout his playing days Hansen disguised chronic nerves to appear the calmest, most assured man on the pitch and became arguably the most accomplished defender the club has ever had.

Out for most of the 1988/89 season – only to be dramatically recalled at Hillsborough – Hansen finally succumbed to a persistent knee injury and announced his retirement just days after Dalglish's resignation in February 1991. Was talked off as a potential managerial successor to Dalglish – and to Graeme Souness three years later – but instead took the opportunity to work for new satellite TV Chanel BskyB and then as a pundit on an Italian football programme. This began a successful media career that now sees him as the most respected match-analyst for the BBC's Match of the Day.

Played 620 times for the Reds, winning eight league titles, three European Cups, two League Cups – and the 1985/86 Screen Sport Super Cup – scoring 14 goals in the process.

1985/86 stats: League: Games 41 Goals 0, Cups: Games 19 Goals 0

Mark Lawrenson

Sadly for Lawrenson, the fourth league title and first FA Cup he won in May 1986 were his last winners medals; an Achilles tendon injury hastening not only his departure from Liverpool but also his retirement from the game in 1988 – at the age of 29. His 356 games and 18 goals in a red shirt only tell only half of the story of one of the most talented footballers to play for Liverpool however, as Lawrenson was an exceptional player - equally adept in a variety of positions in defence and midfield.

Appointed Oxford United manager after leaving Liverpool but left after the club's directors sold Dean Saunders to Derby County without his approval and then made two starts for non-league Barnet, before a last hurrah as a player in the USA with Tampa Bay Rowdies. Had a final crack at management with Peterborough United in 1989/90 before embarking on an alternative path, this time into journalism and a place on the Match of the Day and Football Focus couches, often teaming up with his old sidekick Hansen. Also acts as a BBC co-commentator and radio analyst.

1985/86 stats: League: Games 38 Goals 3, Cups: Games 20 Goals 2

Gary Gillespie

Forging his way into the team on a more regular basis during 1985/86, Gillespie's Liverpool career continued until May 1991 by which time he had racked up 241 appearances. Had won a European Cup medal as a sub in 1984 and, after adding a League winners' medal in 1986, won a further two championships in 1988 and 1990.

One of a number of experienced Anfield professionals fall foul of Graeme Souness's purge of senior players, he was transferred to Celtic in 1991 where he spent a further three seasons before finishing his playing days back at Coventry.

Since retirement Gillespie has served regularly as an expert summariser for Liverpool matches on BBC Radio Merseyside and is a regular member of the commentary team for Liverpool games on LFC TV. He also continues to play for the Liverpool FC Masters side.

1985/86 stats: League: Games 14 Goals 3, Cups: Games 10 Goals 0

Mark Seagraves

Faced with competition from an array of international defenders, Bootle-born Seagraves was unable to add to his surprise debut at QPR in the League Cup semi-final and the following FA Cup tie at York City.

Forced to seek first-team football elsewhere he moved to Manchester City in 1987 before spending the bulk of his playing career at Bolton Wanderers, whom he represented against Liverpool at Wembley in the 1995 League Cup Final. Moved to Swindon Town soon after before taking his coaching badges and working under his former Liverpool FC youth team colleague Paul Jewell at both Wigan Athletic and Derby County. Now lives in Crosby and works as a scout for former employers, Bolton Wanderers.

1985/86 stats: League: Games 0 Goals 0, Cups: Games 2 Goals 0

John Wark

Having ended an injury-plagued Double season on crutches at Wembley, Wark struggled to reclaim a regular place in the team and made just a further 19 appearances in a red shirt. Although he scored 42 goals in 108 appearances for the Reds - testament to his perfectly timed runs from midfield – Wark's spell at Anfield was beset by injuries and if it wasn't for these he would surely have appeared many more times. A vastly under-appreciated contributor to several seasons of success at Liverpool.

With the signing of John Barnes by Dalglish in 1987, Wark moved to back to Ipswich where he continued his amazing scoring record from midfield – 23 goals in just 89 games. Continued to play until he was 40 - via Middlesbrough and a third spell at his spiritual home, Portman Road. In his latter days he underlined his versatility by featuring regularly as a centre-half.

Eventually retired to Suffolk with occasional work in the corporate hospitality department at Portman Road. Continues to play veteran's football and features regularly in the Liverpool FC Masters side.

1985/86 stats: League: Games 9 Goals 3, Cups: Games 9 Goals 3

Jan Molby

Although he remained at Liverpool until 1996, for the man who played such a pivotal role in the Double success, the rest of his time at Anfield was blighted by injury, fitness and personal problems, and disagreements with management. Such was his obvious connection with his adopted City and its people however, that Molby always remained popular with the fans. Scored 61 times for Liverpool in 292 appearances and remains the only Liverpool player to score three penalties in one match – against Coventry in a League Cup tie in November 1986.

Spent spells on loan to Barnsley and Norwich in 1995, before leaving Anfield in 1996 to become player-manager at Swansea. Enjoyed some brief success here, and also held the reigns at Hull City and Kidderminster Harriers. Now an established after-dinner speaker displaying as natural a gift for comedy as he once did in Liverpool's midfield. Also contributes intelligent analysis on radio and TV.

In 2009 Molby finally unearthed the grainy video footage of his legendary 1985 Milk Cup goal against Manchester United and, when it was aired for the first time in 2010, his swashbuckling run and shot certainly didn't disappoint those who had witnessed it live 25 years earlier.

Made an 'Honourary Scouser' by the Lord Mayor of Liverpool in 2009 and another regular in the club's Masters side.

1985/86 stats: League: Games 39 Goals 14, Cups: Games 19 Goals 7

Steve McMahon

A £300,000 acquisition from Aston Villa in September 1985 – Dalglish's first foray in the transfer market - the ex-Evertonian was identified by Dalglish as the man to add the required steel in Liverpool's engine room. McMahon was the perfect foil for the silky skills of Jan Molby, but not without attacking talent of his own - to say nothing of his shuddering tackles and relentless covering play.

McMahon's game flourished as part of Dalglish's second great Liverpool team – the entertainers of 1987/88 – and he went on to add two more League titles and another FA Cup before being sold prematurely (to Manchester City) by Graeme Souness in November 1991. Scored 50 goals in 277 Liverpool appearances. Stayed at Maine Road for three seasons before moving to Swindon Town as player-manager in 1994 - although he was sent off on his debut. Although relegated that first season McMahon took Swindon up as Division Two Champions immediately but left in 1998 to take over at Blackpool where he remained until 2005.

Subsequently moved to Australia to manage Perth Glory but soon moved into the media where he worked as a TV pundit with Asia-based ESPN Star Sports. Joined Singapore-based Profitable Group as head of Strategic Sports Investment soon after but the company ceased trading in 2011.

September 2011 brought an unexpected return to Anfield employment when he was hired to expand Liverpool's 'brand' and scouting into India, where he will also be head coach of a facility there, as the club attempts to leave a footprint in each continent.

1985/86 stats: League: Games 23 Goals 6, Cups: Games 13 Goals 4

Kevin MacDonald

When asked to recall Liverpool's line-up for the 1986 FA Cup Final few fans are able to recall Kevin MacDonald but, although his laboured running style failed to endear him to many supporters and he was often the crowd's scapegoat in defeat, 'Albert's' work-rate and contribution were assets that were fully recognised by Dalglish and his teammates.

Continued to impress in the early stages of the following season but a broken leg at Southampton interrupted his progress for 18 months and, although he returned briefly, MacDonald was loaned to Leicester City (his first club) and Glasgow Rangers before signing for Coventry City in 1989. A loan spell at Cardiff followed before he ended his playing days at Walsall – for whom he scored seven goals in 53 games. He had scored five goals in 64 games for the Reds.

In 1994 his coaching career began at Leicester (including a spell as caretaker manager) before he moved to become reserve team boss at Aston Villa. Following Martin O'Neill's resignation in 2010, MacDonald took charge of the first team at Villa Park for eight games before the arrival of Gerard Houllier. Remains at Villa Park as first-team coach.

1985/86 stats: League: Games 17 Goals 1, Cups: Games 8 Goals 5

Ronnie Whelan

Whelan's Liverpool career continued for a further eight seasons after the Double success of 1986, eventually finishing with 73 goals from 493 appearances.

Featured alongside Steve McMahon in central midfield in the great 1987/88 team and, in the absence of Alan Hansen the following season, was appointed captain - which meant he was on hand to lift the FA Cup at Wembley in the wake of Hillsborough. Another league medal followed in 1990 and, although his appearances grew less frequent under Graeme Souness, he was still a member of the team that played the last game in front of the standing Kop in May 1994.

Left Anfield to take up the player-manger's post at Southend in 1995 - until he was sacked at the end of season 1996/97. Whelan then tried his luck at management abroad, taking Greek side Panionios to the quarter-finals of the European Cup Winners Cup in 1999. Spells in Cyprus with Olympiakos Nicosia (2000-2002) and Apollon Limassol followed.

Returned to his native Ireland to feature as a TV pundit for RTE and makes occasional appearances on the LFC TV Channel. Released an overdue autobiography 'Walk On: My Life in Red: in 2011.

1985/86 stats: League: Games 39 Goals 10, Cups: Games 18 Goals 4

Sammy Lee

The Super Cup semi-final against Norwich in May 1985 was Liverpool-born Lee's last game in a red shirt. Joined QPR in the summer of 1986 but, after a year in London, he enjoyed two seasons with Spanish club Osasuna. Before hanging up his boots in 1991 he also represented Southampton and Bolton Wanderers.

Returned to Liverpool as reserve team coach in 1993, working under Graham Souness and Roy Evans. Later promoted to first-team coach by Gerard Houllier. After a spell coaching England, Lee moved to Bolton as assistant to Sam Allardyce in 2005. When the latter resigned two years later, Lee took over but was in charge for only 14 games and returned to Liverpool once more in May 2008 as Rafa Benítez's assistant manager. Lee survived the coup and internal strife that saw Roy Hodgson replace Benitez. However, just prior to the season 2011/12 it was announced that Lee would be leaving the club, having supported Kenny Dalglish during his caretaker period.

1985/86 stats: League: Games 15 Goals 0, Cups: Games 11 Goals 0

Craig Johnston

After making a further 72 appearances in the two seasons following his Cup Final goal at Wembley, Johnston abruptly made a decision to quit Liverpool – and football - to care for his seriously-ill sister in Australia. His last appearance had been to replace John Aldridge in the 1988 FA Cup Final after the latter had just had a penalty saved by Dave Beasant. Johnston never played football again, but he returned briefly to Merseyside in the aftermath of the Hillsborough Disaster.

Instead of returning to football, Johnston - who stated he could never contemplate playing for anyone other than Liverpool - embarked on a business career which saw him invent a prototype for the Adidas 'Predator' football boot. Clearly a man of man of many gifts, he subsequently established a further niche as a professional photographer. Wrote an illuminating autobiography in 1989 entitled Walk Alone.

Still living in Australia, Johnston's business interests see him travel the world, offering insightful thoughts on football and life to an ever-growing audience of admirers – although a 12-page letter to FIFA in 2010, criticising the official ball used in the 2010 World Cup, will probably not have endeared him to the game's governing body. Made a total of 271 appearances and scored 40 goals for Liverpool, and is fondly remembered for penning 'The Anfield Rap' – Liverpool's 1988 FA Cup Final record.

1985/86 stats: League: Games 41 Goals 7, Cups: Games 20 Goals 3

Kenny Dalglish

If the glorious 1986 Double wasn't enough to convince the most critical observers of Dalglish's genius, then the football played and subsequent league championships won by his teams in 1988 and 1990 rightly elevated his status as a manager to a level equivalent to that he enjoyed as a player. His playing career ended at Anfield in May 1990 when he came off the bench to replace Jan Molby for the last 20 minutes of a game that ended with Liverpool being awarded their 18th League title. Played 515 times for Liverpool, scoring 172 goals.

Dalglish's esteemed reputation among the people of Liverpool is deserved not so much for his deeds as an unparalleled footballer and manager however, but for his impeccable response to the Hillsborough Disaster in April 1989. In the wake of the tragedy; the strength, support, and empathy shown by Dalglish cannot be underestimated or undervalued.

When Dalglish shocked many by resigning the manager's position in February 1991 he took a short break from football before returning as manager of Blackburn Rovers. He led them from the Second Division to the Premiership title in 1995. Left Blackburn in 1995 and took over at Newcastle in 1997. Led them to the FA Cup Final in 1998 but was sacked after just two games of the following season. A short stint as boss of his old club Celtic in 2000 saw Dalglish lead them to success in the Scottish League Cup.

Finally returned to Anfield, as club ambassador and with a role at the club's academy, at the behest of manager Rafa Benitez in July 2009. After the departure of Benitez and the calamitous tenure of his replacement Roy Hodgson, Dalglish was confirmed Liverpool manager for a second time in January 2011, initially in a caretaker capacity before being appointed on a permanent basis on 12 May 2011.

1985/86 stats: League: Games 21 Goals 3, Cups: Games 10 Goals 4

Ian Rush

Liverpool agreed to the sale of Ian Rush for £3.2m to Juventus in the summer of 1986, although he was immediately loaned back for a final Anfield season in which he scored another 40 goals. After just one year in Italy however, he was dramatically re-signed by Liverpool and spent another eight seasons at Anfield, resulting in him becoming the Reds' all-time leading goalscorer with 346 goals in 660 games.

Scored two goals as a substitute to win the 1989 FA Cup, won a fifth league title in 1990, scored again in another FA Cup Final win in 1992, and won the League Cup as captain in 1995. His last appearance for Liverpool came at Wembley in the 1996 FA Cup Final. Had been awarded an MBE the same year. Also holds the record for the most goals (25) in matches between Liverpool and Everton. Continued his playing career with Leeds, Newcastle, Sheffield United and Wrexham before finally hanging up his boots in 2000 after a brief spell in Australia with Sydney Olympic.

A career in management with his first club Chester City stalled in 2005, although 'Rushie' resigned with the club virtually safe from relegation. Has since worked in the media with Sky Sports, Sky Sports News and ESPN, and in 2010 returned to work as Liverpool FC's Soccer Schools ambassador, also working with the club's commercial team. Appears regularly for the Liverpool FC Masters team.

1985/86 stats: League: Games 40 Goals 22, Cups: Games 16 Goals 11

Paul Walsh

After missing the run-in to the Double success in which he had played such a huge part, Walsh overcame an early season injury to become a regular again during 1986/87 as Dalglish continued to scale down his own appearances. However, the goals dried up and he lost his place to new man John Aldridge. His position at the club was further weakened by the arrival of Peter Beardsley in the summer of 1987.

Ironically, Walsh made his first and only start of the 1987/88 season against Spurs at White Hart Lane in November; his last game in a red shirt before accepting an offer to join the North Londoners for a fee in the region of £500,000. 'Walshy' scored 37 goals for Liverpool in 122 games. Fours years at Tottenham - and an FA Cup winners' medal in 1991 - was followed by spells at QPR (on loan), Manchester City and Portsmouth (twice) before he was forced to hang up his boots in 1996 after suffering a cruciate ligament injury in his second spell at Fratton Park.

Appeared as a young-looking 'veteran' in a Liverpool side that dominated the televised Masters series for ex-players in recent years. Although he has taken his coaching badges, Walsh appears comfortable as a pundit in Sky TV's London studios on the acclaimed Soccer Saturday programme. Like a handful of the 1986 Double winning side, yet to publish an autobiography.

1985/86 stats: League: Games 20 Goals 11, Cups: Games 12 Goals 7

Postscript

Sunday 9 January 2011
FA Cup third round
Manchester United v Liverpool

As a double decker bus crammed with vibrant Liverpudlians young and old rolled out of the car park in front of the Johnny Todd pub in Kirkby, Merseyside en route to Manchester, the level of anticipation surpassed even the usual excitement that accompanied an away day at Old Trafford. On a bright, sunny winters' morning the same animated conversations and restored pride and belief were evident on the Spirit of Shankly, LBU, Happy Al's and Irregulars' coaches; on the 'ordinary' trains from Lime Street to Picadilly; and in hundreds of cars and vans as more than 9,000 Liverpool fans made the short trip to Manchester.

Despite a long-awaited change of club ownership, Liverpool FC remained in turmoil. Results were so poor that an open revolt on the Kop against unpopular manager Roy Hodgson made his departure inevitable. However, the identity of Hodgson's successor stirred passions that many Liverpudlians thought had been consigned to the memory of their youth. For the younger Red blood, a chance had come to taste something that they knew of only from stories passed down by their elders. The King was back.

Following the League and Cup Double of 1986, Kenny Dalglish came agonisingly close to repeating the feat on three further occasions. A freakish Wembley defeat in 1988 for the cavaliering team which featured John Barnes and Peter Beardsley at the hands of Wimbledon, and heartbreak at Anfield against Arsenal with the last kick of the season in the aftermath of Hillsborough in May 1989 saw the Reds fall at the final hurdle.

In 1990 the Champions-elect suffered a shock cup semi-final loss to Crystal Palace to again put paid to dreams of a second double. The 1989/90 season witnessed the last of Liverpool's 18 League Championships and, as the emotional burden of Hillsborough took its toll on Dalglish, he resigned the manager's position in February 1991 - despite Liverpool sitting on top of Division One.

His replacement Graeme Souness's flawed policy of revolution over evolution saw Liverpool slip dramatically from the pinnacle of English football - in the space of just three seasons. When Souness's fraught time was up, the club reverted to a homely 'bootroom' philosophy in the shape of Dalglish's former lieutenant Roy Evans. The likeable Evans briefly restored Liverpool's dignity and created an exciting team of young talent – albeit one which ultimately failed to realise its potential, in particular by gifting the 1997 league title to Manchester United through a late-season collapse.

Evans reminded Liverpool how to play, but was unable to deal with the player-power that was a symptom of the modern game; players suddenly becoming almost bigger than their clubs as the Premiership took a firm hold of the English game. Desperate to bridge the gap in years since the club's last league title, the Reds looked abroad for a new approach with the arrival of Gerard Houllier from the World Cup-winning French FA in 1998. The failed joint-management of Evans and Houllier saw the former fall on his sword and the Frenchman subsequently gained sole control of team affairs.

An influx of foreign players and tighter discipline brought rapid improvement, crystallised in a glorious FA Cup, League Cup and UEFA Cup treble in 2001. Houllier's progression saw the club reach the quarter-finals of the revamped UEFA Champions League in 2001/02 but major heart surgery during the same season signalled the end of his mastery and a sharp decline – amid some extremely poor signings - saw him leave the manager's chair in 2004.

Liverpool's Champions League exit in 2002/03 was in no small part down to emphatic defeats home and away to a superb Valencia side, managed by a hitherto unknown Rafael Benitez. It was the Spaniard who Liverpool looked to next in succession to Houllier. Benitez pulled off probably the most remarkable feat in the history of the club when, in his first season, he led an erratic Liverpool team to an unlikely triumph over AC Milan in the 2005 Champions League Final in Istanbul. A second European Cup Final followed two years later and gradual domestic improvement saw Liverpool go painfully close to a yearned-for 19th League title in 2009.

The latter part of Benitez's reign was conducted against the backdrop of a catastrophic leveraged buy-out of the club by American shysters Tom Hicks and George Gillett. Their frightening levels of debt impacted massively on the club's activity in the transfer market – and came perilously close to forcing the club's bankruptcy.

As the size and quality of his squad was reduced, Benitez was distracted by internal political battles resulting in a disappointing seventh place finish in the League in 2010. This was sufficient excuse for the Board to finally rid themselves of Benitez. Before his departure however, he was able to secure one signing which didn't require the transfer kitty so frequently denied him. In July 2009 Benitez invited Kenny Dalglish - after a gap of 18 years - to return to the club in an official capacity as an Ambassador with additional responsibility for the club academy in Kirkby.

The death throes of the cataclysmic Hicks and Gillette ownership which saw Liverpool FC in the High Court and within days of financial meltdown, brought the appointment of Londoner Roy Hodgson to one of the most revered positions in world football – the seat once occupied by Bill Shankly, Bob Paisley, Joe Fagan, Kenny Dalglish, Gerard Houllier and Rafa Benitez.

The folly of boardroom financiers making football decisions - inspired by a willingness to listen to the London media more than their own fans - came home to roost with Hodgson's disastrous six-month tenure. His removal by new American owners, Boston-based Fenway Sports Group (headed by John W Henry) on Saturday 8 January with Liverpool lying 13th in the Premier League was as welcome as it was inevitable. There was only one man capable of healing Liverpool's wounds. After the sorrow of Hillsborough the football club had limped on through the failure of the Souness years, the false hope of the Roy Evans era, and the belated adoption of a modern approach to the sport under Gerard Houllier.

The reign of Rafa Benitez briefly restored Liverpool's name to the summit of European football but never, since 1990, had the club and it supporters been truly united behind a common goal. The split in the club's support was never more apparent during the turbulent period of 2007-2010 when, despite the best efforts of Benitez, the ownership of Hicks and Gillett saw fans squarely at odds over the correct interpretation of a notional 'Liverpool Way'.

Simmering disagreement in the stands and on the Kop over the right way to fight for the future of the club was symptomatic of what had effectively become the nation's most dysfunctional club.

When Liverpool and Manchester United emerged from the Old Trafford tunnel on Sunday 9 January 2011 to play an FA Cup third round tie however, there was renewed hope in Liverpool hearts that the infighting was finally over and, when a familiar figure in an oversized black coat raised two clenched fists towards one end of Old Trafford, the roar that followed said it all.

At the age of 59 and a quarter of a century on from that glorious May day at Wembley in 1986; The King was back.

Bibliography:

John Aldridge, My Story, Hodder & Stoughton, 1999

John Aldridge, Alright Aldo Sound as A Pound: On the Road with Everybody's Favourite Irish Scouser, Trinity Mirror Sport Media, 2010

Nicholas Allt, The Boys From The Mersey: The Story of Liverpool's Annie Road End Crew, Football's First Clobbered Up Mob, Milo Books, 2005

Archbishop of Canterbury's Commission on Urban Priority Areas, Faith in the City: A Call for Action by Church and Nation, Church House Publishing, 1985

Arnie Baldursson and Gudmundur Magnusson, Liverpool: The Complete Record, De Courbertin Books, 2011

Kathy Barham, 194 Radio City – The Heart of Liverpool, Lulu.com, 2006

John Barnes, The Autobiography, Headline Book Publishing, 1999

John Belchem and Brian Briggs, Liverpool: City of Radicals, Liverpool University Press, 2011

Michael Crick, The Mach of Militant, Faber and Faber, 1986

Kenny Dalglish, My Liverpool Home, Hodder & Stoughton, 2011

Kenny Dalglish, Dalglish: My Autobiography, Hodder & Stoughton, 1996

Derek Dohren, Ghost on the Wall: The Authorised Biography of Roy Evans, Mainstream Publishing, 2005

Neil Dunkin, Anfield of Dreams: A Kopite's Odyssey, Know The Score books, 2008

Professor Geoffrey K Fry, The Politics of the Thatcher Revolution,: An Interpretation of British Politics 1979-1990

Bruce Grobbelaar, More Than Somewhat, Collins Willow, 1986

David Goldblatt, The Ball is Round; A Global History of Football, Viking 2006

Alan Hansen, A Matter of Opinion, Partridge Press, 1999

Derek Hatton, Inside Left, Bloomsbury Publishing Plc, 1988

Michael Heatley, Lost league Football Grounds, Ian Allen Publishing, 2010

Mike Herd (editor), The Guardian Book of Football: 50 Years of Classic Writing, Guardian Newspapers Ltd, 2008

Stan Hey, A Golden Sky: The Liverpool Dream Team, Mainstream Publishing, 1997

Peter Hooton, When Football was Football: Liverpool, A Nostalgic Look at a Century of a Club, J H Haynes & Co Ltd, 2009

Simon Inglis. Football Grounds of England and Wales, Harper Collins Willow, 1983

Craig Johnston and Neil Jameson, Walk Alone: The Craig Johnston Story, Collins Publishers Australia, 1989

John Keith, Liverpool Supreme, Cockerel, 1986

John Keith, Bob Paisley: Manager of the Millennium, Robson books, 2001

Alan Kennedy with John Williams, Kennedy's Way: Inside Bob Paisley's Liverpool, Mainstream Publishing 2005

Peter Kilfoyle, Left Behind: Winning Back a Labour Heartland and the Defeat of Militant, Politico's Publishing Ltd, 2000

Mark Lawrenson, Lawro: The Autobiography, Michael Joseph, 2009

Tony McDonald and Danny Francis, Boys of '86, The untold story of West ham's greatest-ever season. Mainstream, 2001.

Andy McSmith, No Such Thing as Society: A History of Britain in the 1980s, Constable, 2011

Steve McMahon with Harry Harris, Macca Can: The Steve McMahon Story, Pelham Books, 1990

Jan Molby with Grahame Lloyd, Jan the Man: From Anfield to Vetch Field, Gollancz (New Edition), 2000

John Motson, Match of the Day: The Complete Record from 1964, BBC Books, 1994

Phil Neal, Life On The Kop: The Phil Neal Story, Macdonald, 1986

Bob Paisley, *My 50 Golden Reds*, Front page Books, 1990

The Paisley Family, *The Real Bob Paisley*, Trinity Mirror Sport Media, 2007

Michael Parkinson, *Liverpool On The Brink: One City's Struggle Against Government Cuts*, Policy Journals, 1985

David Paul, *Anfield Voices*, Amberley publishing, 2010

Brian Pead. *Ee-Aye-Addio, We've Won the Cup! : Liverpool in the F. A. Cup, 1892-1993*, Champion Press, 1994

Darren Phillips, *The Little Red Book of Liverpool FC*, The History Press Ltd, 2010

Mark Platt and Andrew Fagan, *Joe Fagan – Reluctant Champion: The Authorised Biography*, Aurum Press Ltd, 2011

Brian Reade, *An Epic Swindle: 44 Months With a Pair of Cowboys*, Quercus publishing Plc, 2011

Chris Rowland, *From Where I Was Standing: A Liverpool Supporter's View of the Heysel Stadium Tragedy*, GPRF Publishing, 2009

Ian Rush, *Ian Rush: Goals and Glory*, Ebury Press, 1996

Ian Rush, *Rush: The Autobiography*, Ebury Press, 2009

David Sheppard and Derek Worlock, *Better Together*, Hodder & Stoughton, 1988

David Sheppard and Derek Worlock, *With Hope In Our Hearts*, Hodder & Stoughton, 1994

Ian St. John, *Liverpool: The Glory Decade, 1980-1990*, Sidgwick & Jackson, 1990

Peter Taafe, *The Rise of Militant*, Militant Publications, 1995

Peter Taafe and Tony Mulhearn, *Liverpool: A City that Dared to Fight*, Fortress, 1988

Rogan Taylor, John Williams, Andrew Ward, *Three Sides of the Mersey: An Oral History of Everton, Liverpool and Tranmere Rovers*, Robson Books, 1993.

Rogan Taylor, Andrew Ward, *Kicking and Screaming: An Oral History of Football in England*, Robson Books, 1998

Rogan Taylor, *Football and its Fans: Supporters and their relations with the game, 1885-1985 (Sport, Politics and Culture)*, Leicester University press, 1992

Phil Thompson, *Liverpool in the 80s*, The History Press Ltd, 2006

Alwyn Turner, *Rejoice, Rejoice!: Britain in the 1980s*, Aurum Press Ltd, 2010

Clive Tyldsley, *Bob Paisley's View of the Liverpool First Team Squad, 1986/87*, Cablestar Ltd, 1987

Richard Vinen, *Thatcher's Britain: The Politics and social Upheaval of the 1980s*, Pocket Books, 2010

John Wark, *Wark On: The Autobiography of John Wark*, Know the Score Books, 2009

Ronnie Whelan, *My Life in Red: My Autobiography*, Simon & Schuster, 2011

John Williams, *Red Men: Liverpool Football Club – The Biography*, Mainstream Publishing, 2010

John Williams, Catharine long, Stephen Hopkins, *Passing Rhythms: Liverpool FC and the Transformation of Football*, Berg Publishers, 2001

Jonathan Wilson, *Inverting the Pyramid: A History of Football Tactics*, Orion, 2009